Intramural Administration
Theory and Practice

Edited by

JAMES A. PETERSON

United States Military Academy
West Point, New York

PRENTICE-HALL, INC., Englewood Cliffs, New Jersey

Library of Congress Cataloging in Publication Data
Main entry under title:

Intramural administration.

    Bibliography: p.
    Includes index.
    1. Intramural sports. 2. School sports.
3. College sports. I. PETERSON, JAMES A.,
date
GV710.I58   371.8'9   75-30692
ISBN 0-13-477232-6

This text is dedicated to General Frank J. Kobes, Jr., Director of the Office of Physical Education, United States Military Academy, 1953–1974. To General Kobes, the phrase "Every Cadet an Athlete" was more than an institutional goal; it was his lifetime commitment.

Printed in the United States of America

10 9 8 7 6 5 4 3 2 1

PRENTICE-HALL INTERNATIONAL, INC., London
PRENTICE-HALL OF AUSTRALIA, PTY. LTD., Sydney
PRENTICE-HALL OF CANADA, LTD., Toronto
PRENTICE-HALL OF INDIA PRIVATE LIMITED, New Delhi
PRENTICE-HALL OF JAPAN, INC., Tokyo
PRENTICE-HALL OF SOUTHEAST ASIA (PTE.) LTD., Singapore

Contents

iii

III

A LOOK TO THE FUTURE

Foreword

In recent years many intramural sports programs across the country have experienced great increases in interest and student participation. This apparent good health of the profession is attributable not only to the increasingly good administrative work by intramural professionals, but also to the natural evolution of the intramural sports movement in this country.

Activities that could be identified as intramural in nature seem to have taken place at a number of American colleges as early as the late 1850s. Administration of the early intramural programs was left to the students. Subsequently, however, facility and equipment usage problems impelled university administrators to provide professional administrative assistance.

The use of faculty personnel to guide intramural programs soon led to the need for a viable professional association for the exchange of these pioneer intramural administrators. Administrators from Western Conference colleges have met annually since 1920 to formulate policies and programs. The College Physical Education Association created an intramural sports section at its annual meeting in 1933. In 1938, a similar section was set up by the Division of Men's Athletics of the American Association for Health, Physical Education and Recreation.

The emergence of a professional body concerned solely with the administration of intramural sports did not take place for another decade. This organization, the National Intramural Association, was formed as a result of a conference of Negro colleges at Dillard University in 1950. The conference was called to review a comparative study of intramural programs in Negro colleges made the previous year. Since those "embryo" days, members of the National Intramural Association have directed their professional energies toward the goal of providing leisure opportunities for all.

The present text comprises essays by a select group of National Intramural Association members. Each was selected by the editor because of particular expertise in one or more of the areas of intramural administration. The book provides a unique approach to understanding the critical elements in intramural administration: in addition to treating the technical aspects of administration, it examines the theoretical framework within which effective administrative techniques must be formulated. The outstanding individuals who have contributed to this text are in and of the intramural movement, and share the historical background cited in the introduction.

I consider it an honor to have been asked to write the foreword for this text.

WILLIAM N. WASSON
Founder, National Intramural Association
Wayne State University
Detroit, Michigan

Preface

"Do you personally have difficulty making decisions?"
"Well, yes and no!"

Anonymous Intramural Director

Few would deny that college-level intramural programs have proliferated in the last decade or so to an extent far beyond the expectations of most physical educators. On one hand, one of the strongest catalysts for this change in popularity and acceptance has been the perseverance of those individuals associated with the field of intramurals. Their efforts have frequently resulted in a reordering of institutional priorities. On the other hand, the increase in the number and the size of intramural programs has not witnessed a concomitant change in the administrative approaches used to direct such programs. Far too often, the administration of intramural programs appears to be founded on intuition, habits, or trial and error.

Conceivably, the proposition could be advanced that since "traditional" administrative methods have gotten intramurals this far, wouldn't it be better to leave well enough alone? Such a narrow dictum, however, fails to consider the inescapable premise that we are living in a period of continual and accelerated change. The forces that are at work within our society—economic, political, social, and technological—are having and will continue to have profound impact on the field of intramural administration and upon the efforts and responsibilities of intramural directors. Consequently, in the future the intramural administrator must possess more

ix

than merely the technical skills normally identified as the basic responsibilities of the position (for instance, scheduling a tournament). Rather, intramural directors must possess the managerial skills that will enable them to meet the challenge and opportunities inherent in change.

Many efforts have been made and are currently being made to improve the body of knowledge or information concerning the field of intramural administration. A lot has been learned and many things have been accomplished. However, much remains to be done. The training and continued preparation of competent, effective intramural administrators is a relatively new and uncharted area.

Many grave questions can be posed. Are our present approaches to intramural administration good enough? Are our present concepts of the dimensions of intramurals and of the responsibilities of the intramural director adequate to meet future needs and demands? What opportunities are available for preparing the administrator of tomorrow to meet the new demands more effectively? A conceptual exploration of these questions is the purpose of this book.

This text is an effort to present known facts and information concerning intramural administration, to interpret this information, and, more important, to raise new questions and present ideas that may stimulate the thinking of the reader in his own analysis of the future needs and challenges facing intramurals. Some of the basic questions to be examined are the following:

1. What is being done today in the field of intramural administration?

    a. What are the accomplishments? the limitations?
    b. What basic principles appear to have emerged from current and past endeavors?
    c. What are the opportunities for improvement?

2. What fundamental changes have occurred and are now taking place that will affect intramurals and the responsibilities of intramural directors in the years ahead?

    a. What are the implications of these changes for the field and for the work of those in the field?
    b. What changes in thinking will be required?
    c. What will intramural directors need to learn and to do in the years ahead?

3. What do these changes imply for the intramural administrator?

    a. What new knowledge, understanding, and approaches will be required?

b. What changes in thought and action will be essential?

c. How can these requirements be met?

Now is the time to "rethink." It is critical that intramural directors take the time to reexamine their practices, experiences, attitudes, and beliefs. Intramural administrators should return to fundamentals—in order to develop a clear vision of the needs to be filled and the opportunities to be seized. They require conceptual approaches to their tasks that are geared to the needs of the times.

Hammer has suggested that the first step in thinking is the questioning of authority.* It is far more important for intramural directors to question the adequacy of their beliefs, their knowledge, and the quality of their thinking than it is to seek to justify them. In these changing times, what makes sense will change as the administrator gains new knowledge, new experience, and new habits of thought and action.

If this book is helpful in the difficult but desirable task of examining these critical questions, if it points the way to more effective methods in intramural administration, if it stimulates thinking by suggesting new concepts and approaches, if it leads to innovation and progress in the field, it will have accomplished its purpose.

The reader is first introduced to several of the basic aspects of leadership within intramural administration (Part I). In Part II the reader is introduced to a series of position papers dealing with administrative practices and policies. Last, Part III—a look to the future—presents an overview of several of the administrative implications of the road ahead for the field of intramurals.

The editor is grateful to the contributors for their efforts. All are presently involved in administration to varying degrees. The editor thanks William Wasson, not only for writing the Foreword but also for his continuing commitment to the field of intramural administration. Prentice-Hall, and in particular Walter Welch, Assistant Vice-President, are to be commended for their patience and support over the past few years while this publication was being developed. A special thanks and appreciation is extended to Earle Ziegler, a professional in all aspects of life, for his counsel and inspiration. My overriding debt is to my wife Susan, to whom all my energies are dedicated.

JAMES A. PETERSON
West Point, New York

---

* J. R. Hammer, ed., *Logic for Living: Dialogues from the Classroom of Henry Horace Williams* (New York: Philosophical Library, 1951), p. 6.

I

Focus on Leadership

1

Intramurals, Profession, Discipline, or Part Thereof?

EARLE F. ZEIGLER
University of Western Ontario
London, Canada

The main objective of this presentation is to offer to the field of physical education and sport, and specifically to those who are related primarily to the promotion of intramural athletics, some ideas about the past, present, and possible future of that aspect of sport that has commonly been designated simply as "intramurals." Interestingly enough, this term is just about as familiar as the term "PE" on the North American continent. These ideas and thoughts about intramurals ask this fundamental question: "Is Intramurals a profession, a discipline, or part thereof?"

To meet this main objective, the following questions or topics will be considered in order: (1) definition of the terms "profession" and "discipline"; (2) the fractionating influences in physical education today; (3) intramural athletics—then, now, and in the future; (4) a model for the profession; (5) implications for the proposed model for intramurals; and (6) a summary with recommendations for the future.

The ideas to be expressed are the result of long observation of

This paper was presented originally to the Intramural Athletics Section of the National College Physical Education Association for Men, 76th Annual Conference, Pittsburgh, Pennsylvania, January 8, 1973.

intramural athletic programs in two countries; close personal association with several of the field's leading directors; a recent experience as administrator of a faculty of physical education in which both physical recreation and intramurals *and* intercollegiate athletics programs are included; and the writer's study of the philosophy of physical education and sport, which includes a pragmatic orientation and a professional concern with the persistent problems of physical education and sport.

DEFINITION OF THE TERMS "PROFESSION" AND "DISCIPLINE"

The current controversy or problem within the field of physical education and sport about whether this field is a profession or a discipline of necessity applies to intramurals, itself presumably a subdivision of physical education. One simple definition of a *profession* is an occupation or a vocation requiring knowledge and understanding of some department or field of learning. Traditionally, a professional person serves mankind; follows a code of ethics; is licensed or certificated to practice; considers his work a lifetime career; and does not consider the amount of money he earns to be of primary importance. Of course there are other criteria that could be added to this list.

A *discipline* is, on the other hand, a branch of instruction or learning. Thus, a professional person bases his practice upon the knowledge and understanding provided by the disciplinary investigator in one or more fields of instruction or learning.

Based on a preliminary analysis of intramural athletics up to this point in the discussion, intramurals would have to be categorized as a subdivision or subunit within the profession of physical education (which is itself typically thought to be a subdivision of the teaching profession). In responding to the question, "Is your professional practice based on undergirding disciplinary knowledge?" the intramural director would probably hesitate before responding relatively weakly that the field was moving in that direction. By such an answer he would be basing his case on the current effort to orient physical education as a discipline, but he would be hesitant about making any significant claims for the scholarly body of knowledge developed by "intramurals people" for use in the professional practice of intramurals directors. Does this imply that intramurals directors need only be personable organizers with a broad, but possibly superficial, background in sports? No attempt will be made to answer this rhetorical question definitively, but there is a definite problem here.

THE FRACTIONATING INFLUENCES
IN PHYSICAL EDUCATION TODAY

Before proceeding further with the "intramurals case," it is imperative that a look be taken at the field of physical education as it presently exists. (This exposition assumes that the 1960s have been a traumatic experience for most of the population, and that the impact of this past decade has been such that education in general is malfunctioning to a most serious degree.) Whether or not mankind is on a collision course with the future because the tempo of civilization is increasing so fast that many people are unable to adjust satisfactorily, there seems to be ample evidence that the field of physical education is on a collision course with itself: its professional leaders are gradually being *forced* to make an effort to understand what idealistic youth mean when they use such terms as "relevance," "accountability," and "involvement." At the same time, higher education is facing greater financial expenses with seemingly steady-state or declining legislative allotments. This means that certain subject matters and professional faculties on campus will inevitably have higher priorities than others. This problem is compounded further by possibly indefensible required physical education programs, academically inferior teacher education curricula, and intercollegiate athletics programs that have typically lost sound educational perspective in almost all regards.

Furthermore, there are major internal problems within what has been loosely called "the field" or "the profession." These are explained as follows:

1. *Specific-Focus Approach vs. "Shotgun" Approach:* Should the profession now attempt to unite behind the idea that the professional task within formal and informal education is to teach humans to move efficiently and with purpose in sport, dance, play, and exercise within the context of man's socialization in an evolving world, *or* should the present generalist curriculum be retained?

2. *The Physical Education vs. Athletics Encounter:* Does the profession in the United States dare to speak out time and again in a statesmanlike, forcible manner against practices in competitive athletics that don't even have a rightful place at any educational level or in society?

3. *The Male-Female Dichotomy in Physical Education:* Can men's and women's departments at all educational levels be amalgamated equitably, efficiently, and rapidly so that greater professional strength will be gained at the same time that money for the total operation is being saved?

4. *Professional Preparation Wing vs. Disciplinary Wing:* Can the field of physical education make the adaptation to the newer professional-disciplinary approach? This implies that all who teach in the various undergraduate curricula will be scholars (with all that this implies).
5. *The Bio-Science vs. The Humanities–Social Science Conflict:* Is it possible for faculty members teaching the natural scientific aspects of the field to live in peace with colleagues forming undergraduate and graduate options in the humanities and social science aspects of physical education and sport?

As if these problems aren't enough, the profession is additionally confronted with a situation in which the field of health and safety education *and* the field of recreation are successfully earning separate professional status (and would rather not have the term "physical education" on their letterheads). Moreover, the field of physical education can't even decide what to call itself: *required* physical education is in trouble in a great many places, and interphysical education is possibly the subject that is traditionally held in least regard in academic circles. It must be mentioned in passing that intercollegiate athletics is "running on a financial treadmill that is set at an impossible angle" for it to survive in its present form. This brings the discussion around again to the topic at hand—intramural athletics. What is its state of health?

INTRAMURAL ATHLETICS: THEN, NOW, AND IN THE FUTURE

Strangely enough, with all the woes that seem to be plaguing the field at present, intramural athletics *seems to be* healthy and thriving, both ideologically and practically. No matter which educational philosophy is held by the evaluator, intramurals tends to emerge as a program of "sport for all" that defies the onslaughts of campus critics. It is safe to say that since its beginning as an organized entity early in the twentieth century, its popularity has never been higher than it is now. The various theories of play that are extant seem to allow at least a significant place for individual, dual, and team experiences in a form of competitive athletics that is fairly well organized but not overemphasized. Even the use of public funds for the promotion of intramurals meets with general approval, because people sense intuitively that there's potential room in the program for all students, male and female alike.

After painting such a rosy picture of intramurals, however, we must recognize a dark side to the representation. The intramurals function has been taken for granted in the past, and this seems true even today. Intramurals is regarded as a *service* program and not as an educational one. There is still the feeling both within and without the field that intramurals can make do with inferior facilities and equipment. The officials in intramurals contests, for example, can be at the same level as the players, according to the opinion of many—fairly good, that is. After all, it's all for fun anyhow; so what if the official makes a few poor calls? Students just take part in intramural athletics to let off steam, and such emission tends to provide a safety valve for campuses that might otherwise be even more troublesome were it not for strenuous physical activity provided by the "establishment" for the aggressive mesomorphs.

And what about the status of the intramural director and his associates in the athletics or physical education hierarchy? Here we tend to find a similar situation—at least in the eyes of intramurals personnel. Certainly, intercollegiate athletic coaches and officials rarely provide more than lip service to the present intramurals ideal; often, the provision of leisure services is used as an excuse for the continued support of the whole varsity athletic program. Intramurals organizers don't fare much better with their presumably academic colleagues in physical education departments. Promotions and comparable salary levels are somewhat more difficult for the intramural director to achieve because he is usually so busy managing his program that truly scholarly efforts on his part are a rarity indeed. Thus, when the higher administrative posts within physical education and/or intercollegiate athletics are filled, it is almost self-evident that the good old "missionary" running a fine intramurals program is passed by for the proven scholar or the successful coach.

It is at this low point that the main thesis of this presentation emerges. The idea is simply this: the development of physical education and sport on this continent has reached the time when the supposed inferiority of intramurals can be overcome through the use of a revised definition of the field, a definition that can guarantee at least equality of status within the very near future to all properly conceived, well-organized, and adequately financed programs. An explanation about how to arrive at this halcyon state must begin with the presentation of a conceptual model for the entire field.

A MODEL FOR THE PROFESSION

A model for optimum professional development in a field called "X" has been developed. This model can serve for any given field that is based on its broad outline, but here it is designed to encompass what at the present time probably ought to be called "physical education and sport." Such a designation for the field undoubtedly represents only a "holding action" for the period immediately ahead. For the purposes of this discussion, the definition of the disciplinary aspect of the field is as follows: the art and science of human movement as related to the theory and practice of sport, dance, play, and exercise. The position taken here is that it is logical and in the best interest of intramurals to adopt a similar disciplinary definition immediately and to begin the conduct of its professional practice on the basis of the available body of knowledge.

This model (see Figure 1) comprises the following five subdivisions, all of which are applicable to what is presently called intramural athletics: (1) professional practice, (2) professional preparation, (3) disciplinary research, (4) a theory embodying assumptions and testable hypotheses, and (5) operational philosophy.

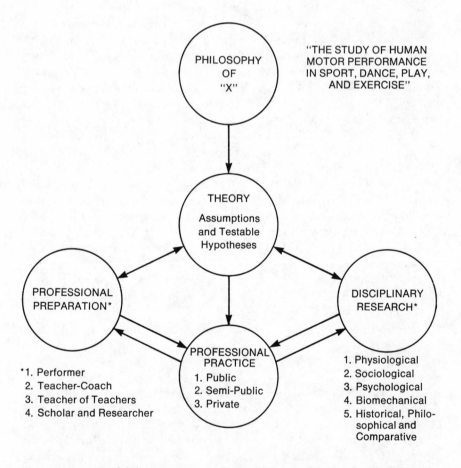

Figure 1. A Model for Optimum Professional Development in a Field Called "X"

Professional practice can be characterized as (1) public, (2) semi-public, and (3) private. *Professional preparation* should be designed to educate (1) the performer, (2) the teacher-coach, (3) the teacher of teachers, and (4) the scholar and researcher. *Disciplinary research* includes (1) the physiological, (2) the sociological, (3) the psychological, (4) the biomechanical, and (5) the historical, philosophical, and international aspects of human motor performance in sport, dance, play, and exercise. The assumptions and testable hypotheses of *theory* should constitute "a coherent group of general propositions used as principles of explanation for [the] phenomena" * exhibited in human motor performance in sport, dance, play, and exercise. Last, inclusion of the *philosophy of* "X" as an overarching entity in the model propounded is based on the belief that the value system of a society will in the final analysis gradually be realized within a developing social system.

IMPLICATIONS OF THE
PROPOSED MODEL FOR INTRAMURALS

Are there certain implications for intramurals that might be drawn from the discussion to this point? It could be argued that intramurals are popular and are making headway—good reasons for leaving well enough alone. On the other hand, the way the world is going today, mere maintenance of a low profile in a period of turmoil is certainly not sufficient planning for the future. With the current decline in the growth curve of higher education, it is inevitable that all programs will be undergoing continual evaluation. Those programs on campus that can stand close scrutiny will be supported increasingly, but those that can't present *evidence* that certain educational objectives are being achieved will be challenged. The mere statement that such and such a percentage of the student population is taking part, or that so many teams are in various basketball leagues, will no longer suffice. Evidence might also be mustered to claim that a certain percentage of the student population masturbates, but on what basis can the case be made that one activity is better than the other?

The argument is, therefore, that it is high time for intramural directors to become thoroughgoing, highly competent professional persons whose professional practice is based on disciplinary investigation resulting in a sound body of knowledge. Until now, the approach has been that of the evangelist ever exhorting his sheep to greater involvement with the flock in an amalgam of physical recreational activities. What does it all add up to? Who knows?

The essence of this position is, then, that intramurals has the

---

* *The Random House Dictionary of the English Language,* 1967.

wrong name and the wrong emphasis; that the old physical education triangle is now terribly dated; and that the intramurals subdivision of the field of physical education is somewhat like the headless horseman— ever ready and willing to ride off in any one of a number of directions at the same time. The recommendation is that intramurals should probably call itself something like "Physical Recreation and Intramural Sport," and that the entire field should direct itself immediately to the matter of hammering out in joint session an acceptable definition for the disciplinary undergirding of the profession that individual professionals are seeking to practice all across the land at all educational levels. Acceptance of new, instructional, and physical recreational objectives that are immediately realizable, as well as long-range goals of a more intangible nature, must become a reality soon. A disciplinary-professional approach stressing the art and science of human movement in sport and play would serve notice to the entire field—and to those outside of the profession—that the second-class-citizen days for intramural directors and their associates are to be relegated to history's trash heap.

Educational institutions can no longer justify the concept that public funds should be used for low-organizational, intramural sports programs that serve as recess periods for those students—men and women— who are presumably not suited for or capable of acceptable human motor performance. Educators do have the responsibility to provide instructional and physical recreational programs of the highest caliber for the ninety-five percent of the student population who should have the opportunity to learn about "the art and science of human movement as related to the theory and practice of sport, dance, play, and exercise." Such achievement—the learning of sound physical recreational skills—is recommended as a part of the good life for all young people, to be used whenever they desire in their later lives. Until now, the finest instruction, facilities, and equipment—and the prime time—have been available to those who needed it the least! Obviously, the needs and interests of the larger majority must be met. This is not to say that the program for the gifted or accelerated man or woman should be eliminated, but it is obvious that better balance is needed.

A SUMMARY WITH
RECOMMENDATIONS FOR THE FUTURE

Looking to the future, the profession of physical education and sport—a name for the field that is being recommended for the immediate future—should emphasize that human movement undergirds sport, dance, play, and exercise. An understanding of the theory and practice of such movement—actually, the "nonverbal humanities"—can come only from knowledge, skill, and understanding of a basic disciplinary core. A division or department of physical recreation and intramural sport can relatively soon demonstrate scientifically that active and creative physical recreation should be a part of a way of life during school and college years—and thereafter! Thus, its program can be either instructional or recreational in regard to physical recreation and sport.

A realistic assessment of the current situation will show that there is a need for improved *cost-benefit analysis.* Those concerned with the administration of programs of physical recreation and intramural sport should explain clearly to all concerned what the realizable objectives of a program are, how these objectives can be achieved by those taking part, and how the result will be evaluated to demonstrate conclusively that further—and possible increased—financial support is justifiable.

With such an approach, it would be possible to respond to our opening question about the possible disciplinary or professional status of intramurals. Physical recreation and intramural sport are important, integral aspects of the profession of physical education and sport. This emerging profession operates in public, semipublic, and private agencies, and it includes performers, teachers and coaches, teachers of teachers, and scholars and researchers. Professional practice is based on a disciplinary core of knowledge developed through scholarly and scientific investigation. The field is developing a theory of human motor performance in sport, dance, play, and exercise—a theory based on study of the physiological, sociological, psychological, biomechanical, and historical, philosophical, and international aspects of the phenomena being investigated.

Based on this analysis of our original question, physical recreation and intramural sport programs are *potentially* integral parts of the educational program offered to all in the department, school, or college of physical education and sport. Whether those concerned with this phase of the program truly achieve such professional status based on a core of sound disciplinary knowledge will depend on many factors in the years immediately ahead. The long-range goals would most certainly seem to warrant a good old college try on the part of us all.

2

Professional Preparation of Administrators of Intramural and Physical Recreation Programs

LAWRENCE S. PREO
Marquette University
Milwaukee, Wisconsin

INTRODUCTION

The primary premise of this chapter is that the preparation of individuals to be administrators of intramural and physical recreation programs is not a process that should be left to the result of fortuitous circumstances or adventitious speculation. Rather, the training of these managers of "sport for all" should proceed in an orderly fashion. The basis for this preparation must be to provide the administrator with both a technical and a conceptual framework that will enable the administrator to direct the intramural organization as effectively as possible.

Relatively few attempts have been made in the literature to describe or identify the process an intramural administrator should undertake to prepare for the task at hand. And yet, the extent and the quality of professional preparation programs for intramural administration may well be the determining factor in whether or not intramural and physical recreation programs continue to prosper.

BACKGROUND

Until recently, the field of intramurals has not seriously addressed itself to the issue of professional preparation of its members. Little or no research exists in this area. This void seems incongruous in light of the history of the growth of the profession. "Intramural athletics appeared in the school long before anyone ever thought about physical education and interschool athletics" (Voltmer and Esslinger, 1958, p. 279). Since the urge to play is generally accepted as being universal, it is difficult to imagine that it was quelled in our earliest educational institutions. Intramural baseball was played at Princeton as early as 1857, and the first intramural departments—consisting of one man each—were organized at Ohio State University and the University of Michigan in 1913. From these modest beginnings in 1913, organized intracampus physical recreation has developed into large-scale, professionally staffed operations. Staffs, programs, budgets, and facilities have increased. Multimillion-dollar facilities for intramural sport and physical recreation have been constructed on campuses across the country (for instance, at the University of Illinois, Oklahoma State University, Michigan State University, Purdue University, and the University of Washington). Many other universities report that they have planned this type of facility, needing only the necessary funding to begin construction.

Early intramural programs are a far cry from what can be found on most campuses today. The first programs were limited in scope; usually only four sports were offered: football, basketball, track, and baseball. Most of these limited programs were directed by a varsity coach. In fact, in those days many coaches gleaned the ranks of intramurals for recruits. It was also a frequent practice to use intramural teams as practice competition for junior varsity and freshman teams. Oddly enough, intramurals provided the impetus that created the position of varsity coach. The early sporting clubs on college campuses, seeking a higher level of competition, eventually scheduled games with "outside" competition. In one sense, this increased emphasis on competition led to a restricted membership: only the highly skilled had the opportunity to participate. Such was the catalyst of varsity teams (Means, 1963, p. 3). As the organization and structure of intramurals assumed new dimensions in the 1920s, the obvious choice for the position of intramural director was the individual who frequently appeared to know the most about the activity—the intercollegiate coach. Eventually, intramural departments frequently became the pasture in which old coaches were placed for their few remaining years before retirement.

Recent studies within the field have drastically altered the stereotyped image of the intramural administrator. Research conducted by the author produced a new profile of the intramural specialist (Preo, 1972). Among other things, the results of the study indicate that the average intramural director is a 38-year-old white male working at a state university with an on-campus student enrollment of under 5,000. He has a

12-month appointment, of which approximately 60 percent is concerned with intramurals; the remaining 40 percent is allotted to teaching. He has almost 9½ years of experience in intramurals, and he has been at his present institution for approximately 8 years. He has the rank of assistant professor but does not have tenure. He earns $10,204 per year ($12,040 with fringe benefits). He has a Master's degree in physical education with a minor in health, and he belongs to three professional organizations— National Intramural Recreation Sports Association, American Alliance Health, Physical Education and Recreation, and state (Association of Health, Physical Education and Recreation). He participated in inter-collegiate athletics (football, basketball, or baseball) as an undergraduate while earning a B— grade-point average. As a graduate student, he participated in intramurals and earned a B+ grade-point average. The preceding traits hardly describe the "old coach."

The same study also provided an overview of the formal professional preparation of the average intramural administrator. As an undergraduate, he probably was in the teaching/coaching option in the physical education curriculum. He took courses in speech, sociology, psychology, educational psychology, administration of health, physical education and recreation, and administration of athletics. He was active in both intramural and intercollegiate athletics. His intramural involvement often consisted of serving as either the captain or the coach of "his" teams. He also worked for the intramural department in the capacity of sport official. As a graduate student, he continued his preparation for a career in teaching and coaching and had aspirations of someday becoming an administrator. His program of study included several graduate-level courses in both education administration and higher education (Preo, 1972, pp. 32–33). In short, although an inspection of the educational background of the "average" intramural director certainly suggests that significant studies have been conducted on the preparation of intramural administrators in the last two decades, much remains to be done.

MODEL FOR ACTION

Intramurals has overcome many problems in the past and will face many challenges in the future. One of the most critical of these challenges is the need to adopt a more sound process of preparing individuals to become intramural administrators. This author rejects the neo-traditional method of selecting individuals to be intramural administrators merely on the basis that they worked for an intramural department during either their undergraduate or graduate student days. On the other hand, employment that evolves from merely fulfilling an arbitrarily derived list of "desired" course work is not the solution.

Until that day when professional standards of knowledges and skills are identified and subsequently required for admission to the profession, this writer proposes the following model as a basis for professional preparation in intramural administration.

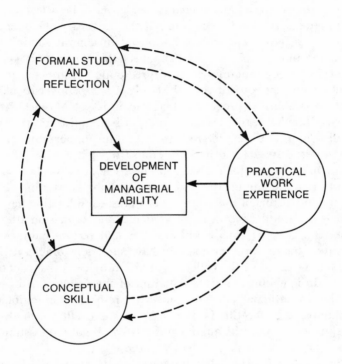

Figure 1. Proposed Model for the Professional Preparation of Intramural Administrators

As you can see, the core of the proposed model is the development of skills and knowledges, collectively referred to as "managerial ability." The objective or goal of such ability is to enable the administrator to develop and regulate the decision-making process within the organization in the most effective manner possible. For the reader who is interested in developing an overview of the dimensions of managerial skills, the writings of Peter F. Drucker (1966, 1974), Chris Argyris (1963), Herbert Simon (1957), and Chester Barnard (1938) are recommended.

For the individual who is interested in using this model as a basis for professional preparation in intramural administration, a logical starting point would be to attempt to identify as many of the factors that influence each of the three primary groups of input. Once identified, the prospective administrator could get his or her "ticket punched" and satisfy as many of the requirements as possible. The reader should note that the model provides for a continuing process, as well as for a comprehensive orientation. All three groups of input are interrelated.

The input area of formal study and reflection has two parameters: (1) the selection of an institution of higher learning and (2) choosing the proper course work. Many factors can govern the selection of the college to attend. It would be desirable if the university offered a degree program with a formal curriculum option in intramural administration. Although the number of schools that satisfy this criterion is somewhat small, the intramural administration degree option is growing in popularity. The University of Illinois and Michigan State University offer two of the more established programs. The University of Massachusetts has recently instituted a degree program in "sports administration." Another preferable option is the undergraduate internship opportunity in intramural administration offered by Kent State University.

A second criterion for the selection of a school in which to prepare to be an intramural administrator is to evaluate the faculty in the major area. If the instructors of the course work under consideration have reputable credentials and have demonstrated credible professionalism, then (all other things being equal) this school should receive more consideration than an institution that does not have similar favorable attributes. The graduate catalog of the college typically provides the credentials of all faculty. Insight into the professionalism of the faculty can be gained by perusing professional journals, by asking respected professionals for their opinions, or by meeting face to face with the faculty themselves.

A third criterion is the quality and relative size of the existing intramural program at the school under evaluation. Although it may or may not be justified, it is a fact that individuals who attended schools that had quality intramural programs (in reputation, at least) and who had the opportunity to work in these programs during either their undergraduate or graduate days have a greater chance for job placement in intramural administration. The proliferation of intramural administrators who had a Big Ten Conference affiliation or background is a good example of this phenomenon. An ancillary benefit of meeting this criterion is the general improvement in the quality of the practical work experience—another of the groups of input in the model.

The second parameter in the selection of the "best" school is choosing the proper course work. Although any such listing is somewhat arbitrary and is subject to debate due to uncontrollable situational factors, the following inventory is proposed as a minimum requirement:

1. Intramural or sports administration.
2. Recreation administration.

  3. Facility planning.
  4. Educational philosophy.
  5. Injury prevention and treatment.
  6. Communications theory.*
  7. Marketing theory.*
  8. Personnel administration.*
  9. Financial management.*
 10. Administrative theory.*
 11. Social science courses (as many as possible—for instance, sociology, psychology, anthropology).
 12. Basic introduction to law.

A traditionalist might object to the lack of a heavy concentration in either physical education or recreation courses. The changing nature of the responsibilities facing the intramural administrator—as an outgrowth of multimillion-dollar facilities, large budgets, the increased involvement of minority groups in physical recreation programs—require that intramural personnel undertake an interdisciplinary education or be partially unprepared to meet the challenges of the job.

The second type of input in the model is practical work experience. Any experience that provides contact with people is recommended. One of the cornerstones of intramural administration is an understanding and appreciation of *human relations*. Obviously, direct intramural experience would also be valuable. This kind of experience could take the following forms:

  1. As an intramural participant at the undergraduate and graduate level.
  2. As an intramural official, sports supervisor, program supervisor, gymnasium supervisor, or field supervisor at the undergraduate and/or graduate level.
  3. As a member of the student managerial system or policy board.
  4. As a graduate assistant working for the intramural department.
  5. As an assistant and/or associate intramural director.
  6. As a member of the NIRSA.

The last of these is particularly encouraged since membership in a professional association is frequently assigned a low priority by students besieged with many demands on their time. The NIRSA has several avenues of potential involvement for students—both undergraduate and graduate.

The third grouping of input into the model is the development and utilization of conceptual skill. Far too often, intramural directors adopt

---

* Usually these courses are offered by the department of business administration.

a bits-and-pieces, seat-of-the-pants approach to solving problems or making decisions. If a decision needs to be made, and it does not accommodate one of the slots on a laundry list of dos and don'ts, the intramural director is lost. Rather, an ability to see the whole problem in a frame of reference that will account for the future, as well as for the present, is needed. This ability is a conceptual skill. Conceptual skill is defined as the ability to develop, understand, and use concepts and knowledges, and to apply or transfer them to a variety of similar or related situations so as to aid in analyzing or understanding these situations, in planning future action, and in predicting the results of such action (Houston, 1961, p. 229). This skill enables the administrator to direct the organization in a dynamic environment—one in which different needs must be met, problems solved, and actions taken.

In sum, professional preparation to be an intramural administrator is an ongoing process. It starts before the individual decides to become an intramural administrator and continues throughout his or her days as a member of the field.

THE CHALLENGE OF THE FUTURE

What must be done now is a critical, in-depth analysis of the field of intramurals. Decisions need to be made concerning what type of intramural director is needed in the field. Decisions must be made about the role and function of the field with respect to the goals and aims of higher education. A determination of the present and the desired status of the field (for example, is it a profession or a discipline?) needs to be made. The final goal that is to be sought is the improvement of the professional preparation of intramural directors and, therefore, an improvement of the total intramural program.

While we are waiting for these decisions to be made, we, the active members of the field, must do everything in our power to improve ourselves and our profession. We must strive to remain aware of the ever changing needs of our campuses. We must become actively involved in our profession at the local, state, and national level. We must consume and produce research related to our work. We must attend workshops and meetings designed to improve and update ourselves as intramural administrators. We must attract graduate assistants who are interested in our area and then cultivate and mold those individuals to be our future leaders. We must develop a student section and promote student involvement in our local, state, and national conferences. Women, both at the student and professional level, must be encouraged to take active leadership roles in our profession. If each of us dedicates ourselves to these means, the end product—the improvement of our profession—will be accomplished. You and I can then say, "We are Number One."

GENERAL BIBLIOGRAPHY

ARGYRIS, CHRIS, *Organization and Innovation*. New Haven: Yale University Press, 1963.

BARNARD, CHESTER I., *The Functions of the Executive*. Cambridge, Mass.: Harvard University Press, 1938.

DRUCKER, PETER F., *The Effective Executive*. New York: Harper & Row, 1966.

————, *Management: Tasks, Responsibilities, Practices*. New York: Harper & Row, 1974.

HOUSTON, GEORGE C., *Manager Development: Principles and Perspectives*. Homewood, Ill.: Richard D. Irwin, 1961.

KLEINDIENST, VIOLA, and ARTHUR WESTON, *Intramural and Recreation Programs for Schools and Colleges*. New York: Appleton-Century-Crofts, 1964.

McCONNELL, JOHN, *Law and Business*. New York: Macmillan, 1966.

MEANS, LOUIS E., *Intramurals: Their Organization and Administration*. Englewood Cliffs, N.J.: Prentice-Hall, 1963.

PREO, LAWRENCE S., "A Comparative Analysis of Current Status and Professional Preparation of Intramural Directors," Unpublished Ph.D. dissertation, University of Illinois, 1972.

SIMON, HERBERT A., *Administrative Behavior*. New York: Macmillan, 1957.

TEAD, ORDWAY, *The Art of Leadership*. New York: McGraw-Hill, 1935.

UHRLAUB, DAVID, "Qualifications and Status of College Men's Intramural Directors," in *National Intramural Proceedings*. Dubuque, Iowa: Kendall/Hunt, 1969, p. 82.

VOLTMER, EDWARD F., and ARTHUR A. ESSLINGER, *The Organization and Administration of Physical Education*. New York: Appleton-Century-Crofts, 1958.

3

Blueprint for Structuring Campus Recreation

MICHAEL J. STEVENSON
University of Michigan
Ann Arbor, Michigan

It would appear that the era of participating rather than spectating has descended upon the nation's colleges and universities. Unprecedented numbers of students, faculty, and staff are presently enjoying campus-sponsored recreational pursuits. This phenomenon, which has been building steadily throughout the past decade, has caused leaders in the campus recreation field to give considerable thought as to how best to meet the enormous challenges of providing recreational opportunities for all individuals within the university family. One of the most critical of these challenges is to determine how best to structure campus recreational efforts in order to maximize the benefits for the recreational consumer, the participant.

HISTORICAL BACKGROUND

Historically, the traditional organizational pattern for campus recreation has been to assign control over such efforts to either the physical education or the athletic department. (Berg, 1969, p. 74). It would appear that several factors might account for this early trend: the great majority of campus recreation administrators had physical education and

20

athletic training; the early intramural programs were, at times, out-growths of formal physical education programs; and, finally, almost without exception the facilities used for campus recreation programs were controlled by either the physical education or the athletic department—or both. Another factor was that some leading physical educators viewed the intramural program as a natural extension of their departmental function. These early administrators appeared to emphasize the concept that campus recreation programs should be laboratory experiences in which students could develop skills acquired during physical education classes. As a result, the authority for intramurals was kept within the department.

In many institutions, part of the vast financial assets of intercollegiate athletic departments have been used to promote campus recreation (Mueller, 1971, p. 34). The provision of funds for the construction and maintenance of facilities used primarily for recreation, as well as funds for programing, salaries, and equipment, was a positive outgrowth of substantial athletic department contributions to campus recreation. Such contributions have generally resulted in the availability of funding to construct and maintain facilities that have been shared, at least part of the time, by participants in both intercollegiate athletics and intramural activity programs. In a limited number of situations, the generosity (obligation?) of varsity athletic administrators has also extended to the provision of monies for the salaries and equipment necessary for the intramural program. The view that intramurals should be responsible to either physical education or intercollegiate athletics has lived a long life. As late as 1971, a majority (57 percent) of the schools surveyed received recreational funds from physical education and/or athletic departments (Mull, 1971, p. 4).

Over the past several years, however, there appears to have been a trend away from assigning organizational jurisdiction over campus recreation to either physical education or athletics. In the past three years, for example, four Big Ten institutions (Iowa, Michigan State, Minnesota, and Purdue) have transferred administrative responsibility for campus recreation from either a physical education or an athletic department to a unit of the division of student services.

Apparently, this trend is the result of several factors. One of the primary reasons is that recreational programs are beginning to be perceived by high-level university administrators as primarily service-oriented rather than academic-oriented. The philosophical incongruity between the assumed responsibilities of physical education (for example, teacher preparation and research) and the primary service role of campus recreation has served to further illuminate potential conflicts. Historically, the competition with other interests within the department of physical education for funds, facilities, and identity has not been conducted in the best interests of campus recreation. Most of the bargaining leverage has rested with interests other than campus recreation. A committee of section chiefs, for example, would typically include only one voice for intramurals. The other individuals—possessing higher salaries, greater faculty rank, and, typically, more departmental esteem—would fight for their own vested interests. Without question, this competition has frequently restricted the growth and development of recreation on college and university campuses across the country.

In the fierce competition for funding, campus recreation personnel have also witnessed a change in their relationship with intercollegiate athletic departments. In some cases, athletics are becoming victims of their own past generosity. When stadiums were full and costs were low, funds provided by the athletic department benefited campus recreation programs. As one example of this generosity, the Intramural Sports Building at the University of Michigan was built entirely from intercollegiate gate receipts. However, costs for all aspects of intercollegiate programming have escalated to such a great extent that only a handful of the nation's college and university athletic programs can be administered without the support of general university funds. In the great majority of cases, the plight of campus recreation programs funded from athletic funds would appear to be self-evident. The growth of intramural and physical recreation programs has reached a state where it is both impossible and inadvisable to depend upon gate receipts.

NATURE AND PURPOSE OF ORGANIZATIONS

Having reviewed the historical background of the traditional means of organizing campus recreation, the next appropriate step is to consider some of the parameters of organizations in general. Our modern society is one based on various types of organizations. We are born in, educated in, and spend our lives working in organizations. We also spend a great deal of our leisure time paying, playing, and praying in organizations (Etzioni, 1964, p. 1). During the last fifty years, our country has become a society of organizations. Every major social task, whether economic performance or health care, education or protection of the environment, the pursuit of new knowledge or defense, is currently entrusted to large organizations, which are designed for perpetuity and are governed to a great extent by their own managements. On the performance of these institutions, the performance of society—if not the survival of each individual—increasingly depends (Drucker, 1974, p. 3).

What are these "units" that govern our lives? If we had no other evidence, we would know that complex organizations were necessary to accomplish great construction tasks—planned cities such as Kyoto, monuments such as the pyramids and temples of Egypt, irrigation systems such as those in ancient northern China (Arrow, 1964, p. 398). But we also know of organization for less material ends, for the preservation of law and order, for the maintenance of peace or the prosecution of war. And yet, organizations exhibit several descriptive commonalities. An organization is a group of individuals attempting to achieve common goals. Each member of an organization has objectives of his own, which in general are not coincident with those of the organization. Each member has some range of decisions to make within limits set partly by the environment external to the organization and partly by the decisions of other members. Finally, formal divisions of labor, power, and communication channels are frequently well delineated.

Since one of the primary characteristics of organizations is the directed behavior of a group of individuals towards the achievement of stated goals, it is probable that some forms of organization are more suitable than others for the administration of intramural programs. The next step, then, is to examine some basic considerations in the design and selection of the most appropriate organizational structure.

CONSIDERATIONS FOR STRUCTURAL DESIGN

The primary considerations for structural design can be categorized in three concerns: specialization of function within the organization; coordination of productive efforts within the organization; and span of managerial control within the organization. To lend order to an examination of these considerations, I have listed nine basic parameters that are identified by Richards and Greenlaw in their book, *Management Decision Making*.

1. Most organizations are designed to provide varying degrees of job specialization for their staffs. The determination of the degree of such specialization is a critical area of concern when designing the organizational structure.

2. Generally, specialization of activity, as opposed to performing a variety of skills, will increase individual productivity.

3. A second aspect that needs attention when considering structural design is the coordination of work to be performed by different individuals within the organization.

4. Managerial coordination is effected by providing subordinates and other organizational members with information, and then influencing these individuals to accept the content of the communicated messages.

5. When designing organizational hierarchies in which managers at various levels coordinate and direct the efforts of subordinates, the structure

must consider not only work content but also such factors as informational flow and power and influence relationships among various members of the organization.

6. A third area of concern when considering structural design is the span of control. Organizations that rely on both specialization and coordination must be structured to include various groups of personnel, each consisting of specialists and a formal leader.

7. The formal leader has such personal limitations as time, knowledge, skills, interests, and motivation, and thus the scope of a leader's activities within any given period of time is considered explicitly in organizational design by the notion of span of control. This concept states that the single manager is limited as to the number of subordinates whom he or she may supervise effectively.

8. Generally, the smaller the span of control, the greater the number of managers, total employees, and both managerial and total organizational levels. However, a wider span of control tends to decrease administrative costs and to facilitate vertical communications.

9. Messages communicated in narrow spans of control may become distorted as they pass from one individual to another, since each individual's knowledge, levels of understanding, perceptions, needs, and so on, are different. On the other hand, a wide span of control may result in the job of supervising becoming so great that the manager cannot perform his or her work effectively.

To this point, our discussion has focused on examining considerations for organizational structure from an industrial or business administration perspective. The next step is to examine factors that individuals who have been identified (by the author) as participants in campus recreation perceive to be the critical considerations in structuring campus recreation.

Haniford maintains that it is essential for the administrator of campus recreation to have a direct line of communication with top-level administrators within the university, if communication is to be effective (1968, p. 17). If the director of campus recreation finds himself in a role that is subordinate to directors of varsity athletic or physical education programs, opportunities to communicate the needs of recreation on the campus to levels where decisions of university finances are generally made can be greatly impeded. The basis of this potential impediment is obvious when the potential self-interests of both physical education and varsity athletics are considered.

Beeman and Humphrey identified another factor (1960, p. 15). They found that control of facilities has a significant influence on the resulting structure of campus recreation. Few schools in the country are afforded the luxury of having separate facilities for physical education, athletics, *and* recreation. The sharing of limited facilities and the determination of who has priority over these facilities seem to constitute a common dilemma for university officials throughout the country. It would appear, logical to assume that whenever one interest is subordinate to another, priority and control of the use of available facilities lie with the interest that is higher on the organizational ladder. In the battle for the autonomy of, or the guarantee of equal rights for, campus recreation efforts, it is interesting to note, however, the large number of university administrators who presently either do not understand this logic or who (for other reasons) have chosen to ignore the obvious rationality of the argument.

Matthews is in basic agreement with both Haniford and Beeman and Humphrey. He states that sources of funds, priority in the use of facilities, and the degree of authority vested in the office of the campus recreation director are the critical factors to be considered when designing a structure for campus recreation (Matthews, 1973, pp. 1–4).

When program funding is not based on a fixed per-student allocation, access to adequate channels of communication is essential. The director of campus recreation must be permitted to submit and defend his budget request at the highest possible administrative level if he is to avoid the traditional problems of conflict of interest, misinformation, and lack of proper information being delivered to the correct channel.

A second aspect of the funding parameter in structuring campus recreation is the problem of competition from other units for limited funds. For instance, competition might occur among several different units within a student services structure, which might lead to difficult times for a campus recreation organization assigned to such a structure. In actuality, this problem is not different than the vested interest in physical education departments discussed earlier. On the other hand, Matthews believes that where the director of campus recreation is located may not be critical. What is more important, he believes, is that the effectiveness of administration is directly related to the strength of the administrator's decision-making power. After receiving guidance from various advisory committees, the director must be given the authority to decide what is best for the total campus recreation program.

Factors considered important by recreational specialists in structuring campus recreation were the necessity for ease of communication with the top-level administration; problems involved with conflicts of interest among physical education, athletics, and campus recreation; concerns as to who will control decisions regarding shared use of facilities; sources of funds; and the degree of authority vested in the position of campus recreation director.

Given this examination of the considerations involved in structuring campus recreation within the university bureaucracy, the next step is to propose a hypothetical model.

HYPOTHETICAL MODEL FOR CAMPUS RECREATION

Traditionally, campus recreational programming has been concerned primarily with physical recreation activities. A few well-written textbooks regarding programming for such activities have been published: Means, 1973; Kleindienst and Weston, 1964; Beeman and Humphrey, 1960; and Mueller, 1971. These authors have generally addressed such technical aspects of programming as history, finances, facilities, equipment, units of participation, activities, scheduling, tournament structure, point systems, rules and regulations, publicity, and sports clubs. Much remains to be done, however, in the expansion of campus recreation's purview of activities. In this author's opinion, it is both logical and desirable to extend our programming efforts to such previously omitted areas as theatre, music, student union activities, arts and crafts, outing activities, and special-interest recreational clubs of a nonphysical nature. Stressing the theory of coordination discussed earlier, it would seem appropriate to centralize the organization and administration of all aspects of campus recreation under the direction of a single administrative unit.

Under the assumption of a coordinated single administrative unit, the direction of competitive intramural activities, sports clubs, informal or "free play" activities, social activities, outing activities, and creative activities should all be considered within the administrative scope of a division of campus sports and recreation. Figure 1 illustrates the proposed model that could accomplish this coordination.

Legend for Model

(1) = Responsible for team, dual, and individual competitive intramural programs for men.

(2) = Responsible for informal/"free-play" activities program.

(3) = Responsible for team, dual, and individual competitive intramural programs for women, and for competitive co-recreational intramural program.

(4) = Responsible for social activities such as nonphysical recreation, dances, parties, and so forth.

(5) = Responsible for music, dance, drama, lectures, and so on.

(6) = Responsible for organization and administration of physical recreation–oriented sports clubs.

(7) = Responsible for orienteering, hunting, fishing, sailing, skating, skiing, and similar activities.

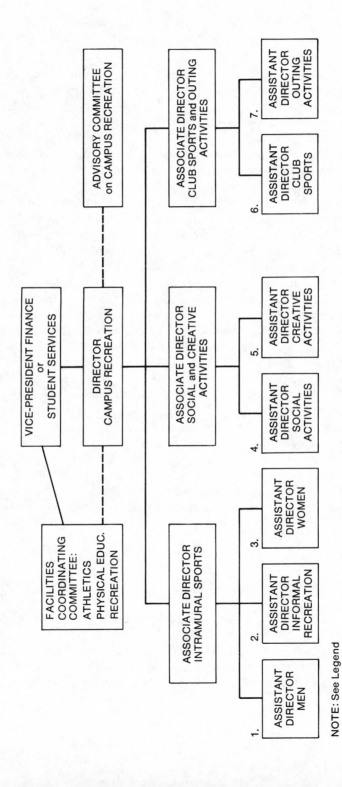

Figure 1. Model for Structuring a Division of Campus Sports and Recreation

NOTE: See Legend

RATIONALE FOR THE PROPOSED MODEL

The rationale for having the director of campus recreation report to either a university vice-president for student affairs or a vice-president for finance is, in this author's opinion, to insure that the director of campus recreation has a direct line of communication to a high-level administrator. This author believes that the closer (in the organizational structure) that the administrator is to the individual responsible for the disbursement of funds, the more likely his chance will be of receiving a favorable response to his budget requests.

Since the problem of joint use of facilities is commonplace, it would seem appropriate to form a facilities coordinating committee, responsible to the vice-president and composed of representatives from athletics, physical education, and campus recreation, which would set priorities and regulate the joint use of facilities.

Consistent with the wide span of our discussion of control earlier in this chapter, it is recommended that there be three associate directors who report to the director and seven assistant directors who report to the three associate directors. The factor of job specialization is also considered in this recommendation.

It must be pointed out that few institutions in the country currently have eleven staff members within their campus recreation division. On the other hand, however, once a consolidation of the various aspects of campus recreation (as defined within the context of the proposed model) were effected, many institutions might easily approach, if not surpass, this recommended number of personnel.

Finally, the reader should remember that various divisions within the proposed model may be either revised or excluded entirely, depending upon the size of the institution and the present and planned-for recreational opportunities for students, faculty, and staff of the institution.

GENERAL BIBLIOGRAPHY

ARROW, KENNETH J., "Control in Large Organizations," *Management Science*, X, No. 3 (April, 1964).

BEEMAN, HARRIS F., and JAMES H. HUMPHREY, *Intramural Sports: A Text and Study Guide*. Dubuque, Iowa: William C. Brown, 1960.

BERG, OTTO, "Future Trends in the Administration of Intramural Sports at the College Level, "Twentieth Annual Proceedings of the National Intramural Association. Los Angeles, 1969.

DRUCKER, PETER F., *Management: Tasks, Responsibilities, Practices.* New York: Harper & Row, 1974.

ETZIONI, AMITAI, *Modern Organizations.* Englewood Cliffs, N.J.: Prentice-Hall, 1964.

Guidelines for Effective Coordination of Campus Recreation. A Report of the National Conference on College and University Recreation. Washington, D.C.; National Education Center, 1968.

HANIFORD, GEORGE, "Future Trends in Intramurals, Organization and Finances," Nineteenth Annual Proceedings of the National Intramural Association. Austin, Texas, 1968.

Intramural Sports for College Men and Women, rev. ed. Washington, D.C.: American Association for Health, Physical Education and Recreation, 1964.

KLEINDIENST, VIOLA, and ARTHUR WESTON, *Intramural and Recreation Programs for Schools and Colleges.* New York: Appleton-Century-Crofts, 1964.

MATTHEWS, DAVID O., "Administrative Structures." Paper presented at the Intramural and Campus Recreation Personnel Conference, Illinois State University, Normal, Illinois, Nov. 14–16, 1973.

MEANS, LOUIS E., *Intramurals, Their Organization and Administration.* Englewood Cliffs, N. J.: Prentice-Hall, 1973.

MUELLER, PAT, *Intramurals: Programming and Administration,* 4th ed. New York: Ronald Press, 1971.

MULL, RICHARD F., "A Survey of Intramural Programs of Colleges and Universities." Paper presented to the School of Physical Education, West Virginia University, Morgantown, W. Va., 1970.

PARSONS, TALCOTT, *Structure and Process in Modern Societies.* Glencoe, Ill.: Free Press, 1960.

RICHARDS, MAX D., and PAUL S. GREENLAW, *Management Decision Making.* Homewood, Ill.: Richard D. Irwin, 1966.

4

Human Relations in the Administration of Intramural Sports and Recreative Services

FRANK BEEMAN
Michigan State University
East Lansing, Michigan

INTRODUCTION

The awareness of the importance of comprehensive and judicious intramural administration was born in this writer in October, 1955. It became clear, as Co-Chairman of the first National Conference on Intramural Sports for College Men and Women held in Washington, D. C., that direction must be provided for those responsible for the administration of the tremendously expanding sports program. One hundred and ten men and women, representing seventy-nine institutions from thirty-nine states and Canada, gathered to formulate guides useful to the preparation of intramural administrators.

Because of the concern to prepare people for intramural administration rather than to continue to accept the "old coach" or the "lame duck" teacher or supervisor as intramural directors, a study exploring the most crucial element, human relations, was completed in 1960.

Administrative skills are universal. Because the common element with which all administrators must work is people, administrative skills,

From *Administrative Theory and Practice in Physical Education and Athletics,* Earle F. Zeigler and Marcia J. Spaeth, Eds., © 1975. Reprinted by permission of Prentice-Hall, Inc., Englewood Cliffs, N.J.

techniques, and concerns cross all boundaries between education, industry, armed services, or government. With this in mind two techniques were borrowed from business and industry. The Harvard University Business School had successfully used the case study method in the administration of business and industry (McNair and Hersum, 1954). Adaptation of this method was made by Bauer (1955, p. 35) in developing the case problem technique. This technique was the primary tool used.

A case problem is defined by Bauer as that type of case that contains two elements, the facts crucial to the problem and the problem itself. "The problem is one easily identified and contains only the facts that have direct and immediate bearing on the problem" (1955, p. 36).

The secondary tool used was the critical incident technique. This was developed by John C. Flanagan (1952), Director of the American Institute for Research. Flanagan describes a critical incident as

> any observable human activity that is sufficiently complete in itself to permit inferences and predictions to be made about the person performing the act. To be critical, an incident must occur in a situation where the purpose or intent of the act seems fairly clear to the observer and where its consequences are sufficiently definite to leave little doubt concerning its effect. (Ibid., p. 327).

Because the universities of the Western Conference involved more than 50,000 students in their intramural programs and because of the similarities among Conference institutions, these ten schools were the subjects of the investigation. To provide potential and practicing administrators with some tangible guidelines to foresee problems and to help solve administrative problems that occur, even with conscious foresight, it was necessary to

1. Determine administrative problem areas;
2. Gather data from the administrative problem areas that could be developed into case problem;
3. Offer alternate solutions to those situations involving human relations;
4. List the "critical incidents" in the cases that led to satisfactory or unsatisfactory solutions;
5. Suggest currently useful generalizations based upon the cases as guideposts for the Western Conference Intramural Directors.

Intramural programs have progressed beyond the stage of small "extras," offered by athletic departments to mollify critics of varsity athletics. The President's Council on Youth Fitness, the AAHPER Youth Fitness Project, the changing emphasis toward do-it-yourself sport activity among all segments of the population, but particularly among girls and women, have created intramural buildings and facilities worth millions of dollars on hundreds of college and university campuses throughout the country. The administrators of these facilities must deal effectively with the student desires and demands for organized and informal participation.

Because many of their administrative problems will be in the area of human relations, it is imperative that some "life experience" be made available to them for professional preparation and in-service training purposes. The establishment of some uniformities or useful generalizations through analysis of research case problems gives the students a clearer insight or understanding of their responsibilities.

Each director employs, trains, and directs hundreds of students each year. Supplies and equipment must be purchased to successfully coordinate participants' use of facilities and areas. Plans for expansion of physical facilities as well as program content must be continually plotted. These responsibilities bring the administration of an intramural program on this level ever closer to the administering of a business or industry.

Directors have had to learn about the responsibilities and intricacies involved in administration largely by trial and error. The responsibilities for thousands of participants and hundreds of thousands of dollars in budgets requires that efficient methods of administration be insured to safeguard the privileges of all individuals as well as to insure the proper use of public funds.

There has been no accumulation of solutions, decisions, methods, or techniques for solving the administrative problems of the Western Conference Intramural Directors. Duties and responsibilities are listed in most intramural texts. No real insight, however, into some of the solutions or methods that are effective in working with people drawn from true-life has been available. As Bauer states,

> There is a great need for material that throws light on the effect of formal and informal organization, interpersonal relations, subgroup behavior, and pressures from the environment surrounding the administrative situation. Finally, there is practically no material available that concentrates on, and contributes to an understanding of, the process of decision-making in the college or university setting. These are the areas in which the development and study of cases may be expected to make a significant contribution (1955, p. 44).

As early as 1955 the College Physical Education Association, AAHPER, and the National Association for Physical Education of College Women recognized the potential of intramural programs to contribute to the students' overall development. To aid in the development of intramural directors administrators, these groups sponsored the National

Conference on Intramurals. The Conference was reminded by Ruth Abernathy, president of AAHPER, to "fit the intramural sports program into the administrative pattern of the colleges" (1955, p. 35).

REVIEW OF RELATED LITERATURE: BRIEF HISTORICAL BACKGROUND OF THE CASE METHOD

The use of the case method to analyze and investigate human relations and problems has been prevalent for many years. As early as 1871 the technique was used in the Harvard Law School to bring more reality to the study of law. Various fields have made extensive use of this method of investigation where the laboratory or experimental methods were not appropriate. Public administration, social services, youth delinquency groups, school counseling departments and, more recently, personnel in educational administration are using the case method to teach, to prepare, and to gain insight into the problems of people.

The use of case histories by the social services and school counselors differs in its objectives from the use of case studies by colleges of business administration and educational administrators. In the first instance, the purpose is to determine factors that cause problems for the individual. Having found the causes, the worker attempts to reduce or remove them and, at the same time, tries to rehabilitate the individual. In the field of business administration and in educational administration, the case study is used to prepare leaders in the respective fields. In these fields, this technique is also used extensively to resolve problems that appear to be reducing the efficiency of a particular staff or department.

In 1920, a significant event occurred in the development of social research studies. The personal document, which may well be considered as the forerunner of the case study, advanced from the uncritical stage to the critical status required of clinical work: "If any line can be drawn between the era of uncritical and the era of the critical use of personal documents, the research of Thomas and Znaniecke, "The Polish Peasant," in 1920 marks the date (Allport, 1942, p. 29)."

Since 1920 the case method has undergone considerable refinement. Improvements have been made in the collection of data and in the interpretation of the information drawn from the data. Educational administrators are exploring this technique thoroughly in attempting to prepare school administrators.

The use of the critical incident technique is also relatively new, particularly in the field of education and especially in the area of intramural administration.

This technique had its origin in the studies of Sir Francis Galton seventy-odd years ago. Interim developments were time sampling studies, controlled observation tests, and anecdotal records. According to John C. Flanagan (1952, p. 325), the critical incident technique grew out of studies in the Aviation Psychology Program of the United States Air Force of World War II. This program was initiated to improve the instruction of pilots, navigators, and other crew members.

Harvard President Conant's enthusiasm for the case method of study in the business school was the result of many years of hard work by the Harvard faculty in both the law school and the business school. C. C. Langdell initiated the use of the method in 1871 for the study of law. The method, which was resisted at first, proved its practical value, and by 1915 all the better law schools in the country were using it (Bauer, 1955, p. 29).

In 1920, Melvin T. Copeland, the instructor at the Harvard Business School who had been given the approval to use the case method, completed a book entitled Marketing Problems. Cases in the book were drawn from the Bureau of Business Research from newspaper items, from business publications such as the Federal Trade Commission Report, and from personal business acquaintances.

In 1932, the Harvard Business School decided to concentrate on collecting cases concerned with a particular administrative problem and to attempt to develop a better understanding of that problem, rather than to try to draw guides from a diversified group of cases about varied problems.

As the refining of cases developed, the business school noted that there were two parts of a research case:

1. Description of a situation observed accurately;
2. Diagnosis of the situation—specific suggestions for action. (Suggestion for action is that order of statement which would be useful to a person who has to administer the situation being described.) It should make sense to those who live in the situation—it is to clarify for them things which they have intuitively acted upon but which they have not previously put into words.

In summary, the case method has been developed and accepted predominantly in the study of law and business. Educational administrators are expanding this technique as more texts and more courses utilizing the method are created. Physical education, intramurals, and athletics, three phases of the educational program particularly concerned with administrative problems, have begun to explore the use of the case method. The technique has developed in the various fields bcause of the concern of administrators who are searching for ways to resolve human relations "bottlenecks" and inefficient administrative practices.

Very little research has been done in the field of education and particularly in the field of physical education using the critical incident technique. The technique itself needs further refining, as do all techniques used in determining human relations factors. Rather than collecting opinions, estimates, and hunches, it obtains a record of specific behaviors from those people in the best position to make the most accurate observations and evaluations.

METHODOLOGY

Selection of Problem Areas

The problems and problem areas were drawn from three sources. The first was from the Western Conference intramural directors themselves, and their predecessors. The minutes of the annual meetings of the conference directors from 1948 to 1958 inclusive, were collected and studied. Those problems that appeared more than once in the minutes and those that gave evidence of difficulty were recorded.

The second source was from those areas in which problems occurred that were recorded in the report of the National Intramural Conference for College Men and Women sponsored by the AAHPER, NAPECW, and CPEA in Washington in 1955.

The third source was from those problem areas which the writer has become aware of in twenty-five years as a university intramural director; four years as Chairman of the Intramural Section of the AAHPER; Co-Chairman of first National Intramural Conference noted above; and co-author of the text, Intramural Sports, for professional physical education students.

The problem areas and outline for the study were presented to the 1959 meeting of the Western Conference intramural directors. Each problem was to be checked as "most difficult to solve" or "most frequently encountered," or in both categories. Space was made available for additional comments adjacent to each response.

Each director and school was assigned a code number to mask the identity of the institutions and the source of any case information. This was necessary to reduce the "halo effect" that might occur when the directors studied the decisions and solutions of their fellow directors.

The directors were supplied with the problem areas they, as a group, had selected as important in their administrative duties. At the same time, the directors were furnished with a case reporting form. The form helped the directors in recording the pertinent facts about the case problems they encountered and also aided in standardizing the recorded interviews.

The writer made arrangements to visit each director personally at his particular school for a tape-recorded interview. Each director collected a number of cases to be prepared for the interview. The reporting form was used as a guide during the interviews to form a basis for questions and to guide each interview along similar channels. The cases were told to the writer in story form. The writer broke into the report only to clarify points or to identify an individual's statements or actions. In some instances original letters and papers were submitted by directors to substantiate the case problems.

Treatment of Refined Case Problems

The writer then refined the thirty-two taped interviews and wrote them in narrative form with all the facts retained. Twenty-three of these case problems were determined to contain sufficient facts and to be in areas of common interest to the directors. With the exception of two case problems, the actions of the directors were not disclosed, because this would have revealed the actual steps and decisions made by them. In these two long cases involving a number of people and considerable time, the complete information was recorded for each director's reaction.

The writer devised alternate solutions for each case problem and listed these solutions, with the actual solution, at the end of each case. Provision was made for the directors to rank the alternatives from best to worst.

The cases with the alternate solutions and critical elements were then returned to all the directors. The actual solutions were included in the list of alternate solutions so that no director (except the person at the school involved) knew what decisions were actually made. The directors were given the opportunity to offer additional solutions in the event they agreed with none of those listed.

In addition to ranking the solutions in order of best to worst, the directors also indicated the incidents they determined to be critical in each case.

Intramural directors, as with all persons in administrative positions, react humanly and thus with some variance, even to very similar situations. The intramural director must act and solve, in one fashion or another, the multitudinous situations he encounters in an efficient and yet individually creative manner many times a week. He does not possess the time, staff, or, in many cases, the desire to collect a case history or even a case report.

The case history requires much background research and additional information not easily accessible to the director. For these reasons, the case problem is more suited to his needs. He is interested predominantly and usually has access only to the "facts that have direct and immediate bearing on the problem" as described on the last page of Bauer's book (1955, p. 213).

This present study is an attempt to examine one segment of the physical education field using this technique. In other words, the plan was to collect cases from those individuals concerned with the administration of intramural programs and to collate the evaluations of the administrative procedures and decisions reached by these directors. From the analysis of these cases, currently useful generalizations were prepared, or as stated by Lombard (in Andrews, 1953, p. 228), "that order of statement which would be useful to a person who had to administer the situation being described."

FINDINGS AND CONCLUSIONS

Intramural programs are conducted for the benefit of the students at the various institutions. The better programs are service programs concerned with the development of the individual as well as with the provision of various activities. In the majority of the cases the directors involved the student participants in the decision-making process. The directors recognized that the students would have additional opportunity for development if they were allowed to contribute to the decisions controlling their actions.

The directors are concerned with those problem areas in which they experience difficulty in determining fair solutions and those which they encounter frequently. The following three tables indicate the areas in which the Western Conference intramural directors find their greatest concern.

Table 1.   The Problem Areas Determined
by the Western Conference Intramural Directors
as "Most Difficult to Resolve"

---

* 1. Enforcement of eligibility rules
2. Publicity in school paper
3. Building management
4. Office management
5. Preparation of fields and facilities
6. Health clinic cooperation
7. Relations with superiors
8. Relations with other departments and faculty
9. Allotment of intramural budgets

---

* Random order

Table 2. The Problem Areas Determined
by the Western Conference Intramural Directors
as "Most Frequently Encountered"

---

* 1. Enforcement of eligibility rules
  2. Publicity in school paper
  3. Building management
  4. Office management
  5. Preparation of fields, facilities
  6. Relations with other departments and faculty
  7. Relations with coaches and physical education staff in the use of activity areas
  8. Selection of supervisors and officials
  9. Control of contestants by student officials

---

* Random order

Table 3. The Problem Areas Determined
by the Western Conference Intramural Directors to Fall in
Both Categories of "Most Difficult to Resolve" and
"Most Frequently Encountered"

---

* 1. Enforcement of eligibility rules
  2. Publicity in school paper
  3. Office management
  4. Building management
  5. Relations with other departments and faculty

---

* Random order

There appear to be acts or omissions of acts that affect the development of administrative problems. An arbitrary number of three repetitions was selected to depict an incident as consistently critical. When an incident occurred in three or more cases, that incident was deemed to be significant and important for a director to consider when conducting an activity. There were a total of sixty-nine critical incidents drawn from the sixteen cases.

Critical incidents initiated by Western Conference Intramural Directors indicate the following points:

1. Inadequately written sport rules and participation regulations create a significant number of the administration problems;
2. Permitting abusive participants or spectators to remain in an activity area will help intensify existing situations;

3. All-year point systems tend to create a pressure that builds tension and induces problem situations.

CURRENTLY USEFUL GENERALIZATIONS CONCERNING WESTERN CONFERENCE INTRAMURAL ADMINISTRATION

There were a total of seventy-two generalizations from the sixteen case problems. Those generalizations repeated as pertinent guides for successful administrative action in three or more cases were summarized into statements useful to individuals administering similar situations. In some instances information found in the incidents determined to be critical by the directors was also found in the generalizations.

The nine generalizations which meet the required three or more repetitions are ranked below according to the number of case problems in which they appear.

1. Directors recognize and seriously consider recommendations from student organizations.
2. Intramural game rules and participation regulations often prove to be incomplete and are not infallible.
3. An equitable all-year point system is difficult to devise, and a point system tends to create tensions among units.
4. Errors caused by supervisory mistakes and inadequate regulations do not cause units or individuals to be penalized.
5. Strict disciplinary action is invoked for direct intentional violations of rules and such problems as the exhibition of personal disrespect for the director.
6. Rulings pertaining to individuals and units are discussed by all concerned before the rulings are invoked.
7. Direct lines of communication are to be maintained among the director, students, and officials concerned with student affairs.
8. Game rules or regulations that have proved unworkable should be modified immediately.
9. Consideration is given to the replay of contests under protest because of rule misinterpretation, rather than determining the winner by rule alone.

Usefulness of the Case Problem Method

The usefulness or value of the case problem method in gaining valid knowledge about human relations in the administration of Western Conference Intramural Programs is demonstrated in the findings following. Questionnaires and statistical studies would not have indicated how the directors might change their decisions after further study of an actual problem (Table 4, item 4). This item indicates that in seven out of the

Table 4. Indication of Cases from which Significant Information about Western Conference Intramural Administration was Drawn

Information Drawn from Directors' Responses	Percent	Cases 1	2	3	4	5	6	7	8	9	10	11	12 A	12 B	13	14	15
1. Human relations are clearly involved in Western Conference intramural administration because fourteen cases out of sixteen were concerned with team or individual conflict.	87	X	X	X	X	X	X		X		X	X	X	X	X	X	X
2. * Inadequate regulations caused eight out of eleven of the administrative problems involving intramural rules and regulations.	73			X	X	X	X	X	X	X		X			X		
3. The student protest is a definite part of the intramural regulation system. There were ten case problems that involved team or individual violations. Seven of these were reported to the director by means of a protest.	70						X	X	X		X	X	X		X		
4. ** The original decision by the director involved was not supported in eleven of the sixteen case problems.	68			X	X		X	X	X	X	X	X	X	X	X	X	X
5. The Western Conference Intramural Directors recommend and encourage student participation in the determination of decisions and regulations concerning eligibility and conduct violations. In ten cases out of sixteen, student participation was required by the directors.	62	X	X	X	X	X	X	X	X	X	X	X					X

Table 4—Continued

Information Drawn from Directors' Responses	Percent	Cases															
		1	2	3	4	5	6	7	8	9	10	11	12 A	12 B	13	14	15
6. Pressures created by point systems are a significant source of problem for the directors. Seven out of thirteen case problems reported that involved team protests, or individuals' problems arose from the all-around point system.	54				X		X		X	X			X	X		X	
7. The directors indicated they were reluctant to award a contest to a team by rule alone. In three of the six games protested, rather than determine the game by rule, the directors rescheduled the game in part, or completely.	50				X			X				X					
8. Student supervisors and officials are a significant source of administrative problems. In seven of the sixteen cases, these student employees were involved.	44	X		X	X		X	X				X				X	X
9. Problems involving the control of participants, such as ineligibility, make up the most difficult single problem area for the directors. Seven of the sixteen cases concerned eligibility.	44		X			X	X				X		X		X	X	

* In each of the eight cases concerning inadequate regulations, the directors modified the regulations. By this action, they indicated that they considered the individual more important than the rules.

** In seven instances directors who had made an original decision to solve a problem changed their decisions after a more thorough study of the problem in an objectively written form. This supports the use of the case problem method as a dynamic means for gaining insight to Western Conference intramural administrative action.

fifteen cases, directors changed their original decisions because of the opportunity for a more thorough and objective study of the problem. In each case the new decision was the one supported by a majority of the other directors. The tensions created by point systems, which may be the basis for innumerable other problems, are clearly brought out by this method of investigation. The modification of rules determined to be inadequate (Table 4, item 2) was best brought out by the directors' investigation of actual life situations. The directors were willing to waive or modify rules in favor of individual fairness and justice. Their responses indicated involvement of students in determination of rules and penalties concerning their participation. These two statements above are well demonstrated (Table 4, item 5) by the case problems.

IMPLICATIONS FOR THE ADMINISTRATOR

Individuals who are responsible for the actions and performance of others are unfortunately often acting only on intuition. This intuition is too often based only upon their own narrow experiences which are limited to the policies of the previous administrator. In many instances there is no chance for the departing executive or director to pass on even what he has learned to the new director.

If each director could record cases concerning various problems he encounters, including those incidents that appear to be crucial to a successful solution of the problems, a tremendous backlog of actual experience would be available. Even the directors gathering the cases would benefit by being able to review their actions and decisions in previous problems of a similar nature.

All scientific investigators keep records of performances of various agents, materials, and conditions. The justice courts and the practice of law give considerable weight to precedence. Is it not even more important that the practice of governing individuals be given the benefit of past methods and results? Is it impossible to envision a case book available to every intramural director? Obviously, no set rules would be prescribed for each problem the director might encounter. Cases similar to those the director must deal with plus guides or generalizations pertaining to these cases would certainly aid in the formulation of intelligent, comprehensive decisions.

The methods and techniques available for other purposes such as experimental, statistical, and questionnaire are more concerned with the end results of certain situations or sets of questions. The recording of life experiences in case form provides more information about the actual process of human action and decision-making. In human relations it is often more important to know why and how the participants reacted than to know what the end result was.

From a growing log of cases intramural administrators may well find that the one common and crucial element in all situations is the relationship between people. Any collection of cases will show the ever-widening relations touching the director and staff, director and student employees, director and participants, director and other colleagues, and all these individuals with their circle of relationships with the director and each other.

Administrators may discover: (1) that efficient and successful human relationships call for attacking the problem a person has—not the person with the problem; (2) that an administrator or director directs best by serving, and serving a staff means, first not to be the bottleneck at which all fresh, new ideas are blocked; (3) that removing obstacles and making decisions, rather than procrastinating, enables a staff to perform unhindered; and (4) that, through a continual study of the human relations involved in every situation, and by the awareness of those critical incidents pinpointing problems, the director may come to the realization that people are more important than things.

Finally, additional work should be initiated to further explore this area so crucial to effective (in terms of people) administration. Some suggestions for further investigation follow.

1. Only one small segment of the administrative areas concerned with Western Conference intramural administration was investigated in this study—a phase of the "controlling" area. The other phases of planning, organizing, directing, and coordinating need to be studied in a similar manner before a comprehensive scheme of the position of intramural director may be recorded.

2. More intensive study should be made over a number of years in order that numerous cases may accumulate additional administrative actions appropriate to similar situations.

3. One school and one director, determined to be competent, efficient, and successful in terms of student participation, growth, and development, might be studied intensively in the same manner.

4. Further study should be made to investigate the development of a system to enable directors to recognize and record immediately critical incidents occurring in their daily administrative duties.

GENERAL BIBLIOGRAPHY

Abernathy, Ruth, "President's Address," AAHPER, NAPECW, CPEA, *Intramural Sports for College Men and Women: Report on First National Conference on Intramurals*. Washington, D.C., 1955.

ALLPORT, GORDON, *The Use of Personal Documents in Psychological Science,* Social Science Research Council Bulletin 49, New York, 1942.

ANDREWS, KENNETH, et al., *Human Relations and Administration.* Cambridge, Mass.: Harvard University Press, 1953.

BAUER, RONALD D., *Cases in College Administration.* New York: Teachers College. Columbia University, 1955.

BEEMAN, H. F., CAROL HARDING, and J. H. HUMPHREY, *Intramural Sports.* Dubuque, Iowa: William C. Brown, 1973.

FLANAGAN, JOHN C., "Critical Incidents in Individuals." Educational Conference, Modern Educational Problems, 1952.

MCNAIR, MALCOLM, and ANITA HERSUM, *The Case Method at the Harvard Business School.* New York: McGraw-Hill, 1954.

5

Communications Theory:
Implications for
Intramural Administration

STEVE NEWMAN and ROBERT WALLACE
Illinois State University
Bloomington, Illinois

INTRODUCTION

Throughout this textbook, various chapters attempt to aid the administrator in planning and scheduling activities, training officials, planning facilities, and so on—all of which have programming application. But once program parameters are determined, how do we get the message of program opportunities to the participant? It is the purpose of this chapter to discuss those basic communicative tools that are most effective in informing the participant of the intramural opportunities available and to examine how communications theory can assist the intramural director in achieving maximum student involvement in the intramural program.

With a vast number of intramural programs prospering throughout the country, administrators can no longer rely on word of mouth or on all-sport point systems to increase participation. Increased participation can no longer be considered solely as a measure of success; it must also be considered an inherent responsibility of administrators. Implementation of proper communication techniques to promote service philosophy and activities will have profound effects on the number of individuals who choose to participate.

Although the major emphasis of this chapter will be on communicative tools, an explanation of the basic principles of communication theory can aid in the identification and selection of the most effective tools. We shall initiate our study of communication principles with an explanation of a basic communication model (Figure 1) and its applica-

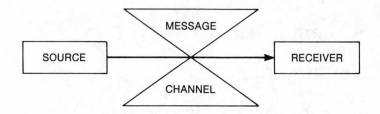

Figure 1. Model of the Basic Communication Process

tion to intramural administration. Most administrators have at least a cursory familiarity with the basic communications model. The source is the encoder of the message, the channel is how the message is transmitted, the message is what is being encoded, and the receiver is the decoder of the message.

When the model is specifically modified for intramural purposes (Figure 2), the source becomes the intramural staff and the receiver be-

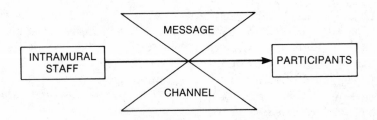

Figure 2. The Communication Process for Intramural Administration

comes the participant. The message and channel remain the same. When the intramural staff applies an appropriate message to a channel, the participant receives the message and responds to it. A large number of messages must be transmitted by the intramural staff: entry information, officiating information, scheduling, postponed games, and so on. The channel may vary according to two major factors: the information to be transmitted and the type of participants to be reached. The most advantageous system is one in which the intramural staff utilizes the correct channel to transmit an appropriate message to the intended participant. The major part of this chapter will deal with the types of channels used.

COPING WITH NOISE

Communication can be extremely effective when the system operates correctly. However, the element of "noise" can interfere with the communication process (Figure 3). Noise is distortion that may lead

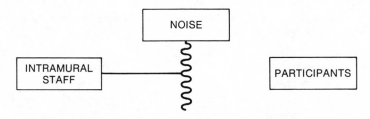

Figure 3.   Noise as an Input into the Communications Model

to hindrance of communication or even to total breakdown in the system itself. Noise may affect either the message or channel, or both, and may be either audible or subliminal. The source (the intramural staff) may affect noise, as may the receiver (the participant). Simple examples of noise that can disrupt the communications system in intramurals are cluttered or outdated bulletin boards, uncomfortable meeting rooms, poor preparation for meetings, or a caller receiving a busy signal when seeking information.

Three methods can be used by administrators to eliminate or overcome totally or partially the problem of noise. The first is the pre-planning of communicative efforts. This is the ideal that is illustrated by Figure 1; unfortunately, this ideal seems to work only through direct contact. In this case, the intramural staff usually transmits to the participant personally, by telephone or personal meeting. This is effective, but usable only for small bits of information.

The second method used to cope with noise is a multichannel approach, whereby the intramural staff anticipates reaching the participants through at least one of the many channels employed (Figure 4). This is

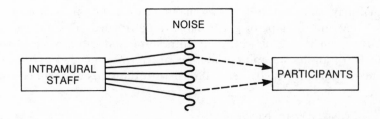

Figure 4. The Multichannel Approach to the Problem of Noise

perhaps the method most often used, because of the relatively large number of available channels: telephone, bulletin boards, radio, newspaper, and others. A scenario for this method is the use of the campus newspaper, student radio, information sheets, and bulletin board announcements to notify participants of an upcoming entry period. In using all available channels, it is hoped that one or two of them will be effective in transmitting the messages.

The final method of counteracting noise is for the staff to develop lines of communication that provide for feedback from the participants (Figure 5). If feedback from the participants can be elicited, the source

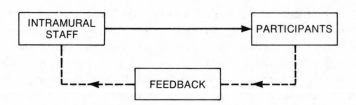

Figure 5. Feedback in the Communications Process

or intramural staff knows immediately if the message has reached the participant, and also which channel was used successfully to transmit the message. The staff can also see whether or not the noise has affected the communicative effort. Feedback is also important in the sense that the participant can reverse the model and become the source of a message transmitted through a channel to the receiver, the intramural staff. In this way the participant can affect the program.

Other elements that may cause communicative breakdown may be traced to the source. It is imperative that a source be a credible one. If the receiver lacks confidence in the source, communicative planning and organization may be perfect, but the decoder (receiver) will lack necessary trust and respect for the encoder (source) and will disregard the message. The source is also responsible for selecting appropriate messages and channels for communication. Messages must be designed for easy interpretation and thorough explanation. It is also imperative that effective channels be explored, tested, and evaluated in order to insure successful transmission by the source. If the breakdown occurs at the source, it is highly unlikely that any message will be received by the receiver.

In this section we have presented the reader with a very brief explanation of elementary communication principles. Since theories and principles are only as effective as their implementation, the next section will deal with an explanation of the tools of communication that may be used to achieve the goal of informing the intramural participants. Administrators should not only attempt to develop new communication tools, but should also use standard means of transmitting messages to the student. The use of bulletin boards, student newspapers, department publications, and other usual channels, along with what are unique practices of transmitting intramural information to the participant, constitute the major emphasis of this chapter.

COMMUNICATION TOOLS

Orientation

Each school year, an initial effort should be made to inform new students and remind returning students of the intramural activities available to them. The usual approach is to arrange meetings between students and a staff member, who presents an orientation program that offers the group opportunities to ask questions and express opinions. A program of this nature can include audio-visual matter, charts, and printed information. The presentation should be of such a nature as to expose the group to the activities but not to answer specifics of the program, thereby stimulating questions and promoting group interaction. One effective method in developing this type of presentation is an audio-visual program showing participants in action; this is likely to stimulate "How do I get involved?" questions, which can be used as a measure of feedback concerning the presentation.

Bulletin Boards

One of the oldest methods of communication used in intramural administration is posting information on bulletin boards. A few basic principles are necessary for effective board use. Boards must be kept up to date. Participants who rely on boards for information will soon disregard this channel if boards contain information that is consistently outdated. Neat and attractive boards will increase readership, as their appearance will aid in catching the eye of passers-by. Consistent maintenance of boards is necessary, as they are often targets of destruction. Finally, posting regular season results and schedules as well as those for tournaments will enhance interest in bulletin boards.

Publications

Printed matter can be designed each year to provide participants with information needed to take part in intramural programs. Intramural handbooks or guidelines that outline activities offered, program operations, eligibility requirements, and available recreation facilities are a must for efficient administration. These may be distributed at all student meetings and should be made available to team captains and individual participants.

Brochures and other materials may be printed and distributed to various interest areas. Monthly calendars with a day-by-day report of intramural events are excellent information sources and are easily posted on bulletin boards. In addition to monthly calendars, a yearly list of activities, entry periods, and dates of play will aid in keeping participants up to date. Activity information sheets that contain complete information necessary for entry and participation in the designated activity must be distributed to all entrants and team captains as well as being posted on bulletin boards.

A weekly or monthly newsletter is yet another means of communicating with participants. In addition to having accurate content, it is imperative that these be published with consistency as to their day of release. Students will quickly learn to expect the publication and will rely on it to assist their participation. Publications are an effective tool insofar as policies of program operations are readily available to the participants and provide for consistency in administration. A note of caution in planning for the production of printed matter is to be aware of the costs involved. Many of the aforementioned publications can be produced by simple duplicating procedures and do not require the added expense of a printing service.

Newspapers

One of the most successful tools available to intramurals is the campus newspaper. It is a relevant publication for students since it is a report of their community. However, it is difficult for intramurals to receive adequate coverage in most college newspapers, since intramural administrators are constantly competing for space that is devoted mainly to intercollegiate athletics.

One approach that may enhance the chances of publication of intramural-related news is for intramural directors to request that articles that report results be the only non-intercollegiate sports articles to appear on the sports pages. Articles concerning general campus activities can be transferred to the campus news pages. The amount of space available on these pages often exceeds that of the sports pages; thus, chances of intramural news being printed are better if the general news can be transferred to other pages.

In working with the student press, one may find that the following techniques can increase acceptance and publication:

1. *Be sure your request is newsworthy.* Constant submission of insignificant news will turn editors off to all your news.

2. *Be your own reporter and writer.* Making copy ready for print requires extra effort on your part but decreases the work load of the newspaper staff. Employment of a student writer by the intramural department will ease administrators' work and lend consistency to the reporting.

3. *Submit pictures whenever possible.* Newspapers will lean toward articles accompanied by an action photograph.

4. *Know your newspaper's deadlines and meet them—they have to.* Student papers usually lack printing equipment, necessitating deadlines one to three days prior to publication.

5. *Stagger the amount of copy you submit.* A deluge of copy decreases chances of publication, not only because editors dislike wading through an overabundance of copy, but also because much of the copy will not be used due to limits on space.

6. *Meet with the editor.* A meeting with the student editor will aid in understanding the problems on both sides. Let the editor know that publicity is important to the intramural program and that without the paper the program becomes less effective. Also, an occasional note of appreciation for coverage received will enhance future acceptance of news.

7. *Finally, don't expect all news to be printed—it just doesn't happen.*

Telephone

Another conventional method of communication is the telephone. Using the telephone to inform participants of program changes, general information, or tournament scheduling is the simplest, most economical method available in terms of accuracy and guarantee of notification. The major goal in handling daily inquiry calls is to satisfy the informational needs of the caller. This goal can be attained more easily by having professional staff members handle as many of these calls as possible and by keeping the general office staff totally informed of program operations in order to prevent misinformation from reaching the participants.

The telephone provides another communication tool for administrative needs. This is an electronic answering device, which provides a variety of services. Some of these devices simply repeat a recorded message; others not only pass on program information but also provide the caller with an opportunity to leave a message. Consulting the local telephone service representative will aid the administrator in selecting the appropriate device for program needs. A necessary follow-up to obtaining this device is promotion of the service to participants. Using established methods of communication for promotion is necessary if the service is to become successful; if no one knows the number to call or even that the service is available, the device is ineffective.

Radio

The radio is not available or even practical for all intramural programs, but when the opportunity exists it can be a dynamic tool for communication. One of the most common uses of the student radio station is that of reporting intramural results. Listeners enjoy hearing their scores, and consistent reporting will increase interest in the intramural program.

Daily reports by administrators who explain program operations may easily be broadcast to potential participants. A unique aspect of radio stations is that this type of broadcast may be done live, via telephone, from a staff member's desk, the only requirement being the availability of a staff member at a certain time each day. One distinct advantage of this program is that information concerning changes in or additions to an intramural program may be announced to students as soon as they are known.

Special-feature programming is another avenue open through the radio stations. Format will vary with each radio station, but programs that should prove interesting are those involving sports club leaders, team captains prior to a championship game, and promotion of special activities. Also, members of the intramural staff may be featured in a series of programs that explain their particular areas of interest and responsibility. These special features may be taped in advance and played at the convenience of the program director.

In addition to regularly scheduled programming, special broadcasts may be used throughout the school year. Half-time interviews at varsity football and basketball games provide additional opportunities for discussion of special program activities. Play-by-play reports of intramural championships can be initiated in order to increase the coverage of intramurals by the student radio station and to maximize the awareness of the university community to the intramural program.

Television and Video Tape

A method of communication that is even less available and perhaps less practical than radio is television and video tape. However, the increased use and the vast impact of this medium has caused it to be available to a greater degree today than ever before. Television and/or video tape is the most effective medium for society as a whole; how can it be used to benefit the intramural administrator and, most of all, the intramural participant?

Television and/or video tape can be used in several ways. The most obvious is the live or taped play-by-play broadcast of an intramural contest by a television station. The added dimension of video makes the broadcast even more effective as a lure to the intramural participant. If a live broadcast is not possible, perhaps a delayed taped broadcast would be.

Another possible use is for special programming by the television station. This can consist of half-time interviews at athletic contests, or it might involve a half-hour program built around the intramural program. Such an orientation program would be most effective at the beginning of the school year.

A more limited use for video tape is within the intramural program itself. Here, video tape can be used for several purposes. Officials' rules and mechanics sessions can be taped and rerun during the season; material is thereby covered in an easy manner. New activities can be taped and then shown in order to orient participants as to how the game is played, and also to demonstrate to officials the signals and positions they should use. Tape can also be used in sessions that are called for a particular purpose. For instance, officials might view the tape of a game in order to detect things in the game that might develop into problems later. In all of these uses, the great advantages of tape are its reusability, its lower cost compared with film, and the fact that it can be stopped, backed up, and run again.

Television and video tape can be and are used in new and valuable ways by the intramural administrator, including new ways of publicizing and orienting the program. Its limits are its availability and the need for cooperation between communication personnel and intramural administrators.

Two-Way Communication

As we suggested previously, communication is most effective when it is two-way: in addition to communication from the source, feedback is channeled back to the source. An advisory board composed of student representatives from various parts of the university community may meet periodically with intramural staff members to discuss various problems and recommendations affecting the program. This board offers the staff an opportunity to react to student feedback and to consider this information when formulating adjustments in intramural operations. A very important consideration of the staff is to make the board feel that they have a real function within the structure of the program and that their thoughts are carefully judged and appraised by staff members. It is extremely important that the staff be good listeners at these meetings and not the mainstays of discussion.

Another channel that may be employed is team captains' meetings held before each team activity. These meetings are not only constructive for dispensing activity information and program philosophies, but also for obtaining reactions to the intramural program. One of the major problems with this tool is lack of attendance by all team captains. One easy way to avoid this problem is to notify team captains that the only time they may turn in an entry is at one of these meetings. To avoid conflicts, more than one meeting should be scheduled, so that students may choose a meeting time that is convenient for them.

Special program presentations by staff members at various student living quarters provide administrators with yet another method of obtaining participant reaction to operations. A letter offering students in each living unit the opportunity to invite staff members to meet with the students at their residence should be sent to all intramural coordinators. Meetings of this nature often arise from a problem that has affected student participation in intramurals. This may cause an uncomfortable situation for the staff members, who should be prepared for feedback that seriously questions the procedures used to formulate intramural policy. Such meetings will ease the situation and more often than not provide a means for absolving dissatisfaction.

A complaint or protest procedure is yet another two-way tool for increasing feedback to administrators. Through guidelines and team captains' meetings, participants are encouraged to submit in person or to write any complaints or protests resulting from their participation, rather than to direct their actions towards officials, supervisors, or fellow participants. All individuals involved must be contacted personally by a staff member after the report is filed. The facts of the complaint are compiled, and if necessary, the parties are called to appear before an intramural hearing or disciplinary board. This board provides multiple source-receiver relationships and affords numerous modes of feedback for the administrator. It is imperative that all individuals receive immediate reports as to the action taken on a complaint or protest filed. If this step is not taken, the credibility of the channel will decrease rapidly.

Open-Office Policy

A final tool, one that requires no special planning or execution, is an "open-office policy." Intramural administrators should encourage all students to feel free to stop by the intramural office to talk with any staff member about questions, recommendations, or reactions regarding any phase of the program. This is basic communication since there is a continuous exchange of ideas and a constant feedback of reaction to program operations and philosophies.

IMPLICATIONS FOR ADMINISTRATORS

In order to discuss how communications theory can assist the intramural administrator in his managerial efforts, it is necessary for the reader to examine the four elements of the communications model. This examination should not be in terms of the *message flow*—from the communicator (intramural staff) to the audience (potential participants), but in terms of *planning flow*—from target audience back to the communicator. The communicator—in this case, the intramural administrator—should start with the audience because the audience determines to a great extent *what* is to be said, *how* it is to be said, *when* it is to be said, *where* it is to be said, and *who* is to say it. The first step is audience segmentation. There are two important dimensions of audience segmentation that the intramural administrator must observe closely.

The first is the *level of audience aggregation*. An intramural department can direct its promotional efforts to an individual, a specific group, or to the school as a whole. Communicating to an individual is usually a person-to-person affair in which the message can be highly tailored to the individual. Group communication is another situation in which the message can be made specific. For example, at many schools the cohesiveness and comraderie of intramural participation is emphasized in the promotional efforts that are directed at the fraternities and sororities. The third level—communicating to the school as a whole—is more apt to utilize mass media, such as radio, television, or public bulletin boards, and is more apt to be directed at the "average" student.

The second dimension of audience segmentation is the *level of audience awareness or interest*. Audiences should be distinguished according to their anticipated level of awareness and interest in the intramural program. Persons at different levels of awareness and interest require different types of messages, and possibly media, for effective influence. For example, in the fall of 1969 the undergraduate black student enrollment at the University of Illinois more than quadrupled. Quite obviously, the promotional efforts of the Division of Intramural Activities to involve and to assimilate these students into the intramural program required some drastic modifications, if for no other reason than that practically all of these individuals had had absolutely no experience with an intramural program of any kind and were unfamiliar with the leisure opportunities available to them.

Once the target audiences are identified, the intramural administrator must next consider the specific channels to be used to reach the audiences. Channels of influence are of two broad types: personal and nonpersonal. Personal influence channels are means of direct interpersonal contact with target individuals or groups. For intramural administrators, two personal influence channels can be distinguished: advocate and social. *Advocate* channels consist of intramural departmental representatives trying to influence potential participants through personal contact. Promotional tools in this type of channel range from simple, one-to-one discussions to prepared speeches or presentations. One of the most effective direct-contact "promotools" to evolve in recent years is the use of multimedia. Multimedia involves the coordination of several types of media—usually, at least slides and sound—to communicate an idea or a message.

The other personal influence channel is the *social* channel. This channel, also referred to as word-of-mouth influence, consists of the student's associates and friends, who may influence him. Unfortunately, the intramural administrator has little direct control over this type of channel. Although one typically does not "hire" students to speak favorably about intramural participation, the coordinated use of the other communication channels—both personal and nonpersonal—can strengthen the resulting word-of-mouth communication.

Intramural personnel can undertake specific steps to stimulate personal channels. Among them are the following:

1. Observe whether certain individuals or groups seem particularly influential in their sector of the audience, and devote extra effort to them, either through personal attention or through direct promotional means.
2. Create opinion leaders out of certain persons by supplying them with firsthand briefings, by soliciting their advice and assistance, or by hiring them as departmental representatives.

3. Work through influential members of the audience, such as residence hall leaders, class officers, and social organization leaders.
4. Develop promotional efforts that are high in "conversational value."

The second type of communication channel is the nonpersonal influence channel. This channel comprises media that carry influence but that involve no interpersonal contact. Three types of nonpersonal media can be distinguished. The first, *print and broadcast* media, consists of flyers, newsletters, handouts, notices, bulletin boards, radio, television, and in some instances film. Print media have the advantages of enduring, being tangible, read at leisure and at one's own rate. Broadcast media are more ephemeral and insistent: they demand more attention, since the medium sets the pace; and they can be utilized in more social circumstances.

The other two types of nonpersonal influence channels are *atmosphere* and *events*. To a varying degree, intramural personnel also utilize these channels. For example, administrators frequently attempt to establish an office environment that is both attractive and enticing to the drop-in student. Action pictures on the wall, pleasant secretaries, and bright wall colors are prime examples of atmospheric stimuli. An example of the third type of channel—events (staged actions designed to create awareness or interest in the intramural program)—would be an intramural contest held at half time of an intercollegiate game.

We have proposed that effective communication calls first, for identifying the target audience and, second, for determining the major channels for reaching the audience. The next step is to design messages about the intramural program that are appropriate to the audience and the channels. Various messages will convey different meanings to different individuals. Messages can attempt to convey information, alter perceptions, stimulate desires, produce conviction, direct action, and provide reassurance. The choice of message depends largely on the audience. Each type of message requires adherence to different principles. Regardless of the exact type, however, if the sent message is going to be the received message, it must be encoded in a way that is meaningful to the receiver. Messages are essentially signs. Intramural directors should select signs that will be familiar to their students. In 1970 at the University of Illinois, for example, when the open basketball league schedules were mailed out, the names of the Greek-letter fraternities were spelled out in full. Less than a month later, one of the winter's most explosive incidents occurred when a black team that was to play Delta Chi surmised that they were being "slipped a ringer" when they saw only "Triangle-X" (the Greek letters) on the sweatshirts of their opponents.

The final element in the communications model is the communicator. From an audience standpoint, the intramural administrator must be viewed as standing firm behind his communications efforts. For that reason, it is important that the intramural director be concerned about his image and that of the various media and spokesmen who represent him. The higher their credibility, the greater their effectiveness.

IN CLOSING

Although the tools and philosophies presented in this chapter are not unique, they will help the intramural director plan and execute his administrative efforts. If any one administrative tip is gained from this chapter, it should be that a need exists to plan, use, and evaluate the communicative tools and philosophies in such a way as to insure that potential participants are adequately informed of the opportunities to become involved in intramurals. With the goal of maximum participation of all students comes the responsibility of maximum communication by all administrators.

GENERAL BIBLIOGRAPHY

CARTWRIGHT, DORWIN, "Some Principles of Mass Persuasion," *Human Relations II,* No. 2 (1949), 253–67.

KLAPPER, JOSEPH T., *The Effects of Mass Communication.* New York: Free Press, 1960.

LASSWELL, HAROLD D., *Power and Personality.* New York: Norton, 1948.

NIERENBERG, GERALD I., *The Art of Negotiation.* New York: Hawthorn, 1968.

ROBERTSON, THOMAS S., *Innovative Behavior and Communication.* New York: Holt, Rinehart & Winston, 1971.

SCHRAMM, WILBUR, "How Communication Works," in *The Process and Effects of Mass Communication,* ed. Wilbur Schramm and Donald F. Roberts. Urbana, Ill.: University of Illinois Press, 1965.

6

Marketing Theory: Implications for Intramural Administration

JAMES A. PETERSON
United States Military Academy
West Point, New York

INTRODUCTION

It might reasonably be concluded that intramural directors aspire to associate themselves with a quality intramural program—one in which their students readily avail themselves of the opportunities to participate. Some individuals surmise that for such participation to occur, all the intramural director has to do is to compile a formidable list of activities and then sit back and wait for the students to walk in and sign up. This author strongly disagrees. The major working assumption of this chapter is that student participation does not automatically come about through any process in nature. Rather, it requires an expenditure of time, energy, skill, and supervision. The framework for these efforts is proper understanding and efficient application of basic marketing principles.

In this light, consider the naïveté of Emerson's famous saying, "If a man . . . makes a better mousetrap . . . the world will beat a path to his door." It is more likely that the grass will grow high on the path to his door, unless he takes positive steps to bring his product to the attention of persons concerned with the problem of rodents and to convince them that the product has superior qualities. All of these steps require planning, energy, and judgment—precisely the qualities that constitute the core of sound intramural administration.

Every individual within the field of intramural administration is cast, by the very nature of the voluntary involvement aspect of intramural programs, into the role of a market manager. As such, not only is it necessary for the intramural director to develop an inclusive offering of leisure activities and programs, it is also his responsibility to encourage participation in those endeavors through whatever managerial means are appropriate.

What is meant by the term "appropriate managerial means"? The literature suggests that administrative efforts are most effective when planned and carried out on an integrated basis. To achieve this goal, the intramural administrator must answer, in his own mind at least, an extremely difficult and sometimes complex question: What is the "product" my department offers to the potential participant? How the administrator answers this question will provide the focal point of his managerial efforts. What is the product that intramural administrators offer to the university community? Is the intramural product merely the opportunity to participate in any of a vast listing of activities? I submit that anyone who tenders this limited interpretation of intramurals seriously panders his professional function. Someone once asked Charles Revson, the cosmetic king, about his product, and he replied, "In the factory we make cosmetics but in the drugstore, we sell hope." In a similar vein, Francis Rooney, a noted shoe company executive, replied when asked the same question; "People buy shoes because of the way they make them feel—masculine, feminine, rugged, different, sophisticated, young, glamorous, 'in.' Buying shoes has become an emotional experience. Our business now is selling excitement rather than shoes."

Like Revson and Rooney, intramural administrators offer more than the obvious "prepackaged product." In a very real (and yet somewhat abstract) sense, participation in intramural activities serves as the means by which different participants achieve different ends: fun, fitness, excitement, diversion, cohesiveness, passion, thrills, brotherhood, masculinity, femininity, friendship, self-esteem, peer acceptance, exercise, leisure —to name just a few. The office stationery of J. D. Parsley, intramural director at St. Thomas College, includes a phrase at the bottom of each sheet that perhaps describes the intramural product most succinctly: "Participation is a plus." I believe it; you as professionals believe it; and, more important, your managerial efforts must make the potential participant believe it. Since numerous divergent extracurricular activities exist on every campus—each one competing for every student's time and efforts—it is imperative that intramural participation be viewed as a positive alternative.

As Newman and Wallace illustrated so pointedly in Chapter 5 of this text, consciously arranging promotional efforts—through a variety of messages and a choice of channels in order to achieve a calculated effect on the attitude or behavior of a specific audience—is frequently a complicated task *at best.* Unfortunately, this task is sometimes complicated further when intramural personnel fail to employ fundamental marketing principles.

This chapter will attempt to illustrate how marketing theory can aid the intramural director in the discharge of his professional responsibilities. Four broad areas will be examined: (1) conceptualizing marketing management; (2) analyzing marketing opportunities; (3) organizing for marketing; and (4) planning the marketing program.

CONCEPTUALIZING MARKETING MANAGEMENT

We, as a nation of over 200 million people, are subject to a wide variety of marketing efforts. From coast to coast (from the "Come on down to Ralph Williams Ford" hourly television bombardments in the metropolitan Los Angeles area to the "What's the story, Jerry?" commercial spiels in the New York/New Jersey area), these efforts permeate almost every facet of our daily life. It is somewhat of a recent phenomenon, however, that marketing efforts have spread beyond the traditional abode of such giant concerns as Colgate-Palmolive, Proctor and Gamble, and General Mills. In fact, the practice of marketing the organization's "product" has become somewhat fashionable in a variety of endeavors. Banks, for example, because of their relatively recent discovery of marketing have adopted new approaches toward their customers and their services. Politicians have also relied more heavily in recent years on marketing, though not all aspects of this phenomenon are entirely new. Candidates are now handled like "product launchings": careful attention is paid to voter polling and research, issue "packaging," communication and promotion media, and the orderly development of "markets." With increasing frequency, school administrators are examining marketing efforts as a means of securing more favorable results in bonding referendums. Some college officials, facing dwindling enrollments, are attempting to attract potential students through marketing as a way to explain and improve their services to people. The New York City program to attract heroin users to its methadone treatment program is an excellent example of "governmental marketing." Cultural concerns are also turning to marketing. Increasingly, museums, symphonies, and libraries are redefining their services and products in terms of people's desires and are turning to more sophisticated conceptions of packaging, distributing, promoting, and communicating in reaching out to the public. The attendance at the Metropolitan Museum of Art in New York City was increased substantially during the late 1960s as a result of the influence that a change in marketing management had on museum management efforts. A listing of examples to show the relevance of marketing efforts is somewhat endless, but the basic implication is the same: whenever ideas and causes compete for attention or any other specified response, marketing can serve a useful purpose.

At this time, it is appropriate to develop a definition of marketing and market management. Although a variety of definitions and perspectives of marketing is possible (and, in fact, is extant in the literature), a core definition of marketing would be as follows:

> *Marketing* is the set of human activities directed at facilitating and consummating exchanges.

This definition of marketing suggests (intuitively) that at least three elements must be present to define a marketing situation: (1) two or more parties who are potentially interested in exchange, (2) each possessing things of value to the other, and (3) each capable of communication and delivery.

Certainly, the campus intramural situation could accommodate these criteria. The parties who are potentially interested in exchange are the intramural staff (as either a total or partial entity) and the various elements of the campus community (students, faculty, staff, dependents, and so on). The reader should note that the definition deliberately avoided specifying what is being exchanged. In the intramural setting, the intramural department offers a variety of consequential by-products of participation (see the aforementioned list of potential intramural "products"). The participant exchanges (in varying degrees) several things on his or her part: time, energy, commitment, sociopsychological attachments, and in some cases money. The pertinence of the last element is somewhat obvious. If the segments of the market were unable to communicate and unable to exchange their "goods," intramural programs would simply *not* exist.

Having identified the core premise of marketing as centering on exchange, market management can now be interpreted as an "action" approach based on principles for improving the effectiveness of exchange. A more specific definition of marketing management is that this approach consists of the analysis, planning, implementation, and control of programs designed to bring about desired exchanges with target audiences for the purpose of personal or mutual gain (Kotler, 1972, p. 13). In short, to the intramural director, marketing management represents increased professionalism in the carrying out of exchange relationships.

Within intramural departments, a variety of attitudes and philosophies can be held regarding market management and its importance in the total picture of the organization's operations. The intramural director can view marketing as largely a problem of influencing others or as a problem of serving others; he can see marketing as a small part of his job or a large part; he can see it as a common-sense task or as a skilled practice. All of these attitudes can be justified to some extent in terms of the goals, resources, and particular circumstances of his department.

ANALYZING MARKET OPPORTUNITIES

Before the intramural director can organize and plan his marketing program, he must first analyze what market opportunities are present in his situation. This responsibility has at least four dimensions: (1) identifying and applying the marketing concept to his administrative approach; (2) examining his school's marketing environment; (3) appraising the concept of "marketing opportunity"; and (4) analyzing the dimensions of his school's intramural market.

The Marketing Concept

On a broad basis, the marketing concept is an administrative approach to achieving organizational goals by meeting customer needs and generating customer satisfaction. This concept is contrasted with the traditional sales approach, which focuses on the product rather than on the needs of the customer. The basic differences between the two approaches in the intramural setting are illustrated in Figure 1. Obviously, the choice of either of the two concepts as a basis for a department's ad-

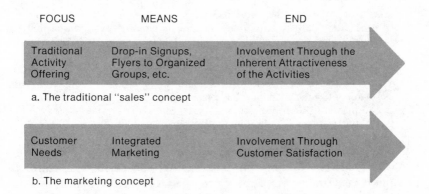

Figure 1. A Contrast between the Traditional Sales Concept and the Marketing Concept in an Intramural Program

ministrative efforts will have a significant effect on the methods employed to run the intramural program. The traditional sales approach starts with the intramural department's existing program of activities and considers the primary task to be one of using promotional means to stimulate student participation in the program. The marketing concept starts with the department's existing and potential participants and their needs; it plans a coordinated set of services and programs to serve those needs; and it hopes to build student involvement by creating meaningful value satisfactions within those services and programs.

Since the marketing approach is relatively new to many intramural directors, it may be desirable to examine the three pillars of the marketing concept in more detail. The first cornerstone is *customer orientation*. The marketing concept requires a basic reorientation by the intramural department from looking inward toward its various service and program offerings to looking outward toward the needs of the department's potential participants. It is one thing to exhort a customer-oriented approach and another to implement it. Several steps should be undertaken by the intramural director who truly wishes to utilize the customer-oriented approach:

1. The intramural department should adopt a basic definition of the basic needs it intends to sense, serve, and satisfy within the university community.
2. Since there are limitations (financial, facility, and personnel) to the efforts of any intramural program, the intramural director must identify the groups—and even the specific needs within these groups—that his department will serve. This practice (described in marketing theory as target-groups definition) establishes an orderly determination of departmental priorities.
3. The intramural director should develop a variety of services, programs, and messages to meet the needs of the groups selected as target groups. For example, if the intramural department wanted to attract and involve students in its programs who did not reside in organized housing (dormitories, or "Greek" houses), its marketing efforts should be varied.
4. An effort should be made to measure, evaluate, and interpret the wants, attitudes, and behavior of the various target groups. Although a number of methods partially achieve this goal, one of the most valuable sources of input for the intramural director could be provided from communication with other professionals and groups on campus (for example, psychologists, sociologists, marketing theorists, and ethnic leaders).

The second pillar of the marketing concept, *integrated marketing*, involves a number of things. First, all sections and personnel within the intramural department must appreciate the fact that "customer (student) satisfaction" is everyone's responsibility. The actions of everyone within the intramural department—from the student employees, the student officials, and the secretarial help to the supervisory staff—may have a profound effect on the department's efforts to attract and sustain student involvement. Integrated marketing also means that the intramural director should rationally and intelligently coordinate all of his department's efforts to facilitate the exchange relationship that was discussed in the previous section. For example, all promotional efforts for a service or program offering should be planned to occur at the most effective time and in the most conducive manner.

The third and last pillar of the marketing concept is the amount of *customer satisfaction* that the intramural department can manage to generate. The barometer for this factor must be more than just a cursory examination of the number of participants. It requires that the intramural director engage in a continual evaluation of his services and programs, and their consequences.

The Marketing Environment

Having taken a look at the marketing concept, the next appropriate task is to examine the marketing environment in which an intramural department exists. The literature suggests that since the rate of change in an organization's environment usually outstrips the rate of change within the organization, the organization is constantly left in a "maladapted" state. The implication for the intramural director is that his department must either continually adapt to the changing environment or be overwhelmed by it. A "passive" intramural department faces severe conflicts and difficulties; an "adaptive" department will survive and enjoy a degree of modest prosperity; and a "creative" department will flourish and, in some instances, contribute to the changes occurring in the external environment.

What is meant by the term "marketing environment"? For an intramural program, the marketing environment is the totality of forces and entities that surround and potentially affect the marketing of intramural programs and services. The four layers of the marketing environment for intramural programs and services are illustrated in Figure 2.

The variety of situational factors attendant to each school makes an inclusive discussion of each potential element in the intramural environment an impossible task. What is necessary, however, is that the intramural director attempt to conceptualize what factors constitute his department's environment. As its environment changes, the intramural department must adapt or respond to these changes creatively. Too often, intramural departments are too rigid in their ways. As the environment changes, more appropriate administrative means must be used to direct the intramural effort.

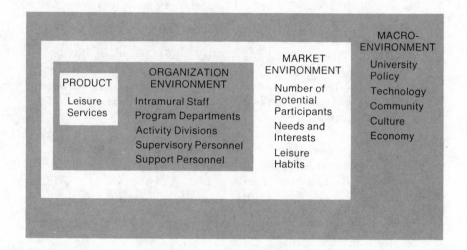

Figure 2. The Four Layers of the Marketing Environment for Intramural Programs

The Concept of Marketing Opportunity

Instead of viewing change as a threatening state of affairs, the intramural director should assume a more positive approach. For example, in the late 1960s when the University of Illinois instituted a series of equal opportunity programs that drastically increased the black student population on its Urbana campus, one approach would have been to view this influx of black students as a potentially disruptive force in the intramural setting. However, instead of viewing these programs as a threat, the Division of Intramural Activities approached them as an opportunity to offer leisure services to a new "market"—the minority student. "Opportunity for all" was more than just a departmental goal. It was a blueprint for action.

The literature suggests that intramural administrators should view change as a veiled opportunity rather than a veiled threat. Bell refers to such opportunities as "marketing opportunities" (1966, p. 29). To deal effectively with such opportunities requires an administrative effort at what can collectively be referred to as opportunity analysis. To accomplish this, the intramural director must develop procedures for identifying, appraising, and responding to opportunities. This task is facilitated greatly when the intramural department has a clear sense of its goals, resources, and capabilities.

The Intramural Market

The term "market" has different meanings and different uses. To a stockbroker, the market is the place where stocks are traded. To a produce merchant, the market is a location in a city where produce is received and sold. Finally, to a market theorist, the market is "all individuals and organizations who are factual or potential customers for a product or service" (Kotler, 1972, p. 89). It is in the latter sense that this section will examine the dimensions of the intramural market. An intramural market consists, therefore, of all the members of the university community (and in some cases, the adjacent community) who are actual or potential participants in the intramural program.

Although intramural markets frequently exhibit vast differences from institution to institution, there are some essential elements of all markets that the intramural director can examine in order to decide how to approach his market effectively. The literature suggests that the major elements of a market can be categorized into mnemonics: the four O's. The four O's answer these questions: What does the market buy? Why does it buy? Who buys? How does the market buy? In turn, the four O's of a market—objects, objectives, organizations, and operations—are interrelated with another set of mnemonics: the four P's of the marketing mix. The marketing mix consists of the major market decision variables.

Figure 3 illustrates the potential relationship between the four O's and the four P's that exists in an intramural setting. Considered together, these elements provide the intramural department with the framework for accomplishing its professional responsibilities. Thus, the intramural director faces two main tasks within the intramural market. First, the target markets must be selected, a task that requires the ability to effectively measure opportunities and assess responsibilities in different market segments (the four O's). Second, the appropriate market mix (the four P's) must be selected, a task that entails the ability to assess the requirements of different market segments.

ORGANIZING FOR MARKETING

The previous two sections of this chapter identified and defined several of the parameters of marketing management and examined some of the dimensions of market opportunities. Having discussed the need and the probably beneficial consequences of "marketing input" in the organization, this section will address the problem of how to provide for such input.

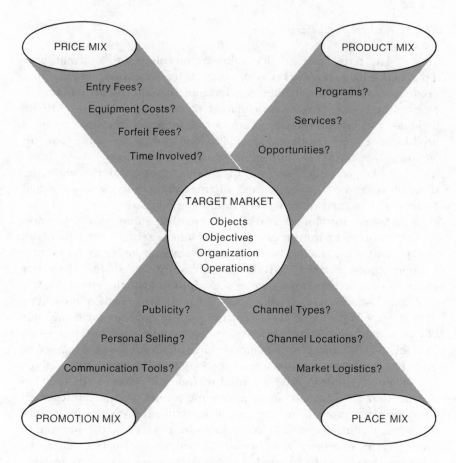

Figure 3.   The Four O's and the Four P's in the Intramural Setting

In these days of fiscal strangulation it would be foolhardy to assume that any intramural department has the resources to employ a staff member who could be assigned full-time to monitor marketing input.* On the other hand, some arrangement should be made to insure that the structure of the intramural department does not inhibit (as opposed to actively soliciting) the influence of sound marketing principles. Marketing organization everywhere is shaped by a host of unique factors: company

---

* It could be argued that all staff members of leisure-service organizations are in fact full-time "marketeers."

objectives; management's philosophy of administration; management's view of marketing; the utility of different marketing tools; the types of products, services, and programs; the character of competition; and so forth.

Within intramural departments, three arrangements to provide for marketing input seem plausible. Each of these three marketing arrangements—by program, by target market, and by function—achieves certain advantages for the intramural department at the price of certain disadvantages. The reader should select the arrangement that best suits his situation.

In the *program* arrangement, the staff member assigned to a specific area of services or programing (for instance, co-recreation, faculty-staff activities, and informal recreation) is held responsible for the marketing strategy within his bailiwick. Interservice or interdepartmental marketing strategy is coordinated either by the intramural director or by the use of staff meetings, departmental policies, or other direct communication efforts.

When marketing input is solicited on the basis of *target markets,* the individuals within an intramural department who are most familiar with the target market are usually assigned this responsibility. For example, a staff member with a fraternity or sorority background would help analyze the "Greek" market; a black staff member, the minority market; and so on.

The third and final arrangement for organizing for marketing input is to assign someone on a part-time basis to coordinate the marketing efforts in all departmental programs. This individual could be a staff member with business orientation or someone solicited from the institution's marketing education program. Another possibility is to have the intramural director contact his counterpart in the marketing program and seek his professional assistance. This person could help the intramural director in a number of ways: by direct personal advice, by assigning one of his classes to examine the intramural department as a case study, or by permitting the intramural director to address the marketing class (preferably one at the graduate level) and seek reasonably competent advice.

Regardless of who is assigned the responsibility for marketing within the intramural department, the arrangement must include a system or a procedure for the orderly collection and utilization of marketing information. Figure 4 presents an overview of the primary elements of a marketing information system constructed within the intramural setting. On the basis of information obtained from the system, the intramural director can develop plans and programs that are consistent with his department's goals.

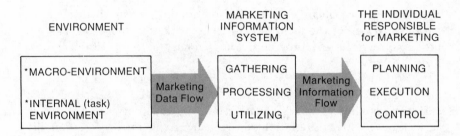

Figure 4. Components of a Marketing Information System

MARKET PLANNING

Before the intramural director can act purposefully and effectively to achieve the goals of his department, proper planning and preparation must occur. This section examines several of the various types, concepts, and tools of market planning that can help the intramural director achieve departmental goals.

What is planning? Planning is deciding in the present what to do in the future. It comprises both the determination of a desired future and the steps necessary to bring it about. In short, it is the process whereby intramural directors reconcile the resources of their departments with their department's goals and opportunities.

All intramural departments carry out some planning. The preparation of the annual budget represents planning. Although all intramural directors plan, they vary considerably in how extensively, thoroughly, and formally they do it. However, no one will dispute the fact that planning yields positive benefits. Though planning can be carried to excess, excess is usually not the problem in the intramural setting. The problem is to develop appropriate planning procedures together with department-wide participation and competence in carrying them out.

The literature suggests strongly that if good procedures are used, several distinct benefits from planning are possible (Branch, 1962, pp. 48–49):

1. Encourages systematic thinking ahead by management.
2. Leads to a better coordination of departmental efforts.
3. Leads to the development of performance standards for control.
4. Causes the (intramural) department to sharpen its guiding objectives and policies.
5. Results in better preparedness for sudden developments.

6. Brings about in the staff who participate in the planning, a more vivid sense of their interacting responsibilities.

It is inappropriate for the intramural director to view departmental planning as if it were a single process. Within the intramural setting, at least five types of planning can be distinguished (not all exist at every institution): long-range planning, annual planning, product (programs and services) planning, venture planning, and activity planning. The five types differ according to what personnel are involved; how they are involved; what is expected from the type of planning; and how the planning is achieved.

Long-range planning undertaken by the intramural department establishes the basic direction of its future goals and operations. For example, does the intramural department want to confine its responsibilities to organized competition, or should it adopt a campus recreation program oriented towards a wide range of services and tasks (for instance, dances, informal rec, and facility management).

Annual planning establishes specific goals and plans for the year. For example, the intramural department wants to achieve "x" number of participants in its programs or attract "x" number of informal-rec users of its facilities or employ "x" percentage of a minority group as student help.

Product planning establishes a long-range plan and a short-range plan for a particular product within the scope of the department. For example, a school decides to offer powder puff football for the first time. The strategy for conducting this activity during its formative stages might vary considerably from the strategy utilized after the activity becomes established. The girls could play flag football, for example, while they were becoming acquainted with the sport. After several years, it would be reasonable to expect that the skill level of the participants would be raised significantly. At this point, safety considerations would necessitate that the "flag" rules be switched to "touch." Proper planning could aid this transition.

Venture planning guides specific ventures—such as new products—from their inception to fruition. The intramural director who offers a new program or service and who wants to maximize its opportunity for success would employ this type of planning.

Finally, *activity planning* establishes a schedule for carrying out the complex interrelated activities within the department. All intramural directors engage in this type of planning to some degree. The allocation of staff, the scheduling of promotion, and the assigning of priorities for the use of facilities are examples of the responsibilities facing the intramural director in this area.

All of these types of planning involve the establishment of a set of planned actions, performance actions, and performance measures. As the planned actions are carried out, the results are checked against the performance measures and the deviations are noted. The deviations then lead to corrective actions. Within a broad context, these corrective actions constitute the final element in the intramural director's control system, which is one of the essential management tools in intramural administration. Figure 5 illustrates the four elements of this system.

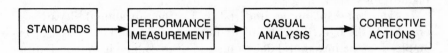

Figure 5.   The Four Elements in an Intramural Director's Control System

The first element consists of the *standards* (targets, participation quotas, and budgets) that are to be met during the school year. The second element is *performance measurement,* which yields information on actual versus expected (desired) results. The third element consists of *causal analysis* which determines the reasons for unsatisfactory results (poor staff actions, lack of participant interest, disruptive interferences, and so forth). The fourth element is corrective action which seeks to bring the actual results back into line with the desired results. Although simple in outline, this model of the control process has many ramifications for the intramural director. The dimensions of each element must be identified, and the steps needed to incorporate each action into the "intramural effort" must be undertaken.

THE CHALLENGE

The past decade has witnessed a rapid growth of quantitative and behavioral tools, concepts, and models that hold great promise for improving the decision-making process used by the intramural administrator. This chapter has attempted to expose the reader to a *broad* overview of marketing principles and ideas that can help today's and tomorrow's intramural administrator. The potential value of marketing tools and techniques to the intramural director is boundless. In closing, I hope that this chapter has made each reader view marketing not as an unnecessary infringement on the traditional seat-of-the-pants approach to intramural administration, but as a *positive opportunity* to develop and offer a quality intramural program to all students.

GENERAL BIBLIOGRAPHY

ALDERSON, WROE, and PAUL E. GREEN, *Planning and Problem Solving in Marketing*. Homewood, Ill.: Richard D. Irwin, 1964.

ANTHONY, ROBERT N., *Planning and Control: A Framework for Analysis*. Boston: Division of Research, Graduate School of Business Administration, Harvard University, 1965.

BELL, MARTIN L., *Marketing: Concepts and Strategy*. Boston: Houghton Mifflin, 1966.

BOYD, HARPER W., JR., and SIDNEY J. LEVY, *Promotion: A Behavioral View*. Englewood Cliffs, N. J.: Prentice-Hall, 1967.

BRANCH, MELVILLE C., *The Corporate Planning Process*. New York: American Management Association, 1962.

BUELL, VICTOR P., *Marketing Management in Action*. New York: Mc-Graw-Hill, 1966.

BURENSTAM-LINDER, STEFFAN, *The Harried Leisure Class*. New York: Columbia University Press, 1970.

CYERT, RICHARD M., and JAMES G. MARCH, *A Behavioral Theory of the Film*. Englewood Cliffs, N. J.: Prentice-Hall, 1960.

DAWSON, LESLIE, "The Human Concept: New Philosophy for Business," *Business Horizons*, December, 1969, pp. 29–38.

DRUCKER, PETER F., *The Practice of Management*. New York: Harper & Row, 1954.

KOTLER, PHILIP, *Marketing Management*. Englewood Cliffs, N. J.: Prentice-Hall, 1972.

LEVITT, THEODORE, *Innovation in Marketing*. New York: McGraw-Hill, 1962.

MASLOW, ABRAHAM H., *Motivation and Personality*. New York: Harper & Row, 1954.

MAUSER, FERDINAND, *Modern Marketing Management: An Integrated Approach*. New York: McGraw-Hill, 1961.

McCARTHY, E. JEROME, *Basic Marketing: A Managerial Approach*. Homewood, Ill.: Richard D. Irwin, 1964.

McLUHAN, MARSHALL, *Understanding Media: The Extension of Man*. New York: McGraw-Hill, 1965.

OSBORN, ALEX F., *Applied Imagination*. New York: Scribner's, 1963.

PETERSON, JAMES A., "Marketing the Intramural Product: Tools and Techniques," paper presented at the annual meeting of the American Association for Health, Physical Education and Recreation, Anaheim, California, March, 1974.

Rodgers, Everett, *The Diffusion of Innovations*. New York: Free Press, 1962.

Stanton, William J., *Fundamentals of Marketing*. New York: McGraw-Hill, 1964.

II

Administrative Practices and Policies

7

Black Involvement in Intramurals

The Black Employee

ROSS TOWNES
North Carolina Central University
Durham, North Carolina

INTRODUCTION

The unprecedented growth of intramural programs, due in part to the increased participation of minority students, stands in direct contradiction to the sometimes snaillike pace of the employment of black individuals in the administration of such programs. A significant number of blacks are employed as intramural administrators at *all-black institutions,* but my section of this chapter will address itself to the need for recruiting and utilizing black personnel in intramural positions at *predominantly white institutions.* Although I strongly believe that job selection should be based on qualifications—not on race—the facts suggest that this has not been the case.

In the predominantly white institutions, the number of black intramural administrators closely parallels the number of black head coaches

---

Editor's Note: Because of the complexity of the many aspects of black involvement in intramurals in this country, this chapter comprises three sections. The first section, "The Black Employee," deals with increasing the number of black personnel at all levels of intramurals. The second section, "The Black Athlete," offers an overview of the black student's perspective of black involvement in intramurals. The third section, "Balance of Pride: Basis for Interaction," presents suggestions for the improvement of human relations.

of intercollegiate sports: there are only a handful of each. Although a large number of schools have at least one black assistant coach in certain sports (for instance, football and basketball), the lack of progression by these assistants into the head positions frequently prompts allegations that some of these assistants have been hired as "window dressing" to attract black athletes or to quell advocates of affirmative action. Intramurals, as a field of professional endeavor, needs to guard against similar criticism by hiring blacks and providing them with the opportunity to advance to positions at all levels of intramural administration. Intramurals must not become a closed fraternity in which the top positions are reserved for white cronies and friends.

A BLUEPRINT FOR ACTION

Any examination of the scope, range, and intensity of the problems involved in attempting to employ more blacks at all levels of intramural administration would be far-reaching, at the least. To assist the reader in this task, I propose the following framework. The basis of this framework is a series of fifty questions (in outline form) that will hopefully provide the administrator with the information needed to proceed equitably. The questions are grouped into five sets of potential problems: problems in employing blacks; problems in orienting and motivating black personnel; relationship problems; problems in the training and development of blacks; and administrative problems. Except in a few instances, the framework is not specific to a certain level or position within the field of intramural administration.

Problems in Employing Blacks

A. Bases for Employing Black Personnel
 1. Does data exist regarding black interest in positions in intramural administration? If not, how can the intramural administrator develop and acquire such data?
 2. How can the intramural director inform blacks within the university community of employment opportunities? How can the intramural director convince blacks that such efforts are sincere?
 3. How can the intramural director improve the image of the intramural department among blacks within the university?
 4. Does the intramural director have an obligation to employ local applicants for staff positions, or should he hire from the outside?
 5. How can the director create the right image in his employment efforts? How can the intramural department encourage the feeling that it is *dealing with people,* not merchandise?

6. How can the intramural director increase the number of "walk-ing delegates" who work individually with university blacks giving them evidence that his department cares?

7. What techniques can the intramural director use to offset neg-ative images blacks have about the intramural department?

B. Inventory

8. What percentage of blacks have been hired in the past five years? What can be said about turnover among blacks?

9. How can the intramural director deal with such turnover?

10. How can the number of blacks hired at "senior-level" staff po-sitions be increased?

C. Recruiting

11. How can the intramural administrator develop a recruiting pro-gram for both staff positions and technical positions (gym su-pervisors, student officials, and so forth)?

12. How does the intramural director find out who is available for jobs?

13. What can be done to motivate black interest groups to provide applicants for vacant positions?

14. What are the most effective methods of attracting black appli-cants from outside the university for staff positions?

15. What resources within black groups on campus can be used to broaden the department's recruiting program?

16. How can communications with minority applicants be im-proved? How can they be persuaded that the intramural depart-ment wants them to apply?

D. Qualifying

17. Should the intramural director review job qualifications for the various jobs?

18. How can applicants be ranked? If the merit system is not used, what system should be employed?

19. How can the "trainability" of job applicants be assessed?

E. Placement

20. How can blacks be assisted through the hiring process?

21. How can the amount of time required for an employer to con-sider applicants be reduced?

22. In order to improve the "affirmative-action" statistics of the in-tramural department, the intramural director may be tempted to turn the hiring program into a numbers game. How can indi-viduals be brought into jobs realistically, so that their oppor-tunities for success are maximized?

23. How can the intramural director know more about black appli-cants for staff positions, ahead of their interviews?

24. What can be done to improve feedback on the reasons for attrition of black employees?
25. How can the job interview process be improved?

Problems in Orientation and Motivation

26. How can the intramural director prepare present employees for a black coming into the group?
27. How can the problem of employee attitudes that are not compatible with job requirements be attacked?
28. How can more motivation on the job for blacks be provided? What changes in environment and in perception can be made?
29. In a failure case, how can the intramural director make sure that the employee was sufficiently trained for the job?
30. What steps can be taken with black employees to improve motivation for work, self-discipline about jobs, and maintenance of a good performance record?

Relationship Problems

31. How can the work climate within the intramural department be improved? What can be done to establish a favorable climate for black employees? What can be done to improve working conditions and climate for the new employees?
32. How can the intramural director overcome "fear of the unknown" in relations between new and old employees, peers and superiors?
33. Is it a fair assumption that both blacks and whites have biases? How can these biases be overcome?
34. How should the intramural department go about training and preparing white supervisors and employees to accept black employees?
35. How can prejudices in supervisors be overcome? Apathy?
36. How can the intramural department reach the point of treating black employees the same as all others?
37. How can the intramural department instill insight into their white employees about their biases, which are perhaps unknown to them but are quickly perceived by blacks? How can individuals learn to avoid terms that carry "bad" connotations?
38. What can be done concerning individuals with a chip on their shoulder?

Problems in Training and Development

39. How can opportunities be provided for blacks to progress to higher-level jobs within the intramural department?

40. Could the intramural department develop long-range programs for training blacks for high-level supervisory positions?
41. What changes in compensation and prerequisites would lead to better training and promotion?
42. How can supervisors be persuaded to take the responsibility for guiding and training new employees?
43. Is the affirmative-action program of the intramural department compatible with the university's program?
44. Could training programs from other sources assist the intramural department?

Administrative Problems

45. What can be done to improve coordination with university groups interested in encouraging affirmative action? How can communication be improved with all groups working on the problem?
46. How can the intramural director arrive at goals and objectives compatible with the university's stated program?
47. How does one release incompetent employees? What methods for adjudicating differences can be devised?
48. How should a supervisor meet the pressures (perhaps the threat of physical reprisal) of an unsatisfactory relationship with an employee?
49. How can the intramural department collect data about employment sources in order to attract blacks?
50. How can the time and expertise within the intramural department be used to solve difficult cases?

EPILOGUE

According to Harold Titus, prejudice is a mental bias that leads us to make a judgment in advance without examining the evidence; it is not inborn, but rather is acquired during the process of our development and training (1936, p. 400). Race prejudice is one of the most serious evils in our social life. Group selfishness, a by-product of prejudice or racism. is exceedingly dangerous. The polarization of all-black or all-white groups in an intramural activity program may well harm the social welfare in general. Those who have sympathy and affection for the members of the "in-group" or "we-group" may harbor feelings of avoidance, suspicion, hatred, or fear for the "out-group" or "other-group." Attitudes of the "in-group" toward the "out-group" are often those of indifference, dislike, disgust, suspicion, or possibly warfare. We should strive to make the "in-group" the human family as a whole. The truly integrated society must be the ultimate objective of black and white alike.

Codes of ethics are important means of social control that define conduct. Every profession has its particular problems of conduct. Virtues are the good character traits, and vices are the bad traits. The professional is expected to render his best service quite apart from the amount of reward, whether it is much, little, or even nothing. The professional is expected to give the public a social outlook and a type of service not demanded of the businessman. The ideal of a profession is that the individuals who expect to gain a living from it measure their success in terms of the service they perform. The physical educator who directs intramural activities is a professional.

These important attributes of the intramural director are not peculiar to any distinct race or ethnic group. The selection of individuals to administer the program of intramural activities should be based upon desirable personal *qualifications,* not on any other factor.

The Black Athlete

ANTHONY CLEMENTS
University of Illinois
Urbana, Illinois

INTRODUCTION

In this section of Chapter 7, an attempt is made to illustrate the necessity for administrators of intramural programs (in fact, all university-level administrators) to be able to foresee (whenever possible) and to react in a positive manner to the problems incurred by black students. Instead of proposing a specific model with which to deal with the problem at hand, I will present a case study involving a not-too-atypical situation in which *black involvement* in the intramural program is more than just an empty phrase. I hope that by presenting an overview of the program at the University of Illinois during the years 1968–1974, you will be able to gain a better understanding of how to approach the task of integrating the black athlete into the intramural arena at your school. The material

This section is based largely on a paper presented to the twenty-fourth Annual Meeting of the National Intramural Association, Tampa, Florida, March 26, 1973.

used in this section is all firsthand. The events and occurrences are re-layed to you as I witnessed them. As a result, it is left to your discretion whether to utilize this information as a point of reference or to wait until you are face to face with similar problems.

The basic scenario is that of a large, multistudent university (in this case, with a semirural atmosphere) having to come to grips with a succession of entering freshmen classes containing substantial numbers of urban-area, minority students. Because this influx of minority students into the University of Illinois witnessed a corresponding increase in the minority group participation in all facets of university life, the Division of Intramural Activities became quickly and integrally involved in racial tensions and their concomitant problems. It should be pointed out that although the solutions used to meet these problems may not be the most appropriate for all institutions or all situations, the administrative philosophy of ignoring matters that may later become problems can be a costly approach.

A CASE STUDY

This part of the paper examines in semioutline form the steps taken by the University of Illinois to ensure that all members of the university community receive an equitable opportunity to participate in a quality program. This discussion consists of six topics: an introduction to the background of the author in dealing with this problem, and his perception of what a black athlete is; an overview of the black perspective of sport; an examination of the traditional patterns of black participation in the intramural program at the University of Illinois; a delineation of some of the problems that arose as a result of the increased involvement of blacks in the intramural program; a presentation of the actions taken to "solve" these problems; and a discussion of the situation at the University of Illinois today.

The Black Athlete: Introduction

1. Author's background in dealing with the problem.
    a. University of Illinois (Urbana): black student; varsity athlete; intramural participant; intramural official; first black student supervisor; graduate assistant in the intramural department; full-time staff position with the Division of Campus Recreation.
    b. Precollege days: raised in a college town (Raleigh, North Carolina —St. Augustine's College); father was the head basketball coach at an all-black school; extensive participation in athletics at all levels.

2. Definition of black athletes.

   a. All black students who participate in some facet of the intramural program (limited view).

   b. All black students within the university community (less widely held but more operational view).

Black Perspective of Sports

1. A number of studies indicate that blacks excel in certain sports not because of physical differences, but because of different philosophical, psychological, and environmental factors.

   a. Blacks have used sports as a means of escape, and they still do.

   b. Blacks know that only the most qualified athletes advance. Those who do not advance can best be categorized as frustrated athletes. Frequently, these are the athletes who participate. in the intramural program.

The Influx of Black Students into the University of Illinois

1. Illinois was a typical (predominantly white) institution with regard to black involvement in intramurals until 1968.

   a. Very few blacks participated in any aspect of the intramural program.

   b. There was possibly one black on a team. (What else could be expected when only 900 out of 30,000 students were black?)

   c. In 1968, however, the University of Illinois started Equal Opportunity Programs to recruit minority students (500 minority students per year).

      1. Illinois initiated a new program to recruit minority law-school students.

      2. These law students acted as a catalyst in the drive to recruit more black students (including varsity athletes).

      3. The black students who were enrolled under the EOP were primarily from Chicago, Philadelphia, East St. Louis, Washington, D.C., Florida, and Mississippi.

2. The influx of these relatively large numbers of black students resulted in the formation of black teams in the intramural program.

   a. Blacks from the same areas entered open basketball leagues.

   b. Because of housing procedures, blacks in many cases established situations where everyone assigned to a dormitory area was black.

   c. Black fraternities that had previously never participated in intramurals became involved.

d. At the same time, many black law students and other black graduate students began to participate in intramurals.

e. The amount of black students on campus increased in 1968 and 1969 from 900 to approximately 2,500. The percentage of black participation in the intramural program increased over 2,000 percent.

The Problems That Arose as a Result of Increased Black Participation

1. The first basketball season.
    a. Blacks noticed the almost total lack of black officials and gym supervisors.
    b. Blacks were involved in a series of misunderstandings regarding the policies of the Intramural Division.
    c. As a result, numerous black students and black groups became embroiled in disputes (argumentative and physical) with the Intramural Division.
2. The 1969–1970 basketball season was the test season.
    a. A white student official was assaulted by blacks and required hospital care for several days.
    b. A female official was chased by a mob of approximately fifty blacks. (We were able to sneak her out of the gym's back door).
    c. Our playoffs were disrupted by black participants throwing eggs, cherry bombs, and water balloons on the courts.
    d. A game had to be stopped because of packs of sugar thrown on the court to show dislike for an official who had refereed a previous contest in which a black team had lost.
    e. A white team was attacked in their locker room before a game by a black team they had filed a protest against and had won.
    f. Players were beaten in hallways after games.
    g. Players and officials were constantly threatened.
    h. An atmosphere of constant antagonism and apprehension between blacks and whites existed.
3. Facts the department began to realize.
    a. Of our officials, 99.9 percent were white.
    b. No blacks were members of either the student protest board or the policy-making body.
    c. Blacks had no input into the decision-making process of the Division.
    d. The lines of communication between black students and the Intramural Division were practically nonexistent.

What We Did

1. We held weekly meetings for about four weeks with captains of all teams.
2. We initiated a program to recruit black students to be officials.
3. We initiated a program to recruit black gym supervisors. (Such students contributed significantly to a lessening of the tense courtside atmosphere.)
4. We included pictures of black involvement in the intramural program in the intramural handbook distributed to students.
5. We analyzed the existing program and developed new activities to meet the needs of blacks.
6. We recruited blacks into the men's and women's student manager programs and assigned blacks to be members of both policy and protest boards.
7. We had black faculty, advisors, and counselors view games and officials.
8. We initiated extensive publicity efforts to attract black students into the intramural program.
9. We had both the law and sociology departments evaluate our program in terms of equitable opportunities and potential negative aspects regarding black involvement.

What We Have Today

1. Fights involving black basketball teams have been virtually eliminated (only one occurred in 1973).
2. About one third of our gym supervisors are black.
3. Approximately 10 percent of our officials are black. (That percentage has been as high as 25 percent in certain sports).
4. Our Protest and Policies Board has been chaired by a black man for the past two years.
5. In the quarterfinals of our open league basketball program, six of the sixteen teams were predominantly black, but only one was totally black.
6. No all-black graduate teams were entered in any team sport.
7. Black students are now conducting their own athletic tournaments and are inviting white teams to them.

THE CHALLENGE

Intramural personnel must redefine and redirect their efforts to involve black students in the intramural program. Then, and only then, will we—as intramural administrators—be fulfilling our professional task of providing *sport for all!*

A Balance of Pride: Basis for Interaction

FLOYD H. McAFEE
Lieutenant Colonel
United States Army

The first and most significant overt black boycott in the sports world occurred during the 1968 Olympics.* Before the "age of boycott" the problems of black athletes were expressed less openly and were labeled as "dissension among the players." Since 1968, there have been many overt expressions of discontent by black athletes. These expressions, which have had various causes, have occurred in all sports. The 1969 football season was, for example, highlighted by the problem of black boycotts in major colleges and universities throughout the United States.

An underlying cause of this situation is the feeling of black awareness taking place in the United States today. All of our black people, including black athletes, are undergoing a struggle to take their real place in society. This feeling of black awareness is not violent, nor is it aimed at the "establishment." It is centered more within black people and is not a battle between black and white.

There once was a time when black people were ashamed of the color of their skin and were sensitive to the overtones of racial imbalance. The word "black" was used very sparingly in conversation and was never used when referring to the color of a person's skin. To not use the word "black" was part of an unwritten code of ethics and mutual understanding that has been shared by black and white people in our country since the landing of the *Mayflower*. During this same span of time, the black man's racial problems could not be intelligently discussed openly because of the "sensitivity of the subject." This feeling was shared and respected by both black and white people.

This section of Chapter 7 is based largely on the article, "Balance of Pride," *Journal of Health, Physical Education, and Recreation,* XLI, No. 7 (September, 1970), 24–27.

* *Editor's Note:* Although Colonel McAfee frequently addresses his comments to athletic coaches and speaks of the "threat" of acts of civil disobedience, his thoughts have considerable relevance to the intramural administrator who is interested in understanding the black student.

However, because of some strange and unexplained act of faith, a black woman with tired feet sat in the wrong seat on a city bus in Montgomery, Alabama, in 1955 and refused to move. This incident caused the spark that was needed to energize a new feeling of black unity among black people. This feeling awakened black people. They grew in both pride and awareness. They began to recognize and appreciate the beauty of the God-given shades of the ebony tint of their skin. This feeling also motivated black people to air their grievances in public and inspired them to want to be heard. Black people had fought a battle and finally freed themselves of the bonds of sensitivity that for generations had restricted their struggle for manhood and freedom.

Today, black people are no longer ashamed of either their black skin or their black heritage. Most black people sincerely realize that "black is beautiful." Black people now flaunt their black music, black clothes, black history, black food, black language, black hair, and other aspects of their blackness. Black people have a feeling of identity and freedom that they never before experienced.

Although the brunt of the feeling of black awareness has been centered within black people, there is an overflow that is aimed at deleting racism. The ultimate goal is to maintain this new-found dignity and honor of black people.

Now, if an administrator or an educator (whatever his responsibility) fails to recognize and understand this feeling of black awareness within black students, he will be unable to meet the needs of these students. A failure to satisfy these needs often causes black students to become hopelessly frustrated and to manifest these frustrations by rejecting continued participation in a program they consider to be a cause of such feelings. The use of a boycott by black athletes is an excellent example of such consequences.

The problem of black boycotts has caused great concern among the involved personnel—school administrators, teachers, coaches, and players. They realize that the impact of a black boycott can be detrimental to the school's name, can cause the team to finish the season below the expected win level, can create an extra burden for the coach, and can ruin the players' futures in the sports world.

Great efforts have been made by college administrators and coaches to solve the problem. The head coaches of colleges and universities have met with their assistant coaches, with administrators and teachers, and with the head coaches of similar colleges and universities, such as those in the same athletic conference. The black coaches, both the head coaches in predominantly black schools and the assistant coaches in predominantly white schools, have also met to try to solve the problem. Yet the problem still exists, and no solution has been found.

There is a tendency for the involved personnel to state the problem by attempting to determine who is right, who is wrong, and who caused the problem—the coach, the white players, or the black players? The answers to these questions result only in the involved personnel offering stronger justifications for their actions. The incident in question is then investigated by school officials and discussed by the public, but eventually the issue fades away—until the next season.

After making a continual study and a detailed analysis of interracial conflicts for more than two decades, and as a result of becoming involved in black boycotts in intercollegiate sports, the author has concluded that the basis of the problem is *pride*. "Pride" has been defined in *Webster's New World Dictionary* as "an overhigh opinion of oneself; exaggerated self-esteem; conceit."

The late Martin Luther King, Jr., preached a sermon entitled "The Drum Major Instinct" at the Ebenezer Baptist Church in Atlanta, Georgia, on February 4, 1968. In this sermon Dr. King vividly and candidly transformed his biblical text into "how man's pride affects the social relevancy of today's world." He pointed out that "the dominant impulse—the basic drive of human life—was the quest for recognition; the desire for attention; the desire to be important; the desire to be first." His major point was that we must recognize the fact that "we all have the 'drum major instinct' in us, and that its use must not be perverted." Dr. King further pointed out that "if the 'drum major instinct' is used right it is good, because one's pride runs the whole gamut of life!"

In relating this theory to the problem of black discontent with either the varsity or the intramural athletic program, it is evident that there is often a "conflict of pride" between the individual in a position of authority (for example, an intramural administrator or coach) and the black student. Although the nature of this imbalance in human relations may vary from situation to situation, the author has chosen to categorize it simply as "pride." The solution to this dilemma for the intramural director lies in achieving a "balance of pride" in the relationship between black students and his department. The "scale of pride" (Figure 1) suggests that the actions of the intramural director and his representatives and the "needs" of black students are the basic factors in the achievement of a "balance of pride." The foundation of the scale, on which this balance rests, includes these factors: departmental policies, lines of communication, an appreciation of individual differences, and a commitment towards understanding. External factors that may tip the balance one way or the other are the news media, public opinion, and the community contiguous to the university.

What causes an imbalance in the scale? Although many reasons are possible, such a tilting generally results from an administrative neglect

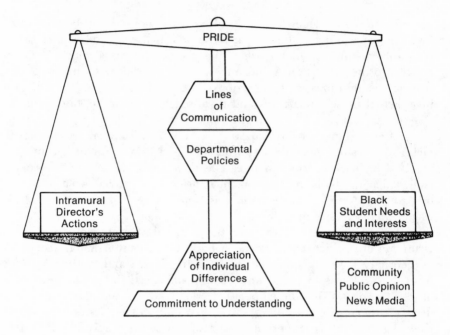

Figure 1. Scale of Pride

of one of the foundation blocks on the scale. In short, the actions of the intramural department are not completely in tune with the needs or basic dignity of the black participants in the intramural program.

Here are ten techniques that can be used by the intramural director who wishes to maintain a balance of pride in the relationship between his department and his school's black students:

1. Recognize potential areas of conflict in human relations.
2. Be an outstanding educator.
3. Be an outstanding individual.
4. Train and supervise departmental personnel to perform their tasks effectively.
5. Treat the individual as an individual.
6. Be impartial in expressing or discussing in public any disagreement or conflict with black students.
7. Recognize and make an attempt to understand the feeling of black awareness in the black students.
8. Be willing to listen to the grievances of the black students, and make every attempt possible to guide them in solving their problems.

9. Be more willing to exercise teacher-learner authority when helping the students solve their problems.
10. Make every effort to ensure that a balance of pride is obtained and maintained, and have a strong desire to solve all conflicts that affect the effective functioning of the department.

Regardless of the technique or method used by the intramural director to guide his department, the basic framework is clear: all departmental efforts and actions must be compatible with the *inherent worth and dignity of every individual.* Then, and only then, will a balance of pride be achieved.

GENERAL BIBLIOGRAPHY

BRINK, WILLIAM, and LOUIS HARRIS, *Black and White.* New York: Simon & Schuster, 1967.

BROOM, LEONARD, and PHILIP SELZNICK, *Sociology.* New York: Harper & Row, 1963.

CLEMENTS, ANTHONY J., "The Black Athlete in Intramurals," *National Intramural Association Proceedings,* XXIV (1973), 71–73.

EDWARDS, HARRY, *The Revolt of the Black Athlete.* New York: Free Press, 1969.

JORDAN, PAT, *Black Coach.* New York: Dodd, Mead, 1972.

MCAFEE, FLOYD H., "A Balance of Pride," *Journal of Health, Physical Education, and Recreation,* XLI, No. 7 (Sept., 1970), 24–27.

———, "A Balance of Pride: A Follow-Up Survey," *Journal of Health, Physical Education, and Recreation,* XLIII, No. 6 (June, 1973), 9, 70.

OLSEN, JACK, *The Black Athlete: A Shameful Story.* New York: Time-Life Books, 1968.

REEVES, DONALD, "Supplements for Campus Racism," *Ebony,* March, 1974, p. 114.

ROBERTS, OZZIE, "Where Are the Coaches," *Ebony,* December, 1973, p. 160.

SCOTT, HARRY A., *Competitive Sports in Schools and Colleges.* New York: Harper & Brothers, 1951.

SCOTT, JACK, *The Athletic Revolution.* New York: Free Press, 1971.

SUGAR, BERT R., "Star-Spangled Mixup," *Black Sports,* II, No. 2 (May, 1973), 36–37.

TITUS, HAROLD H., *Ethics for Today.* New York: American Book, 1936.

8

Intramurals for Women

Women's Intramurals: Issues and Directions

CAROL HARDING

Michigan State University
East Lansing, Michigan

IM is a logos representing intramural sport and game services for the entire university community and this community includes women.

INTRODUCTION

The woman student is clearly aware of herself and her own potential in relation to sport, game, and physical activity. She is requesting increased, equitable sport services and recreational facilities. Due to the traditional separation of men and women's intramural departments, men's intramural services have developed more rapidly. Concurrently, more men have occupied sports administration positions, and men have enjoyed better intramural facilities. A doubling of effort is needed to provide better sports administration and services for the waiting women on American campuses. Special care must be taken to serve the majority of women, who look to intramural sport to provide services, and to at

---

This chapter contains three sections: (1) "Women's Intramurals: Issues and Directions," (2) "A Pragmatic Examination of the Issues Confronting Intramural Activity Programs for Women," and (3) "Sexism, Discrimination, and the Laws."

least parallel the current investment in women's intercollegiate athletics. Increasing emphasis and popularity of participatory sport among all Americans has given impetus to the need for an efficient sport service delivery system for all. Because only a minority of students wish to be a part of intercollegiate athletics—with the resulting rigid practice schedules, games, and pressured performances to win—women cannot wait for "powerhouses" to be built by women in athletics.

New interest in sport psychology and the questioning of playing to win, what losing really means, and professional, high-paying athletics place all students at the threshold of curiosity, debate, and experiment concerning cultural values of sport, game, and play. The "hot" intramural competitor who wishes to run away with an award or an all-university championship is looked upon critically for playing only to win. Students expect comraderie and play for play's sake in IM games. Women are particularly critical of high-pressure, high-stakes male sport and the commercialization of athletics, and they ask, "Is this what sport is all about?" The woman IM participant wants sport to remain relevant for her daily physical and emotional need for recreation, pleasure, and relaxation. The woman undergraduate and graduate student, the sixty-year-old professor's wife, and the forty-five-year-old woman faculty member want sport and activity to be available on their own terms: extensive pool hours, training room opportunities, and open courts offered with a philosophy of community service.

More and more women are using and requesting facilities traditionally used only by men. Steam and sauna areas, weight training rooms, paddleball courts, football fields, and an occasional men's locker room are entered by women as a means of bringing attention to the local campus need for more women's sport services. Although the majority of women students want sport for sport's sake, there are many women who would like a good, competitive IM game, and these women even enter teams or become individual competitors in men's leagues in order to obtain better competition, better officiating, or better courts. Women students request and appreciate the designation of professional women sports administrators to represent their campus recreational needs and to be responsible for developing new comprehensive and equitable IM sport services and facilities for women. Important questions are asked: What is the current investment in women's IM sport services on the campus? Who are the women IM participants. What program considerations can be made?

A CASE STUDY

Table 1 illustrates several of the important indicators of the increased growth in intramural sport services for women that has occurred

Table 1. Growth in IM Sport Services
for Women * in the Big Ten Conference

Year	Women Students Enrolled	Investment in IM Sport Services	Available Open Hours for IM Per Week
1965	74,061	$ 19,350	30.4
1971	146,779	$349,194	64.4

* Parallel figures for men's IM programs are not available, but each university's investment and participation in men's programs far outreaches existing programs for women. At least two of the universities had budgets for men during the academic years 1970–71, 1971–72, 1972–73 that equal the total for women in all ten universities.

Table 2. Growth of Participation
at the Women's Intramural Building
at Michigan State University

Years	Total Number of Participations in the Informal Recreational Use of the IM Building	Total Number of Participations in IM Scheduled Competition	Pieces of Equipment Issued
1962–63	2,000	2,515	1,400
1963–64	7,271	2,335	2,352
1964–65	8,260	2,538	9,190
1965–66	8,400	2,496	11,354
1966–67	9,200	2,420	12,342
1967–68	13,480	2,378	15,890
1968–69 *	52,779	1,860	12,622 †
1969–70	90,618	2,301	22,155
1970–71	122,217	2,906	32,493
1971–72	150,598	3,202	37,109
1972–73	165,725	4,630	34,177 ‡

* This was the first year the building was open during the summer session (5 weeks).

† This reduced figure was due to the separation of physical education and intramural equipment.

‡ During this year, the supplying of swimsuits and caps on a sign-out basis was discontinued.

in the Big Ten Conference. Table 2 provides a specific examination of the growth patterns at Michigan State University.

The rise in the female student population on the Big Ten campuses has been accompanied by increased investment in intramural sport services for women and by more than double the number of available hours for women's open recreation. This statistical evidence displays the apparent efforts of women in the development of IM sport services for women on ten large campuses in the United States. These statistics also reflect the changing concept of women's role in sports participation. Women are interested in daily workouts and the leisure enjoyment of sport. Women of all ages and backgrounds are looking to intramural sports centers and administrators to represent women's interest in traditional sports and to develop innovative sports experiences as well. An examination of the profile of the women involved in these intramural sport services yields interesting results. Similar to their male counterparts, women participants have a wide range of sports and activity interests. The extent to which they can pursue their interests in the existing programs varies according to each woman's daily work schedule, outside responsibilities, and so on. Female students (both undergraduate and graduate) receive priority attention in existing administrative efforts because (1) they seek such sport services, and (2) they contribute toward sport services when they pay their university registration fee. However, the total female clientele requesting sport services is much greater. Other women within the university community also need an equitable opportunity to participate in intramural activities.

THE FORGOTTEN WOMEN

Secretarial staff, faculty wives, faculty women, and student wives constitute a substantial group of women in the campus community, and all of them should be included in the sport service arrangement. All of these women have had limited opportunities to exploit their prowess in sport, dance, or related physical activity. This is the issue needing the most attention by the hierarchy in sport administration. There are far more women responsible for putting student husbands through the university than men putting wives through degree programs. Also, there are many less husbands of faculty women on campus than wives of faculty men. These student and faculty wives must be regarded as contributing and important members of the university community, and they must be served equally well as student women. From the standpoint of participatory sport, women cannot have pools, tracks, gyms, and courts closed to them because they do not belong to the student body. These women can contribute to the intramural financial income by contributing slightly more for lockers, towel service, and entry fees. Whatever the financial requirement, these women should be included. They have not had equal opportunities in sport, and if services for women exist on a campus, they cannot continually be excluded from using the facilities. Because of the diversity in age and interests of these individuals, special programming considerations must be made.

SCHEDULING

Effective scheduling for delivery of services is imperative. Women employed by the university as secretaries, clerks, and support staff (food services, health services, and maintenance services) do not have a flexible daily work schedule. The 8 A.M. to 5 P.M. employment pattern must be enhanced by an "early bird" program from 6 to 7:50 A.M. and an early evening service at 5 P.M. These programs will permit the women to enjoy a regular workout before or right after the rigid day's employment. Care must also be taken to have facilities available in the evening hours, for this is a time of high participation by students. Excessive crowding of the intramural center must be resolved with scheduling that permits a positive atmosphere for enjoyable activity. The schedule can be made appealing when the sports administrator knows the clientele and profiles of the individual or groups to be served.

THE FUTURE

The major emphasis in this decade will be on sport services— court reservations, studio reservations, length swimming, open tracks, well-equipped fitness rooms, steam and sauna facilities. Women will come regularly to the intramural facility if they are welcomed and served in a consistent, effective manner. Scheduled games and contests will remain popular, but the expected growth will be in the daily drop-in recreation services. Table 3 provides an overview of the characteristics of current female IM participants at Michigan State University. Although such descriptive data have obvious limitations for application elsewhere, they do provide some basis for evaluation and planning.

Challenge courts for pickup games on a drop-in basis will remain popular, and increasing emphasis will be placed on establishing game service boards that will permit the individual woman to challenge other men and women informally at a convenient time in whatever sport she is most interested in. Finding a court partner, a challenger, or a team to

Table 3. Profile Analysis of the
Intramural Participants at the Women's Intramural Building
at Michigan State University, Winter, 1973 *

Participants using the Women's IM facility::

92%	female	15%	freshmen
8%	male	15%	sophomores
21%	married	27%	juniors
79%	single	22%	seniors
88%	students	21%	advanced degrees

42% live in residence halls
58% live off campus or in married housing

Previous term point averages of the IM participants:

1.5–2.0	15%
2.0–2.5	8%
2.5–3.0	26%
3.0–3.5	34%
3.5–above	30%

Ages of participants:

18	19%	24	4.5%
19	11%	25	5 %
20	20%	26	3.8%
21	20%	27	3.8%
22	5%	28–32	6 %
23	5%	33–65	5 %

42% of the participants come alone to the Intramural Building
24% of the participants come with others
74% have no intramural team affiliation
26% play on intramural teams
23% come to intramurals three times a week
19% come more than five times per week

Participants believe they are overweight:

0 to 10 pounds	36%
10 to 20 pounds	53%
20 to 30 pounds	10%

* Detailed data from the survey of intramural participants was analyzed through Bastat, Chi-Square, and correlational routines on the 6500 Computer at Michigan State University. The use of this computer was made possible through support, in part, from the National Science Foundation.

play on may be difficult, and a very simple posting system and telephone service can be utilized for pairing. This sport service results in a very good mix of age groups and backgrounds—administrator and student, student and professor, wife and student or professor—a mix that enhances community rapport and understanding.

Within this decade, men's and women's IM services will merge. They will serve all people, regardless of sex. The courts, the games, the clubs, and all IM services will be open to all students, faculty, and staff without discriminatory bounds. Future emphasis will be placed on the concept of "intramurals for you." The informal, drop-in program, including clubs, will increase in participation and popularity and will become the focus of the most innovative programming in the intramural field. The services will not be sexist, and the label of men's and women's IM will become passé in rendering or identifying services or facilities. With this nonsexist momentum, women must concern themselves with being included in the services and placing administrative representatives in an all-male hierarchy of administrators of sport. No program of IM services will be completely equitable without women performing in responsible sports administration positions.

Currently, Ohio State University and Purdue University are combining women's IM sport services and intercollegiate athletics in a women's center for sport services. Special attention and care must be exercised to prevent the athletic-oriented minority from having better services than the majority of women IM participants. Responsible sport administrators can make this innovative concept work and perhaps alter the direction of an athletic program for women toward a locked-in tradition parallel to big-time college athletics for men. The concept of all women in sport and athletics is most favorable, and this decade will determine the direction and success of this concept.

Dr. King McCristal, Dean of the College of Physical Education at the University of Illinois, challenged IM sport administrators to regard themselves as the architects of a new form of IM administration, one that will serve the mass of participants waiting for sport services on American campuses. This new form will deliver mass sport services to the entire campus community, of which women are an integral part, both as recipients and as sport administrators.

A Pragmatic Examination of the Issues Confronting Intramural Activity Programs for Women

JAMES A. PETERSON

U.S. Military Academy
West Point, New York

It is with a strong degree of personal satisfaction and some sense of irony that I learned that—as a faculty member at one of this country's most noted all-male institutions—I would have the good fortune to address such a distinguished group. When I first learned several months ago that this conference was to be held, one of my initial thoughts was whether or not this forum would concern itself with the various issues attendant upon intramural programming for women—and if so, how. This concern emanated both from my professional interest, which began with my experience as the director of the intramural program for women at the University of Illinois, and from my observation that other professional meetings that also examined "women and sport" have almost totally ignored this vital aspect of women's involvement in sport.

As several of the speakers this week have pointed out so explicitly, in these times of redefined values and changing attitudes women are demonstrating an ever increasing interest in sport and physical activity. One of the more cogent manifestations of this interest has been the rapid growth of intramural activity programs for women. This growth is the reason that one of the most difficult problems I encountered when preparing my presentation for this forum was to make a decision on how to introduce my topic effectively. Frankly, I strongly believe that many individuals within our profession are not familiar with the extent and nature of the existing efforts to provide intramural programming for women. As a result, they are unaware of the need to examine the issues attendant upon such efforts and to formulate guidelines for appropriate administrative action.

Although I do not wish to belabor or manipulate numbers, indi-

This paper was presented at a conference on "Women and Sport," Western Illinois University, Macomb, Illinois, June 28, 1973.

vidual participation in women's intramural programs is currently being counted—not in the dozens or the hundreds, but in the thousands—at several universities. Competition between women's teams is being conducted in such previously sanctimonious male athletic domains as football, soccer, and ice hockey. At the University of Illinois, for example, the number of women's touch football teams is expected to exceed one hundred this fall. At Illinois, women's involvement in the intramural program has reached the point where in the interest of fair play, teams are placed into competitive leagues on the basis of prior experience in the particular sport.

What import does this unabated development of intramural programming for women have for administrators? At the least, it should call attention to several matters that must be considered if such growth is to continue and if the extant student interest is to be channeled in a manner that provides quality programming opportunities for the participant. The primary purpose of this paper is to present a discussion of several of these critical issues and to suggest possible administrative guidelines for future action.

ISSUE 1: PROFESSIONAL PREPARATION FOR ADMINISTRATORS OF INTRAMURAL ACTIVITY PROGRAMS FOR WOMEN

The substantial growth of intramural programs for women has not induced a corresponding increase in either the extent or the quality of professional preparation programs for administrators of intramural activity programs for women. On the contrary, a dismal situation exists. Only a few schools offer a graduate program that includes specialization in physical recreation or intramural administration. The student seeking an undergraduate education in physical education encounters an equally slack footing in this regard. Although the curriculum of the major may include a basic course in intramural administration, this course typically offers nothing more than a cursory examination of the technical duties of administering an intramural program—scheduling, promoting, equipment procurement, and so forth. In addition, the number of women enrolled in these courses has been minimal, except in a few isolated instances.

Of equal concern is the minuscule amount of time allotted in these courses to a discussion of the unique aspects of intramural programming for women. Knowing how to set up a double-elimination tournament, for example, is of little assistance to the intramural administrator confronted with an ill-conceived administrative concern over an "epidemic" of breast injuries if contact sports are included in the women's program offering. What guidelines influence the formulation of a policy regarding the inclusion or exclusion of highly skilled women in the program? How should the intramural administrator handle a request or a demand that DGWS-ordained rules be used to govern all competitive activities within the women's program? At the University of Illinois, to offer one example, we were unable to develop a successful women's program until the rules in some activities were modified to coincide more with the rules the men were using and with the women's perceptions of what the rules should be. These women were unwilling to accept rigid adherence to a set of rules that they believed pandered their status as participants. The list of aspects unique to women's programming is boundless. The point I would like to make, however, is that a basic survey course in intramural administration —with its attention to the "rhesus monkey" details of the job—is, at best, inadequate preparation for the intramural administrator.

The existing status of professional preparation programs and courses in intramural administration appears to be attributable to three interrelated factors:

a. The first is the relative indifference of top-echelon physical education administrators to the entire question of intramurals. A corollary to the postulate that physical education occupies one of the lowest rungs on the academic ladder is the presumptive caste system that assigns the lowest rung on the physical education ladder to the intramural department. In the precipitant haste to legitimize the "academic" aspects of physical education, intramurals—as a service program—is accorded second-class citizenship, with its attendant lower salaries, fewer opportunities for promotion, limited access to needed departmental resources, and so forth.

b. The second factor is the lack of competently trained faculty to teach a course in intramural administration. This situation appears to be particularly acute for individuals involved with intramural programming for women. With the exception of schools that offer a separate unit for their women students interested in intramural administration, the prevailing practice is to have the intramural course taught by the director of the men's program. The field of intramural administration is inundated with ex-coaches who have been farmed out to serve their remaining days as intramural personnel and with individuals whose experience encompasses only intramural programming for men. What insight regarding progressive intramural programming for women can these individuals offer?

c. The third factor is the relative absence of adequate reference material concerning intramural administration. If an individual's frame of reference regarding intramural programming for women is not founded on personal experience, then on what is it founded? Containing minimal information concerning women's intramurals, much of the extant reference materials can best be classified as nothing more than a layperson's how-to-do-it manual. Little effort is made in these works to provide the intramural administrator with a framework for solving substantive problems.

ISSUE 2: ORGANIZATIONAL RESPONSIBILITY FOR WOMEN'S INTRAMURAL PROGRAMS

In general, women's intramural programs appear to be administered under either of two types of organizational structure. Under one structure, responsibility for the various activity divisions within a physical recreation program—women's intramurals, men's intramurals, corecreational activities, and unorganized recreation—are combined into a single department. Depending on the budget and the extent of the overall program, responsibility for administering each of the activity divisions will be assigned to someone on a full-time basis. Within the limitations outlined in the discussion of the first issue, these individuals will usually have both a strong professional interest in intramurals and some background, however limited, in the administration of activity programs.

Under the other method of administering intramural programs for women, the responsibility for the women's program is assigned—on a part-time basis—to a woman faculty member of the physical education department. In this case, it is not atypical that the individual undertaking the direction of the women's program would have little, if any, prior experience in intramurals for women and would be allocated only a nominal portion (5 to 10 percent) of her full-time employment work load for her intramural responsibilities.

An analysis of the merits of the two types of administrative setups suggests that the combined department provides a more desirable structure for women's intramurals. Under the combined department, the women's intramural program is integrated into the overall campus physical recreation program. This integration provides for a feasible framework within which to effect a more equitable allocation of existing facilities, monies, and support personnel among the various activity programs. The numerous discussions that this writer has had with directors of women's programs—including those from the Big Ten schools—reveal that a similar distribution of resources simply does not occur when responsibility for women's intramurals is assumed on a part-time basis by someone not associated with the intramural department.

An absurd yet unfortunate aspect of the combined organizational structure is the blatant discrimination that is practiced in the selection of administrators for the various activity programs. As infrequent as it is for a woman to be appointed to the chairpersonship of a combined intramural department, it is equally improbable that a male would receive just consideration for the directorship of a woman's program. Certainly, there are far more important professional and personal qualities characteristic of the successful intramural administrator than simply or primarily that of gender.

ISSUE 3: THE RELATIONSHIP BETWEEN INTRAMURAL ACTIVITY PROGRAMS FOR WOMEN AND WOMEN'S INTERCOLLEGIATE ATHLETIC (EXTRAMURAL) PROGRAMS

At many schools, the relationship between the intramural and extramural programs for women is characterized by an administrative atmosphere of cooperative coexistence. Such an atmosphere is predicated on a commitment to provide an opportunity for an athletic experience for all of the school's women students. At some schools, however, an unfavorable association exists between the two programs. As in the relationship that has either been encouraged or tolerated at most universities for many years between men's intercollegiate athletics and men's intramurals, the university allocates the women's intercollegiate program a disproportionately large share of the available resources—monies, facilities, equipment, and personnel. Inherent in this unconscionable condition is an administrative willingness—be it passive or active—to subordinate the opportunities of the majority to the needs of the few.

Another intemperate interpretation of the relationship between the two programs is that the women's intramural program should serve primarily as a "farm system" for the women's intercollegiate program. When held, this perspective has a particularly negative influence on the women's intramural program at schools that assign one individual to administer both the intramural and the extramural programs.

At one time or another, many of you have coached an athletic team. Unquestionably, during that period you discovered that one of the most overriding characteristics of coaching is the tremendous amount of time it requires from the individual. Coupled with teaching duties, professional involvement, and the general business of daily survival, it is not only unlikely but also highly improbable that an individual could do a creditable job in a position of dual responsibility. If the women's athletic programs of the Western Athletic Conference provide a reliable indication, the women's intramural program is the one—of the two—most likely to suffer when a single individual attempts to handle both programs.

ISSUE 4: ENCOURAGE MINORITY GROUP INVOLVEMENT
IN THE INTRAMURAL PROGRAM

Although on many campuses there appears to be an encouraging trend to the contrary, the smattering of minority group involvement in intramural programs represents a major contradiction to the intramural credo of "sports for all." This veritable lily-white state appears to be particularly pronounced in the intramural programs for women. Although a number of reasons could be offered to explain why this inequitable condition exists, a more expedient path to pursue would be to examine what steps can be taken to rectify the situation. Three steps lend themselves to a meaningful effort in this direction:

a. Conduct meetings between intramural personnel and members of the campus minority groups—faculty and student alike. Unfortunately, under the traditional methods for administering an intramural program, viable lines of communication simply do not exist in many cases. Too many intramural personnel misconstrue their open-door policy as constituting an all-encompassing effort to relate to their student constituency. At Illinois, for example, during most of my first year as director of the women's program, the doors of the intramural department were open to all students, and yet the minority group participation in the women's program was negligible. It was not until we met with minority group members—and explained the opportunities that were available for *all* women, determined the basis of the reticence of these individuals to participate in the program, and ascertained what policy changes would induce increased minority group involvement—that progress was achieved in this area.

b. Evaluate the activity offering to insure that sports and activities that are of interest to minority group members are included in the women's intramural program. Such an evaluation implies a two-way thrust: first, a determination of the athletic interests of minority groups; second, an administrative commitment to include activities in the program that satisfy those interests.

c. Adopt personnel practices that result in the employment of minority group individuals in all phases of the administration of the intramural program. In addition to opening the lines of communication between the intramural office and minority students, such a policy offers favorable consequences. It provides the minority group students with a tangible indication that the invitation extended to them to become involved in the program is not a shallow administrative gesture. Equally as important, when minority group students actually participate in the program, the opportunity to express their opinions and grievances to minority group personnel—be they staff, student officials, gym supervisors, or whatever—enhances the validity of the idea that the intramural department can be sensitive and responsive to the viewpoints of minority group members. A sea of white faces among the various intramural personnel can only serve to reinforce the apprehensions that minority group members have toward such organizations.

Drawing from the discussion to this point, a number of recommendations for the future can be advanced:

1. Based upon the realization that intramural athletics—in particular, intramural programming for women—are important, integral aspects of physical education, it is time that a comprehensive professional-preparation program be instituted for those interested in intramural administration. Such a program should be equipped to produce thoroughgoing, highly competent professional administrators whose approach to their jobs reflects a sound disciplinary background. Perhaps then, the practice of hiring ex-coaches or anyone else on the basis of expediency rather than qualification will come to a judicious end.

2. The intramural program for women must shed its bonds of second-class citizenship. Until now, the finest equipment, the best facilities, and in some cases the most competent support personnel have been provided to those who need it least—the highly skilled athletes. Quite obviously, however, the needs and interests of the majority must be given greater consideration. This is not to insinuate that the program for the intercollegiate or extramural performer should be eliminated. Rather, a better balance is needed.

3. Intramural administrators must be held more accountable for their programs. An effort should be directed to ascertain what the realizable objectives of a program are; how these objectives can be achieved by those taking part; and how the results will be evaluated to determine if the objectives are being met. As Earle Zeigler surmised so explicitly in a recent address to the intramural section of the National College Physical Education Association for Men:

> The mere statement that such and such a percentage of the student population is taking part, or that so many teams are in the various basketball leagues, will no longer suffice. Evidence might also be mustered to claim that a certain percentage of the student population masturbates, but on what basis can the case be made that one activity is better than the other?

The implication for the administrator of an intramural program is that more valid assessment criteria need to be employed.

4. A vigorous effort should be undertaken to increase the extent

and improve the quality of intramural programming for women at the high school level. The frequently dismal attempts to provide intramural programming for college women shines with excellence in comparison with the abysmal state of intramurals for secondary school women. In light of the significant number of women who will not continue their formal education, the lack of an adequate intramural program represents a host of lost opportunities. The relative negative state of high school intramural programs can be attributed to most of the same woes that plague the college-level programs—the inequitable distribution of extant resources, the lack of competently trained support personnel, and the administrative indifference to making a strong commitment to "sports for all."

After offering such a negative view of intramurals, I would like to close with the statement that I firmly believe in intramurals—their subordinating past, their encouraging present, and their optimistic future. To paraphrase O. Henry, who once said, "Turn up the lights, I don't want to go home in the dark," intramural personnel would hope that after so many years in obscurity and relative darkness, the intramural light will continue to shine brightly, both ideologically and practically.

Sexism, Discrimination, and the Laws

HAZEL SMITH VARNER
University of Rochester
Rochester, New York

SEXISM

Sexism refers to all those attitudes and actions which relegate women to a secondary and inferior status in society. Sexism further indicates a preference by society for one sex over the other. Society then attributes to that selected sex various preferred qualities and attitudes at the expense of the other sex. According to Thomas Boslooper and Marcia Hayes, authors of *The Femininity Game*, the qualities necessary for success in today's culture—competitiveness, aggressiveness, the desire to achieve—are considered unwomanly. Femininity is defined as passivity, as emotional dependence and physical weakness, as recreation instead of action—the portrait, in short, of a loser (1973, p. 15 and 17). Audrey Van Deren states in "Tonka Toys for Boys," "A female is born into a pre-determined existence—the student, wife, mother, grandmother syndrome. This is beginning to change, but it takes a gut-level change of consciousness concerning what being a human being is all about, to end the conditioning of females and males. Males, too are channeled into roles and ways of behavior which need not be. Too long the 'masculine' and 'feminine' mystique has determined how one must behave and what one must do if one wishes to 'fit in' to society as it has been predetermined" (1973, p. 9).

Sexism, as practiced in its everyday form, may be conscious or unconscious. It may take the simple form of sexist language which demeans, ignores, patronizes, or puts women in a special class. For example, to say, "Arthur Ashe is one of the best tennis players in America, and Billie Jean King is one of the best women players" is sexist. An alternative would be to say "Arthur Ashe and Billie Jean King are among the best tennis players in America today." Sexism in one of its most blatant forms appears as discrimination in the professional career world when women work for less pay and are still unlikely to be promoted to positions of authority.

Sexist attitudes and discriminatory practices must be changed if we are to have a society in which both sexes can derive pleasure from all the roles human beings can play, a society with sufficient flexibility to allow both men and women full expression of their talents. Attitudes are best changed by a process of education whereby each person reaches a state of awareness. Discriminatory practices can be changed by legislation: the passing of laws which forbid discrimination on the basis of race or sex.

DISCRIMINATION AND THE LAWS

Many federal laws and regulations speak to discrimination. Four important federal laws affect the employment policies of educational institutions.

Title VII of the Civil Rights Act of 1964, as amended by the Equal Employment Opportunity Act of 1972, prohibits discrimination in employment (including hiring, upgrading, salaries, fringe benefits, training, and other conditions of employment) on the basis of race, color, religion, national origin, or sex. It is administered by the Equal Employment Opportunity Commission, Washington, D.C., and regional EEOC offices.

Executive Order 11246, as amended by 11375, prohibits discrimination in employment by institutions with federal contracts of over $10,000.

It is administered by the office for Civil Rights, U.S. Department of Health, Education and Welfare, Washington, D.C. 20201, and regional HEW offices.

The Equal Pay Act of 1963, as amended by the Education Amendments of 1972 (Higher Education Act), prohibits discrimination in salaries, including almost all fringe benefits, on the basis of sex. It is administered by the Wage and Hour Division, Employment Standards Administration, U.S. Department of Labor, Washington, and regional Wage and Hour Division Offices.

Title IX of the Education Amendments of 1972 (Higher Education Act) covers the employment practices of education institutions. It is administered by the Office of Civil Rights, U.S. Department of Health, Education and Welfare and regional offices.

In addition, there are many state and local laws and regulations which prohibit discrimination. These should be reviewed with state and local authorities. Complaint procedures are inherent within each of the federal laws and regulations. Information on procedures for filing complaints may be obtained from the specified agencies.

AFFIRMATIVE ACTION ISSUES

Today, college administrators face many affirmative action questions. The *Journal of Law and Education* has identified many of the major issues:

1. *Affirmative action plans:* Required of all institutions with federal contracts totaling $50,000 or more and having 50 or more employees. The plan must be written; Revised Order No. 4 details what these plans must cover.

2. *Numerical goals and timetables:* Required of all institutions with federal contracts covered by the Executive Order. The institution must document its "good faith" efforts in recruiting women and minorities.

3. *Salary equalization:* Women and minorities cannot be paid less because of their sex and/or race. Criteria for raises must be applied equally. Numerous institutions have set aside specific sums for "equity adjustments."

4. *Back pay:*
   Title VII—allows up to two years, but not prior to date of coverage for professional staff (March 24, 1972).

   Equal Pay Act—allows up to two years for unwillful violation, three for willful violation (July 1, 1972).

   Executive Order—time limit not clear.

5. *Pensions such as T.I.A.A., which pay women less on a monthly basis*

because of actuarial differences. Under Executive Order, employers either make equal contributions or provide equal benefits. Under Title VII, equal benefits must be provided regardless of contribution.

6. *Nepotism:* Under Title VII and the Executive Order policies or practices which restrict the employment of spouses are prohibited.

7. *Maternity leave:* Both Title VII and the Executive Order apply. Title VII guidelines require that the part of pregnancy and childbirth when a woman is physically unable to work be treated like all other temporary disabilities in terms of sick leave, health insurance and job retention. *Childrearing leave:* Under HEW guidelines, this leave should be granted if leave is available for other personal reasons.

8. *Internal grievance procedures:* HEW does not require this but recommends that there be written procedures whereby individuals who feel aggrieved because of sex or racial discrimination can ask for an investigation and if necessary, redress.

9. *Child care:* Not required by any laws, but recommended by HEW guidelines.

10. *Recruitment and hiring:* HEW requires that standards and criteria be "reasonably explicit" and be accessible to employees and applicants. Under the Executive Order, new recruiting practices must be developed if old methods result in low representation of women and minorities in the applicant pool.

11. *Affirmative advertising:* All job notices should indicate that applications from women and minorities are sought. Employers cannot state that only members of a particular sex or race will be considered.

12. *Policy statements:* Under the Executive Order institutions are required to have in writing a policy of non-discrimination in employment. This statement must be disseminated throughout the campus.

13. *Conditions of employment, salaries and benefits:* Federal regulations require that there be no discrimination in all conditions of employment, including:
   recruiting, hiring, lay-off, in-service training,
   opportunities for promotion,
   participation in training programs,
   wages and salaries,
   sick leave time and pay,
   vacation time and pay,
   overtime work and pay,
   medical, hospital, life and accident insurance.

14. *Search committees:* HEW recommends that all search committees, whenever possible, should include minorities and women.

15. *Marital and parental status:* Discrimination on the basis of marital status is forbidden by Title VII when applied to only one sex. Criteria concerning parental status would also be a violation if applied to one sex.

16. *Monitoring and accountability:* System required by Executive Order.
   a. There must be an institution-wide office that maintains records and monitors individual departments and units and reports annually.
   b. Individual departments and units are required to maintain records

of applicants and persons hired, as well as records of attempts to recruit women.

17. *Job analysis:* Under Executive Order all job classifications must be reviewed in order to identify "underutilization" of women and minorities.

18. *Work assignments:* Teaching load, research responsibilities, etc. cannot be assigned on the basis of sex.

19. *Termination and reduction in the work force:* Termination is prohibited unless the employer is able to demonstrate reasons unrelated to race, sex, or national origins. Lack of seniority cannot be used as a reason for termination when the person laid off has been found to have less seniority because of previous discrimination. (1973, pp. 631-635).

INTRAMURAL RECREATION

A major issue in the area of sport and athletics, including intramural recreation, is the merger of male and female departments. Physical education, intramurals, and athletics hold a peculiar position in the educational system, being the only programs that have remained highly segregated by sex since the age of colonialism. Departments have been administered and staffed by a single sex and designated "Women's Division" and "Men's Division." With integration, the department administrative structure will change. How these changes occur and the resulting effect on women staff members is of great concern to the professional women in our field and to leaders in the area of women's rights. A significant resolution was passed at the National Women's Equity Action League Convention in Washington, D. C., on December 18, 1974:

Whereas educational institutions throughout the country are frequently merging their girls' and women's physical education and athletic programs with their boys' and men's programs under the guise of responding to the equal rights movement and

Whereas in reality many of these mergers are male take-overs of the women's physical education and athletic program,

Be it resolved that where merger occurs, an affirmative action plan be written to insure that women employees are not demoted or removed and that they retain decision-making authority, and that opportunities for women and girls be strengthened.

This affirmative action resolution deserves support from all persons interested in the equality of human beings. Furthermore, it deserves support from all professional organizations involved in education and in all aspects of sport connected with education, including the National Intramural Recreation Sports Association and the National Intramural

Sport Council of the American Association of Health, Physical Education and Recreation.

While there has not been a study of professional women employed in intramural recreation, there have been studies of women physical educators in higher education. It is likely that the issues and the problem areas confronting both professional groups of women would be somewhat the same. According to a study by Anne Ingram of 425 professional women in collegiate physical education, the following issues were foremost: unequal pay for equal work when qualifications are equivalent, promotion practices, unequal opportunities for advancement, practices in granting tenure, and recruiting and hiring practices. The sexist attitudes of male co-workers surfaced in the study as "male cronyism, buddy system shutting out female participation and derogatory remarks and attitudes toward females" (1973, pp. 1–2).

Discrimination against women staff members in sports and recreation also has an impact on the female student, who suffers from lack of programming and leadership. Such discrimination often means that women students are denied the benefits of athletic opportunity (Sandler, Dunkle, et al., 1973, p. 16).

It has been strongly recommended to the National Intramural Recreation Sports Association by this author that funds be made available immediately for a national study of the employment of women in the field of intramural recreation.

LEGAL DECISIONS

Dr. Bernice Sandler, Director of the Project on the Status and Education of Women, states that many of the issues now being debated, somewhat ex post facto in the Halls of Ivy, have already been decided in the courts. According to Sandler (1973, p. 624), the following points are among those which are likely to have the most impact:

The existence of intent to discriminate is irrelevant. The effect of a policy or practice is what counts.

Statistics can be used to document a pattern of discrimination. Institutions cannot simply say no women or minorities applied. An institution may have a reputation as discriminatory which has a "chilling" effect on applications.

Any individual, including a third party, has standing to raise class allegations and charge a pattern of discrimination, using statistics as evidence. Persons can make a general allegation without having to name names and incidents. The appropriate agency then investigates to see if the charges are substantiated.

All hiring and promoting policies must be based on objective, job-related criteria. A policy implemented by predominantly white males using subjective opinions can be held to be discriminatory.

If an administrator ends up with only white males, when there is a pool of qualified women and minorities available, the institution may well be discriminating and may be called upon to prove it is not.

Any policy or practice that has an adverse or disparate effect on a protected class (e.g. women) and cannot be justified by business necessity is considered discriminatory. (Enunciated by Supreme Court Decision, Griggs vs. Duke Power Co.)

Seniority systems such as tenure which have been previously discriminatory may come under review. Termination of women who do not have tenure because of prior discrimination may well be illegal.

Equal pay for equal work does not necessarily mean identical work, but only substantially equal work. Women may not be paid less simply because they often command a lower market value.

The law does not prohibit bona fide differences in pay based on merit or seniority.

Numerical goals have been upheld and ordered by the courts in numerous discrimination cases. Goals are set after there has been a finding of discrimination. Goals are not punitive; no one is required to be fired. Goals are an attempt to remedy present discrimination and give relief to a specific class that has been discriminated against in the past.

The courts have also maintained, clearly, that affirmative action and goals are not preferential treatment when undertaken to remedy past discrimination. (1973, pp. 627–630)

REVERSE DISCRIMINATION

What is *not* at stake is the hiring of lesser qualified persons or reverse discrimination. A very real economic threat is present: for every woman or minority person hired, one less white male is hired. If affirmative action were to be enforced, it would become more difficult for white males to get jobs, but it cannot be called "reverse discrimination."

There has been a great deal of "flak" recently from the white male establishment, causing HEW to issue a new directive stating that universities may not discriminate against white males, or lower standards, to attract women or minorities, advertise specifically for women or minorities, or create minority slots. We should keep in mind that the opponents of affirmative action are the same tenured white male professors directly responsible for the unjust and discriminatory hiring system in academia.

Washington Post columnist William Rasberry comments that "The HEW memo sent to 3,000 college and university presidents by Peter Holmes, tells them they can hire anybody they damned well please, as long as they make it look good." Rasberry concludes that "Affirmative action quotas and the rest don't make any sense if you assume a rational, fair world to begin with. But they make a good deal of sense if you assume that bigotry, conscious or otherwise, is a fact of American life, and that we ought to do what we can to overcome it." [1]

James A. Harris, President of the NEA, states that "complaints of reverse discrimination against white men reveal a peculiarly ingrained type of prejudice" indicating that some people "simply can't bring themselves to believe that white males aren't always more qualified." He warned that we must not allow the HEW statement to be used as a new defense for the old bigoted thinking." [2]

THE FUTURE

Looking to the future, the prospect for increased litigation is strong. Women's groups can be expected to use the courts with increasing frequency. The EEOC can take to court employers who are found to be in violation of Title VII, and under the Executive Order, hundreds of institutions have been charged with the pattern and practice of sex discrimination. The Equal Pay Division of the Department of Labor is expected to file suit against numerous universities in the next few years.

As of now, while the financial crisis appears to be the primary focus of concern on most college campuses, sex discrimination is the next largest issue. "Women are the fastest growing and potentially the largest advocacy group on campus. They are challenging policies and practices, and using the law to its full extent. The hand that rocked the cradle has learned to rock the boat" (Sandler, 1973, p. 630).

In conclusion, sexism and discrimination will vary in amount and degree from one institution to the next. Some colleges and universities began taking steps to improve equality as soon as the laws were passed; others still have done nothing. According to Dr. Sheila Molnar, sociologist and educator, "Discrimination is no longer simply a moral issue—it is a legal issue. The only remaining question is: Will the institutions make the necessary changes themselves, or will they wait for someone else to force them to do it?"

---

[1] Rasberry's comments are taken from a column in a quarterly two-page bulletin entitled, *Women Today,* and distributed by Today Publication and News Service, Washington, D.C. This bulletin was the Vol. V, No. 1, January 6, 1975 edition, page 2.

[2] From *Women Today,* V, No. 1 (Jan. 6, 1975), 2.

GENERAL BIBLIOGRAPHY

BEEMAN, HARRIS, CAROL HARDING, and JAMES HUMPHREY, *Intramural Sports: A Text and Study Guide.* Dubuque, Iowa: William C. Brown, 1974.

BIRD, CAROLINE, *Everything a Woman Needs to Know to Get Paid What She's Worth.* New York: David McKay, 1974.

BOSLOOPER, THOMAS, and MARCIA HAYES, *The Femininity Game.* New York: Stein and Day, 1973.

CARLSON, REYNOLD, THEODORE DEPPE, and JANET MacLEAN, *Recreation in American Life.* Belmont, California: Wadsworth, 1972.

DUMAZEDIER, JOFFRE, *Toward a Society of Leisure.* New York: Free Press, 1967.

EPSTEIN, CYNTHIA FUCHS, *Woman's Place.* Los Angeles: University of California Press, 1971.

GENDEL, EVALYN S., "Women's Bodies," *NCPEAM Proceedings*, LXXVII (1974), 49–55.

GORNICK, VIVIAN, and BARBARA K. MORAN, eds., *Woman in Sexist Society.* New York, Basic Books, 1971.

HEWATT, CAROLYN, "Women's Athletics," *NCPEAM Proceedings*, LXXVII (1974), 56–58.

INGRAM, ANNE GAYLE, "Problem Areas Confronting Women Employed as Physical Education Faculty in Higher Education." Paper presented to the First Canadian Congress for the Multi-Disciplinary Study of Sport and Physical Activity, Oct. 1973, Montreal, Canada.

JEULTE, GEORGE, and JAY SHIVERS, *Public Administration of Recreational Services.* Philadelphia: Lea and Febiger, 1972.

Journal of Law and Education, II, No. 4 (October, 1973). Washington, D.C.: National Press Building. Reprint Appendix II.

MOLNAR, SHEILA, *Ending Sexual Discrimination in the Schools.* Unpublished paper.

NORTON, ELEANOR HOLMES, ed., *Women's Role in Contemporary Society.* New York: The Hearst Corporation, 1972.

SANDLER, BERNICE, "Sex Discrimination, Educational Institutions, and the Law: A New Issue on Campus," *Journal of Law and Education*, II, No. 4 (October, 1973). Washington, D.C.

SANDLER, BERNICE, MARGARET DUNKLE, et al., *What Constitutes Equality for Women In Sport?* Project on the Status and Education of Women, Association of American Colleges, Washington, D.C., 1973.

STEWART, SHERRI, "Women in Sports," *NIA Proceedings*, XXV (1974), 30–35.

VAN DEREN, AUDREY, "Tonka Toys for Boys," *Sexism in Education.* (Emma Willard Task Force). Box 1429, Minneapolis, Minnesota, 1973.

VANDERZWAAG, HAROLD J., *Toward a Philosophy of Sport.* Reading, Mass.: Addison-Wesley, 1972.

WEISS, PAUL, *Sport: A Philosophic Inquiry.* Carbondale, Ill.: Southern Illinois Press, 1969.

WHITE, JANICE L., "Women's Intramurals—Past, Present, and Future," *NIA Proceedings,* XXIV (1973), 73–82.

ZEIGLER, EARLE F., "Women in Sport as Administrators: or How to Avoid the Watergate Syndrome," *Women and Sports Conference Proceedings,* Western Illinois University, Macomb, Illinois (1973), 130–39.

9

Student Leadership:
The Student Manager Program

RAYMOND J. McGUIRE
University of Illinois
Urbana, Illinois

INTRODUCTION

Intramurals have sometimes been referred to as "the great arena of student service." Certainly, there can be little question as to the value of providing for the leisure needs of students. It is truly a most exciting and rewarding profession. The students of today provide the intramural director with the challenge to constantly innovate and update intramural programming. In attempting to do this, one must not fail to realize the importance of student input into the program. Just what form this input might take is usually up to the discretion of the intramural director. Present-day intramural programs run the broad spectrum from little or no student involvement to total student involvement. Regardless of the degree, some form of student involvement is a definite advantage to an intramural program.

Students can assume a number of roles in the administration and operation of an intramural program. They can serve as members of advisory, policy, or protest boards; assist in the supervision of sports activities; or actually be responsible for conducting the various sports. The latter may take the form of a student manager program.

One must not underestimate the leadership opportunities that are

116

open to students who are involved in intramurals. Many students attempt to identify with the institution they are attending by participating in various campus activities. They continually seek the opportunity to involve themselves in various campus programs and become a part of the decision-making process. These experiences are invaluable to students, as they afford them the opportunity to broaden and expand their abilities in the area of leadership and responsibility.

There are a number of advantages to student involvement in an intramural program. One is the fostering of student support for the intramural program. As students are introduced to the operations of the intramural program and as they become involved in the decision-making process, they develop a positive attitude toward the aims and goals of the program and in turn give it their support. Another advantage is the growth of increased communication between the students and the intramural department as the students communicate the various policies, rules and regulations, and decisions that they themselves have formulated. The decisions of students who are members of protest and policy boards are accepted more readily by their peers. Also, the student is most often the best judge of the opinions of his fellow students, since he samples them in everyday contacts with classmates. Responsibilities that are delegated to students in an intramural program can result in continuity in the program from year to year because of student input and evaluation of policies.

THE STUDENT MANAGER PROGRAM

One of the finest forms of student involvement in intramurals is a student manager program. Originally, student manager programs were established primarily to assist the intramural administrator with the operation of a program that was inadequately staffed. However, in addition to entailing administrative duties, the program has also developed into an excellent means for student input into the intramural policy- and decision-making processes.

There is no one best design for the structure of an intramural manager program. Each school should tailor its program to meet its particular needs and structure. Figure 1 illustrates the structure of the current student manager program at the University of Illinois at Urbana-Champaign. Annually, approximately twenty-five students participate in the program as student managers. There are positions for sixteen sophomores, six juniors, and three seniors. Selection of new managers and the promotion of managers to the next level is conducted by the managers themselves. Thus, the students are given complete control of the manager

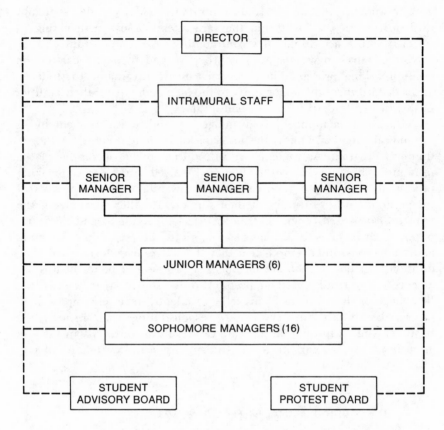

Figure 1. The University of Illinois (Urbana) Student Manager Program

program; the intramural administrator acts as an advisor to the students. Prior to becoming a manager, the student is oriented thoroughly by other managers and by members of the intramural staff as to all aspects of the program. The manager program is entirely voluntary and only at the senior level is a monetary award of $100 given to each senior manager. The seniors divide the responsibilities into three areas—program, policy, and publicity—and in general assist the Men's Intramural Supervisor in overseeing the entire operation of the other managers and the program.

An outline of the basic responsibilities of each person in the manager program is as follows (this outline is also applicable to a women's intramural program):

Definition of Manager's Duties

I. Senior Managers
   A. General Duties for All Senior Managers
      1. Represent the Division of Intramural Activities at meetings of the Interfraternity Council, Independent Housing Association, and Men's Residence Hall Presidents Council, as requested.
      2. Represent the Division of Intramural Activities at meetings of student, faculty, and alumni groups which students are asked to attend.
      3. Serve as members of the Intramural Policy and Protest Boards.
   B. The Senior Manager in Charge of Publicity
      1. Serve as editor of the Intramural Calendar.
      2. Draft news releases and send them to the *Daily Illini* and other news media.
      3. Obtain the publicity release sheets from all winners and send them to the Public Information Office of the university.
      4. Serve as chairman of special committees for selection of all-star teams.
      5. Keep records of the Achievement Point System.
      6. Plan informal activities for the managers at least once per semester.
      7. Take charge of the Top Ten Poll in touch football and basketball.
   C. The Senior Manager in Charge of Program
      1. Conduct the Sophomore Orientation Program.
      2. Supervise the work of the junior and sophomore managers.
         a. Supervise the preparation for a sport by the junior or sophomore manager.
         b. Supervise the conducting of the sport and the posting of results.
         c. Receive and review the sport's summaries from the junior or sophomore manager.
   D. The Senior Manager in Charge of Policy
      1. Serve on the Student/Faculty Intramural Advisory Board.
      2. Chair the Protest and Policy Boards.

3. Schedule and conduct meetings with the intramural chairman of each residence at least once each semester.
4. Save as an ex officio member of all Policy Board committees.
5. Determine times for committee meetings.
6. Receive monthly reports from each committee.
7. Edit all Policy Board rules and the rules for each sport.
8. Send all forfeit warning letters.

II. Junior Managers
   A. Responsible for the conduct of sports assigned to him.
      1. Notify house intramural chairmen when entries are due.
      2. See that entries are properly recorded.
      3. Draw up schedules and distribute rules, field diagrams, and so forth.
      4. Supervise the conduct of sport assigned to him.
      5. Arrange and supervise play-offs.
      6. Turn in progress reports and publicity releases to the senior manager in charge of publicity.
      7. Turn in a summary to the senior manager in charge of program.
      8. Tabulate and turn in Achievement Points for his sport to the senior publicity manager.
      9. Serve as a member of the Intramural Policy Board and Intramural Protest Board.
    10. Assist in taking entries at the Intramural Office on the Thursday and Friday of the week when entries for his assigned sport are being taken.

III. Sophomore Managers
   A. Responsible for the conduct of the sport assigned to him.
      1. Notify house intramural chairmen when entries are due.
      2. See that entries are properly recorded.
      3. Draw up schedules and distribute rules, field diagrams, and so on.
      4. Supervise the conduct of the sport.
      5. Arrange and supervise play-offs.
      6. Turn in progress reports and publicity releases to the senior manager in charge of publicity.
      7. Turn in a summary to the senior manager in charge of program.
      8. Tabulate and turn in Achievement Points for the sport to the senior publicity manager.

9. Assist in taking entries at the Intramural Office on the Thursday and Friday of the week when entries for his assigned sport are being taken.
B. Participate in the Sophomore Orientation Program.
C. Work as an official at all meet sports.
D. Learn officiating techniques.
E. Attend Protest Board meetings.
F. Perform various necessary functions while in the Intramural Office.

In order to assist the managers who are directly responsible for supervising a sport activity, a managers' check list has been developed by both the University of Illinois intramural staff and past student managers. This list is based upon basic intramural administrative procedures and can easily be followed by the student manager. A check list of this type could take the following form:

Managers' Check List

A. Advance Work
1. Check last year's sport summary and files to acquaint yourself with the general operation of the sport. Pay particular attention to the recommendations.
2. Check with the Supervisor of Men's Activities to see that the new entry blanks (if needed) are mimeographed.
3. Have a newspaper article released.
4. Check to see if officials are being lined up.
5. Submit a list of special equipment needed to the Supervisor.
6. Talk to the Senior Manager and get a general OK of plans.
7. To publicize the sport, place posters in prominent places on campus and distribute flyers to house intramural chairmen.
B. Work When Entries Are Coming In
1. Check the eligibility of all entries.
2. Release another news article and include in it the entry deadline.
3. Make a final check on equipment.
C. After the Entries Are In
1. Make up a schedule.
2. Make a list of available facilities and a list of the times that are available at these facilities. This will be kept up to date so that games can be rescheduled immediately if the need arises.
3. Make a list of the team captains and their addresses and phone numbers.

D. Work During the Sport

1. Post information sheets and league standings. Post one set on the bulletin board and keep one set in the file.

2. Record scores and sportsmanship and file scoresheets. (See that sophomore managers are doing this.)

3. Prepare scoresheets in advance, and make sure special equipment is supplied when needed.

4. Issue publicity releases daily.

5. Check with the Assistant to the Supervisor of Men's Activities when officials are needed.

E. Post-Competition Work

1. Make sure championship teams have their pictures taken.

2. Tabulate points and give the totals to the senior manager in charge of points.

3. Return all equipment that was taken out for the sport.

4. Fill out a summary sheet for the sport and complete the file and a scrapbook so that next year's manager will know what to do and why.

5. Be sure to make recommendations and comments.

THE INTRAMURAL PROTEST BOARD
AT THE UNIVERSITY OF ILLINOIS

The Intramural Protest Board at the University of Illinois is composed of members of the Student Manager Program. They decide protests filed as a result of possible incorrect rules interpretations in intramural contests. They do not consider protests based upon officials' judgment decisions. They also act as a disciplinary board for those individuals or teams who commit unsportsmanlike acts during intramural contests.

THE INTRAMURAL POLICY BOARD
AT THE UNIVERSITY OF ILLINOIS

The Intramural Policy Board at the University of Illinois is composed of junior and senior managers plus representatives of various housing units involved in the intramural program. By opening up the Policy Board to a designated number of fraternity, residence hall, and independent house representatives, the board is much more representative of the campus student population. This board decides the policy that governs the intramural program. Rules and regulations concerning eligibility, sports activities, and program operation are developed by this decision-making body. Their decisions are subject to the review and final approval of the intramural administration.

SELECTION OF STUDENT MANAGERS

The continued success of any student manager program depends on the identification and subsequent selection of responsible individuals to serve as managers. At Illinois, our existing student managers recruit, interview, and select the students who will enter the program for the first time as sophomore managers and those who will fill the vacant junior and senior manager positions. This system has been used at Illinois primarily because of the "human relations" benefits accruing as a result of giving our existing managers this fundamental responsibility. Since the student manager program is their program, it is felt that they should be accorded the opportunity to select those who will assume the reins of leadership in the future.

Regardless of the method used to select the manager—student selected or staff appointed—certain factors should be considered. First, every effort should be made to insure that the makeup of the managers as a whole is representative of the student body. Minorities, particularly blacks, should be included. A variety of sources of publicity should be used to attract potential and interested applicants: campus contacts, referrals, posted notices, circulars to campus groups, and so on. Whenever possible, specific criteria should be used to aid the selection process. Individuals with desirable traits (such as dependability, reliability, loyalty, responsibility, integrity, courtesy, perseverance, and intelligence) should be given strong consideration. Above all, each selected student must have an interest in serving his or her fellow students, doing a good job with a minimum of supervision, and improving the intramural program in any way possible. The intramural director should be totally honest in explaining and interpreting the responsibilities of the manager's position to all student applicants and should expect the same degree of frankness and honesty in return. This accomplished, the selection process consists merely of choosing the students who best fill the standards the intramural director expects of the managers.

TRAINING OF STUDENT MANAGERS

Intramural directors should not expect that students selected to be members of the manager program are automatically prepared to assume during their initial (sophomore) year a major role in the administration of the intramural program (significant, yes; major, no). At Illinois, students in their first year in the manager program are not given major leadership responsibilities. Rather, the emphasis is on an overall orientation to the program and on providing the student with welcome assistance in the myriad tasks of the manager's daily routine. Sophomore managers are expected to learn general office and program procedures. Each new manager is put through a complete program designed to acquaint him with both organizational and leadership techniques. Through this training, it is hoped that the student learns not only the technical aspects of his responsibilities, but also the philosophical undergirding on which intramurals is based. Because of this training program, the intramural staff feels confident that the student managers are capable of making major policy and administrative decisions during their last two years in the manager program. Proper training also enables the students to relate better to the staff. A by-product of such a relationship is mutual understanding on many problems and issues and, hopefully, more fruitful interaction between staff and students.

STUDENT INPUT

Intramural programs need not utilize a student manager system to insure student input. Student policy and protest boards can develop from situations other than a manager system. Regardless of the form student input takes, the concept of using a formal structure for student input is still important.

A director can certainly assess student opinion by informal polls of participants. In terms of demonstrating genuine concern for student input into decision making, however, informal input (though important) does not carry the impact of formally structured boards. The esteem commensurate with election or appointment to a policy board represents to the students a tangible, viable means of input. In comparison, informally polling student opinion seems to carry much less importance. Essentially, it does not involve the student in the decision-making process.

Though the important aspect here is student input (regardless of its form), many times the conceptual difference we have noted between formal and informal avenues of student input can make a world of difference in terms of enthusiastic student support and open channels of communication between administrators and students. Obviously, such support and communication are paramount if the intramural staff desires to do more than merely maintain the status quo.

SUMMARY

Intramural departments are generally ideally suited to give students numerous opportunities to develop skills of leadership and responsibility. Intramural administrators have a golden opportunity to lead instead of follow in the development of new, relevant, and exciting programs that can bring out the creative best in today's student and, at the same time, meet the leisure needs of the entire student population. On many occasions when I have discussed the student manager program with members of our profession, their reaction was to be impressed with the efforts of the Illinois students but also to be skeptical as to whether such a system could work elsewhere. These individuals underestimate the basic fiber of today's students, who want to be involved in programs that affect their lives. Give them the opportunity and everyone will benefit.

GENERAL BIBLIOGRAPHY

ANDERSON, BRUCE, "Student Power: Student Policy Boards and Advisory Committees," *National College Physical Education Association for Men Proceedings,* LXXII (1969), 20.

FREDERICK, NORMAN, "Selection of Student Leaders," *National Intramural Association Proceedings,* XIX (1968), 59–60.

HEFFINGTON, MARVIN D., "Training and Responsibility: The Combination to a Successful Manager Program," *National Intramural Association Proceedings,* XVII (1966), 24–26.

HOLSBERRY, WILLARD M., "Remuneration of Student Leaders," *National Intramural Association Proceedings,* XIX (1968), 60–61.

JAMISON, H. TOI, "The Organization of a Women's Intramural Policy Board and Manager Program," *National Intramural Association Proceedings,* XXV, (1974), 35–37.

McGUIRE, RAYMOND J., "Student Power in a Positive Direction: A Student Manager Program," *National College Physical Education Association for Men Proceedings,* LXXII (1969), 21.

MILLER, HARVEY, "Student-Administered Intramural Programs," *National Intramural Association Proceedings,* XXIII (1972), 120–21.

SCHUMACHER, DICK, "Student Involvement in Intramural Sports," *National Intramural Association Proceedings,* XXII (1971), 60–61.

SHERIFF, AL, "Training Student Leaders," *National Intramural Association Proceedings,* XIX (1968), 61–63.

TOWNES, ROSS, "Student Leadership," *National Intramural Association Proceedings,* XIX (1968), 58.

WILKERSON, JAMES, "Duties of Student Leaders," *National Intramural Association Proceedings,* XIX (1968), 63–64.

10

Programming for Student Unrest

WILLIAM G. MANNING
University of California
Berkeley, California

INTRODUCTION

The last decade in American education has been extremely try-ing, not only for those on the campus but for the nation as well. We have experienced the greatest upheaval in the history of our educational system (Carnegie Commission Report, 1971, p. 103) and witnessed the metamorphosis of tranquil campuses into battlegrounds for social and political wars.

That our programs of intramural sports and recreation have been somewhat peripheral to most themes of campus disturbances has not exempted us from their repercussions. As members of the campus com-munity, we have shared in the confusion and disruptions wrought by activist students and concomitant administrative reactions. Perhaps the most significant of these movements—that for black identity—has con-fronted us with stark reality in our own programs.

Much of what has occurred in the past ten years has evoked a depressing sense of administrative inadequacy in dealing with problems of substantial proportions. At times, what has seemed to be rational administrative procedure has inflamed and further complicated tense situations. The free speech movement at Berkeley in 1964 was an excellent example. The protest began with a few relatively minor student rule infractions. It was escalated by a series of administrative and student over-reactions into a disruption of far greater proportions than the original infractions warranted.*

This is not to suggest that had administrators at Berkeley in 1964 taken a different tack, the nation would have been spared the campus strife of the 1960s and 1970s. Had it not been Berkeley in 1964, the starting point for such student-administration confrontations would un-doubtedly have occurred within a short time at any one of a number of other universities. The rapid spread of confrontations from Berkeley to institutions throughout the country suggests that the general student mood was ripe for such action. In the six years between the free speech movement at Berkeley and the Kent State demonstrations against the bombing in Cambodia, over 300 campuses experienced disruptions of varying degrees (Wolin and Schaar, 1970, p. 8).

Administrative "groupings" in the midst of such chaos would seem to have stemmed quite naturally from the lack of historical precedence and prior experience in dealing with problems of such complexity. Those who were intimately involved on either end of the spectrum—student or administrator—have had the unique though not entirely pleasant role of adding a significant chapter to the history of American society and its educational system.

For educators, perhaps the most critical question that must now be asked is, "Where to from here?" For the administrator who wishes to approach this problem, the initial step must be to determine where we (referring to the nation in general and to educators specifically) have been, why we were there, and where we are now.

Though the tragedies of Jackson State and Kent State seem to have shocked most campuses into a return to a relatively peaceful state, many of the factors that created the original environment for dissent have not changed appreciably. Consequently, the undeclared "armistice" that exists on the nation's campuses could evaporate at any time and erupt into a new state of belligerent conflict.

A chronicle of recent problems affronting the sensibilities of many Americans would appear to indicate that society, even given such violent impetus, has failed to make meaningful changes. Consider the following examples: the Watergate fiasco and subsequent revelations of White House "horrors"—enemy lists, secret telephone buggings, transgressions of the law in the name of "national security"; the resignation of the top two elected officials in the land, President Nixon and Vice-President

---

* For an enlightened account of the Berkeley movement in 1964, see Sheldon S. Wolin and John H. Schaar, *The Berkeley Rebellion and Beyond* (New York: The New York Review, 1970), pp. 19–42.

Agnew; the indictment and subsequent conviction of many high-level government officials, including the highest law enforcement officer in the land, former Attorney General John Mitchell; the post–Vietnam war revelations of "secret" bombings in Cambodia; the continued major role of multinational corporations in the formation of United States foreign policy; the staggering ramifications of the energy crisis; the critical economic situation, with rampant inflation and record high unemployment levels; the unconscionable treatment accorded our nation's elderly; and the continued corporate contempt of our nation's environment. Such a list readily illustrates that America has yet to emerge from the dark abyss of neglectful ignorance.

Although such situations are symptoms of social and moral problems of such immense scope that individual action seems ineffectual, all Americans, particularly those individuals (such as college administrators) who by virtue of their professional function come into contact with American youth, can undertake many positive acts. One of the first steps must be an attempt to understand the anger and frustration that created the environment for dissent. As administrators, we must endeavor to discern how (and why) we react to student dissent. Regardless of their moral, political, or social persuasion, individuals must view one another as human beings rather than as radicals, conservatives, reactionaries, and so forth. Labels tend to dehumanize. A strong case can be made that such depersonalization lays the groundwork for atrocities such as those at Jackson State and Kent State.

In order to offer the intramural administrator a framework for structuring his administrative approach to dealing with student unrest, the remainder of this chapter consists of four sections: a review of the history of organized student movements in the United States through 1964; a discussion of the scope of student protest in the United States from 1964 to 1973; an examination of the dimensions of student dissent; and, finally, a presentation of the implications of student conflict for the intramural administrator.

ORGANIZED STUDENT MOVEMENTS IN THE UNITED STATES THROUGH 1964

The series of student protests that evoked such administrative concern and public outcry during the 1960s began at Berkeley in 1964 (Seidenbaum, in *Confrontation*, 1969, p. 3). Though these protests constituted a student movement of national significance that was unparalleled in the history of our educational system, there are numerous instances of student revolt sprinkled throughout the past 200-odd years.

Examples of student rebellion can be found as early as 1766, when students and administration confronted each other at Harvard (Feuer, 1969, p. 327). Though this initial conflict at Harvard was relatively peaceful, others during the following 70 years created disruptions that were seemingly more appropriate to the 1960s. Such rebellion was characterized by student expulsions and by acts of violence, including the destruction of buildings in 1802, the bombing and burning of buildings in 1814, and the destruction of furniture and windows in 1834 (*Ibid.*, pp. 326–30).

The first sit-in on a college campus occurred at Oberlin in 1834 (Angela Davis, in Aptheker, 1972, p. 13). The protest succeeded in achieving one of its major demands—the admission of blacks. That one of the most overriding issues of student dissent in the 1960s was the continued question of black identity (Aptheker, 1972, pp. 20–21) reflects the major historical significance of this demonstration. Similar abolitionist movements occurred at about the same time at Lane Theological Seminary, Phillips Academy (Andover, Mass.), and Marietta College (Feuer, 1969, p. 320).

General conflict between students and faculty occurred during the period 1881–1894 at Dartmouth, Union, Bowdoin, Wesleyan, Williams, and Amherst colleges. These early disturbances were concerned with such familiar issues as rules of student conduct, autocratic administrative power, and freedom of speech (*Ibid.*, pp. 318–40).

Though such early disturbances occurred on many American college campuses and involved a relatively large percentage of each school's student population, they failed to be more than local in scope. In comparison with confrontations of the 1960s, the total number of students involved was quite small. In addition, these disturbances did not reflect a commonality of discontent within society (*Ibid.*).

The 1930s gave rise to student movements that were more national in scope but that still lacked the impact of those to follow three decades later. The onset of the depression provided the impetus for students to organize and demonstrate. Though there were early attempts to tie student rebellion with labor and economic problems, the chief issue in the 1930s, as it was to be some 30 years later, was the nation's potential involvement in war, the primary target of student unrest being the existence of ROTC programs on college campuses (*Ibid.*, pp. 353–63).

Campuses remained relatively peaceful throughout the 1940s and early 1950s. It was not until the late 1950s and early 1960s that campus activists began to identify with the civil rights question, which had previously been concentrated in the South. The push for equal rights became the key issue that propelled student movements into national, organized efforts.

Dale Gaddy views the United States Supreme Court decision of

Brown v. Board of Education of Topeka in 1954 as a pivotal point in the history of student movements (1970, p. 1). Combining with the existence of the legal framework necessary to force school integration and the heroic actions of a few southern black students, white students in increasingly greater numbers began allying themselves philosophically with the issue of civil rights. By the early 1960s, a few hundred such white students were combining action with empathy and spending their summers in the South striving for the attainment of basic human rights by all black Americans (*Ibid.*). Those students who traveled south in the early 1960s and risked their lives in freedom rides, sit-ins, and black voter registration can lay parental claim to the years of student rebellion that followed. Civil rights provided the spark for movement at Berkeley in 1964 (Davis, in Aptheker, 1972, p. 11), and became the most prevalent focus of protests during the student movement in 1964–65 (Peterson, 1966, p. 41).

THE SCOPE OF STUDENT PROTEST, 1964–1973

The Extent of Student and Institutional Involvement

The newspaper headlines during the early period of intense student unrest (1964–1969) bombarded the public with the image that college campuses throughout the nation were coming apart at the seams. On the day following a very peaceful (in the author's opinion) rally at Berkeley in 1964, the huge red-letter headline of a local newspaper flashed the news—"RIOT at U.C." With such sensational news treatment throughout this period, the average citizen would have been shocked had he visited college campuses, most of which were untouched by such chaos (Foley, 1969, p. 49). Prior to the spring of 1970, less than 10 percent of the 2,500-plus college campuses (*Ibid.*) and less than 40 percent of the junior college campuses (Gaddy, 1970, p. 11) had suffered the agonies of "organized" student dissent. Of these, only 4 percent had experienced any form of violent protest (Carnegie Commission Report, 1971, p. 21).

Only a small number of students were actively involved at those campuses that did experience disruptions. At Berkeley in 1964, for example, no more than 3 percent of the student population were committed enough to risk arrest (Sampson, et al., 1970, p. 30).* Without question, however, one of the major factors that tended to misrepresent and mislead observers in the determination of the proportion of "student" involvement was the large number of *nonstudents* who participated in practically every exercise of dissent on the campus. At the junior colleges

---

* From personal observation, it was apparent to me that a somewhat larger number (perhaps 15 percent) were to some degree actively involved.

during the year 1968–69, only 6 to 10 percent of the students were actively involved at any one time (Gaddy, 1970, p. 12).

Richard Peterson estimated that 2 percent of the national student population in the year 1967–68 could be considered actively involved, whereas another 8 to 10 percent were "strongly sympathetic" (1968, p. 39). It is interesting that this movement, touching but a small percentage of students and campuses, could have painted a picture of such general campus disorder. Among the reasons that could possibly account for such a misconception are the following:

1. The institutions that were most often involved (and received the greatest news exposure) were large, selective universities that were considered to be among the finest centers of education—Michigan, Wisconsin, Columbia, Berkeley, and Stanford.

2. Though relatively small as a percentage of total campus enrollment, 3,000 massed students presented a formidable picture to the administration and to the public, especially when viewed in sensational photographs.

3. The violence of the 1968–1970 protests—bombs, fire bombs, fires, "trashing"—though executed by a handful of students on only 4 percent of college campuses, provoked general public indignation and in some cases repressive authoritarian reactions.

4. Some news reporters displayed a penchant for concentrating upon (and stretching at times) the most sensational aspects of these disturbances.

5. As we noted above, many nonstudents were involved in the disturbances.

Possibly the most incredible result of these disturbances was that a relatively small number of concerned students were able to create "waves" that radically changed the educational methods of American colleges and universities. Undoubtedly, many individuals (like myself) faced a dilemma during the early days of student dissent. On one hand, many of the movement's objectives (for instance, human dignity for all) obviously had great merit. On the other hand, some of its goals and methods (such as the burning of buildings and the throwing of rocks) were not totally acceptable. As a result, it was easier for many people to dismiss the whole thing rather than to reflect on the merits of each aspect of the student movement. Eventually, a new sense of maturity or consciousness freed the "repressed" sensibilities of many individuals who were mired in traditional values and perspectives.

These newly awakened sensibilities were assaulted by the events of the spring of 1970. The decision to invade Cambodia, the killings and apparently indiscriminate firing into groups of students by the National Guard at Kent State, and the killing of two students by police at Jackson State provoked the largest wave of student disruptions in this nation's history. Sympathetic protests erupted simultaneously on approximately 1,350 college campuses (57 percent of American college campuses). Enough students were involved to shut down over 500 (21 percent) of all campuses (Peterson and Bilorusky, 1971, p. 17). The Carnegie Report completed in June, 1971, indicated that the proportion of college students who participated in campus disruptions grew to 31 percent (Carnegie Commission Report, 1971, p. 17).

Ironically, it took these same repressive, insane actions at Kent State and Jackson State to shock students into the realization that violence begets *only* violence. Dissent and disruption do not necessarily beget meaningful change. To their credit, many students recognized the need for a shift in the thrust of student energies from ineffectual campus disruptions to a more active political involvement. To date, this shift has had varying degrees of success. The students at Berkeley were able to elect a number of radical members to the city council. The University of Michigan student body effected a change in local drug laws. Across the country, there are numerous reported instances of younger people being elected to governing bodies.

The relative peace on campuses since 1970 may indicate that the nation has weathered the worst of such disruptions. It would be foolhardy, however—considering the frequent failure of student political activity to effect change, the continuing transgressions against civil liberties by government at all levels, and the new levels of student social consciousness—to assume that the nation should now relax and that the campuses will return to the "normalcy" of the 1950s. There appears to be sufficient cause to maintain at least a partial state of administrative awareness that the fight for human dignity may again disrupt in violent dissent.

The Issues Involved

The administrative nightmares created by student disruptions were compounded by the large number of complex issues involved. Studies by Peterson assessing the nature and scope of student protests at over 800 institutions in 1964–65 and 1967–68 pinpointed 81 and 92 different issues, respectively; these were grouped in five broad categories—instruction, faculty, freedom of expression, student administration, and off-campus issues (Peterson, 1966, pp. 52–54; Peterson, 1968, pp. 44–46). A similar study by the Urban Research Corporation in 1969 also indicated that several issues were involved (Urban Research Corporation, 1970, p. 3).

Though issues found in other studies were categorically similar, most were triggered by specific campus-related or local problems. For example, the following list illustrates but a few of the many issues in each of the Peterson categories that led to student protests during the academic years 1964–65 and 1967–68:

1. *Instruction.* Faculty evaluation; enrollment limitations; inaccessible faculty; exams; course revisions.
2. *Faculty.* Faculty salaries; hiring and firing policies; loyalty oath; concerns about faculty involvement and nonuniversity interests.
3. *Freedom of Expression.* Freedom of speech; use of university facilities; CIA interviews on campus with prospective employees, censorship; appearances by high-ranking government officials.
4. *Student Administration.* Student employee salaries; discrimination against black athletes; required physical education; student rights; personal regulations, such as student conduct and smoking policies.
5. *Off-Campus Issues.* CIA interviews; 1964 presidential election; civil rights problems; war-related activities.

(Peterson, 1966, pp. 52–54; Peterson, 1968, pp. 44–46).

Faced with problems of such immense proportions, it is not surprising that campus administrators were relatively unprepared for each new disruption. Even with the benefit of hindsight, it is difficult to envision guidelines that would have prevented this movement from completing some similar cycle.

The Students Involved

Typically, activist students were viewed and labeled by the public and many educational and government leaders as hoodlums, bums, reactionaries, communists, or a combination thereof (Peterson, 1968, p. 5). It has been well documented that with few exceptions, quite the opposite has been the case. Those most active in the protests were among the most intellectually gifted and sensitive of college students during this period (Harris, 1970, p. 68). At Berkeley in 1964, for example, the students most active in the movement were judged to be more individualistic, socially committed, and intellectual than their classmates (Trent, in Sampson et al., 1970, p. 36).

Though some student leaders either belonged to communist organizations or expressed communist sympathies, the early illusion created by many government leaders that student movements were communist-connected has never been substantiated. Art Seidenbaum, a columnist for the *Los Angeles Times,* spent the 1968–69 school year on troubled campuses in California. He found no evidence that student movements were part of a "communist conspiracy" (Seidenbaum, 1969, p. 144).

It would appear that to a great extent, student protests were perpetuated by committed, intelligent, and sensitive young Americans. Their discontent with established society and their unwillingness to either await or accept the slow process of traditional change were among the key factors responsible for this movement.

Distribution of Protests by Institution

The studies by Peterson (1966, 1968) and the Urban Research Corporation (1970) indicate that those campuses with a higher incidence of student protests tended to be large, selective universities with emphasis on a liberal arts (as opposed to a professional or technical) education. In the 1967–68 Peterson study, an analysis of the 50 largest public universities in the sample indicated that on a majority of the 27 issues, students on these campuses exhibited greater personal concern than did the average student at other schools (p. 38).

The reasons for such distribution are not difficult to understand. The activist student, who is profiled as highly intellectually oriented, would likely attend those universities offering outstanding programs in "intellectual" liberal arts fields—philosophy, history, sociology, and so forth. The size of the institution would seem to contribute to campus revolt in two ways: (1) the depersonalization and subsequent alienation of students in overly large institutions, and (2) the increased potential for student revolt as a simple function of the increased numbers of students who might dissent from a specific act or action. (Peterson, 1966, p. 19).

A PERSPECTIVE ON
THE NATURE OF STUDENT DISTURBANCES

The period of intense campus unrest from 1964 through 1970 evoked a great volume of literature attempting to explain the phenomenon of student rebellion (see Aptheker, 1969). To summarize briefly, such rebellious behavior seems to have stemmed from the increased awareness and sensitivity of today's youth (*Crisis at Columbia*, 1968, p. 4), an inherent youthful restlessness combined with indignation over the civil rights struggle (Sampson et al., 1970, p. 2), and a society that denies "personal idealism and self-definition" (Kristol, in *The Troubled Campus*, 1966, p. 78).

Many of us have no doubt felt occasional frustration with societal problems. To understand how such frustrations could produce the rebellion of the 1960s, it is important to attempt to see society as it is conceived by students in today's world—a world that has changed radically in the past few decades.

At the outset, it is necessary to consider the contribution of the unique college environment. Falling between the security of parental homes and the impact of adulthood, the college years provide what may be the greatest transitional phase in a person's life. Unhindered by many of the responsibilities that force nonstudents to compromise ideals for the sake of reality, students are generally free to closely examine society and their relationships to it. In addition, students are increasingly becoming aware of and concerned with the disparity between what they are taught in the classroom and what they perceive to be the reality of the world outside the cloistered university community. Although this gap has undoubtedly existed for numerous generations, many relatively recent societal changes have highlighted for today's students a number of moral conflicts inherent in the American way of life. The shifting emphasis of student movements from issue to issue serves to illustrate a general discontent with society, one that is produced in large part by these conflicts.

As administrators of student programs, it is imperative that we attempt to identify and understand the frustrations caused by such moral conflicts. It is not necessary to share students' frustrations with these societal problems. However, if we are to maintain mutual trust and communication with students, we must respect their feelings of concern and their right to channel such dissent into viable means of protest. Obviously, it is difficult to condone the violence that often accompanies such protest. If the attempt is made to view these problems from the student perspective—the intense frustration of individual ineffectiveness—perhaps the collective behavior that often leads to violence will become more understandable.

Moral Conflicts in American Society

If one looks closely at the issues that have commonly triggered student dissent, many conflicts of a moral nature are apparent. The two most readily identifiable are the struggle over civil rights and American military involvement in Southeast Asia.

The civil rights struggle highlighted for many students a moral conflict that is deeply rooted in American society. The concepts of freedom and equality are the bases upon which this country was founded. "We hold these truths to be self-evident, that all men are created equal.

. . ." "O'er the land of the free. . . ." These exemplary ideals are held in high esteem by most Americans. The intense and often violent struggle by Americans of all ethnic and religious backgrounds to lay claim to these birthrights creates a conflict of major proportions for many students. On the one hand, the student has learned the importance placed upon these concepts of freedom and equality by American society. On the other hand, many minorities have obviously been unable to achieve even the basic rights of their American heritage.

The realization of such a conflict, coming at the same time that students are searching for identity and some degree of individual worth within the complex structure of society, creates moral indignation toward what is viewed as a societal failure. That the struggle for civil rights became an issue of importance to students at a time roughly coinciding with the escalation of American involvement in Southeast Asia (the early 1960s) must not be overlooked as a possible factor in pushing student frustration to the breaking point.

Though American history is concerned substantially with military conflict, the basic premise of war is itself a great moral conflict. One of the fundamentals of a religious, tolerant people would seem to be love of their fellow man. The horror and indignities accompanying war certainly contradict this basic tenet. Societal justification of war—in terms of safeguarding freedom or defending democracy—does not change this fundamental issue. Obviously, it is much easier to make peace with such a conflict when direct threat to personal and collective freedom is evident. Prior to the Vietnam war, such threat was sufficiently felt to override this conflict.

Because American involvement in Vietnam was escalated at a time when many students were already questioning the priorities of society, a great many Americans, both young and old, felt that this involvement was not adequately justified. Since war was never declared officially by Congress, the lives of those not directly involved strayed little from normal routine. Because the necessary justification of the war was absent, public opposition to American involvement existed in many sectors. Students were opposed more vociferously because many young Americans were used as pawns in this encounter.

Though war and civil rights constituted two of the most identifiable moral conflicts, other concerns have no doubt also contributed to the frustrations underlying student unrest: poverty; ecology; the energy problem; the health care crisis; and the plight of elderly Americans. In each case, conflict has arisen from societal priorities that relegate these issues to a position of secondary importance.

The questions asked by students seem to be these: How can a society with the technological knowledge to put a man on the moon not apply some of that same knowledge to provide more jobs for the poor? To safe-guard the resources upon which we depend for survival? To find clean, safe sources of energy? To provide at least a basic affordable level of good health? And to find answers to the problems of growing old in a society geared for the young? Obviously, it is much easier to raise these questions than to propose solutions to them. In the minds of students, at least, it is inconceivable that American technology can make such rapid progress in so many areas while progress in the battle for human concerns moves at a snail's pace. The technology that placed a man on the moon while others were hungry here on earth is but one, though very poignant, ex-ample.

Such moral questioning is certainly not unique to the generation of Americans who expressed their frustrations during the 1960s. Many of the same questions have no doubt been asked by other sensitive men and women of earlier generations. Perhaps the reason that such issues have become so critical and of such major concern as to result in the student reactions of the 1960s is the frightening levels to which they have evolved. Several of the societal changes unique to the last twenty-odd years have rendered these concerns more urgent to today's students.

Recent Societal Changes

The vast technological growth in the United States since the be-ginning of the twentieth century has conditioned young Americans to the idea of rapid change. This concept has brought into sharp focus the very gradual rate of social change that has occurred during the same period. On one hand we have changed from a rural, horse-and-buggy nation into a mechanized, space-exploring society. On the other hand, even considering the civil rights legislation of the late 1950s and early 1960s, we have remained fairly stagnant in areas of human concerns.

Though progress toward the solution of social problems is infinitely complex, the frustrations causing student disenchantment with society are not as naïve as they might appear. Government has been quite slow in enacting strong and favorable legislation in the areas of civil rights, the environment, health care, and welfare. The economy and strong lob-bies seem to wield sufficient strength to delay meaningful social legisla-tion.

At an earlier point in this chapter, I indicated that the increased awareness and sensitivity of today's youth have constituted a major con-tribution to student unrest. Such awareness—politically, socially, and sex-ually—has been too well documented recently to warrant discussion. One of the primary causes for such increased awareness would seem to be a recent major change in our communications system.

Prior to the 1950s, Americans relied upon the network of radio, newspapers, and magazines for local, national, and worldwide news. With the introduction of television to American homes in the 1950s a great change took place. Images previously "visualized" from printed and audio cues leapt from the television screen at today's youth. The drama of world problems were realistically portrayed in millions of American homes. The impact of this stimulus on the maturing and searching youth cannot be minimized.

By providing such instantaneous and realistic news coverage, television has made national and world problems very personal and of more immediate concern. Though this medium has yet to be utilized as intelligently as it might be, its informational value to children and young adults has been a major factor in increasing their awareness of the world outside their immediate environment.

Relatively recent changes in the educational system have contributed to student disillusionment. Keeping pace with technological growth, many institutions have grown beyond reasonable size. In the process, they have become computerized, depersonalized, and populated by far more students than can be comfortably educated. The higher incidence of student rebellion at institutions of this size might be attributed at least partially to the frustration and disorientation that students develop in interacting with such an environment. One's individual ineffectiveness is highlighted by an educational giant mirroring the complexities of a society that is likewise overgrown.

Compounding the effects of size has been the changing educational emphasis in technical and professional fields. Many of these fields have become so specialized that preparatory education is squeezed into a very narrow and vertical sphere. Within this limited framework, interpersonal relationships become distorted and individual worth is harder to pinpoint.

The increasing involvement of these same institutions with federally funded and war-related research projects has not helped. To many students, this is evidence of a lack of social consciousness by the university—a consciousness that by the nature of a liberal arts education this same institution fosters in its students. An apparent conflict exists between what the institution teaches and what it practices. Allied with this is the increasing role of money in dictating university policy (Wolin, 1970, p. 8). Such funding provides additional evidence to the students that the university is mirroring society and prostituting its expressed ideals.

The relatively recent focus on our ecological problems has added a time-squeeze to existing frustrations with society. With high pollution levels surrounding our urban centers and with increasing encroachment into the natural environment, a policy of faith in gradual change is hard for students to understand. Many see all too clearly that the time for action is overdue. They have little of the faith placed by earlier generations in the ability of American ingenuity to provide miraculous cures. Historically, relationships with the natural environment seem to point, unfortunately, to quite the opposite conclusion.

A side effect of technological growth has resulted in a somewhat different time-squeeze. Commensurate with rapid material expansion has been an equally rapid increase in the pace of living. Compare the rate of public transportation at the turn of the century with that of today—the difference is staggering. Distances traveled by pioneers in months now take but hours. This has drastically reduced the concept of global size. A foreign war in 1918 was in another world; the same war today is but an arm's length away. The extreme change in this time-space relationship has brought national and world problems into a more personal perspective for recent generations.

Coupling the increased pace of living with the relatively easy acquisition of material goods, another recent change affecting interpersonal relationships and bearing upon the individual's conception of society is found. With increasing wealth and mobility, Americans have grown away from inter-individual dependence, a dependence much more necessary for earlier generations. Expanding urbanization and accompanying increases in crime have had the effect of wrapping a cocoon even more tightly around the individual. The result has been a growing suspicion of strangers and a retreat from interpersonal relationships. The lack of such relationships has created a society seen by many of its young as dehumanized and in need of change.

When all of these various inputs to individual conscience formation are added together, it should not be difficult to understand the student's feelings of a need for some form of individual and collective action. The disagreeable aspects of such action are, of course, the forms of expression—particularly, violent behavior—chosen by some of the students. In all fairness to those students, it should be mentioned that transgressions resulting in violence have occurred on both sides of the struggle.

The Issue of Black Identity

Intentionally missing from the foregoing analysis was a focus on the issue of black identity. During the period 1967–1970 this issue provided intramural administrators at many institutions with a very direct involvement in the problem of student rebellion. This issue has been separated from others that are responsible for student unrest, because it is a disservice to define it as part of a general student movement. Black identity extends beyond the scope of student unrest. It should be viewed rather as a "human movement" for it encompasses a much greater dis-illusionment with society, one that is held by most black Americans—black students being but the tip of the iceberg.

Being a product of white, middle-class America, I shall not pretend to know the experience of black Americans in this society. I can only empathize with what must be an anger so much deeper than my own as to be beyond my comprehension. It is just such a lack of comprehension that distinguishes the issue of black identity from other student movements. Though concern over the civil rights of black Americans moved both white and black students to action, a motivational distinction must be recognized. Whereas white students, empathizing with black problems, reacted against an unjust society, black students represented those who have been victimized by this injustice. A great difference exists between the two approaches. Black identity is an issue that white students can empathize with temporarily (as illustrated by the shifting emphasis of student unrest to the Vietnam war), but an issue that black students must continually confront. As leisure service administrators, it is important that we recognize this distinction. With increasing minority enrollments and program participation, we must evaluate programs carefully to insure that they meet the needs of all student groups. If they do not, we have probably not heard the last from minority participants.

ADMINISTRATIVE IMPLICATIONS

Though much of the preceding discussion does not bear directly upon the administrative operation of the intramural recreation program, I think it is necessary for the individuals responsible for programming to have a full understanding of the possible reasons for student unrest. As intramural administrators, we have but one major responsibility: to provide a recreational program that includes leisure opportunities for all members of the campus community. That which affects various members of this community will also have direct and indirect ramifications for our programs. The closing and class reconstitution of numerous colleges during the spring of 1970 provides a good illustration of this point. Though the problems causing such action were not within the immediate jurisdiction of the intramural administrator, the effects on many programs were pronounced. Such effects ranged from the complete shutdown of spring programming (at Berkeley, for example) to relatively minor sched-uling inconveniences.

The complete shutdown at Berkeley merits examination. Though the particular disturbances of the spring of 1970 were obviously different from campus to campus, the environment at Berkeley was such that complete shutdown was a necessity. As administrators, we were forced to recognize that students were involved with moral questioning so great as to make normal routine impossible. To have continued normal operations during such protest would have been to affront a great many Berkeley students. Given these conditions, the decision was made to respect the students' expressed desires to curtail programming.

Because we are primarily responsible to the student community for funding as well as participation, it is imperative that we attempt to understand student behavior causing such educational disruption. It is not necessary that we agree with the reasons for, or methods of, student dissatisfaction. It is important, however, that we respect the right of students to disagree and to express this disagreement. If we cannot respect or attempt to understand their viewpoint, then perhaps we are not open-minded enough to administer *their* programs. It is with such a perspective that I have attempted the foregoing analysis of student movements. It would seem that direct administrative action must follow understanding if it is to be effective.

Racial Harmony

The violence that occurred in many programs as an adjunct to the unrest related to racial unrest was all but impossible to control administratively. Even with attempts at understanding and some form of positive administrative action, black-white confrontations and acts of violence were not uncommon. In the heat of the battle, rational communication and problem solving were next to impossible. Since we are now in the midst of a relatively peaceful period, perhaps it is a wise time to reflect, evaluate, and effect any needed change in the hopes of promoting harmonious minority participation. The term hope is used intentionally, for I think that the roots of this problem, as it confronted us in the late 1960s, were so deeply imbedded in societal discontent as to be at times beyond the scope of administrative management.

In 1971 at the National Intramural Association Conference at Blacksburg, Virginia, I naïvely presented administrative suggestions for dealing with racial tension in intramural programs. During the following discussion, an administrator from one of our predominately black colleges made a prophetic statement. In effect, he commented that regardless of the shape it assumes, the issue of black identity is no more than a plea for equal treatment. He advised us that if we were to make sure black and white students are treated equally, the problem would take care of itself. In other words, stand firmly behind rules and guidelines and distribute punishment and rewards equitably. At the time, I thought the statement somewhat naïve, coming from a black administrator who had obviously never had to deal with militant blacks while strapped within a white, middle-class perspective. Subsequent reflection and application of his theory, however, proved him to be quite correct.

Once the initial reactions to strict and equitable rule enforcement were weathered, the problem defused itself to within reasonable limits. Though occasional flare-ups (which have to be expected with a problem of such proportion) still occurred, the feeling of impending doom began to recede and more effective lines of communication were established with the black student community.

Three administrative implications are readily apparent: (1) written program rules and guidelines are a must; (2) these rules and guidelines must be evaluated periodically to insure their effectiveness and relevance to student participants at each evaluation period; and (3) they must be enforced firmly and judiciously. With the firm base of written rules and guidelines, the justification for administrative action is at hand. Without such justification, we encourage student dissatisfaction. Though the topic will be covered later in the chapter, it should be pointed out here that student input into the formation, evaluation, and enforcement procedures that make up such guidelines is imperative if intramural administrators are to establish and maintain effective communication with the student population. Without such input, the best guidelines are sometimes ineffectual.

The point here is that minority students should be given equal access to the responsibilities as well as the advantages of program participation. It should be clear that participation demands individual and group responsibility for conduct and interpersonal relationships. Transgressions by groups or individuals will be dealt with by strict interpretation of both program and university rules.

It seems a good idea to review these rules not only with immediate staff and participants, but with university officials at higher levels to whom grievances might eventually be brought. A major contribution to the racial problems at Berkeley in 1967–68 was the failure of higher levels of administrative authority to enforce disciplinary action taken by our Student Advisory Board (nine students). An important point concerning advisory, protest, and other student boards became apparent when the university administration explained its failure to uphold this student board's decision. Of the nine students elected to this board, none were black; hence, the black student who had been brought before the board "had not received a fair hearing." Election, though certainly democratic, does not necessarily insure the representation of all participants. It is perhaps more prudent to appoint members, or to define election procedures in such a manner as to require minority group representation. Such representation on all policy and grievance committees (both student and staff) seems critical to maintaining a reasonable degree of harmony.

A few preparatory steps might be taken to either avoid or lessen the consequences of racial confrontations. Perhaps the most important is a thorough training of student supervisors and officials. In many trouble situations the immediate action taken by student employees can help determine the eventual outcome of the situation. Poorly trained or qualified supervisors are often more of a hindrance than a help in these situations. Similarly, poor officiating can often spark or add fuel to such confrontations.

Though the use of campus police to restore order following racial confrontations was common on many campuses, the longitudinal effectiveness of such police is questionable. A survey of Big Ten intramural administrators conducted in 1970 by the author indicated that the use of police was helpful only in the immediate situation; it did nothing to solve the underlying problem. Since the use of police to quiet campuswide disturbances had generally a negative effect, it might prove equally undesirable to use police to help moderate an intramural conflict. It seems wise to make every possible attempt at internal management before requesting outside help.

It is necessary to reiterate one important point. It is possible, even with ample training, supervision, and forethought, to be administratively ineffective in racial confrontations. In 1968 at Berkeley, two teams—one black, the other white—met for the All-University Touch Football Championship. Because previous problems had occurred during the same season, the potential for trouble was recognized and appropriate measures were taken. The four best officials (unfortunately, all were white; no blacks would agree to referee during this particular season) were assigned to the game. The game was supervised by the Intramural Director, the Assistant Director, and the head student referee. During the game, a loose ball scramble resulted in a dislocated knee suffered by a star black player. This incident sparked a fight among the students that must have lasted at least fifteen minutes. Because of the fight and an administrative mix-up by campus police in securing ambulance service, medical help did not arrive for some forty minutes. Subsequent mismanagement and questionable medical practice by the campus hospital resulted in the amputation of the young man's leg. When the resulting suit was tried in 1970, the verdict found the hospital staff guilty of medical malpractice. More important, the intramural staff was found guilty of lack of adequate supervision—an interesting judgment, considering that every possible step had been taken to insure just such supervision. Even with the advantage of hindsight, it is difficult to think of any supervisory innovation that might have kept this particular situation under control. The only corrective step that would have been effective seems to have been to cancel the game.

Other Student Issues

At many large, overgrown institutions a common complaint by students is that they become computerized nonentities whose identification number is as important in attaining graduation as the courses they take. Individual class enrollment at Berkeley in required courses—basic chemistry, political science, basic physics, and so forth—number in the hundreds (and in some cases, almost one thousand). The preenrollment procedure for classes with limited enrollment is a mad scramble with long waiting lines and depressing conditions. Our physical education preenrollment is unfortunately one of the saddest examples: with enrollment "supply" far below student demand, lines form as much as twelve hours ahead of time—a simple function of too many students and too few classes. Such crowding is quite common at many of the larger colleges and universities in this country.

This depersonalized environment is heightened by the overworked and often unfriendly staff in many campus administrative and departmental offices. In the face of what is sometimes a depressing student environment, the intramural-recreation program is a potential oasis. Having direct contact with a great number of students, intramural sports is afforded the opportunity to provide a friendly, cooperative atmosphere and what may be the closest personal relationship many students have with university programming.

To insure this type of treatment of students, intramural office guidelines should dictate that students seeking help and information have priority over other work. Though it is not always possible, the staff member should make the initial gesture to the student ("May I help you?"), rather than forcing the student to seek assistance. The difference in attitude is important: by making the initial overture, the staff person demonstrates a willingness to help; to keep working and force the student to ask for help conveys a lack of concern for the individual and his or her problems. It is important to create an environment in which the student feels comfortable and important. One might look at it as good business practice—"selling" our programs to students. Without their interest and enthusiastic participation, the justification of expenditures during these economically disadvantaged times is next to impossible.

Intramural programs afford students the opportunity for direct involvement in another area that has caused student frustration with the educational system. Throughout the troubled years of the 1960s, the demand for student representation on policy boards affecting their education was evident. The demand went beyond the scope of the black student's call for equal representation. Students collectively demanded a voice in determining the content and quality of their education. Intramural directors can offer an avenue for the partial realization of this goal.

Though the intramural director is indeed the professionally trained administrator, it must be remembered that the program exists primarily for, and is often funded by, students. Students must have key roles in policy and decision making whenever possible. At numerous campuses, recent problems in constructing recreational facilities have illustrated the impact of the failure to involve students. The aim should be to guide student energies into decisions and actions dictated by personal conscience. In doing so, it seems necessary to maintain sufficient flexibility to meet changing needs. Communication and flexibility may be the keys to maintaining compatible relationships between administration and students. Flexibility and program evaluation seem closely related. Periodic program evaluation by staff and students, and the necessary administrative flexibility to effect change when it is called for, is important in insuring that the program meets the needs of changing students.

It also seems important that all staff members get out of the office in order to be seen by, and become involved with, student participants. The nature of intramural-recreation programs dictates personal involvement if the staff member is to be administratively effective. Personal contact is perhaps most important in programs involving many thousands of students and numerous full- and part-time staff. Such contact is an indication of personal concern and interest in student activity. For today's student, such concern seems to be of significant value.

SUMMARY

As it was difficult to assess campus disturbances during the years of turbulence, so it is difficult to determine what the past few years of relative quiet mean. Perhaps we have weathered the worst and an investigation such as this is purely academic. As a college administrator, I hope this is so. As a somewhat disenchanted citizen, however, I am not so sure I wish for an end to student discontent.

As I have tried to point out (from a somewhat necessarily biased viewpoint), very little has changed within society in the past decade. Certainly, we have made some progress. Attempts at legislation in a few areas—for instance, school busing and pollution control—have been encouraging. But effective change has been agonizingly slow.

If in their discontent students can continue to focus on these problems, perhaps quicker solutions will have to emerge. I do not wish a return to the violent confrontations of the late 1960s. Their effect was extremely detrimental to the realization of change. Because these confrontations polarized divergent viewpoints into warring camps, rational discourse and the focus on societal problems needing remedy was lost.

I have made one very important personal realization during the research and writing of this chapter. In being forced to express sometimes nebulous dissatisfaction, I was surprised to find the depth to which many of these feelings had grown in me. Were I twenty and beginning at Berkeley in 1964 again, I might have been throwing rocks too . . .

GENERAL BIBLIOGRAPHY

Aptheker, Bettina, *The Academic Rebellion in the United States*. Secaucus, N.J.: Citadel Press, 1972.

————, *Higher Education and the Student Rebellion in the United States, 1960–69, a Bibliography*. New York: American Institute for Marxist Studies, 1969.

The Atlantic Editors, *The Troubled Campus*. Boston: Little, Brown, 1966.

Bell, Daniel, and Irving Kristol, eds., *Confrontation*. New York: Basic Books, 1969.

Campus Tensions: Analysis and Recommendations. Report of the Special Committee on Campus Tensions. Washington, D.C.: American Council on Education, 1970.

Carnegie Commission on Higher Education, *Dissent and Disruption*. New York: McGraw-Hill, 1971.

Crisis at Columbia. Report of the Fact-Finding Commission Appointed to Investigate Disturbances at Columbia University in April–May, 1968. New York: Vintage Books, 1968.

Feuer, Lewis S., *The Conflict of Generations; the Character and Significance of Student Movements*. New York: Basic Books, 1969.

Foley, James A., and Robert K. Foley, *The College Scene*. New York: Cowles, 1969.

Gaddy, Dale, *The Scope of Organized Student Protest in Junior Colleges*. Washington, D.C.: American Association of Junior Colleges, 1970.

Harris, Janet, ed., *Students in Revolt*. New York: McGraw-Hill, 1970.

Hart, Richard L., and J. Galen Saylor, *Student Unrest: Threat or Promise?* Washington, D.C.; Association for Supervision and Curriculum Development, National Education Association, 1970.

LEVITT, MORTON, and BEN RUBENSTEIN, eds., *Youth And Social Change*. Detroit: Wayne State University Press, 1972.

PETERSON, RICHARD E., *The Scope of Organized Student Protest in 1964–1965*. Princeton, N.J.: Educational Testing Service, 1966.

————, *The Scope of Organized Student Protest in 1967–1968*. Princeton, N.J.: Educational Testing Service, 1968.

PETERSON, RICHARD E., and JOHN A. BILORUSKY, *May 1970: The Campus Aftermath of Cambodia and Kent State*. A Technical Report Sponsored by the Carnegie Commission on Higher Education. Berkeley, 1971.

SAMPSON, EDWARD E., et al., *Student Activism and Protest*. San Francisco: Jossey-Bass, 1970.

SEARLE, JOHN R., *The Campus War*. New York: World Publishing, 1971.

SEIDENBAUM, ART, *Confrontation on Campus: Challenge in California*. Los Angeles: Ward Ritchie Press, 1969.

URBAN RESEARCH CORPORATION, *Student Protests 1969: A Summary*. Chicago: Urban Research Corporation, 1970.

WOLIN, SHELDON S., and JOHN H. SCHAAR, *The Berkeley Rebellion and Beyond*. New York: Vintage Books, 1970.

11

Intramural Sports Programming for the Community and Junior Colleges

WILLIAM A. THOMPSON
Long Beach City College
Long Beach, California

William Rainey Harper, president of the University of Chicago at the turn of the twentieth century, drew the line between the second and third years of college. The first two years were designated as "collegiate," all further study as "university." Shortly thereafter, he made the distinction by using the terms "junior" and "senior" college. Although Harper did not originate the idea of the junior college, he gave the idea enduring appeal (Brubacher and Rudy, 1958, p. 248). The development of the junior college depended not only on multiplying its facilities but also on bringing these facilities within geographical reach of the masses. The further growth of the junior college as a local or "community" college, therefore, was of utmost importance. Such an institution brought higher education within reach of many students who would otherwise have found the expense of board, room, and travel away from home prohibitive. The student planning to complete a four-year education could take his first two years locally and save that much of his expense. Many overgrown universities were relieved to have their work decentralized to this extent. To remain a "community" college for the masses, however, the junior college had to beware concentrating on preparation for the senior college. Its most pregnant possibility lay in orienting itself to the needs of the great mass of people who would not be going on to senior college (*Ibid.*, p. 251). The rapid growth of the junior colleges, from eight in 1900 to more than one thousand today, has had a profound effect on higher education. Continued growth in the number of these institutions and increased enrollment in them are expected in the next decade (Reznik, 1972, p. 1).

The community colleges in California enroll more students than the four-year colleges and universities. The Master Plan of Higher Education for California tentatively calls for the community colleges to assume the responsibility for educating the public student for the first two years; the state university system is to complete their education in the final two years.

There is no doubt in my mind that the community college is the most dynamic segment of higher education.

THE CLIMATE FOR PROGRAMMING

In light of the dramatic growth of the community colleges, we cannot assume that intramural programming has automatically followed suit. In fact, professional progress at the community college can only be traced back to the 1950s. However, actual programs were in existence, in modest forms, as early as 1920.

At present, 75 percent of junior and community colleges conduct intramural programs, according to a report by John Reznik (1972). Of the colleges that lack intramural programs, 75 percent reported inadequate facilities or equipment. Program growth in the past two decades can be attributed to student pressure to make provisions for all students in the recreational area. As at the four-year college and university, "something for everybody" became the byword of the community college intramural movement. Student sensitivity is more pronounced today. With the unprecedented growth of athletic programs and the continued diminution of the number and extent of required physical education programs, greatly expanded intramural programs are inevitable. Stephenson Parker predicts further that "enlarged intramural sports stressing mass participation will become paracurricular activities in the early 1980s" (1970, p. 29).

THE CORNERSTONES OF PROGRAM DEVELOPMENT

The basic ingredients in the formation of a community or junior college intramural program should include the following:

1. *Director of Intramural Sports*. The convenient coach-director is not the answer. Split loyalties prevent excellence in either area. A director

with or without a partial teaching load is capable of effectively guiding the program through the school year. Continuity and momentum are essential to success. It should be obvious that only professional directors can devote the time and energy necessary to achieve program quantity and quality control. Professional participation in local, state, and national workshops and conferences is essential to program growth and vitality. From a statistical standpoint, only 6 of the 236 schools responding to the Reznik survey had full-time directors. Other pertinent data indicated that 50.6 percent of these directors had part-time secretarial help, 75.8 percent taught classes, 46.9 percent coached varsity teams, and 40.6 percent conducted intramural programs in addition to coaching and teaching. The majority of programs were the responsibility of the department of physical education, the department of student affairs, or both.

2. *Activity Hour.* In that most community or junior colleges are commuter colleges, after-school scheduling is extremely difficult. To engage the majority of students, it is suggested that a minimum of two sessions per week at 11:00 or 12:00 A.M. be designated as activity hours. This provision will allow a program to accommodate round-robin tournaments in the major sports with a minimum of conflicts. These conflicts will be limited to competing student activities, not to credit classes. Probably the most effective strategy to gain the activity hour is to appeal for it as a part of the student affairs program. If the hour is granted, clubs, forums, and other activities besides intramural events could also be scheduled at this time, allowing the student the freedom of choice. The recognized need for meaningful student activities should improve your chances of having the activity hour accepted. Two days per week will be adequate for most programs. One- or two-day tournaments and special events meet with success at the 3:00 P.M. hour, on or off campus. Possibilities for short-term activities include the 7:00 A.M. and Saturday morning time slots. Tournaments in soccer, badminton, volleyball doubles, bowling, golf, pool, rope tug-of-war, and surfing, among others, have been successful outside the activity hour structure. Because a special interest is involved, along with a minimum commitment of time, student interest is high.

3. *Sports Officiating.* The majority of colleges (62.6 percent) reported that the director selected game officials and that clinics were the primary method utilized to train them (Reznik, 1972, p. 4). The quality of competitive programs depends on the professional instruction provided for the student officials, whether in the form of a clinic or a class. In addition to providing an invaluable experience for majors in physical education and recreation, credit classes appear to produce student officials who are better prepared and more reliable. Constant review of

game situations, general observations, and official rating forms have been incorporated to refine the efforts of these student officials. Needless to say, institutional savings can be appreciable. Depending on the size of the program, it may be necessary to use both student and paid officials. When it is not possible to use student and/or paid officials, your promotional talents will be tested. Two remaining options that have been successful are using participants as officials and scheduling games without officials. In the first instance, each participating team in a league must provide one or two officials for training and assignment to games played on their off days. If teams want officials badly enough, they will readily adopt this procedure. The last resort is to play the games without officials. Several schools do not use officials in team sports and report fewer conflicts as a result.

4. *Facilities and Equipment.* Reznik reports that the facilities of the community and junior colleges were slightly above average, compared with colleges as a whole. In addition to competing with varsity teams, outside agencies shared the facilities, but only when they were not used by campus groups in structured activities. Facility conflicts and inadequacies are most commonly offset by scheduling events in the off-season. For example, when the varsity football team is playing, intramural basketball should be scheduled, and vice versa. The absence of programs in 43 colleges was attributed directly to inadequate facilities or equipment.

5. *Budget.* Assuming that most equipment needs can be satisfied through the department of physical education, budget needs will be minimal. Basic costs include officiating, awards, special game equipment, promotional materials, and expenses for professional conferences. According to the Reznik study, the most common source of intramural program financing was a separate intramural budget. Budgets ranged from $100 to $18,000 but could be interpreted in many ways. For instance, one budget might include some staff salaries and/or equipment; other budgets might have these expenses assumed by another college support category. Consequently, comparisons are not reliable without extensive research. The number of dollars expended has little relationship with the effectiveness of a program. The three major areas of expenses are officiating, awards, and equipment, not necessarily in that order. Finances should be obtained from dependable sources in order to guarantee the continuity that a program needs to develop. Community colleges' intramural programs have progressed without entry fees, in keeping with the "no-cost" policy. Exceptions are off-campus commercial facilities used for special events, such as bowling, golf, riflery, pool and so on. In these activities, the student assumes the basic costs of participating in the event. Most colleges seem to prefer the "built-in" services that enable sound programming to continue with limited budgets.

6. *Participants.* The major objectives of the intramural-recreational programs of all schools were directed toward the recreational values of the students (Reznik, 1972, p. 3). Participants definitely favor the major round-robin team sports, such as basketball, football, volleyball, and softball. For many years, the organized clubs on campuses provided the nucleus of program support. The majority of the teams now participating in community and junior college intramural programs are independent groups. It must be remembered that national fraternities are not active on the community or junior college campuses. Unattached or independent student participation is also increasing rapidly in the special events. The average participant is a student from a middle-class family who has a background of organized sports in secondary school. Participation is on the increase in the open or noncompetitive recreational activities scheduled on the campuses in the late afternoons, in the evenings, and on Saturdays. These unstructured recreational offerings are extremely popular.

CONTEMPORARY PROGRAMS

Community or junior college programs have very traditional offerings. Most programs are oriented toward major sports. The men's program is dominant, but the coed program is growing. Women's programs have not been successful for several reasons: the popularity of the coed program, co-recreational competition with other colleges, and the upsurge of women's athletic programs. Programming for the handicapped and for night students has been limited.

Statistically, the program offerings break down as follows: 95.5 percent competitive, 67.8 percent coed, and 53.1 percent faculty-staff. Independent groups and individuals constituted the largest unit of participation—83.6 percent of all participants. Some 80 different activities were offered in the men's programs, 62 in coed programs, and 42 for faculty and staff. The most popular men's event is basketball; the most popular activity for women and coeds is volleyball. Traditional events might include basketball, football, softball, volleyball, track, swimming, tennis, badminton, handball, and archery. Unique events might feature wrist wrestling, Sigma Delta Psi, bike racing, obstacle courses, a hole-in-one contest, a tug of war, basic olympics, jogging 100 miles, surfing, three-man basketball, and inner-tube polo.

Sports clubs appear to be gaining momentum but have failed to assert themselves in the competitive intramural program.

Equipment checkout and open recreation programs are limited. For the most part, most nonstructured recreational activity is not college-supported.

PROMINENT CONCERNS

The Physical Recreation Concept

The intramural program must establish a position in the college structure before it can be viable. The most common position finds intramurals joining varsity athletics and physical education in a triumvirate. In this program concept, each area has very definite responsibilities. The varsity athletic program provides a competitive outlet for the highly skilled student, the physical education program provides skill instruction, and the intramural program provides the laboratory opportunity for the inclined student to test those skills in competitive experiences. Most strong college programs boast healthy athletic, physical education, and intramural programs, each contributing to the others.

Objectives

Program objectives must be developed. A typical list provides the following objectives:

1. To maintain better health through exercise. With the pressure of world problems and modern living requirements, it is important that the individual take time out periodically for recreational pursuits in order to maintain a healthful mental equilibrium.
2. To make social contacts and friendships that could not readily be developed in the classroom.
3. To learn the important values developed through team spirit and cooperation and a sense of belonging to a group.
4. To relax from strenuous school work and the rapid pace of modern living
5. To develop sportsmanship of the highest order. Everything that sportsmanship implies should be developed on the playing fields.
6. To realize for every individual, regardless of ability, the joy and fun of participation in one's favorite sport against good competition. (Thompson, 1973, p. iv.)

Communication

Active communication practices must be employed in program promotion, publicity, and public relations in order to stimulate student participation and to sell the merits of the program (Means, 1952, p. 373). Although we tend to think of public relations primarily as communication with the public in order to gain public understanding and support, communication from the public is equally important (Streloff, 1961, p. 141). Public administrators should consider promotion, publicity, and public relations as a single endeavor, rather than divorcing one facet from another. What do the professionals have to say on the subject? On March 10, 1969, personal interviews with men in the field yielded the following:

Ben Cunningham, San Francisco 49er advisor:

1. Appeal to the strengths and the following of your program participants.
2. If coverage in the student newspaper is lacking, ask for an explanation.
3. Utilize student input in writing your releases.
4. Provide special interest and highlight releases to capture filler space.

Jim Brochu, Publicity Director, Los Angeles Lakers:

1. Establish rapport with your communication colleagues.
2. Don't become subservient in an attempt to gain space.
3. In the early-season competition for space, the proof of your ability is to provide unique picture layouts and special interest items.

Don Drury, News Bureau, Long Beach City College:

1. Provide something the news media needs (service).
2. Avoid high pressure: if your program is sound and your publicity efforts are sincere, coverage will come. Don't become a defeatist.
3. Continually strive to sustain a positive relationship with individuals in the various media.

Communication advances should be positive in nature. Make no apologies. Gimmicks—methods that bring positive results for us individually—must be practiced diligently. This is extremely essential in that we are not all blessed with the influence and persuasion of a Tom Paine or a Thomas Jefferson.

Communication possibilities are numerous. Student newspapers, weekly board meetings, and word of mouth will be discussed at length. I agree with the professionals that your success in communication is directly related to your rapport with the newspaper staff, the experience of those who write your releases, and your punctuality in meeting deadlines. In writing publicity releases, you must strive to attract students, ensure that the releases are consistent with departmental goals, and present an accurate and objective view (Harral, 1940, p. 104). Experience leads me to recommend that if you can't find a competent reporter on your own staff, you should make arrangements to meet the assigned reporter once a week, on the same day and at the same time, to discuss the release. While developing a mutual understanding, you will provide the dependable service that is required in a student newspaper.

The most effective means of communication experienced is the weekly meeting of club and independent team representatives. This meeting affords the occasion to review in detail the schedule for the week, explain procedures, offer critiques of past events, and resolve problems. The advent of this meeting has refined communication at my college immeasurably.

In an interview, Jack Kent Cooke—owner of the Forum, the Los Angeles Lakers, and the Los Angeles Kings and majority owner of the Washington Redskins—stated emphatically that he expects all his employees to be salespersons. Our intramural staffs and representatives must also subscribe to this theory. Feasible communication gimmicks include calendars of semester events, polaroid pictures of winners and game action, instructor announcements, stag nights, banquets, record boards, handbooks, result sheets, club visits, spot announcements on campus radio and television, video and slide shows and a firm commitment to the open-door policy. Make a point to schedule and post hours during which either the director or another staff member is available to answer questions raised by students, faculty, and staff. Intramural directors must take the position that nothing can be assumed. Constant reminders through as many media as possible are necessary to reach the majority. Remember that more than half the responsibility in communication rests with the listener. Publicity is a constant, ongoing process. Sell the merits of your program, but don't hesitate to grow with your students. Give credence to the notion that listening to student interviews may not only serve to bridge the communication gap and help the student express his concern, but at the same time may minimize our communication problems (Wittenberg, 1949, p. 110). Contemporary students are imbued with the idea of service. They are most likely to respond to those of us who are genuinely interested in and like people (Whyte, 1957, p. 80).

Physical Examinations and Insurance

Medical clearance for participation is a continuing dilemma. Pressures to waive the required physical examination in keeping with the "no-cost" community and junior college philosophy leaves the programs extremely vulnerable. Students must be informed that as voluntary participants, they must assume all risks. Low-cost deductible medical insurance is often made available through the student affairs office. Directors should be fully covered to offset potential liability in suits.

Minority Involvement

Minority involvement is the concern of every college. Sincere efforts must be made to engage minority students in the full scope of the program. This includes participation in a wider range of activities, as well as officiating and leadership. Ethnic isolation retards the growth of all participants and the program itself.

College Committee Involvement

The recognition of the intramural program depends on the director's involving himself in the affairs of the college. Involvement in general committee work will afford the director the opportunity to educate his peers as to the philosophy and objectives of the intramural program. Favorable reaction to budget proposals is often the result of positive feelings by faculty toward our programs.

Professionalism

Directors must be encouraged to share their successes and assist in the problem-solving effort at the local and state conferences and workshops. Professionalism should be extended to membership in the National Intramural Association, the only "all-intramurals" professional organization. Membership entitles you to attend the national conference and to receive the annual conference proceedings and the quarterly newsletter. The most important purpose of the organization is to help new programs get off the ground. If you are sincere in your dedication to the intramural philosophy, you will want to become an active member of the National Intramural Association.

FUTURE CONSIDERATIONS

Physical Education Requirements

Diminishing physical education requirements will have a severe impact on community and junior college intramural programs. The current intramural program of volunteer participation is expected to become a more formal program in the near future. Colleges must take immediate action to prepare for this eventuality. Professionally trained, experienced directors are now available and will be in demand to institute sound programs. Colleges that must utilize existing staff members are encouraged to provide these men and women with professional training through area, state, and national workshops and conferences and through university intramural organization and administration courses.

Needs and Interests

There is a distinct necessity to offer a wide series of activities to meet the needs and interests of a diverse student body. Community and junior college students represent every socioeconomic level and ethnic group, range in age from 17 to 70 and have leisure interests which are as diverse as the differences in their backgrounds. For these reasons, numerous activities and events—active and passive—are required. It is hoped that exposure to the intramural program through a familiar activity will promote further participation in other events, which will in turn provide new experiences for the individual student. The commuting student must also be considered. Every effort should be made to schedule activities throughout the day, so that all students can sample them.

National Trends

The national trends in the intramural sports movement are very definite. They include rapidly growing coed programs, the expressed need for more unstructured recreational opportunities, and the increasing popularity of lifetime leisure sports. Coed programs in volleyball, tennis, and badminton have experienced great success, and many other sports are gaining momentum. Unstructured recreational activity is a must. We should realize that not all students are competitive by nature. In fact, the majority welcome a chance to participate without the constant pressures of the competitive program. Increased interest in lifetime sports—tennis, golf, badminton, and others—has been induced by increased leisure time. The fact that our students are now becoming active participants in intramural activities is one of the healthy signs of our time. Directors must keep ahead of national trends and gear their programs accordingly.

High School Programs

Intramural programs flourish at the junior high school level but are deficient or nonexistent in senior high schools. However, most school districts are anxious to provide constructive leisure time activities for their students. Physical education staff assignments could be adjusted to make instructors of both sexes available for after-school programs. The program offered should serve student interest in both individual and team sports and make provisions for unstructured activity. What could be more advantageous in the concept of the total physical education program than involving the majority of the student body in wholesome, positive activity? Local and community support for physical recreation programs would be greatly enhanced. The promotion of high school programs could be proposed through the leadership and expertise of the community or junior college directors.

Student Unions

The advent of student unions on the community and junior college campuses prompts intramural action to coordinate programs. Mutual cooperation should provide additional organized recreational outlets for the student body. Student union successes include recreational and competitive play in table tennis, billiards, bowling, chess, checkers, and card games. An added bonus is the inherent cross-promotional benefit of program exposure. For example, video tapes or slide shows of activities might frequently be projected for student viewing. Other traditional promotional endeavors, such as strategically placed announcement boards, may be used to publicize records, results, and coming events. Staffing is generally the dual responsibility of both the intramural and student affairs departments.

Facility Planning

Most community and junior colleges have encountered appreciable increases in enrollment over the past decade. In order to serve more students and community participants, facility planning must be more realistic. We have not kept up with the demand on our facilities. College intramural directors must take the lead in studying facility innovations that will accommodate the continual growth of programs. Preparedness is a combination of facility and program research for the future.

In-Depth Studies Are Needed

In order to meet the challenges of community and junior college intramural programs of the future, in-depth studies should be conducted in the areas of:

1. Financing junior college intramural programs.
2. Patterns of participation in junior college intramural programs.
3. Qualifications and training of personnel for administering junior college intramural-recreational programs.

4. Administrative problems peculiar to the administration of junior college intramural-recreational programs. (Reznik., 1972, p. 8)

THE CHALLENGE

Contemporary students are bewildered by numerous forces. Dissipation could become the most popular pastime. Whether or not you move forward in intramurals depends upon upgrading your programs and upon your dedication to these young people, not to yourself. It's your move!

GENERAL BIBLIOGRAPHY

Brubacher, John S., and Willis Rudy, *Higher Education in Transition.* New York: Harper & Brothers, 1958.

Harral, Stewart, *Publicity Problems.* Norman, Okla.: American College Publicity Association, 1940.

Means, Louis E., *The Organization and Administration of Intramural Sports.* St. Louis: C. V. Mosby, 1952.

Reznik, John W., "Junior College Intramural-Recreational Programs: A Survey and Analysis." Doctoral dissertation, University of Illinois, Champaign, 1972.

Streloff, Alexander N., *Guide to Public Relations.* Burlingame, Calif.: South-Western Publishing, 1961.

Thompson, William A., "Intramurals Handbook." Associated Student Body, Long Beach City College, August, 1973.

Whyte, William H. *The Organization Man.* Garden City, N. Y.: Doubleday, 1957.

Wittenberg, Rudolph M., *So You Want to Help People.* New York: Association Press, 1949.

12

Intramural Programming
for a Commuter College

PETER R. BERRAFATO
University of Illinois at Chicago Circle
Chicago, Illinois

INTRODUCTION

This chapter focuses on problems peculiar to commuter college programming. To outline a typical college intramural-recreation program would be an unforgivable redundancy. However, because some problems are common to resident and commuter institutions, some overlap is unavoidable. Nevertheless, the effort will be made to consider only those problems whose impact is more crucial on the commuter campus.

The chapter will be divided into four units: historical background and development, unique aspects of programming, the scope of the program, and implications for the administrator. In order to deal effectively with these units, we need to clarify certain terms.

Definition of Terms

1. *Commute:* to travel daily to and from a commuter college.
2. *Intramurals and intramural activities:* those sports activities engaged in by students, faculty, and staff within the boundaries of an institution. Unless otherwise specified, this term connotes structured competitive activities.

161

3. *Commuters:* students, staff, faculty, and administrators who travel daily to and from a commuter college.

4. *Commuter colleges:* Colleges, universities, and institutions of higher learning to and from which commuter personnel travel daily. For our purposes, a commuter college is arbitrarily classified as an institution to which all, or almost all, personnel commute daily. (Logically, other arbitrary percentages of commuters—such as 50 percent or more, 75 percent or more, and so on—may be used.)

5. *Recreation and recreational activities:* Nonstructured or "less"-structured sports activities, usually noncompetitive in nature.

6. *Co-Recreation:* Those sports activities, structured or unstructured, highly competitive or "free-play," engaged in by men and women together.

HISTORICAL BACKGROUND AND DEVELOPMENT

European Influence

The antecedents of the American urban college were colleges in continental Europe. Universities were first founded in medieval towns such as Bologna and Paris, and later in London, Manchester, Berlin, Hamburg, Frankfurt, and other large cities. In France and Italy, cities competed with one another for leadership in the development of fine urban universities. This trend has continued into modern times.

It is important to note that two exceptions to the trend were Oxford and Cambridge. "In flight from the harassments of Paris, scholars in the twelfth century chose a provincial town rather than a city" (Klotsche, 1966, p. 3). This is important because of the profound effect that the Oxford and Cambridge pattern subsequently exerted on the development of higher education in America. The American pattern had to develop in the countryside, due to the fact that when the first American universities were founded there were no urban centers.

State Universities

The state universities, the first of which was the University of Virginia, established by Thomas Jefferson in 1825, were the immediate predecessors of the urban university in America. The University of Virginia can be considered the first state university because it was "by the express intent of its constitution a thoroughly public enterprise rather than a private or quasi-public one" (Brubacher and Rudy, 1968, p. 148). Following the early American tradition, state universities and land-grant institutions were founded for the most part in rural, open settings.

Urban Universities

Finally, and very recently, the state universities contributed greatly to the development of urban institutions by initiating programs in the heavily populated centers of their respective states. "In 1962 almost 150 such branches were being operated by 43 universities in 31 states" (Klotsche, 1966, p. 15). Many of these institutions, and of course many other, older schools, constitute the modern commuter colleges of America.

UNIQUE ASPECTS OF PROGRAMMING

Programming for the urban commuter institution is unique for many reasons. These reasons can be categorized as follows:

1. Time considerations.
    a. Commuting practices: virtually all of the students, staff, and faculty live off campus.
    b. Employment practices: 86 percent of the students are employed (Klassen, 1971, p. 40).
    c. Time spent on campus: the students spend a comparatively short period of time on campus (*Ibid.,* pp. 45–46).
2. Units of competition.
3. Facilities and schedules.
4. Out-of-school recreational opportunities.

As we examine these unique aspects of the urban commuter institution, we may be inclined to suspect that such an institution is not a true community of scholars and teachers, as is its resident school counterpart—at least not in terms of time. The commuter community emerges each morning at 8:00 A.M. and vanishes at 5:00 P.M. each weekday of the school year. Like much of the workaday world, it is an 8-to-5 community with an hour for lunch. This, of course, has significant implications for the intramural sports program.

Despite these obvious disadvantages, commuter institutions can develop, and indeed have developed, well-rounded educational programs that range from adequate to outstanding. Klotsche has observed of urban institutions that "some are prestigious, with worldwide reputations" (1966, p. 8).

Similarly, high-quality extracurricular activities of a diverse nature can be developed. But the obstacles are many and formidable! And the effects of these obstacles, individually and collectively, tend to limit the size of the program. It follows, then, that in order to develop and operate a quality intramural program worthy of an important place in the overall educational pattern of the institution, we must examine each of the obstacles, or group of obstacles, and attempt to minimize their negative effects.

The Factor of Time

The time dimension presents a very critical obstacle. Whereas the resident institution's population spends virtually all of its time on the campus or in its immediate environs, the commuter personnel spend a considerable amount of time off campus. The average time spent commuting to and from school in a typical institution is 90 minutes (Klassen, 1971, p. 51). Approximately another 30 to 60 must be added for traveling to and from places of employment. The final dismaying statistic is that in this same institution the median number of hours spent on the campus is a mere 27 per week—17 in classes and labs, 5 in the library, and 5 in the student union.

Obviously, we cannot change the amount of time spent in commuting to school and to work, nor the time spent in classrooms, laboratories, and libraries. We must, however, commit our energies and strategies to effect some changes in the use of the remaining weekday hours. Supposedly, the 14 percent of the students who are not employed have ample time for some extracurricular activity. And since the average number of work hours for the remaining 86 percent of the students is 14 hours per week (Ibid., p. 41), we may conclude that many of those who work fewer than 14 hours per week (43 percent of the student body) would have some time for extracurricular pursuits. Additionally, we may estimate that relatively few of those who work more than 14 hours per week would have sufficient time for intramurals or other activities. Many of those in this group would have to "steal" time in order to participate. In summary, we may conclude optimistically that in spite of the many time demands on these commuter students, there is a substantial number of potential participants.

Units of Competition

Certainly, one of the positive motivating factors for the intramural participant is the opportunity to represent his or her own group: dormitory, college or department, religious group, professional society, military group, and so forth. Unfortunately, many of these types of groups do not exist on the commuter campus, and some that do exist are not close-knit, well-organized entities. On many commuter campuses there are, however, several categories of groups that can become effective, workable units of competition. These include (not in priority ranking) varsity teams, fraternities, sororities, groups with a high school and/or neighborhood affiliation, physical education and recreation majors, and physical education classes.

The viability of intercollegiate squads as units of competition depends to a large extent upon the attitude of the coaching staff, particularly the head coach, and the leadership capabilities within the squad. Whenever there is a positive feeling about, and a respect for, the intramural program on the part of either or both of these two forces, the intramural program will benefit from varsity squad participation. It is interesting to note that this type of involvement lends prestige and excitement to the intramural program. Students are happy for the opportunity to compete with varsity athletes.

When they are present, fraternities and sororities can be excellent units of competition. They are usually well structured and their organizational philosophy specifically promotes participation in various aspects of the college community's extracurricular activities. The intramural department should encourage wide participation by these groups, either in separate leagues or in the existing leagues—and in some cases, both.

A word of caution is in order at this point. It seems that some fraternities, for diverse reasons (some apparent, some obscure), tend to exert pressure upon administrators to permit them to adopt special rules, play different types of schedules, and receive special privileges. Certainly, efforts to meet the unique needs and interests of special groups must be made. However, it is highly recommended that administrators resist the temptation to promote two distinctly different types of programs in order to cater to the whims of certain groups or, as is often the case, to a few vocal individuals within these groups.

Initially, some freshmen tend to retain their high school and neighborhood friendships. The teams that result from these relationships are usually excellent, if ephemeral, units of competition. Unless the group is fairly large, these units tend to disband upon the termination of their respective schedules. Occasionally, a nucleus survives and adds participants for the forthcoming intramural activity. The intramural department should encourage this practice whenever possible. A key to this situation is the distribution of information and entry blanks for the next scheduled activity, prior to the termination of the current tournament or league. This practice makes it easier for the captains and/or managers to retain some of their squad members for the next activity.

Historically, physical education and recreation majors have supported intramural programs as managers, officials, *and* participants. For them, the intramural program is a laboratory for experience, practice, and of course fun. They should be encouraged to participate in the program in each of these roles.

Finally, physical education classes can be utilized to help recruit teams and individuals. The instructor's attitude is of paramount importance in this aspect of the program. If he holds the intramural program in high esteem and if he believes that the physical education and intramural programs should be closely related, then he will be a positive force in the development of units of competition. These efforts will not detract from the class work; rather, they will enhance and supplement it. With this philosophy and approach, the instructor can provide his students additional opportunities for enriched experiences in physical education and intramurals.

Intraclass competition—that is, competition limited to members of various sections of a specific activity, such as handball, racquetball, volleyball, or bowling—provides excellent opportunities for many students of similar ability levels. In addition to providing the opportunity for valuable experiences, such competition can serve as an initiation to, and maturation for, participation in other activities on the intramural calendar. The possibility of including intraclass activities in the intramural program should be seriously and thoroughly explored. The results of this type of programming as an integral part of the intramural offering can be very fruitful and rewarding.

Facilities and Schedules

The problem of facilities on the commuter campus is not merely the presence or absence of adequate space, equipment, and so forth; it is the priorities established for the use of the existing facilities. Traditionally, intramural activities are conducted each day after the physical education program and the intercollegiate programs have been concluded. On a commuter campus the prime times for intercollegiate sports and intramural sports are frequently identical. To compound the problem, the physical education program and the intramural program also may be in conflict in this respect. The prospects for intramurals may be dismal, but they are never hopeless.

The intramural administrator has some options in his scheduling practices:

1. Activity hour(s), if available.
2. Late afternoon and early evening.
3. Saturday morning and early afternoon.
4. Sunday morning and early afternoon.

5. Scheduling, in part, "around" an intercollegiate squad—for instance, intramural basketball games whenever the varsity team is away.
6. Scheduling, in part, "around" the physical education programs—for example, whenever the physical education program does not require the use of every teaching station.
7. Off-season scheduling—basketball in the spring, softball in the fall, and so forth.
8. Recess or holiday tournaments.

Regardless of the patterns that are adopted, the primary consideration in scheduling for intramural sports on a commuter campus is the availability and the convenience of the participants.

Out-of-School Recreational Opportunities

The commuter college intramural program in an urban setting must compete for participants with many other agencies, some of which provide excellent facilities and quality programs. These agencies include park districts, the YMCA, the YWCA, community centers, settlement houses, and others. It is this writer's observation that many of these agencies provide programs largely for the highly skilled participants, particularly the high school "stars," who can't or won't participate at the varsity level.

In view of this situation, and inasmuch as the intramural program should provide opportunities for *all,* we must remember not to neglect potential participants of poor, modest, or moderate skills. In fact, we must make special efforts to attract them. Furthermore, if we may generalize, many elementary and high schools in large urban centers, because of a shortage of adequate facilities (and sometimes other factors), produce young people whose sport skills are inferior to those of their suburban and rural counterparts. The commuter college intramural program must try to provide this group with opportunities for participation.

THE SCOPE OF THE PROGRAM

The Structured Competitive Program

This program should include as wide a range of activities as is feasible. There should be a variety of individual and team activities, which will appeal, hopefully, to all interests and tastes. The intramural calendar should include mild, moderate, and vigorous activities. The number of offerings must be given careful consideration. Mueller suggests that "a better program will result from a few well-chosen and properly administered activities than a hodgepodge of less meaningful, poorly organized activities" (Mueller, 1971, p. 81). In our efforts to meet the needs and interests of all the students, staff, and faculty and to attract as many as possible to the intramural program, we tend to offer too many activities within a limited period of time. This is especially true when the quarter system is in use.

Each activity should be subjected to the following questions:

1. Is the activity popular locally? Is it popular as a *participant* activity?
2. Is it taught in the physical education program? Do the potential participants have the opportunity to learn the basic skills and rules?
3. Does the activity contribute to the realization of one or more of your objectives?
4. Does it require preliminary training and/or practice sessions? (Rarely will individual teams subject themselves to adequate conditioning regimens for a very demanding activity.)
4. Is it financially feasible to conduct the activity? Consider, for example, the potential expense of a golf, hockey, or baseball program.
6. Are the necessary staff and/or student "experts" available for any particular activity? This question must be given special attention when new activities are being considered.
7. Are adequate facilities and space available?
8. Is there adequate time for the activity?

The activities offered on commuter campuses will depend upon the foregoing considerations and also upon the location and climate of the institution. It may be appropriate to list a very few of the more universally popular activities in urban areas. The team sports would probably include basketball, touch football, softball, and volleyball. Soccer, speedball, hockey, water polo, and lacrosse would be examples of team activities that are popular in certain areas of the country. Individual activities with widespread appeal would include archery, badminton, bowling, table tennis, tennis, handball, and racquetball. Other individual activities with a more limited appeal might include riflery, fencing, squash, and cycling.

The intramural administrators must be receptive to participant needs and interests. Every suggestion should be given careful consideration.

Recreational, Free-Play, and Unstructured Activities

The current trend toward "doing your own thing" is perhaps a healthy sign. On all campuses, commuter as well as resident, many students, staff, and faculty are expressing the desire to participate at their leisure in sports activities of their choice. This participation involves a minimum of organization or formal structure. The activity may be highly competitive or almost devoid of competition in the usual sense of the term. Whatever it is, it is important! For many, such activities may well constitute a better vehicle for self-expression than our rigidly structured, highly competitive programs.

The unstructured program may be especially appealing to the commuter student who can sometimes "steal" a few minutes to "shoot some hoops" or play thirty minutes of volleyball, badminton, or racquetball or play five innings of one-pitch softball. Whatever the demands, it behooves the administrator to provide the opportunities for these types of intramural-recreation experiences.

Co-Recreational Activities

This aspect of the total intramural-recreational program is currently undergoing a vast change. The demands for co-recreational activities are enormous. It is quite likely that in this decade and in the 1980s the development of co-recreational activities will accelerate at a tremendous rate. This development will help to satisfy an important need in our educational programs. "For the student's emotional well-being, a wholesome adjustment to the opposite sex is imperative. To enable more men and women to meet under wholesome conditions is one of the most important purposes of college life" (Means, 1973, p. 270).

Some activities are naturally and easily adapted to co-recreational play. The most notable examples of these include tennis, badminton, racquetball, table tennis, archery, bowling, and golf. Participation may be by the individual, by mixed-doubles teams, or in tournaments in which men and women compete. Handicap systems may be introduced when different levels of ability suggest their use. Two notable examples of team events that lend themselves readily to co-recreational play are volleyball and softball. Modifications of rules may be useful, depending upon the skill levels of the participants.

In general, co-recreational sports should flourish on commuter campuses. Conceivably, current late-afternoon and evening women's intramurals will essentially become programs of co-recreational activities. The women's activities that survive in the urban setting will be those offered during the regular class hours.

Programs for Staff and Faculty

Teachers, administrators, and staff personnel on the commuter campus experience the same types of difficulties as students in gaining access to on-campus recreational or intramural activities. However, this group as a whole spends considerably more time on campus than the students. Consequently, many of these individuals can schedule periodic recreational or intramural sessions. Their needs may parallel those of the students in many respects, but their interests are generally quite different. They are attracted to activities such as jogging, swimming, fitness programs, handball, racquetball, squash, table tennis, and tennis.

The intramural-recreational department is responsible for providing space, facilities, and programs for this segment of the university population. Admittedly, students must be given priorities in many instances, but staff and faculty must not be neglected. As important members of the university community, they must be afforded their fair share of recreational-intramural opportunities.

IMPLICATIONS FOR THE ADMINISTRATOR

Many of the observations that follow are applicable to all intramural programs. However, they have special significance for the commuter college program. Perhaps they can best be described as guidelines for the commuter college administrator.

1. Students, staff, and faculty must be afforded opportunities to participate in activities of their choice at times *convenient to them.*
2. Time commitments must be relatively short. Additional opportunities for those with great interest and adequate time should be provided— for instance, "perpetual" tournaments.
3. Cooperation of coaches and administrators of intercollegiate programs should be solicited.
4. In order to retain units of competition and to attract new ones, try to control the environment so that each intramural experience is enjoyable and meaningful.
5. Solicit the cooperation of the physical education program director and instructors, especially in the promotion of intraclass activities.
6. Be receptive to new ideas and new interests.
7. Experiment with various scheduling patterns.
8. Provide opportunities for participation at various skill levels.
9. Use the activities popular in a particular campus location and develop schedules around them.
10. Provide adequate opportunities for unstructured, free-play experiences.
11. Make special efforts to augment the co-recreational program with appropriate activities.

GENERAL BIBLIOGRAPHY

BRUBACHER, JOHN S., and WILLIS RUDY, *Higher Education in Transition,* rev. and enlarged ed. New York: Harper & Row, 1968.

KLASSEN, PETER P., *Commuter Students in an Urban University.* Master's thesis, University of Illinois at Chicago Circle, 1971.

KLOTSCHE, J. MARTIN, *The Urban University.* New York: Harper & Row, 1966.

MEANS, LOUIS E., *Intramurals: Their Organization and Administration,* 2nd ed. Englewood Cliffs, N. J.: Prentice-Hall, 1973.

MUELLER, PAT, *Intramurals: Programming and Administration,* 4th ed. New York: Ronald Press, 1971.

13

Co-Recreational Programming: More than Social Contact

JOHN REZNIK
New Mexico State University
Las Cruces, New Mexico

INTRODUCTION

Less than 75 years ago it was unheard of for a woman to vote. Today it is not only a *fait accompli,* but in many elections a deciding factor. Similarly, it was only a very short while ago that women began to encroach upon the "male" domain of athletics and sport. Yet, the accomplishments of many female athletes—both Olympic (for example, Cathy Rigby) and professional (for instance, Billie Jean King)—are well known the world over. The field of intramurals has also witnessed many changes in the scope and the nature of women's increased interest in sport.* Not only are women participating in ever growing numbers, they are engaging in such previously all-male game areas as the football field and the ice hockey rink. On many campuses the programming thrust is, in fact, aimed at achieving "sport for all."

The goal of "an activity for everyone and everyone in an activity," however, requires more than an offering of separate programs for men and women. The intramural director should attempt to offer those activities that meet the diverse interests of a heterogeneous student com-

---

* *Editor's note:* See Chapter 8 of this text for a more inclusive examination of this interest.

munity. Among the programming efforts attendant upon this responsibility are those involved with co-recreational activities.

HISTORICAL BACKGROUND
AND A REVIEW OF THE LITERATURE

Although progress in co-recreational activity programming has been relatively slow until the last fifteen years or so, over these years there have been numerous recorded instances of men and women engaging together in some form of play or sport. Many of the earliest efforts were the outgrowth of social gatherings between residential groups on college campuses. Since many of these social mixers were held outdoors, it was only natural that athletic games were frequently included as part of the effort to have a good time and to break the social ice. Among the most popular of such games were volleyball, softball, badminton, and tennis.

In recent years, as many of the social taboos that have occasionally inhibited the involvement of women in sports have been eliminated, co-recreational activity programs have expanded in popularity across the country. The current status of programming efforts in this area can best be described as healthy and growing. In fact, at least a partial co-recreational intramural program can be found on almost every university and college campus. Several intramural administrators have recognized the need for such programming. Shirley concluded that a recreational program worthy of its name must include co-recreational activities (1964, p. 9). Frye observed that coed activities are an established part of the scheme of American education (1964, p. 12). Haniford wrote that collegiate administrators were aware of the need for coed recreation programs (1963, p. 19). In an address to the National Intramural Association, MacIntyre suggested that co-recreation programs can help meet the challenges of an automated society (1966, p. 128). Caldwell stated that "nationwide trends indicate that co-recreational programs are growing faster than any other type of intramural activity" (1974, p. 43). In short, the literature supports the need for an administrative commitment to co-recreational programming.

ADMINISTRATIVE CONSIDERATIONS

On most campuses, co-recreational activity programming is merely an extension of the regular intramural (campus recreation) program. Only minimal adjustments of administrative techniques and procedures are necessary to implement a co-rec program. As in other intramural programming areas, it is desirable to have accountability and responsibility for the co-rec program assigned to someone with the necessary managerial acumen. The skills required include an ability to assess the interests and the needs of both men and women; an awareness of how activities can be structured to preclude male dominance of the contest; and a commitment to providing a program whose primary emphasis is on individual enjoyment rather than on one of the traditional competition-oriented goals. And as with other intramural programs, co-rec activities should be granted equitable consideration when policies are scheduled for the prime-time use of existing recreational facilities. Over the years, one of the prime factors that has limited the growth of quality programs of co-recreational activities has been a reluctance on the part of intramural directors to accord co-rec programs a share of departmental resources that is equal to those enjoyed by the men's and women's programs. Without apparent justification, co-rec programs have been assigned second-class citizenship. As such, these activities have frequently been relegated to Friday nights and Sunday afternoons only.

Co-rec activities that require officials should be refereed by both male and female students. In addition to reaffirming the coed nature of this program, the use of men and women officials contributes to the activities by providing a valuable source of public relations, competent help, and heterogeneous student input.

Possibly the most challenging aspect of co-rec programming is the task of team formation. Because teams are composed of both male and female students, the residential unit (with the exception of coed living arrangements) is not the standard organizational basis, as it typically is in both the men's and the women's programs. Although many living groups readily arrange to "go in" with another group to form a co-rec team, the intramural director should make some provision to form teams composed of individuals or groups who are unable to organize a team. Even though some directors are unwilling to engage in such matchmaking efforts, the opportunity to participate in a co-rec program should not be limited to those fortunate enough to know someone of the opposite sex who is also willing to participate. "Fun for all" should not mean "fun only for the socially active." Perhaps the simplest approach to this problem is a procedure used by the University of Illinois. On that campus, all individuals who are not on a team or do not have a partner for a co-rec activity register with the intramural department and are subsequently assigned arbitrarily to a team on a first-come, first-served basis.

CO–RECREATIONAL ACTIVITIES

What constitutes a co-rec program? A well-organized co-rec intramural program can include almost any activity that a specific campus will support. Table 1 provides a listing of some of the activities that are frequently found in a co-rec program.

Table 1.   Co-Rec Activities

archery	free throw shooting	par three golf
badminton	frisbee football	ping pong
basketball	frisbee softball	racquetball
billiards	golf	softball
bowling	ice hockey	special events
broomball	inner-tube basketball	squash
fencing	inner-tube volleyball	swimming
field hockey	inner-tube water polo	touch football
flag football	inner-tube water relays	volleyball
floor hockey	kickball	water polo

The determination of which activities to include in the co-rec program depends both on the available staff, facilities, and equipment and on the interests of the students. Regarding the latter criterion, Johannes Van Hoff (director of intramurals at New York State University at Binghamton), in a presentation to the second annual New York State Intramural Directors Meeting, advised intramural personnel to be patient when they evaluate the effectiveness and the worth of newly instituted co-rec activities. It has been his experience, stated Van Hoff, that it occasionally takes a while for some co-rec programs to catch on. The intramural director who is easily discouraged may abandon a potentially successful activity.

CO–RECREATIONAL RULES

"The activities offered by the creative intramural director are important to the overall effectiveness of the program; but, the uniqueness of the co-rec program seems to be keyed in the effectiveness of the rule modifications." (Caldwell, 1974, pp. 43–44) Co-rec rule modifications constitute perhaps the most important dimension of co-rec programming. In each activity, the intramural director must modify the rules so that the contest is not dominated by the male team members. At the same time, the basic concept of the game must be maintained so that the participants do not feel that their efforts are being pandered.

An example of how this problem might affect the efforts of the intramural director is illustrated in a study undertaken recently at the Berkeley campus of the University of California. The opinions of coed participants in the co-rec softball program were surveyed in an attempt to identify what direction rule modifications for co-rec softball should take. The rationale for the inquiry was that men often play "around the women." For example, a male shortstop may take *all* throws to second base, thereby preventing a woman second baseman from taking the throws that a second baseman would normally handle. Another example would be the intentional walking of male batters to set up an easier "out" or "double play" situation. Such efforts tend to detract from the coed nature of the activity. About 60 percent of the women surveyed responded in favor of establishing rules to keep male players from overplaying the situation. In the second example, one solution might be to eliminate walks entirely.

The basic premise to be followed in considering co-rec rule modifications is that an enjoyable activity should be insured for all participants. All changes should be kept as simple as possible. The rules should be specific to each situation and compatible with the interests of the students. To help provide an overview of how co-rec activities are structured at other schools, I have outlined below the basic regulations for four co-rec activities.

Coed Flag Football

At the University of California (Davis), four men and four women constitute a team (Colberg, 1972, pp. 129–30).* Advancement of the ball is restricted as follows:

1. Scrimmage play via the run: advancement from behind the line of scrimmage to beyond the line of scrimmage is restricted to women only.
2. Scrimmage play via the pass: (a) a male passer cannot penetrate past the line of scrimmage under any circumstances; (b) female passers have no limitations on their advancement behind or beyond the line of scrimmage.
3. There are no advancement restrictions to a male once he has obtained possession beyond the line of scrimmage.
4. A male or female may execute any number of laterals to receivers of either sex behind the line of scrimmage, but only females may advance the ball beyond the line of scrimmage.
5. A male cannot advance a punt or kickoff forward from his point of contact with the ball, but may, however, move backwards or laterally from that first point of contact. Advancement via a punt or kickoff is possible only by a female ball carrier. (Usually, the man catches the ball and then laterals to a woman).
6. If the passer is female, she can complete her passes to either sex, but if

---

* Colberg suggests that this number be reduced to six (three of each sex) in order to increase the number of scoring opportunities and to reduce the frequency of inter-sex matchups.

a pass is completed to a male, he must be beyond the line of scrimmage at the time of the reception.

7. If the passer is a male, he can complete his toss only to a female, anywhere on the field. This modification will be changed next year to allow one male-to-male beyond-the-line-of-scrimmage attempt every four downs (four downs are allowed to advance the ball from one 20-yard zone to the next 20-yard zone).

Co-Rec Basketball

At Illinois State University (Normal), the rules of the co-rec basketball program were formulated to answer at least three major areas of concern: the question of officiating; the problem of establishing equitable competitiveness between the women and the men; and the minimization of injuries (Wallace, 1972, pp. 134–36). The first was solved by requiring all teams to provide their own officials during the season. Wallace surmises that although the "quality of play was lowered," the spirit and enjoyment was raised as a result of the lack of a "formal" official. Three major rules provided an equalization of the competition: the scoring system, the rule barring men from entering the lane, and the elimination of the three-second rule for women. Injuries were reduced by restricting the number of players in the front court. The rules and regulations follow:

1. Players
   a. Each team consists of 6 players—3 men and 3 women.
   b. Substitutions are allowed on a man-for-man and woman-for-woman basis only.
   c. Each team must have at least one extra player to assist in the scoring and timekeeping on the sidelines.
   d. Each team must provide an official for the game.

2. Timing
   a. Each game consists of four 6-minute quarters, time running continuously except for time-outs.
   b. Each team is allowed one 1-minute time-out per quarter, nonaccumulative. The clock will be stopped on all time-outs.
   c. There will be a 1-minute break between quarters and between overtime periods that are required.
   d. There will be a 5-minute break between halves.
   e. Overtime periods will be 2-minutes continuous running time, with no time-outs allowed.

3. Scoring
   a. Field goals scored by men are worth 2 points each, field goals scored by women are worth 4 points each.
   b. Free throws scored by men are worth 1 point each, free throws scored by women are worth 2 points each.
4. Fouls and Free Throws
   a. All personal fouls are charged against the violator; a player who commits a fifth foul shall have fouled out of the game.
   b. All personal fouls are taken out of bounds by the offended team, except for those committed in the act of shooting. In these instances, if the field goal attempt is missed, two free throws are awarded to the offended player. If a foul is committed against a player in the act of shooting, and the shot is made, the field goal is awarded and the foul charged to the violator, but the ball is taken out of bounds by the scored-upon team as would be the case following any successful field goal.
   c. All technical fouls (1 shot plus possession), intentional fouls (2 shots), and flagrant fouls (2 shots) result in free throws.
5. Special Regulations
   a. Each team can never have more than 4 of its players on any one half of the court at any time. Of the minimum 2 players left, there must always be at least one man and one woman. A violation of this provision awards the ball out of bounds to the other team.
   b. Men players are not allowed in the entire area of the free-throw lane from the free-throw line to the baseline at any time on either end of the court. This holds true for offensive driving, defensive guarding, rebounding for both field goals and free throws, and all other cases without exception. A violation of this provision is treated as follows: (1) if the encroachment is in the violator's offensive court, the ball is awarded out of bounds to the other team; (2) if the encroachment is in the violator's defensive court, it is treated as basket interference (whether a shot has been attempted or not) and 2 points are awarded to the other team.
   c. The game begins with a jump ball between a woman player from each team.
6. Rules of the Ilinois High School Association for Men's Basketball shall govern all other aspects of play. In addition, all rules of eligibility stated in the Co-Recreational Activities pamphlet shall apply.

Co-Rec Softball

   Bill Manning, assistant intramural director at the University of California, states that the Berkeley co-rec softball program follows all

American Softball Association rules governing slow-pitch softball, with a few exceptions. These include:

1. Team makeup: 5 men and 5 women. Teams can play with less than 10 players, but at no time may the number of men exceed the number of women. The minimum number allowed to play is 8.
2. The batting order must be male, female, male, and so on. Choice of leadoff batter is left to the team.
3. Teams may set their own fielding positions—no restriction as to gender apply.*
4. Teams are encouraged to keep in mind the coeducational nature of the game and to avoid "playing around" women team members.
5. Eligibility rules are to be followed.

Coed Inner-Tube Water Polo

Colberg reports that this sport is the most popular "co-intramural" event in the University of California (Davis) program (1972, p. 132). The rule modifications for this activity include the following:

1. Seven players constitute a team. Either combination of 3 and 4 make up a team—3 men and 4 women, or 4 men and 3 women (the latter is more popular).
2. Only men may be goalkeepers.
3. One or two hands may be used to propel the ball goalward.
4. Two points are awarded for each goal scored by a woman and one point for each goal by a man.
5. After scoring, equilibrium must be maintained by the individual in his or her inner tube or the goal is nullified.
6. All penalty shots must be taken by a woman and count only one point.

SUMMARY

Co-recreational activities should be an integral part of every intramural program. Although these activities offer opportunities for both social interaction and structured competition, their primary emphasis should be on having fun. Because they are based on this concept, they offer the intramural director a good opportunity in which to try innovations. The number of innovative ideas developed and the resulting level of participant enjoyment is limited only by the imagination of students and program staff.

---

* *Editor's Note:* Several schools that conduct a co-rec softball program require a male to be the catcher since this position is frequently the area of injury-causing collisions.

GENERAL BIBLIOGRAPHY

BUCK, CHARLES R., "Coeducational Intramurals: Trend or Topic," *National Intramural Association Proceedings*, XX (1969), 52–56.

CALDWELL, SANDRA, "Co-Rec Intramurals: Emphasis Fun," *National Intramural Association Proceedings*, XXVI (1974), 43–44.

COLBERG, GARY, "Co-Ed Flag Football," *National Intramural Association Proceedings*, XXIV (1972), 129–31.

————, "Co-Ed Innertube Water Polo," *National Intramural Association Proceedings*, XXIV (1972), 131–33.

FRYE, ROSEMARY, "Coeducational Intramurals," *National Intramural Association Proceedings*, XV (1964), 12.

HANIFORD, GEORGE, "Co-recreation and Intramural Sports," *National Intramural Association Proceedings*, XIV (1963), 19–22.

MACINTYRE, CHRISTINE M., "Co-Recreation: A Must for the Future," *National Intramural Association Proceedings*, XVII (1966), 126–28.

SHIRLEY, MAX, "Coeducational Programs," *National Intramural Association Proceedings*, XV (1964), 9–11.

TURNER, EULA D., "Co-Educational Programs," *National Intramural Association Proceedings* XV (1964), 16–17.

WALLACE, ROBERT, "Co-Rec Basketball at ISU," *National Intramural Association Proceedings*, XXIV (1972), 133–36.

14

Intramural Programming
for Faculty and Staff

RODNEY J. GRAMBEAU
University of Michigan
Ann Arbor, Michigan

Intramural and recreative sports programs on our university and college campuses—and, to a lesser degree, at the secondary level—are experiencing a growth of interest and participation unmatched in the history of the intramural program. Participants and intramural directors are challenging university administrators to provide the necessary finances, facilities, and personnel to insure a quality program. Program growth and interest has resulted in the building of many new facilities and the development of programs whose major emphasis is on providing recreational opportunities for all members of the university community.

One important segment of the university community is that of faculty and staff and their families. Although budgetary, facility, and personnel restrictions may limit the extent of some programs, leading intramural directors throughout the country agree that they are responsible for providing a quality faculty-staff program. Many rewards can be realized for the program as a whole, as well as for the participants, through the good university relations that it engenders.

The inclusion of faculty and staff in intramural programming has been apparent since the beginning of intramural programming within our schools. By reviewing its literature and history one can view the development of various aspects of faculty-staff programming.

HISTORICAL BACKGROUND
AND RELATED LITERATURE

Considered by many the father of intramurals in America, Elmer D. Mitchell, author of the first text concerned with intramural administration at the college and university level, recognized the importance of providing a program of recreation for faculty and staff. In his text he suggested that a faculty advisory committee

> is a body which it may prove well to organize, though it meets but a few times a year. The members appointed to this committee are faculty men sympathetic with the program. In a practical way, their services amount to little; but, in such matters as policies and influence with the school proper, their support is very helpful. At any special function of the intramural department, such as an annual banquet, the presence of faculty members makes the occasion more worthwhile for the students. (1939, p. 79)

Faculty and staff enjoy challenge games with student teams or community teams; such games could make up one area of competition. Where facilities are available, faculty league competition is possible. The sports that have been the most popular include softball, volleyball, tennis, handball, squash, golf, and horseshoe pitching. In addition, Mitchell states that wherever possible, a special recreation area with dressing facilities should be provided to allow for "drop-in" exercise programs.

Leavitt and Price offer additional programming areas for faculty and staff. They surmise that mixed teams of faculty men and women playing against mixed student teams in co-recreational activities, and faculty family nights with facilities reserved for faculty and their families can be excellent faculty-staff activities (1949, p. 90).

Another prolific author in the field of intramurals, Louis E. Means, states that "the enterprising director and his staff are always awake to the possibility of serving the faculty group recreationally" (1973, p. 66). According to Means, bowling and golf are perhaps the easiest sports to introduce in a faculty program. Like Mitchell, he also suggests the provision of a separate building unit including shower and dressing facilities, reading and smoking rooms, and an opportunity to obtain food.

At the National Intramural Association's tenth annual conference, C. B. Meyers suggested that we need to bring the faculty into the cultural sphere of the students. One of the ways of doing this is to interest faculty in physical and recreational activity. One of the best morale builders in faculty-student relationships is the promotion of faculty teams that compete not only among themselves but also against student teams.

Meyers suggests open-house or fun nights during which faculty men and women can compete, swimming classes for faculty and their children, faculty sponsors and coaches for intramural teams, and recreational programs for children of faculty (1959, p. 6).

In a survey conducted in selected colleges and universities in North and South America in 1959, I found that 45 percent of the American schools that replied to a questionnaire and 33 percent of the Canadian respondents had an organized faculty-staff program. Of the 23 sports participated in, volleyball was found to be the most popular. I concluded that there was a need for a study of faculty-staff intramural programming in order to better determine attitudes resulting from faculty-staff participation (1959, p. 144).

Larson and Hyatt suggest that faculty recreation programs help build *esprit de corps* and keep the faculty fit for teaching through both physical and mental stimulation. They suggested gearing the program to the needs, interests, capacities, and abilities of a particular faculty group and being sure that both husbands and wives are involved and that activities are presented in a casual, relaxed way that is suitable for participants of all ages and skills (1961, p. 57).

In their text, Kleindienst and Weston indicated the need for an awareness among staff members of the importance of providing worthwhile programs for the faculty, preferably individual and dual sports (1964, p. 56).

Matthews reports that many faculty positions are accepted or retained on the basis of fringe benefits, and one of these benefits is the recreation program provided for faculty and staff and their families. He indicates that many activities are available for faculty, but cautions that injuries constitute a possible problem because of the question of liability. Other problems cited by Matthews include scheduling, financing, providing adequate supervisory personnel, taking care of children left by faculty parents, and poor attendance at some activities (1964, pp. 33–35).

Murphy notes that one of the purposes of our intramural programs is to offer recreational activities for the complete university family, which includes faculty and staff. It is as important for the instructors to relieve themselves of academic pressures by "relaxing" in an activity as it is for the students. Furthermore, the activity provides an opportunity for faculty and staff members to become acquainted with one another in an informal setting.

A faculty-staff council, selected from different areas of the university, helps determine and implement the faculty-staff programs. The council's use of questionnaires and a suggestion box is suggested by Murphy. In addition to the regular program offerings, a medically supervised faculty fitness program, which includes conditioning, jogging, and a monthly fitness letter with humorous anecdotes, enriches the faculty-staff program (Murphy, 1966, p. 119).

Gunsten suggests the use of the basic public relations principles of perseverance, responsibility, initiative, dependability, enthusiasm, and pride as guidelines in promoting programs. He emphasizes the need for a faculty intramural council that promotes participation by faculty and staff and provides total program support (Gunsten, 1967, p. 5).

Rivets points out a number of trends, including programming for faculty during the summer, faculty involvement in sports clubs, informal and family activities, and faculty clubs. He notes that summer programs are successful because student programs are minimal at this time; this serves to release the facilities for faculty and staff use. Demands on faculty and staff members' time are also reduced, and this results in greater time for recreational pursuits. Rivets sees sports club participation increasing. One result of this trend is that faculty and staff have a better chance of becoming involved in the administration of the clubs and thereby obtaining a voice in scheduling and conducting the programs and an opportunity to work with the students in these areas.

In schools with adequate facilities and services, informal participation is increasing. Faculty and staff may set up their own schedules and make their own arrangements for facilities and equipment. Another approach Rivets mentions is a faculty-staff club, which may offer opportunities such as tennis courts, swimming pools, handball and squash courts, sauna baths, and locker and dining facilities (1969, p. 56).

An article written in 1971 supports the idea that spouses and families of faculty and staff must all be provided opportunities for play. It suggests that some opportunities should be available for men and women jointly, some just for men, and some just for women (Hewatt, p. 41).

McGuire includes graduate students, faculty, and nonacademic staff in a co-recreational activities program designed to bring men and women together in a recreational atmosphere that includes a free-play program for informal leisure desires, an extensive club program, and unstructured clinics in various activities. He indicates that much-needed program support from university administrators can be fostered by their participation in a faculty-staff recreation program (McGuire, 1971, p. 33).

Mueller notes that members of the faculty and staff of an educational institution have the same needs and desires for physical recreation as students. He indicates that it is necessary to develop flexible scheduling patterns because of the unpredictability of faculty-staff professional commitments.

He suggests that faculty-staff sports clubs and fitness forums create and maintain interest in intramural participation, and that instruction may be provided for those who wish to learn or improve skills. Other methods that he suggests include distributing newsletters periodically, electing officers, and sponsoring award banquets and other social functions (1971, p. 34).

PROGRAM AREAS

By reviewing the literature, one can see that an extensive faculty-staff program should cover many areas, including the competitive, recreational, physical fitness, social, and family-oriented areas.

The competitive program involves scheduling faculty-staff teams in leagues and tournaments in a number of activities. Championships in various sports are played, and overall faculty-staff division champions are determined.

The recreational program involves providing opportunities for faculty and staff to participate in a variety of activities, indoors and outdoors, such as handball, paddleball, tennis, and jogging. Participation is self-initiated and program responsibility mainly involves providing facilities, either through reservation or on a first-come, first-served basis.

The physical fitness program may involve exercise classes, scheduled swim periods, scheduled jogging periods, or other forms of fitness, usually on a supervised basis and sometimes in conjunction with the health service of the institution.

The social program may involve recreational activities of a nonphysical nature, such as card playing, billiards, pool, or get-togethers after some physical activities.

Family-oriented programs include providing facilities, programming, and in many cases instruction in sports activities such as swimming, paddleball, tennis, and gymnastics for the children of faculty and staff. The program should also provide for families to participate together in a variety of activities.

PROGRAM COMMUNICATION

To provide a quality program, it is important to know the needs of the faculty and staff. A number of methods have proved successful in determining these needs. One method is the use of a questionnaire designed to provide the information needed. The questionnaire may also function as a publicity tool by bringing the existence of a program to the attention of all of the faculty and staff.

Another excellent method is to develop a faculty-staff intramural council with representation from various segments of the faculty-staff community. This council can provide the program director with first-hand information on the needs of the various faculty and staff groups.

It is also an effective vehicle through which program information can be disseminated to the faculty and staff.

The use of a suggestion box has proved successful in a number of institutions as a means of relaying information to the program director. In some institutions, suggestions and replies are posted on a bulletin board. This maintains interest in the use of the suggestion box and shows good faith on the part of the administration toward those who will take the time to make suggestions.

Perhaps the most successful method of communication is a periodic newsletter, which can be used to announce coming activities as well as covering results of various programs. A newsletter may be one of the most effective public relations methods that a faculty-staff programmer can use because it shows the program in action and because it helps provide important information about the needs of the program to those within the administration.

FACILITY USE

Some institutions look upon the faculty-staff program as a fringe, faculty benefit, in which programming and facility use are provided with no additional cost to faculty and staff members. In other institutions, a trend that appears to be gaining considerable acceptance is that of assessing faculty and staff a yearly user fee. Most faculty and staff are willing to pay a nominal fee for the opportunity to use facilities and to have a quality program provided them.

In many schools, handball courts, tennis courts, swimming pools, and other areas have been opened up for joint use of students and faculty-staff on a first-come, first-served basis. This has provided an opportunity for faculty-staff and students to participate together, which has proved enjoyable to both groups.

The concept of equality for all, including men and women and students and faculty-staff, appears to be the accepted and desired procedure in intramural programming. The practice of providing separate facilities and separate programming for students and faculty-staff no longer appears to be necessary, or indeed practiced. Although some activities and programs require separating these goups in most program areas, no priority for facility usage or progam planning is necessary.

TYPICAL PROGRAM

A sample faculty-staff program is presented below. It may be used as a guideline in the development or enlargement of a program.

A typical program in a large institution could involve a constituency of approximately fifteen to twenty thousand participants, including academic appointments, research assistants, administrative personnel, teaching assistants, and their families. A specific portion of the overall facility usage should be programmed for faculty-staff participation.

Competitive Program

The competitive program involves leagues and tournaments, with points awarded to teams representing departments. Sports organized into leagues, followed by a playoff, are awarded points ranging from 50 to 150, depending on place of finish. Elimination tournaments award between 35 and 100 points; the number is determined by the number of teams and/or places in the competition. Only the entry advancing the highest may earn points in any given sport for a department. If two partners on a team represent different departments, the highest earned point total for the team will be split equally between the two departments.

A faculty-staff sports calendar might be as follows:

First Semester:	Second Semester:
1. Softball	12. Basketball
2. Tennis (singles)	13. Volleyball
3. Golf	14. Bowling
4. Touch Football	15. Tennis (doubles)
5. Bowling	16. Handball (doubles)
6. Badminton (singles)	17. Paddleball (singles)
7. Paddleball (doubles)	18. Badminton (doubles)
8. Squash (singles)	19. Racquetball (singles)
9. Handball (singles)	
10. Volleyball	
11. Racquetball (doubles)	

Eligibility

All faculty, administrative staff, research assistants, and teaching assistants, and their families are eligible to compete in the faculty-staff division. Members may compete on teams from other departments, if they so desire.

Awards

Where the budget permits and the situation merits their use, individual or team trophies can be awarded to members of winning teams in each sport. The intramural department may also select one faculty-staff member each year to receive a faculty-staff intramural honor award. This individual is selected on the basis of sustained interest, athletic ability, participation, and leadership.

Fees

A $5.00-per-team fee, payable at the time of entering, is required for softball, touch football, basketball, and volleyball. There is no fee for entering individual or dual sports tournaments.

Equipment

Equipment for team sports will be provided by the department. Racquets and balls may be checked out at the equipment cage for a small rental charge. ID cards are required when checking out equipment.

Sports Club Program

Faculty-staff sports clubs can be established in such activities as tennis, squash, water polo, and sailing. Faculty and staff are also eligible to join any of the many student-sponsored sports clubs.

Informal Program

All recreational facilities are available for faculty and staff on an informal basis. These include facilities for jogging, gymnastics, swimming, conditioning, paddleball, handball, racquetball, squash, badminton, tennis, golf, and other activities.

Faculty-Staff/Student Competition

In each sport top performers from the various IM tournaments throughout the year are selected to represent both the faculty and staff and the students. The matches are selected to assure both a high skill level and an equal match for the participants. In scoring, one point is awarded to the winner of each match and no points to the loser. The total points are then tabulated to determine whether the faculty or the students have earned the higher overall score. Competition is held in tennis, softball, golf, paddleball (singles and doubles), squash, handball (singles and doubles), basketball, billiards, water polo, badminton, rifle shooting, and volleyball.

NEW DIRECTIONS

In addition to the regular faculty-staff programming, a number of interesting and exciting faculty-staff recreation facilities and programs have been developed in different areas of the country. Examples of these are a faculty-staff recreation association, a faculty-staff club, a faculty-staff women's program, a faculty-staff recreational site development, and a faculty-staff family recreation program.

Faculty-Staff Recreation Association

The University of North Carolina at Chapel Hill has witnessed the development of a faculty-staff recreation association involving a group of faculty-staff personnel who have united in an attempt to provide a high-quality and varied recreation experience for themselves and their families at a reasonable cost. The program includes instruction in certain sports and an opportunity for fun, fellowship, competition, and relaxation. The association is run by a board of directors and comprises about 550 members, who pay an initiation fee and low annual dues. The facility is operated by a manager and is located approximately three miles from the campus.

Faculty-Staff Club

At Michigan State University, land donated by the university and a donation from an alumnus provided the incentive for the development of a faculty-staff club. The club presently has approximately 1,100 family memberships, is located a mile from the campus, and is open to all faculty and staff and their children. The club includes tennis courts, shuffleboard courts, a pool, meeting rooms, a dancing area, a bar and grill, locker rooms and showers, and offices.

The club is operated by an elected board and a manager with a house committee. Initiation fees were originally $175 but have increased to $225, and there is a monthly charge of $30 per month per family. Instruction is available for swimming and tennis, and competition is provided with other clubs in the area. The club is used a great deal by young people with children, as well as by the older faculty-staff members, who enjoy the luncheon and card facilities.

Faculty-Staff Women's Program

Because of the limited number of women faculty and staff on most campuses, very little programming has been provided for this segment of the university family. At the University of Michigan, the Women's Division offers all university women—students, faculty, and staff, regardless of their ability—an extensive program of individual, dual, and team sports.

Competition is divided into two divisions: the Competitive Division for teams interested in a high degree of competition, with participation points and awards, and the Recreative Division for teams who desire organized competition at a more "recreative" level, with no participation points or awards. Individual and dual sports do not award team points. A woman may play on only one team in either the Competitive or Recreative Division in a given season.

Each team pays a $15 entry fee when entering its first sport. This fee covers all subsequent sports. If a team enters more than one team, each pays a separate fee. Green fees for golf and per-line costs for bowling are paid by the participant. Other all-campus events require no fees.

WOMEN'S SPORTS CALENDAR

Fall Term:	*Winter Term:*
1. Softball	13. Basketball
2. Tennis (doubles)	14. Paddleball (doubles)
3. Badminton (singles)	15. Badminton (doubles)
4. Water Polo	16. Bowling
5. Golf	17. Racquetball (singles)
6. Track (outdoor)	18. Swimming
7. Powder Puff Football	19. Foul Shooting
8. Cross Country	20. Track (indoor)
9. Ice Hockey	21. Table Tennis (doubles)
10. Paddleball (singles)	22. Tennis (singles)
11. Volleyball	23. Relays
12. Racquetball (doubles)	

A special instructional program is organized through a faculty women's group. Total membership has a potential of 3,000 persons. Ten special-interest sports groups are organized. The Intramural Department schedules facilities and helps find instructors for these groups. These groups can participate during morning hours, which eases the demand on facilities during "prime-time" afternoon and evening hours.

In addition to these organized and instructional programs, faculty and staff women are eligible for a number of co-recreational sports clubs and may use the facilities for open recreation, when available, by showing a faculty-staff ID card.

Faculty-Staff Recreational Site

Land and substantial development funds were donated to finance a faculty-staff recreational site, the initial development being an eighteen-hole golf course. Memberships are available to faculty and staff for $150 per individual or $200 per family, which includes all greens fees. Individual greens fees for guests are $10 per guest on weekends and $7.00 per guest weekdays. The golf course includes a pro shop and luncheon area. Locker rooms for men and women are presently being developed. Future development plans include a picnic site, tennis courts, swimming pool, bridle paths, and a nine-hole golf course.

Faculty-Staff Family Recreation Program

"The family that plays together stays together" is the motto of a faculty-staff family recreation program. Programs are held on Sunday afternoons from 1:30 to 5:30 P.M. Admittance is by presenting a membership card, which costs $20 per family for twenty sessions. Guests may be sponsored by member families for $1 per visit; families are limited to four guests per card, per session. Parents *must* accompany children and must remain with them during the sessions.

Activities include badminton, basketball, gymnastics, handball, paddleball, racquetball, table tennis, trampoline, squash, swimming, and volleyball. All equipment is furnished including lockers and towels.

ADMINISTRATIVE IMPLICATIONS

Greater emphasis on participation at all age levels for enjoyment as well as physical well-being has resulted in increased demands for programming and facilities within the university community. Intramural programming for faculty and staff and their families has become a major area of responsibility for intramural administrators.

Faculty-staff participation in the planning process of councils or committees will assist the program as well as gain support for it at the administrative level.

Esprit de corps and fitness are positive outcomes of a faculty-staff program. It is as important for faculty and staff to relieve themselves of academic pressures as it is for students.

A medically supervised faculty-staff fitness program that includes jogging and conditioning will enrich the program. Faculty-staff fitness forums create and maintain interest in the program.

Sports club participation by faculty and staff will continue to increase as faculty-staff members not only participate but become involved in the administration of these clubs.

Program areas should include a competitive program with leagues and tournaments, a recreational program with self-initiated activities, a physical fitness program with exercise classes and supervised fitness activities, and a family-oriented program including instruction for faculty-staff children as well as family participation.

Faculty-staff program needs can be determined through the use of a questionnaire, through a faculty-staff council, through a suggestion box, and through a periodic newsletter.

Faculty usage should be on a first-come, first-served basis, with recreational areas used jointly by students and faculty-staff. There should be equality for all, including men and women students and faculty and staff.

Where faculty-staff programs are not financed by the general funds of the university, a nominal user's fee has proved acceptable and helps provide a quality program.

New directions include the development of faculty-staff recreation associations, faculty-staff clubs, extensive faculty-staff women's programs, the development of faculty-staff recreational sites, and faculty-staff family recreation programs.

The job is there—are you willing to tackle it?

GENERAL BIBLIOGRAPHY

BUCHANAN, EDSEL, "Interpreting Intramurals to the Faculty," *The Physical Educator*, XXIII, No. 2 (May, 1966), 6.

DELON, E. E., "Intramural Sports for College Professors," *School and Society*, May, 1931, p. 30.

GRAMBEAU, RODNEY J., "Faculty-Staff Intramural Programming," *National Intramural Association Proceedings*, XXI (1970), 137–43.

————, "A Survey of the Administration of Intramural Sports Programs for Men in Selected Colleges and Universities in North and South America." Doctoral dissertation, University of Michigan, 1959.

GUNSTEN, PAUL, "Public Relations with Faculty and Administration," *National Intramural Association Conference Proceedings*, XVIII (1967), 5.

HEWATT, CAROLYN, "A Women's Viewpoint of Men's Intramurals," *National Intramural Association Proceedings*, XXII (1971), 41.

KLEINDIENST, VIOLA K., and ARTHUR WESTON, *Intramural and Recreation Programs for Schools and Colleges*. New York: Appleton-Century-Crofts, 1964.

LARSON, LORRAINE, and RONALD HYATT, "Faculty Recreation Programs," *Journal of Health, Physical Education and Recreation*, XXXII, No. 4 (April, 1961), 57.

LEAVITT, NORMA M., and HARTLEY D. PRICE, *Intramural and Recreative Sports for High School and College*. New York: Ronald Press, 1949.

MATTHEWS, DAVID O., "Family Recreation for University Faculty," *Journal of Health, Physical Education and Recreation*, XXXV, No. 3 (March, 1964), 33–35.

McGUIRE, R. J., "Comm-University Programming," *National Intramural Association Proceedings*, XXII (1971), 33.

MEANS, LOUIS E., *Intramurals: Their Organization and Administration*. Englewood Cliffs, N.J.: Prentice-Hall, 1973.

MEYERS, C. B., "The Product of Intramurals and Selling the Program to the Academic Faculty," *National Intramural Association Conference Proceedings*, X (1959), 6.

MITCHELL, ELMER D., *Intramural Sports*. New York: A.S. Barnes, 1939.

MUELLER, PAT, *Intramurals: Programming and Administration*, 4th ed. New York: Ronald Press, 1971.

MURPHY, M. OSBORNE, JR., "Faculty-Staff Programs," *National Intramural Association Conference Proceedings*, XVII (1966), 118–19.

RIVETS, RUSSELL L., "New Directions in Faculty Participation," *National Intramural Association Conference Proceedings* (1966), 56–59.

SLIGER, IRA, "A University Recreation Program," *National Intramural Association Conference Proceedings*, XXI (1970), 153.

15

Intramural Programming
for the Public School

THOMAS P. SATTLER
University of Illinois at Chicago Circle
Chicago, Illinois

In this chapter, an attempt will be made to provide the reader with an understanding of public schools, the transformation of educational objectives, and the emergence, development, and current status of intramural programs. Consideration will then be given to the types of administrative problems, organization of programs, current activities, and policies affecting participants. The final segment of the chapter is a discussion of the analysis and its implications for the practicing intramural director.

EVOLUTION OF PUBLIC SCHOOLS

Historical Background

During ancient times schools were virtually nonexistent. Sons of the rich men received private tutelage while the poor found themselves maturing in an atmosphere of slavery with no opportunity to learn how to read or write.

The available evidence indicates that the first schools originated in ancient Greece approximately 2,500 years ago. Students were males from families of nobility. Instruction was provided by one teacher, either in the instructor's home or in outdoor areas where the boys also had an opportunity to exercise. Girls, as well as the sons of the deprived class, were ineligible for formal schooling. The segregated process of education for the male elite was perpetuated throughout the Greek and Roman eras.

An addition was made to the formal process during the Middle Ages, but free equality of educational opportunity was still far from reality. The daughters joined the sons of the noblemen in the only schools that were available in Europe at this time—the monasteries and convents of the Roman Catholic Church. When the Church of England changed to Protestantism during the seventeenth century, isolated attempts were made by clergymen to open "public schools." These schools retarded, rather than advanced, equality of opportunity because they returned to a policy of educating the sons of rich families who could afford to pay tuition. In a broad sense, the title of "public schools" during this period was a misnomer.

During the Renaissance and the Age of Enlightenment there was a rebirth of emphasis on humanity instead of divinity, and a revolution was initiated to challenge the powers of the church and state. The classical languages were recalled, and the various philosophies of idealism, realism, and pragmatism offered various and sometimes conflicting views on the educational process. Despite the multiplicity of changes that were awakened and generated during this time, universality of educational opportunity in public schools was not realized.

Ever since the English colonists first landed at Plymouth Rock, there have been shouts for the implementation of democratic education. Unfortunately, this ideal did not become realized until the late nineteenth and early twentieth centuries in America. Colonial education was virtually dominated by the western European influence of denominational control and a prescribed curriculum. Students were not educated according to their abilities and interests, nor was anyone concerned with vocational training or the generation of new knowledge. It was important that knowledge be absorbed and not criticized by any student. Boys and girls from an assortment of socioeconomic backgrounds were afforded an elementary and secondary education. The girls rarely attended at either level. Public schools were provided for the paupers, but the majority of students received instruction from private tutors or district schools. The Law of 1647 required towns with fifty families to establish "grammar" or secondary schools (Rice, 1969, p. 138). The secondary schools continued their adherence to the policy of England and demanded tuition to support their operation.

The pendulum of thinking toward "public schools" moved in a

new direction after the Revolutionary War. American educators became impressed with the French ideals of more practical subjects, secular instead of denominational control, and increased centralization. The academy that stressed a utilitarian education for living replaced the grammar school that advocated educational preparation for the ministry. Coeducational experiences became more commonplace and denominational control rapidly lost its influence. Formal schooling was also provided for blacks.

The most radical swing of the pendulum occurred after the Civil War. This was due mainly to the industrial revolution, child labor laws, increased urbanizaion, compulsory attendance in public schools, and the German influence based on their scientific discoveries. The democratic ideal of free public schools for all was rapidly approaching reality.

The last swing of the pendulum, as we know it today, was a result of the resurgence of British influence regarding the education of the whole student. It was finally realized that "public schools" would never be effective in a democratic society unless they considered the needs, desires, and abilities of all students, regardless of their grade level or aspirations. Current thoughts by educators on the importance of education in a democratic society through the medium of public schools have been expressed as follows:

> In a democratic society, education has a unique place and quality, for democracy is not so much rule by majority as it is attaining "majority" through education, information, and free communication. Unlike dictatorial forms of government, democracy has everything to gain and nothing to lose from the intelligence of its citizens. Democracy is defined as the method whereby men and women from all walks of life gain confidence in themselves and their fellow humans, and thereby move from force to persuasion, from restriction to liberty, and from blind obedience to creative effort. (Ehlers and Lee, 1959, p. 2)

Classification of Public Schools Today

From this brief historical account, it should seem obvious that the term "public school" is a rather recent phenomenon, even though the title was used centuries ago. The word "public" by its very definition means "for the use or benefit of all." The word "school" pertains to a location where people come together to learn something. Although some people would consider institutions of higher learning as public schools, the term does not apply here, because everyone does not qualify for admission. In the broad sense, elementary, junior high, and high schools fall into this classification.

The elementary public schools are provided for children between the ages of five and eleven. Levels of education range from kindergarten through the sixth grade. The public junior high schools deal primarily with adolescents in the twelve-and thirteen-year-old range. Grade levels are seven and eight. Many communities also offer "middle schools," consisting of grades seven through nine. The public senior high school is a four-year institution consisting of grades nine through twelve. Students in these grades are commonly referred to as freshmen, sophomores, juniors, and seniors, respectively, and they range in age from fourteen to eighteen.

Transformation of Educational Objectives

The turn of the twentieth century not only marked the beginning of equitable educational opportunity, it also changed the emphasis of the objectives of the school. The most important transformation was in the nature of educational objectives. In the past, the traditional goal in the education of a child was adherence to a prescribed curriculum of formal discipline. The individual was perceived as possessing a mind that was capable of memory and reason. Educators agreed that these faculties could be disciplined through exercises. From this rationale, it logically followed that the objective of the school was to train the mind. The curriculum was concerned only with experiences that would provide the student with opportunities for reasoning and rote memorization. Latin was selected because the content was sufficiently difficult to tax the memory and was organizationally structured to allow utilization of the reasoning powers. The evaluation was simply a verbal regurgitation of the material that had been logically reasoned and remembered. The dualistic philosophy, with its insistence on separation of mind and body, could not conceive of bodily expression or activity as part of the process of formal discipline. Educational objectives were concerned with training only the mind, not the body. This theory has been termed "faculty psychology" (Sawrey and Telford, 1964, p. 240).

The concept of formal discipline was attacked and eventually abandoned shortly after the turn of the twentieth century. Educators challenged the retention and transfer of learning abilities of the children who had been educated by the traditional system. Mounting evidence confirmed that mere exercise of the mind to tax the memory and excite the reasoning abilities was a questionable practice, because most of the children in the elementary and secondary schools could not understand concepts when the same concepts were introduced from a different perspective. The only contributions that had been made by formal discipline (or faculty psychology) were the development of acceptable attitudes and feelings and the practice of acting properly.

Transfer of training became the objective of the school in the twentieth century. Simply stated, transfer of learning occurs between something that has been learned and something that is to be learned (Sawrey and Telford, 1964, p. 260). The concept received its greatest thrust from John Dewey's now legendary phrase, "learning by doing." The evidence that he publicized emphasized the reactions of the learner, not the teacher. In other words, learning could be evaluated in terms of what the learner was doing. The theory of transfer provided the crushing blow to the proponents of the dualistic philosophy who perceived of all education as mind training. The holistic view was a return to the Greek ideal that the mind and body are one. The new insistence on behavioral objectives was predicated on the assumption that education should include all individual reactions, such as knowledge, understandings, attitudes, and practices.

With the emphasis on the formal disciplining of the mind in schools during the nineteenth century, inroads were made into the curriculum by the advocates of bodily training. Just as the training exercises of memory and reasoning neglected the body, the early physical educators concentrated on a program of bodily development with total disregard for the intellect. Formal physical education during this era was termed "education of the physical" (Williams, 1930, pp. 279–82).

After the holistic view of the unity of mind and body was introduced during the early twentieth century, education of the physical was challenged as vigorously as faculty psychology. The new concept of physical education regarded the individual as an integrated or whole person. This concept was centered in Gestalt psychology, which stated that "the phenomenon we perceive is the whole and not the sum of the parts" (Thorpe and Schmuller, 1954, p. 205). More specifically, in regard to education it has been stated as follows:

> When mind and body were thought of as two separate entities, physical education was an education of the physical. In similar fashion, mental education made its own exclusive demands. With the understanding of the nature of the human organism in which wholeness of the individual is the outstanding fact, physical education becomes education through the physical. With this view, physical education has concern for and with emotional responses, personal relationships, group behaviors, mental learnings and intellectual, social, emotional and esthetic outcomes. (Williams, 1959, p. 2)

In order to effect the desirable behavioral objectives that were being sought for all students in the public schools, the English system of sports and games was selected by the proponents of the new philosophy. Sports and games were incorporated into the curriculum in the early 1900s to challenge formal gymnastics in the famous "Battle of the Systems" (Weston, 1962, p. 53). For two decades, the two systems coexisted in physical education programs. The battle ended after the termination of World War I, and sports and games emerged as the principal emphasis for future curriculums.

Up to this point, we have considered three major conflicts that have shaped the development of public schools as we know them today. First, universality of educational opportunity has finally been realized after a long struggle over the programs designed for the sons of nobility. Second, the faculty psychology of mental exercise has been abandoned in favor of behavioral objectives and transfer of learning. Third, the formal gymnastic system of physical training has been overshadowed by the view that "doing" requires "thinking"; therefore, the mind and body cannot be considered separate entities. The only remaining conflict in the operation of the public schools is between intramural and extramural sports.

Emergence and Development of Intramural Sports

The exact origin of intramurals is difficult to ascertain. Competitive tests of prowess can be traced chronologically from the ancient Olympic games through the chivalric games for squires during knighthood. Evidence is also available that impromptu games and contests were staged during the colonial period despite strict church rulings that prohibited such activity. In 1701, "His Majesties Justices" passed a law prohibiting footballs, squibs, and snowballs (Rice, 1969, p. 141). Any of these activities could have been intramural in nature. Competitive activity became more highly pronounced and structurally organized during the nineteenth century. Concentrating on formal discipline of the mind on one hand, and rigid bodily training through gymnastics on the other, school officials ignored the competitive instincts of their students during or after the school day. As a result, the students provided their own organization and scheduled their own contests. The idea became so popular by the twentieth century that the indifference of the school officials mutated into concern, and all programs were brought under school authority. Even though the original intent of the students was probably to provide a competitive outlet for everyone, the scope of the programs that were offered in the schools during the early part of this century resulted in varsity competition for only a few.

Although intramural activities were initiated on a small scale in public high schools in 1925, they did not begin to assume a major role in the secondary school until the intramural directors of the Western Intercollegiate Athletic Conference (the Big Ten) discussed high school intramural programs at their annual meeting in 1930 (Mueller, 1971, p. 18). Prior to this time, emphasis was placed on the development of interscholastic athletics. These interscholastic programs grew rapidly, but the development of athletics for everyone in the public school through intramural sports was only marginal.

After World War II, there was a new emphasis on the value of intramural sports in educational institutions. The war had demonstrated the importance of participation in sports. Physical activity was utilized as a means of training for the development of physical efficiency and teamwork. Wholesome social attitudes were also derived from the recreational programs that were made available here and abroad. A mutual conclusion was reached that intramurals should be afforded all students who did not possess the skills for extramural competition (Voltmer and Esslinger, 1958, p. 280).

In 1964 a group of educators and consultants were summoned to the Kellogg Continuing Education Center at Michigan State University to discuss a structural program of intramurals for the elementary, junior high, and senior high public schools. Three publications were released, one for each of the three levels. These publications dealt with a multiplicity of considerations and aspects of program operation and development (Athletic Institute, *Intramurals,* 1964, pp. 1–37).

Two years later, the National Intramural Sports Council was instituted as a coordinating structure of the Division of Men's Athletics and the Division of Girls' and Women's Sports of the American Association of Health, Physical Education and Recreation (AAHPER). Their sole mission was to generate intramural programs at all education levels.

The conflict between intramurals and extramurals in the public schools was finally brought to the attention of concerned educators in two position papers prepared and published in 1970 by the AAHPER as a national affiliate of the National Education Association. The first paper was directed specifically toward the upper elementary grades. The AAHPER recommended that interscholastics could be provided, but only after a sound physical education and intramural program had been established (AAHPER, 1970a). The second paper, which concerned high schools, recommended that intramural and interscholastic programs be equally available to all boys and girls, provided that a sound instructional program of physical education exists (AAHPER, 1970b).

The Current Status of Intramurals

Even though public schools throughout the nation cannot currently claim "intramural availability for everyone and everyone in intramurals," there is evidence that programs are developing, and the future looks optimistic. Someone once said, "An optimist is someone who sees an opportunity in every calamity; a pessimist sees calamity in every opportunity." Prognostications for the future of intramural sports in the public schools are not made in light of achieving such universal results. The conflicts that have been considered and the manner in which they have been resolved can only generate enthusiasm for more and newer possibilities.

Since the advent of universality of educational opportunity, we find that enrollments have increased drastically in the elementary and secondary schools. Figures were approximated in 1972 to be 36 million and 16 million, respectively. These figures prompted the Carnegie Commission on Higher Education to recommend in 1967 an "open-door policy" for junior colleges (Carnegie Commission, 1971, p. 22). The commission was concerned about postsecondary opportunities. At present, we must be concerned with youngsters who are still in public schools. A wide range of needs, abilities, and interests would seem to dictate variable, equal-opportunity programs. Intramural sports not only offer a wide variety of experiences, but are far reaching because they are available to everyone.

The transitions from mind training to transfer of learning, from a command style to a problem-solving style of teaching, and from bodily training to movement education have placed the public school student in a new light. They have also enhanced the importance of intramural sports. A youngster's knowledge, understandings, attitudes, and practices can be observed more readily when he or she is engaging in an intramural activity out of personal interest.

Available evidence would also indicate that the "golden age" of interscholastics is on the decline. Students are becoming more concerned with co-recreational experiences and with recognition that is based on active participation—not on passive observance. Athletes enjoy the games, but they are shying away from the long, grueling practices. At present, we are finding fewer students waving their pennants at varsity interscholastic events. Poor attendance is not indicative of decaying morality or rebellious spirits but is merely another reminder from students that "there are different strokes for different folks." Intramural sports are founded on this premise.

ANALYSIS OF INTRAMURAL STRUCTURE

In this second division of the chapter consideration is given to the various types of administrative problems, the organization of programs, current activities, and policies affecting participants.

Administrative Problems

Before any attempt can be made to advertise the availability or promote the participation of an intramural program, numerous factors must be weighed carefully. Success or failure is predicated largely on the director, available finances, facilities and equipment, a student leadership corps, an intramural council, health and safety aspects, insurance, the scope of the program, and time allotments in scheduling.

The Director.   A prerequisite for the success of any enterprise is competent leadership. It is assumed that the leader has been properly trained for the assigned responsibilities, possesses the talent to delegate authority, displays enthusiasm about the product, and is skillful in appealing to the interests of the potential user. It is further assumed that compensation will be adequate for duties rendered.

The enterprise in this case is the administration of intramural activities, and the leader is commonly referred to as the intramural director. Since the venture is concerned primarily with sports and games for public school students, the director should have an educational background in physical education or recreation. The director should be able to communicate effectively with superiors, colleagues, and subordinates. A commanding knowledge of the place of intramurals in education and the needs, abilities, and interests of students at a particular level should also be present. Compensation should take the form of a reduced class load or monetary remuneration that is comparable to the stipend received by a head coach in the interscholastic program.

The present practice in the majority of the public schools is to appoint a physical educator or coach as the director. The director is answerable to the chairman of physical education in the larger school districts and to the principal in the smaller schools. Other schools employ municipal recreation directors or an individual from another academic area within the school who possesses an interest and background in sports.

Finances.   There is little disagreement among public school directors that the most desirable approach to financing a program is a specific allocation from the school board. The most logical argument for this type of budgetary consideration is accountability. This approach will discourage the practice of misappropriation of funds, which is common when many programs derive their revenue from a department budget. A second justification for individual program allocations is the position of importance that is derived. Securing finances from supplemental sources such as car washes, bake sales, and raffles is demeaning because it attaches a "second-class citizen" stigma to the program.

The cost of program operation for intramurals is minimal when one considers the vast population of students that the program is designed to serve. School administrators and boards of education probably realize more benefits to pupils per dollar invested in a well-planned and well-directed intramural program of sports than in almost any other activity in which pupils participate (Brammell, 1932, p. 63). Finances are required merely in order to pay for leadership, equipment survey and repair, use of community facilities as needed, and supplies that are essential to record keeping, officiating, and promotion. It is recommended that students not be charged for participation in the program unless community centers are utilized.

Facilities and Equipment. Probably the greatest deterrent to "intramurals for everyone and everyone in intramurals" is the lack of activity areas and suitable equipment. State evaluators who have questioned administrators about poor-quality programs or the lack of intramural opportunities have often heard the justification, "We just don't have the facilities or equipment."

Fortunately, the situation is improved in many quarters by school boards that understand the need for intramurals and are encouraging the development of new facilities and allocating funds for intramural equipment. It is also encouraging to note that many innovative directors are seeking the use of supplemental facilities located in neighboring communities, such as parks, ice rinks, church assembly halls, and commercial recreational centers. In New York City, for example, intramural activity can be observed on the roof tops of certain buildings.

All we really need to become operational within the schools is a main gymnasium, a multipurpose room, hard-surfaced playgrounds, and a parking lot or reasonably level barren land surrounding the institution. Since intramurals is an outgrowth of physical education, a stern look must be taken at the sports and activities that are being offered in physical education classes. Joint school and community planning can also enrich opportunities and can eliminate the redundancies in trying to create programs in facilities that currently exist to meet the needs of district inhabitants.

Equipment should be purchased on the basis of durability. Stencils should be prepared to properly identify each item according to program by means of a sequential numbering system. Inventory lists should correspond with the identification system, and periodic examinations of the various items should be conducted to ascertain safety or need for replacement. The most basic inventory would include bats, bases, vertical uprights, mats, nets, and various types of balls and rackets.

Student Leadership Corps. The success of the program can be correlated with a multiplicity of variables. In terms of the participants, the most important variables are the degree to which the students understand the opportunities that are available, the rules and regulations of participation, the score during competition, and their individual or team standings throughout the course of the various tournaments. The director cannot meet these needs alone.

Many schools have adopted a student leadership corps or managerial program. Regardless of the term employed, the intent of the leadership program is to activate the plan that has been designed by the director. The use of students in authoritative positions is sound from an educational standpoint. The experiences involved in this type of assignment include organizational planning, policy making, public relations, and respect for equipment, and they afford the opportunity for the leaders to gain recognition. Leaders can be derived by a vote from the student body, from an honors class in physical education, or by selecting the top performers in intramurals of the previous year. The organizational structure of responsibilities and the number of leaders will be determined largely by the size of your institution and the scope of the program. You may also wish to establish a hierarchy of command by appointing student directors in certain areas of responsibility; the student leaders would be directly responsible to these individuals. The various duties that will be assigned to the student directors include:

1. Inventory, care, and distribution of equipment.
2. Record keeping.
3. Tournament promotion.
4. Scoring, officiating, and judging.
5. Organization of groups into teams.
6. Notifying students of schedules, postponements, and forfeits.
7. Supervision of activity areas to check for safety hazards.

Intramural Council. An intramural council can function in two ways. First, it increases the efficacy of organizing and administrating the program. Second, it is an integrative approach that can enhance support by everyone in the school. The council could consist of an educational administrator, the chairman of physical education, the athletic director, faculty members, student government, student directors, student leaders, and the director of intramurals.

Health and Safety Aspects. Every physical activity involves a certain amount of risk. Some games and sports are more hazardous than others because they involve more vigorous activity and bodily contact. A simple solution would be to remove the risk activities but then we would be depriving the youngsters who enjoy such challenging contests. And even if these activities were removed from the program, youngsters might engage in them on their own, thus opening themselves to greater risk of injury. The answer is found in the removal or control of the risk factors, not the termination of activity.

Before we consider the risk factors, it is important to recall that intramural administration is charged with a legal and moral responsibility for promoting sound health practices and safeguarding the welfare of its participants. In law, the term "tort liability" encompasses a large variety of acts causing unreasonable interference with the rights and interests of others. Compensation is rendered to the individual for damage to person, property, or reputation (Prosser, 1941, p. 8). One form of tort liability is negligence. Negligence is a breach of legal duty causing damage, which, though unintentional, should have been reasonably foreseeable (Van Der Smissen, 1968, p. 51). In order for the injured party to collect for damages, the tort, or wrongful act due to negligence, involves proof of four essential elements: (1) the actor had a duty to avoid unreasonable risks to others; (2) the actor failed to conform to the standard required or failed to observe the duty; (3) there was a connection between the actor's conduct and the resulting injury to the other party; and (4) damage actually resulted (Fahr, 1958, p. 12). Based on this type of liability and these four essential conditions, the law imposes an obligation on teachers acting as intramural administrators to perform as a reasonably prudent and well-trained teacher would act under similar circumstances. Simply stated, a director should attempt to remove as many risks as possible for the participants. The most common sources of negligence are inadequate instruction, improper supervision, defective or absent equipment, and failure to administer proper first aid (*Ibid.*, p. 76).

Evidence seems to indicate that the highest number of injuries in public schools occur in physical education, intramurals, and varsity athletics (Voltmer and Esslinger, 1958, p. 451). Of 168 legal cases involving pupils from public schools in 1941, 76 involved the departments of health and physical education (Poe, 1941, p. 5). In 1956, reports were more encouraging. Accident records indicated that even though participation had increased, the incidence rate was dropping. The downward trend was attributed to safety consciousness, improved equipment, closer supervision, and enlightened leadership (Grambeau, 1956, p. 151). In 1972, an area survey in Michigan found intramural accidents minimal in comparison with those in interscholastics and physical education. In the words of one school administrator, "We have so few injuries it is not worthy of mention" (Dzenowagis and Sierra, 1972, p. 65).

Returning to the removal and control of risks, it is safe to assume that the downward trend will continue if the following precautions are taken:

1. Medical examinations for the participants.
2. Close supervision and inspection of play areas and equipment.
3. Utilization of activities that have been properly taught in physical education classes.

4. Use of protective equipment.
5. Good officiating, emphasizing the rules and regulations of the game.
6. Maintenance of proper lighting, heating, and ventilation.
7. Modification of the activity to avoid overcrowding and inappropriate play areas.
8. Utilization of weight classifications in sports such as wrestling.
9. Spotting in gymnastics, tumbling, and stunts.
10. Providing the necessary first aid and transportation for emergencies.

Insurance. In the past, school districts were immune from suits due to negligence because they were protected by the doctrine of governmental immunity. This doctrine's origin traces back to England and the divine rights of kings, which claimed that the "king can do no wrong." After the American War of Independence, the doctrine was maintained in the United States for governmental units at the federal, state, and local levels. Since a school functions as a governmental agency, it was immune to tort liability, regardless of the negligence committed. The doctrine remained unchallenged until the middle of the twentieth century.

Since 1960, the immunity doctrine has been challenged in courts of law. There are two overriding considerations in the decisions being made today. First, there is a moral obligation to provide redress for a party who is injured due to another's negligence. Second, there must be protection for the schools from unreasonable claims, which could unduly deplete the financial resources. Liability insurance provides the solution for the latter problem (Van Der Smissen, 1968, p. 37).

There is always the possibility that accidents will occur as a result of negligence, regardless of the precautions that are taken to remove risks. Schools are encouraged to provide liability insurance for their staff members, and it is recommended that accident insurance be maintained by the parents or schools for their children who are responsible for their own injuries.

Scope of the Program. Many schools claim that an intramural program is available for their students. In many of these instances the term "intramural" is a misnomer, because the activities are predominantly male-oriented, the needs, abilities, and interests of all the students within the school have not been considered, and the handicapped students are either avoided or are relegated to the tasks of timing, scoring, or observing. When the program is thus limited in scope, the conflicts between boys and girls and between handicapped and nonhandicapped, in terms of opportunities to participate, are as real as the conflict between intramurals and extramurals.

Intramurals are by nature designed to be all-inclusive, with unlimited potential and varying opportunities. The intramural program is not the "farm club" for interscholastic athletics or an arena for the sports and games that are the prominent interests of the director. In order to be all-inclusive, the offerings must appeal to both sexes, to both skillful and poorly coordinated players and to the trainably, educably, and multiply handicapped. Very few experiences during the school day include the various segments of the school population in social encounters. Development and display of skill is secondary to the atypical child who is provided the opportunity to develop camaraderie with classmates as a team member. This is not to advocate the inclusion of all students in all activities in the program. Certain activities, by their design, are not compatible with the restricted mobility caused by certain handicaps.

Time Allotments in Scheduling. There are two major difficulties in the task of time allotments in the scheduling of intramural activities. First, there is usually a busing problem for elementary and junior high school students. Second, the age-old problem of interscholastic priorities continues to plague directors at the junior and senior high levels.

Commitment to a bus schedule severely restricts the amount of time that is available outside the regular schedule of classes. Simply stated, intramural opportunities are contingent on the availability of the students. If students aren't there, they can't participate. Boards of education frown on long bus schedules because they entail an appreciable increase in operating expenses. Isolated attempts are being made to provide such service, but the practice is minimal in relation to the number of districts utilizing the busing system.

It is becoming more difficult to justify interscholastic priority for the use of facilities, in light of lower attendance at games and fewer varsity participants; nevertheless, the situation remains unchanged. Intramural directors find themselves having to work around interscholastic practices and games, rather than receiving equal consideration from those who plan all activities in the school. This seems ironic, since the intramural program appeals to a larger number of students than all interscholastic sports can ever hope to attract.

The ideal time for scheduling is still thought to be the end of the school day. If that time is not available or if it is insufficient to meet the demands of the program, the director may consider any of the following:

1. Before school: Parents and administrators prefer supervised activity for the children who are scheduled for early arrival. It is a more useful antidote than crowded halls or idleness for the hyperactive youngster.

2. Noon hour: Schools that provide lunch hours in excess of thirty minutes

could stagger lunch and physical activity. At present, most youngsters finish their lunch in fifteen minutes and join the mammoth crowds in the gymnasium or playgrounds in the fight to get the only available ball.

3. Activity hour: Schools could establish the practice of providing an activity hour for the child during the school week. Each day, one fifth of the student population would have an hour for intramural participation. Students who did not wish to participate could work as officials, observe the games, visit the library, or work on a project in the laboratory.

4. Physical education class: After the instruction, drills, and relays of the class, a small portion of time could be allocated for competition. This approach is recommended only if no other time slots are available.

5. Vacation periods: Short tournaments could be held on school grounds at this time. Conflicts over the use of facilities at this time should be minimal.

6. Odd-hour scheduling: Activity can be offered on Saturdays or Sundays.

7. "Eternal" programs: This system is effective when use of facilities and available time is severely limited. The students sign up for the activity and are given available time periods during which they may compete. Each participant then contacts his opponent, and the two mutually decide on a time. This system is particularly suited for dual sports.

8. Lighted schoolhouse programs: Participants can return to school after the dinner hour.

Organization of Programs

After the administrative problems have been carefully considered, the next stage in the development of the intramural structure is the organization of the program. This includes determining the needs, interests, and abilities of the students, establishing competitive units, classifying for equalization, and selecting the types of competition.

Needs, Interests, and Abilities. Program planning is much more complex in the public schools than in the junior colleges or universities due to the disparate growth patterns of students, particularly those in the intermediate elementary, junior high, and senior high grades. Successful implementation of a program requires an understanding of the particular student population. In this discussion of the various developmental levels, the reader must keep in mind that the abilities, needs, and interests of youngsters do not change drastically from one age to the next. An attempt is being made merely to approximate the traits at the various stages.

The elementary school child ranges in age from six to eleven. Intramural programming relates primarily to the intermediate grades—four through six—because the primary child—grades one through three—has relatively low endurance, a short interest span, and muscular control confined to large-movement activity. His activity urge is strong, but he fatigues rather quickly. Furthermore, primary children exhibit competitive spirit but are not emotionally prepared to respond rationally in play or social activities. Anger, fear, or temper tantrums may be displayed when they are under pressure. The interests at this level are mimicking others and engaging in small-group activity among members of one's own sex. In contrast, the intermediate child displays better endurance, is more receptive to practice for the acquisition of skills, and is beginning to develop manipulative muscular control. Furthermore, he exhibits a strong desire for group membership. Emotional and mental maturity is more sophisticated, and the child will conform to group standards out of fear of peer ostracism. At this stage, there is a need for competition in low-organized team games and in individual contests of speed, strength, and tumbling.

The junior high student experiences a rapid growth in muscular, skeletal, and organic development. New interests are developed for the opposite sex, stress activities, and best friends instead of gang memberships. The desire for competition in more highly organized games is so keen that individuals may continue participation beyond the fatigue point. Development of manipulative skills is more pronounced. The students in this age bracket could assist in program planning and policy making. Activity should be offered in individual, dual, and team sports, and allowance should also be made for co-recreational opportunities.

A desire for adult status is particularly evident in senior high school students when they achieve the sophomore grade level. In most cases, the awkward stage of an earlier age is replaced by improved coordination, complete bone growth, and the termination of the puberty cycle. Conformity to peer influences is much more significant than response to adult guidance. There is a desire for adult status, but not adult responsibilities. Girls are more mature than boys of the same age, but boys are usually taller and stronger. Young adults in high schools need highly competitive games for the release of excess energy. There is also a need for co-recreational experiences and for skill-oriented activities that will provide an opportunity for recognition.

Competitive Units. A wide range of possibilities exists for the natural organization of competitive units in the public schools. The availability of predetermined participation or organization groups will depend largely on the grade level of the participants, size of enrollment, geographic location, and the types of activities offered. Utilization of a natural breakdown will enhance communication, develop *esprit de corps,* and provide opportunities for recognition within each unit. Here are some examples of competitive units:

1. Classes or Grade Levels: This type of unit can be found in any educational institution. It is particularly suited for schools that have two or more classes at a specific grade level. In the larger schools, numerous teams can be formed at a specific level and names can be adopted for identification. Competition between different grade levels, such as fourth and sixth, is not encouraged because the younger group will usually be handicapped by a relative lack of physical development.

2. Physical education classes or sections: If few opportunities are available within the school due to scheduling or facility limitations, this type of unit is possible. Take care, though, that the physical education class does not become merely an intramural program. In the larger schools, many sections of physical education classes may be found at the same grade level and may be involved in the same instructional sport or game. Competitive units can be made of these sections.

3. Homerooms or divisions: This unit is usually found in larger schools that do not have self-contained classrooms. Students are brought together in the homerooms to hear announcements about educational programs or school activities, among other things. There are usually enough members to provide an assortment of representative teams.

4. Clubs or special-interest groups: Many schools provide students with the opportunity to organize special-interest clubs. Examples include math, art, biology, and church clubs. Care should be taken to avoid extreme group rivalries, which could obviously have a deleterious effect on the program.

5. Interscholastic athletes: Competitive units can be formed of athletes whose sport is not in season.

6. Performance groupings: As a result of classification and tests of skills, competitive units can be formed from various ability groups. Such groups would be ranked at "A," "B," or "C" levels of competition, for example.

7. Make-up teams: Captains can be appointed to select among individuals who desire to compete and have signed the roster. Provision should be made for students on the roster who are not selected.

Classification for Equalization. Even though some sports and activities do not pose a safety threat due to age, height, and weight differences, there are many contests in which the incidence of injury can increase if the groups are heterogeneous. The alert director will assess the risk potential of the various offerings and strive for homogeneity where it is warranted.

Types of Competition. Another consideration in the organization of the program is the selection of the types of competition that would be most appropriate for your particular program. Some activities are conducive to tournaments, others require leagues, and still others are more suitably organized by combinations. Selection is based on type of activity, availability of facilities, degree of competition desired, and anticipated number of participants. A well-organized program will include elimination tournaments, leagues, perpetual challenges, and variable combinations.

The most common forms of elimination tournaments are the single and double elimination. In the single elimination, the participant continues to compete until he loses or until he defeats all the other entrants. Competition is in the form of brackets based on a power of two—2, 4, 8, 16, 32, and so on. The double elimination tournament provides a second chance for the loser. The competition starts as in the single elimination tournament. But when a participant loses a match in the winners' bracket, he is placed in the losers' bracket for another chance against the other losers. A defeat in the losers' bracket constitutes elimination. If the loser defeats everyone in the losers' bracket, he faces the winner of the winners' bracket. Since the winner of the winners' bracket has not lost, the winner of the losers' bracket must defeat his opponent twice.

Single and double round robins are the principal types of league competition. Individuals or teams can compete against every other entrant either once or twice. Leagues are not the same as tournaments because no one is eliminated in league play. The winners are determined from final standings based on wins and losses. This form of competition is particularly suited for high-interest activities. The greatest disadvantages are the amount of time required for competition and forfeits resulting when individuals or teams become disinterested due to an appreciable number of losses.

A variety of perpetual-challenge tournaments are available. The two types commonly used are the ladder and pyramid. Competition commences after players are randomly assigned to a position. In the ladder (Figure 1), a player may challenge those who are one or two rungs above. For example, player C can challenge either B or A. If C defeats either one, the two positions on the ladder are exchanged. A player must play one match each week or he automatically drops to the next lower level. In the pyramid (Figure 2), any player in position E can challenge any D, the Ds can challenge the Cs, and so on. After a determined period of time, the player who is occupying the A position is declared the winner.

The combinations can be formed according to the design of the director. For some sports, it may be beneficial to use heats to reduce the number of entrants to the best performers, who compete in a final heat. A top percentage of individuals or teams from round-robin leagues may be placed in single or double elimination playoffs. An innovative director can formulate an endless number of possibilities to meet the objectives of the program.

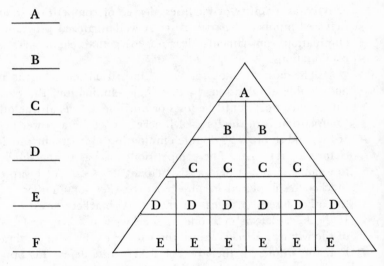

Figure 1. Ladder   **Figure 2.** Pyramid

Types of Activities

We have already discussed the needs, interests, and abilities of youngsters in the public school at various developmental levels. In Tables 1 and 2 recommended activities are listed for the elementary and the junior and senior high grades.

Policies Affecting Participants

Since the main function of the program is to serve the participants, certain policies must be firmly established to insure enjoyable participation. The intramural department is responsible for controlling undesirable practices that adversely affect program operation and the rights and privileges of qualified competitors. The policies should be constantly stressed, adequately enforced, and subject to change as the situation warrants. In this section of the chapter many guidelines will be recommended.

Eligibility. Any individual who is enrolled in a particular public school is eligible for competition within that institution as long as he or she is not subject to any disqualifying factors: Ineligibility results from:

1. Lack of parental approval: elementary school administrators require parental consent for children in grades four through six.
2. Competition in a varsity sport during its active season.

Table 1. Elementary Program (grades 4–6)

Activity	Girls Only	Boys Only	Coed	Individual and Dual	Team	Indoor	Outdoor
Aerial Darts			X	X			X
Archery			X	X		X	X
Badminton			X	X		X	X
Bowling			X		X	X	
Basketball (one-on-one)	X	X		X		X	
Basketball (ten-count)	X	X			X	X	
Bat Ball			X		X	X	X
Cage Ball			X		X	X	X
Checkers			X	X		X	X
Croquet			X	X			X
Dart Games			X	X	X	X	
Free Throws	X	X		X		X	
Hand Hockey			X		X	X	X
Horseshoes	X	X		X			X
Kickball	X	X	X		X	X	X
Kite Flying			X	X			X
Marbles			X	X		X	X

Table 1. (cont.)

Activity	Girls Only	Boys Only	Coed	Individual and Dual	Team	Indoor	Outdoor
Newcomb			X		X	X	
Paddle Tennis			X	X		X	X
Relays			X		X	X	X
Roller Skating			X	X		X	
Rope Jumping	X			X		X	X
Shuffleboard			X	X		X	X
Soccer (modified)	X	X			X	X	X
Softball (modified)	X	X	X		X	X	X
Speedball (modified)	X	X			X	X	X
Stunts and Tumbling	X	X	X	X		X	
Swimming Events			X	X		X	
Table Tennis			X	X		X	
Tennis			X	X		X	X
Tetherball			X	X		X	X
Track and Field Events	X	X			X	X	X
Tug of War		X			X	X	X
Volleyball			X		X	X	X

Table 2. Junior-Senior High Programs

Activity	Girls Only	Boys Only	Coed	Individual and Dual	Team	Group	Indoor	Outdoor
Achievement Tests	X	X	X	X			X	X
Archery	X	X	X	X			X	X
Badminton			X	X			X	X
Baseball		X	X		X			X
Basketball	X	X	X		X		X	
Billiards			X	X			X	
Bowling			X		X		X	
Canoeing			X			X		X
Checkers			X	X			X	X
Chess			X	X			X	X
Cross-Country Runs	X	X	X	X	X		X	X
Curling			X				X	
Cycling			X			X		X
Deck Tennis			X	X			X	X
Field Ball			X		X			X
Field Hockey	X	X			X	X		X
Fishing			X					
Floor Hockey	X	X			X		X	
Free Throws	X	X		X			X	

Table 2. (cont.)

Activity	Girls Only	Boys Only	Coed	Individual and Dual	Team	Group	Indoor	Outdoor
Golf	X	X		X				X
Gymnastics	X	X		X			X	
Handball	X	X		X			X	
Hiking			X			X		X
Horseback Riding			X			X		X
Horseshoes	X	X		X				X
Ice Hockey		X			X		X	X
Ice Skating			X			X	X	X
Kickball			X		X		X	X
Lacrosse		X			X			X
Newcomb			X				X	X
Paddle Tetherball			X	X			X	X
Paddle Tennis	X	X	X	X			X	X
Physical Fitness	X	X	X	X			X	X
Quoits			X	X			X	
Roller Skating			X			X	X	
Rope Climbing		X		X			X	
Scuba Diving			X			X	X	

Table 2. (cont.)

Activity	Girls Only	Boys Only	Coed	Individual and Dual	Team	Group	Indoor	Outdoor
Shuffleboard			X	X			X	X
Skiing			X			X		X
Soccer	X	X			X			X
Softball	X	X	X		X			X
Speedball	X	X			X			X
Swimming	X	X	X	X			X	
Table Tennis			X	X			X	
Tetherball		X	X	X			X	X
Tennis	X	X	X	X				X
Touch Football		X			X			X
Track and Field	X	X	X	X				X
Tug of War		X	X		X		X	X
Tumbling	X		X	X			X	
Volleyball			X		X		X	
Water Polo		X			X		X	X
Weight Training		X		X			X	
Wrestling		X		X			X	

3. Lack of a medical examination within the past two years.
4. Suspension due to a gross violation of the rules.

In addition, students who compete on one team are ineligible for participation on another team within the same activity.

Postponements. Every attempt should be made to adhere to the assigned schedule. Unnecessary delays and cancellations will not only frustrate the anxious participants, but may create new scheduling difficulties. Unavoidable postponements should be made only by the director. Announcements concerning delays and rescheduling can be made available to the participants on a bulletin board in a central location of the school.

Forfeits. There are two basic types of forfeits. The first is awarded when an individual or team member who is ineligible for competition participates. The second type involves individuals or teams who fail to arrive for competition within a prescribed time limit, due to indifference or to lack of knowledge of the scheduled event because of poor communication by the administration. Indifference is more serious, because it displays a lack of respect for the opposition. In this case, a forfeit is automatically awarded to the individual or team in attendance. When participants are not available due to communicative error, the situation is subject to review and possible rescheduling. A conscientious leader can help prevent this type of situation by posting the schedule and notifying the participants before the contest.

Protests. Individuals are entitled to dissent from decisions that are contrary to the rules. The protest should be made immediately. If the official refuses to rescind the decision, and if there is clear indication that the decision was wrong, the protesting captain can appeal to the director. Protests should not be considered on judgment calls, only on misinterpretation of the rules. It is recommended that all protests be submitted in writing. The emphasis of the report should be on the action leading to the decision that was rendered and on the decision that should have resulted. The director should review the situation with the game official and answer the protest within a twenty-four-hour period.

Officiating and Record Keeping. Program success and participant enjoyment are largely contingent on the selection and training of the officials and record keepers. In the elementary schools it may be necessary to utilize teachers and volunteer parents in the more highly organized games. Officials and record keepers may also be drawn from the interscholastic athletes in junior and senior high schools. Regardless of the solution, workshop training is vital. There should be numerous training sessions prior to the commencement of each sport season.

During the contests, officials should be attired so as to be clearly distinguishable from the players. Every attempt must be made to utilize scoreboards, so that the results during the contest can be seen. The results of the contest should be recorded immediately after the termination of each activity.

Rule Modifications. There are many instances in a particular school setting when the inherent dangers of interscholastic sport must be overlooked because certain rules that have been established for that sport cannot be met. This is not the case in intramurals. Any sport, game, or activity can be modified to protect the safety of the participant, adapted to the existing facilities, or economized on the duration of the contest as long as the contestants are aware of the alterations. The only word of caution is to avoid modifications so drastic that the nature of the sport is changed.

IMPLICATIONS FOR THE INTRAMURAL DIRECTOR

In the first segment of this chapter, we examined the evolution of public schools into what they are today, the transformation of the psychological bases of educational objectives, the new emphasis in physical education, and the emergence, development, and current status of intramural programs. The second segment of the chapter treated administrative problems, program organization, recommended activities, and the policies that affect the participants. The last segment of this chapter focuses on controversial issues facing intramural directors. Certain issues have been purposefully avoided thus far in our discussion because they involve traditions that are currently subject to controversy at professional meetings of directors. These controversial issues will be discussed, as will promising new trends in activities, effective promotional aids, and program evaluation.

Controversial Issues

Point Systems and Awards. At the 1972 National Intramural Conference, opposition to the use of a point system was reported in the form of a position paper (Curry, 1972, p. 59). Even though the attack was directed toward the colleges, the concept is just as applicable to the public schools. The speaker's major premise was that "a well-planned opportunity for play makes a successful program, not a well-planned system for making points" (*Ibid.,* p. 60).

The use of a point system is negative when the participants are extrinsically motivated to gaining points instead of intrinsically motivated to gain enjoyment and realize the objectives of the program. Directors in the public schools need to reassess the value of points and awards when it is obvious that ineligible participants are being utilized, rivalries are being created, and the safety of individuals is not being safeguarded. As an example of the latter, a nonswimmer was entered in a relay race so that his team would gain necessary points in a swimming competition. The fact that a drowning may have occurred was incidental.

On the positive side, "points offer a system of giving awards" (Endres, 1971, p. 103). Another writer has stated that "valid point systems are measurements of athletic progress just as school grades are an indication of academic standing" (Pederson, 1963, p. 58). In this book, an entire chapter is devoted to awards and participation incentives. The author of this chapter is merely attempting to alert the public school director to the problems that can be created if the point system is not objectively based, educationally sound, and carefully scrutinized.

Relationship of Intramurals to Physical Education and Athletics. The intramural director has assumed the position of defense for more years than anyone cares to remember. In many school systems, when money, facilities, and time are allotted, physical education receives top priority, interscholastics are second, and the remains go to intramurals. Fortunately, the rather recent emergence of many outstanding intramural programs has prompted school administrators and boards of education to reassess existing inequities.

Physical education, intramurals, and interscholastics are designed to complement rather than aggravate each other. In physical education, the student is exposed to the various skills involved in individual, dual, and team sports. Intramurals supplement the physical education curriculum and provide the opportunity for everyone to compete according to their individual interests and abilities. Students who possess a high degree of skill and interest in a sport have the interscholastic program available to them. It should seem obvious that the administrators of the three programs are in positions of equal stature and should work together, since service to the student is their mutual consideration.

Professional Growth of the Director. It is alarming to note that most intramural directors happen into the position. Most physical educators who graduate from college aspire to teaching and coaching, not to intramural positions. It was reported in 1965 that 34.2 percent of the colleges and universities sampled offered a course in intramural sports, but only 40 percent of that number required the course to be taken (Cable, 1965, pp. 77–83). However, there are signs of encouragement on the horizon, particularly in the public schools, where federally financed projects are making it possible for intramural leaders to operate without major diversions that distract from their leadership (Means, 1972, p. 379). For example in Fort Worth, Texas, a city director, working with the superintendent and board of education, has been able to add a trained intramural coordinator for each district middle school and senior high school. Salaries are derived from a special budget allocated for that purpose (*Ibid.*, pp. 379–80).

Intramural directors can enhance their professional growth in various ways. There are opportunities to achieve a master's degree in intramural sports, develop workshops and clinics among various public school districts, attend national conferences, subscribe to proceedings, and "tune in" to the suggestions of the National Intramural Sports Council.

New Trends in Intramural Activities

Just as teachers and educational administrators are charged with the responsibility of seeking new content and techniques for the enrichment of the educational program, intramural directors have a mutual obligation to incorporate new activities that aid in the development of youngsters toward the ideals that are established in a changing society. Here are some ideas that are worthy of the director's consideration.

Giant Gym Nights. Leisure time in this day and age is at a maximum for the students as well as their parents. Families spend more time in front of television sets than in activities that could bring them and other members of the community closer together. The school can serve as an effective agency to accomplish this task. On Friday evenings, the school could be opened for intramural family activity. Fathers, mothers, brothers, sisters, boyfriends, and girlfriends can engage in activity of an impromptu nature. Opportunities are unlimited for recreational swimming, jogging, social dance, tugs of war, mass volleyball games, sports club instruction, fitness programs and so forth.

Physical Fitness Through Intramurals. At the twentieth national intramural conference, the author presented a program of fitness through intramurals. Although the program was presented for the colleges, it is also applicable to junior and senior high schools.

The activity consists of two phases: Phase I is the "timed circuit" and Phase II is the "individual event."

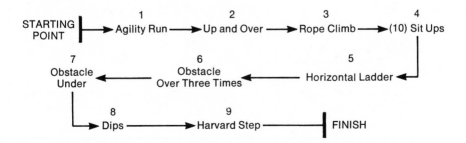

The purpose of Phase I is to serve as a physical conditioner and classification process for Phase II. All participants are timed from the start to the finish. The resulting times are equitably divided to produce three divisions. The top 25 percent of each division compete in Phase II as "A," "B," and "C" level competitors, respectively. The Phase II program consists of an objectively measured physical fitness test. The items consist of push-ups in a handstand position, sit-ups on 45-degree-incline board, chin-ups, a peg board climb, and a 250-yard run.

Sports Clubs. Sports that are not available for the skilled and interested students in the interscholastic program can be made available through intramurals. Sponsorships could be provided by a volunteer teacher, parent, or individual from the community. Competition could take place between schools in the district. Since the clubs are intramural in nature, rule modifications can be applied as the situation warrants.

Record Days. In the various sports, games, and activities that are based either on successful attempts or established times, students are given an opportunity to demonstrate their skill and break the existing records. This approach is particularly applicable to the intermediate elementary and junior high grades, levels at which youngsters are intrinsically motivated to practice their skills. The competitive days are designed as a means of evaluation. Records for each grade level are established and centrally posted. Some possibilities are:

1. Times in track events.
2. Times in swimming events.
3. Rope climb.
4. Number of free throws and lay-ups.
5. Passing a ball through a target.
6. Throwing for distance.
7. Kicking for distance.

Promotional and Communicative Aids

The following is a list of motivational, communicative, and promotional gimmicks designed to "pass the word" about program opportunities:

1. Publish a yearly calendar that includes the dates on which entries are due and competition begins.
2. Establish an intramural bulletin board.
3. Contact the sports editor of the school newspaper for weekly announcements and results.
4. Take pictures of all championship contests and post the pictures on the intramural bulletin board as soon as possible.
5. Create an intramural symbol (for instance, IM LAZY or IM ACTIVE).

6. In the high schools, place intramural schedules and announcements on the inside of toilet stalls or above urinals in the washroom.
7. Place a large piece of plexiglass on the floor in a well-traveled area. Insert all pertinent intramural information under the glass.
8. Use art media developed by art students as eye-catching advertisements.
9. Prior to incorporating a new sport in the schedule, try a free sports instruction program. The participants will enjoy learning the correct skills necessary for a high level of competition, and this desire to improve can lead the students into the program.
10. Make announcements in homerooms and divisions.
11. Hold championship contests during half times of interscholastic events.
12. Prepare slides of intramural competition. During orientation week of the new school year, the slides can be shown along with contemporary background music.
13. Appeal to the community newspapers to publish results and photographs of championship contests.
14. Consider open-recreation opportunities. There is a need for physical expression without competition.

Evaluation

Many statements have been made regarding the need of the evaluative process, but here is one that says it all: "Fiscal responsibility and accountability, the 'tight fund' squeeze in education, common sense and the need to implement planned changes to improve the quality of the intramural program for the students and other participants, all indicate the need for evaluation" (Hyatt, 1971, p. 39).

It is difficult, if not impossible, to justify a program merely on numbers of participants and statements from participants who claim that they had fun. Evaluation is based on the degree of realization of the objectives that have been stated. Activities that are successful in fulfilling goals are retained and possibly expanded; activities that have not been functional are disregarded, and new considerations are investigated. Evaluation also pertains to every other consideration that has been discussed in this chapter. Every director should establish a rating list based on the objectives of his or her program. Objective evaluative ratings according to a scale can be made periodically by students, teachers, volunteer consultant groups composed of parents, the intramural council, or educational administrators.

GENERAL BIBLIOGRAPHY

AMERICAN ASSOCIATION FOR HEALTH, PHYSICAL EDUCATION AND RECREATION, "Essentials of a Quality Elementary School Physical Education Program: A Position Paper." Washington, D.C.: National Education Association, 1970a.

———, "Guidelines for Secondary School Physical Education: A Position Paper." Washington, D.C.: National Education Association, 1970b.

THE ATHLETIC INSTITUTE, *Intramurals for Elementary School Children.* Chicago, 1964.

———, *Intramurals for the Junior High School.* Chicago, 1964.

———, *Intramurals for the Senior High School.* Chicago, 1964.

BRAMMELL, R. P., "Intramural and Interscholastic Athletics," in *National Survey of Secondary Education,* p. 63. U.S. Office of Education Bulletin 17. Washington, D.C., 1932.

CABLE, DONALD L., "Intramural Sport Courses in Selected Institutions of Higher Learning," in *Proceedings: National College Physical Education Association, 1974.* Washington, D.C.: American Association for Health, Physical Education and Recreation, 1974.

Carnegie Commission on Higher Education, *A Digest of Reports and Recommendations.* New York: McGraw-Hill, September, 1967–October, 1971.

CURRY, NANCY L., "What's the Point of Points?" *National Intramural Association Proceedings,* XXIII (1972), 59–63.

DZENOWAGIS, JOSEPH G., and LAWRENCE SIERRA, "Injuries in Intramural Sports," *Journal of Health, Physical Education and Recreation,* XLIII, No. 7 (September, 1972), 65–66.

EHLERS, HENRY, and GORDON C. LEE, *Crucial Issues in Education,* rev. ed. New York: Holt Rinehart & Winston, 1959.

ENDRES, ART, "Intramural Point Scoring System," *National Intramural Association Proceedings,* XXII (1971), 103–5.

FAHR, SAMUEL M., "Legal Liability for Athletic Injuries," *Journal of Health, Physical Education and Recreation,* XXIX, No. 2 (February, 1958), 12–13, 75–76.

GRAMBEAU, RODNEY J., "Developing Safety in Intramural Sports," *College Physical Education Association Proceedings,* (1956).

HYATT, RONALD W., "Evaluation in Intramurals," *Journal of Health, Physical Education and Recreation,* XLII, No. 6 (June, 1971), 39.

MEANS, LOUIS E., *Intramurals: Their Organization and Administration,* 2nd ed. Englewood Cliffs, N.J.: Prentice-Hall, 1972.

MUELLER, PAT, *Intramurals: Programming and Administration,* 4th ed. New York: Ronald Press, 1971.

PEDERSON, ELDON E., "The Intramural Point System," *National Intramural Association Proceedings,* XIV, (1963), 58.

POE, ARTHUR, *School Liability for Injuries to Pupils.* New York: Bureau of Publications, Teachers College, Columbia University, 1941.

PROSSER, WILLIAM L., *Handbook of the Law of Torts.* St. Paul, Minn.: West Publishing, 1941

RICE, EMMETT A., JOHN L. HUTCHINSON, and MABEL LEE, *A Brief History of Physical Education,* 5th ed. New York: Ronald Press, 1969.

SAWREY, JAMES M., and CHARLES W. TELFORD, *Educational Psychology: Psychological Foundations of Education,* 2nd ed. Boston and New York: Allyn and Bacon, 1964.

THORPE, LOUIS P., and ALLEN M. SCHMULLER, *Contemporary Theories of Learning.* New York: Ronald Press, 1954.

VAN DER SMISSEN, BETTY. *Legal Liability of Cities and Schools for Injuries in Recreation and Parks.* Cincinnati: W.H. Anderson, 1968.

VOLTMER, EDWARD F., and ARTHUR A. ESSLINGER, *The Organization and Administration of Physical Education,* 3rd ed. New York: Appleton-Century-Crofts, 1958.

WESTON, ARTHUR, *The Making of American Physical Education.* New York: Appleton-Century-Crofts, 1962.

WILLIAMS, JESSE FEIRING, "Education Through the Physical," *Journal of Higher Education,* I (May, 1930), 279–82.

———, *The Principles of Physical Education.* Philadelphia and London: Saunders, 1959.

16

Sports Clubs:
Organization and Administration

RONALD HYATT
University of North Carolina
Chapel Hill, North Carolina

INTRODUCTION

Sports clubs are different things to different people: a puzzle to college administration, a pseudo threat to varsity sports programs, an opportunity for leadership for campus recreation and intramural directors, and fun for the participants.

Sports clubs pose unique administrative challenges because of their philosophy, their potential for legal liability, their excellent student leadership, which may or may not be responsive to guidance, and their administrative challenges of finding funds, facilities, and guidelines or policies for their organization and administration.

The areas of finance, legal liability, program coordination, cooperative use of facilities, transportation, scheduling, and total program coordination have indeed caused problems for the club members, the intramural director, and the institution's administration. The lack of a plausive comprehensive sports club program on many campuses has lessened the quality of play opportunities for club members, presented a severe administrative challenge to campus recreation leaders, and given the institution new lessons in possible legal liability. These problems can be avoided by establishing a comprehensive sports club program.

Sports clubs—or club sports, as they are known in some schools—are a group of students or students and faculty or students, faculty, and townspeople who have united to participate in and promote a specific sport or recreational activity. These clubs may or may not be co-recreational and may or may not be competitive on an extramural basis. In general, club sports are undertaken on a voluntary basis and are controlled by (or coordinated with) other programs and activities of the school. Some sports clubs possess excellent student leadership and have a relatively long history of stable operation, whereas others are very temporal and reflect the presence or absence of student leadership, support, and concern for a particular program. Extensive funding may be needed by some clubs; others require a minimum amount of funds. The danger element and the risk may be high in some competitive clubs and extremely low in others. Likewise, the sports clubs may represent team or individual activity interest and efforts.

OBJECTIVES OF SPORTS CLUBS

The objectives of sports clubs, then, appear to be for members to pursue their competitive and recreational needs in an informal and unstructured manner without the formal directions of a coach. They seek the value of the play or recreation experience itself without appealing to spectators' needs or interests. Sports club members appear to be more interested in what the player derives from sports participation rather than what the player gives to a sport.

The administration model used to coordinate and control sports clubs varies from school to school. Figure 1 illustrates one possible model for organizing sports clubs. The administrative pattern ranges from programs that are highly centralized, coordinated, led by one administrator, well funded, and recognized as an integral part of the campus recreation program to programs in which no one funds the clubs or claims administrative responsibility for them. As a result of this variation among sports clubs, the philosophy (or the lack of one) for their growth, and the legitimate pressing administrative challenges and opportunities that they present to the administration, sports clubs need to be studied and administrative policies and procedures need to be established for them. Without some control or coordination, chaos can result. Sports clubs have too much to offer to too many people to permit administrators to take them lightly or campus recreation and intramural programs to continue to ignore them. The historical use of sports clubs may provide clues as to the contribution they can make and as to why they present administrators with so many unique opportunities for leadership.

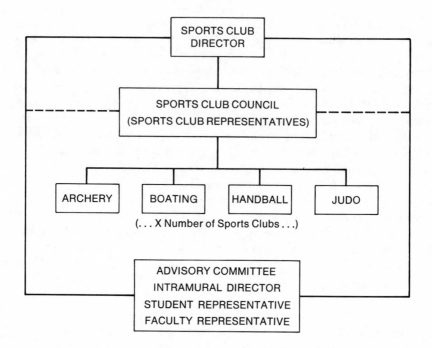

Figure 1. An Administrative Model for Sports Clubs

SOCIAL AND HISTORICAL PATTERNS

Although sports clubs appear to be a recent phenomenon in campus sports programs, they are not! Sports clubs programs underwent a tremendous revival in the late 1950s and early 1960s. This metamorphosis was both a reaction to big-time varsity sports and a sincere attempt on the part of students to participate in sports programs or recreational activities of their own choosing at times convenient to them. Despite these recent changes, sports clubs have a rich heritage and history. Although the theories that "sports clubs arose as a reaction to big-time sports," "sports clubs are simply a manifestation of the existentialist philosophy in action sports programs on the college campus," "sports clubs represent the involved generation doing their own thing in sports," and "sports clubs are people who want all the benefits of participating in a sport without 'paying the price'" may all contain some validity, there are other factors in the resurgence of sports clubs. The student population on college campuses exploded in the 1960s. Varsity athletic programs dragged their feet in their efforts to add to and develop more sports in their arenas. Student bodies were relatively affluent. A final and perhaps critical factor that contributed to the explosive growth of sports clubs was the failure of many campuses' recreational and intramural programs to initiate and maintain leadership for such clubs. In short, sports clubs are a sports phenomenon now, as they were in the 1850s and 1860s.

Early American colleges were patterned after their English counterparts, and as a result they emulated these institutions in their efforts to provide curricular and extracurricular activities. The students of those times probably participated in what are now considered to be "sports clubs" before intramurals, varsity sports, or formal physical education were introduced into college programs. These clubs were founded on the idea of play for the sake of play. According to some writers in the field, sports clubs were one of the earliest forms of sports competition in early American colleges and universities.

Sports clubs grew in number on American college campuses after the 1860s. They flourished for a time, but were eventually overtaken by the rise of varsity sports programs and the development of early physical education and hygiene classes. Those sports clubs that did not become varsity sports either ceased to exist or lost their status to the more "visible" varsity sports. The success of the varsity programs was the result of several factors: the rise in the number of newspaper sports pages, the increase and improvement in means of transportation, the increased number of colleges, and the natural desire of students to compete against other schools. Although sports clubs may have existed in some limited form on college campuses from the late 1800s to the late 1950s, little mention is made in the literature of their existence during this period. An exception to this was the outdoor sports club and camping activities group that developed at Dartmouth.

The explosive rebirth of sports clubs and their play opportunities in the late 1950s and early 1960s are a major contributing factor in what one writer has described as "the new intramurals." Indeed, sports clubs are historically an integral part of the sports scene on American college campuses. The administrative questions presented by sports clubs in the past are equally relevant today.

A REVIEW OF THE LITERATURE

Haniford was one of the early writers to identify the rebirth of sports clubs and to state that they were an administrative responsibility of intramurals (1958, p. 105). Matthews has provided excellent organizational guidelines for sports clubs (1965, pp. 50–53). The problems attendant to sports clubs have been a frequent topic of discussion at the annual meetings of the National Intramural Association, the National Intramural Sports Council, and the National Collegiate Athletic Association. Functional models of the administration of sports clubs have also been identified in the literature. Such models range from a coordinated, closely controlled body under the auspices of the intramural staff to a very broad program of sports clubs that depends almost entirely on student efforts.

TYPES OF SPORTS CLUBS

There are at least three types of sports clubs, with several variations of each type. One type is the competitive sports club, which is organized around a particular sport or activity. This type of club comprises moderate to highly skilled players who desire to participate in a vigorous activity in extramural competition, with (or without) their school's consent and support. Rugby, contact football, and other such team sports are examples of this type of club. A second type is the recreational club, a major objective of which is leisure recreation. At the most, competition in this type of club is restricted to an individual competing against himself in order to improve his performance in the activity. The activities of these clubs would be considered vigorous and physically demanding of a sort. Outdoor recreation, scuba diving, camping, and other such endeavors would fit into this category. A third type of sport club embodies activities that are less physical. This type of club is founded on the premise that the individual can enjoy an activity that is more challenging intellectually than physically. Chess, checkers, and horseback riding are good examples of such an activity. A combination of all three types of clubs would likely be found in the comprehensive sports club program, but an excellent program could be provided with just one category if that was all that was demanded by the interests of the students.

SPORTS CLUBS IN PUBLIC AND SECONDARY SCHOOLS

The club sport movement has made some progress in the secondary schools, but this progress has traditionally been only on a limited basis. Special-interest groups such as skiers, outdoor campers, and aquatics enthusiasts have united under a faculty advisor to participate in such activities. In both junior high and elementary schools, programs have developed to accommodate special-interest clubs of a sports, recreational, or fitness nature. The age of the participant, the pressure on school systems to show legal concern for sports participation and safety, and the lack of funds and facilities are among the factors that may slow the growth of sports clubs in public schools. Other factors are the lack of adequate public exposure for such clubs, the low priority sports clubs receive at the public school level, the tremendous pressures on public school officials to limit any program that might involve the school district in a legal conflict with the participant, and the lack of interested, qualified individuals to help monitor the clubs.

SPORTS CLUB PROGRAMS OF ACTIVITIES

The range of activities and interests offered by legitimately recognized sports clubs varies from campus to campus. The size (number of participants) of the program is not always indicative of the quality of the program services offered to participants. An old adage that can be applied to sports club programs (as well as to the total intramural program) is this: "The quality club sport program is that program that best serves its constituents' needs with regard to providing facilities, funding, and leadership." The Universities of Purdue, Minnesota, Tennessee, and Michigan and the Virginia Polytechnic Institute are examples of schools that have excellent sports club programs. The sports clubs that can be found on the university level range from a few activities to over fifty. One commonality that seems to be present at all schools that have a quality sports club program is the administrative commitment to serve the students in a safe, logical, responsible manner. Some of the more popular sports and activities that are frequently the basis of sports clubs on college campuses are listed in Table 1.

Table 1. Activities of Sports Clubs

archery	field hockey	polo
badminton	gymnastics	rifle shooting
bicycling	handball	rugby
billiards	horseback riding	sailing
boating	ice hockey	scuba
bowling	jogging	skeet shooting
camping	judo	soccer
canoeing	karate	squash
crew	lacrosse	tackle football
cricket	orienteering	team handball
dance	outing	volleyball
fencing	paddleball	water skiing
figure skating	parachuting	weightlifting

A PHILOSOPHIC FRAMEWORK FOR
THE ADMINISTRATION OF SPORTS CLUBS

The diverse nature of colleges and universities, the college population explosion of the 1960s, the rapid rebirth of sports clubs, and the social conflicts (such as demonstrations) that beset colleges in the 1960s have combined to delay many campuses from developing an administrative philosophy and posture toward club sports. In those situations where excellent, stable leadership has been provided by the existing intramural staff and where the varsity sports program has not vigorously opposed their development, sports club programs have been established on a sound basis. Some college and university administrators, however, have either failed to grasp the importance of sports clubs or have ignored the unique challenges and opportunities for leisure fulfillment that are inherent in them. As a result (with very few exceptions), these schools have frequently failed to integrate sports clubs into the total program of campus recreation. In other schools, sports club administration is nothing more than a seat-of-the-pants operation. Anything less than providing an effective policy of integrating students who wish to participate in sports clubs into the total campus program of leisure services is an affront to the idea of "sports opportunities for all students."

SPORTS CLUB PRINCIPLES, CHARTERS, AND OPERATING CODE

The literature suggests that certain principles should be followed in initiating and administering sports clubs. Although any listing of such principles is somewhat arbitrary, an examination of the ones that follow may, assist the intramural director.

1. The sports club program should be coordinated and administered by one person who is trained and qualified in physical education or recreation. He or she should enjoy sports and be people-oriented.
2. In most cases, this person should be organizationally responsible to the intramural staff.
3. An advisory council on sports clubs is desirable.
4. A sports club association, council, or board should be formed as a focal point for sports clubs. This organization should be roughly comparable to the intramural sport council. A charter should be drawn up for this group. The function of this group is to provide policies, approve budgets, approve schedules, establish rules and regulations, and evaluate existing and proposed sports clubs
5. An operating code and guidelines should be drawn up for the clubs and club members. These guidelines should contain written policies

and procedures that the clubs must ascribe to in order to be legitimate clubs. The guidelines and the charter should provide an easy means for clubs to become inactive or become active, depending upon student needs, interests, and leadership.

6. Care should be taken to remember that sports clubs are only one important facet of the campus recreation or intramural program and that other segments of the program also merit equitable concern.

7. Student leadership should be used and developed in administering sports clubs.

8. Whenever possible, a faculty advisor who is willing to assist in monitoring the actions of the club should be selected by each club's membership.

9. Sports clubs should be funded from the general budget or student fees on a fair and equitable basis.

10. All funds should be administered by the sports club director.

11. The safety and health of each participant should be the *primary* concern of both the sports club members *and* the sports club director.

12. Membership in sports clubs who use institutional facilities should be limited to students, faculty, or administrators if any policy of facility use restricts the opportunity of other groups to participate.

13. The coordinating and administrative functions of all the sports clubs should be executed by the sports club director. In coordination with guidance provided by the advisory committee, this person will carry out the policies and procedures established by the club association. The next higher administration officer above the sports club director should be the campus recreation director or intramural director.

14. A sports club handbook should be developed and published for all sports club members. It should contain the charter, policy and guidelines, and other administrative information.

15. All aspects of legal liability should be studied. Medical exams should be required. Insurance should be provided by either the university or the student.

16. A priority program for use of facilities by all interests within the total program of campus recreation should be established.

17. Reasonable administrative supportive services should be provided for each club, such as a mailing address and a typewriter.

18. Each club should be required to submit a detailed, justified budget request.

19. The sports club program needs to be continually evaluated to insure that the program merits student interest and that it is serving the needs of the participants.

There are a number of tools that can assist in the administration of sports clubs. Similar to organizations of other types, the utilization of a charter or constitution by the club can offer the "collected" individuals the degree of administrative direction that is desirable. A sports club charter or constitution is essential to the sports club members, to the campus recreation director or intramural leader, and to the administration. The charter provides a philosophical and administrative framework for the legitimate function of sports clubs. Although a single constitution or charter is not appropriate to every institution, a sample charter (in outline form) is presented below as a guide. This guide is not intended to be inclusive, but it can serve as a starting point.

A Sports Club Charter or Constitution

_____ Sports Club Constitution for a Sports
(Institution)
Club Association (Council, Board)

Introduction (Purpose, Preamble). Sports clubs provide competition and recreational opportunities for larger numbers of students. They enhance, complement, and supplement the intramural program but do not replace it as they are but one part of the total program of activities. Sports clubs provide opportunities for students (and faculty) to participate in a quality program of activities of an intramural, extramural, and recreational nature. Club sports are an integral part of the total program of recreational service and are equal to other parts of the total program.

The purpose of this constitution is to recognize the validity of sports clubs contributions and to provide the administrative framework necessary to ensure equal access to facilities, equipment, supplies, and services by all sports club members.

Section I. Name.

The name of this organization is the _____
Sports Club Association (Council).

Section II. Purposes.

The purposes of this association (council, board) are:

1. To provide and administer a coordinated program of sports club activities.
2. To provide administrative leadership and administrative service to support clubs.
3. To serve as a single voice for sports club needs.

Section III. Membership.

1. Any valid student, faculty member, or administrator is eligible for membership in the association (council, board).
2. Only sports clubs that are members of the association (council, board) can represent the institution as legitimate sports clubs and be provided administrative support, including funds and facilities.

3. If a sports club becomes a varsity sport, it is no longer eligible for membership in this organization. An exception to this is contact club football.

4. Clubs and club members can be removed from the organization by a two-thirds vote of the entire organization. Possible grounds for expulsion are a breach of the campus honor code, hazardous and unsafe conduct, noncompliance with the operating code, and other activities not conducive to a safe program.

5. Clubs and club members may, depending upon the amount of interest in the clubs, become inactive or active simply by relinquishing their charter or by asking the association to reactivate their charter at the beginning of the year.

Section IV. Organization of the Association (Club Council, Advisory Committee).

1. The _____ Sports Club Association will be composed of the president or club representative from each sports club, the sports club coordinator or director, a representative from the student affairs office, a representative from the sports medicine program, a representative from the athletic program, a representative from physical education, a representative from the faculty committee on athletics, a representative from student government, and an intramural council representative. A faculty advisor from each club sport may attend the meeting.

2. The faculty committee on athletics, the sports club director, and the president of the sports club may serve as an advisory body to the association.

3. Duties of the association.
   a. To establish policies in regard to sports clubs.
   b. To act as a hearing body and as the final authority on administrative matters such as funds, facilities, and schedules.
   c. To supervise, along with the campus recreation director, the association policies formulated by the sports club director.

4. The association will hold scheduled monthly meetings and will be available for call meetings as necessary. A quorum, which shall consist of a simple majority of association members, must be present to carry on the business of the association.

Section V. Requirements for Establishing New Clubs or for Reactivating Old Clubs.

1. Any new sports club or any old sports club seeking to be reactivated must fill out the standard application form for clubs used by the department of student affairs. This form is filled out in three copies: one for the association, one for the club, and one for the student affairs department.

2. The application must then be approved by the sports club association.

3. The application must be accompanied by the following items of information found in the club sports application (see Form # 1).

Form Number 1

Sports Club Membership Application

Date _____

New Club _____ Old Club _____

Name of Club _____   President _____

Address _____

Phone Number _____

Sport _____

Faculty Advisor _____   Address _____

Phone Number _____

Purpose(s) of Club _____

_____

_____

Projected Budget
    a. Equipment
    b. Supplies
    c. Transportation
    d. Lodging

Projected Schedule (limit of five away games)

Date _____ Opponent _____ Location _____

Date _____ Opponent _____ Location _____

Date _____ Opponent _____ Location _____

Date _____ Opponent _____ Location _____

Date _____ Opponent _____ Location _____

Equipment Needs: Initial

Continuing

Facilities Needed _____

The Most Convenient Time for Us to Meet _____

Section VI. Finances

Budgets for sports clubs will be approved and allocated through the office of the sports club director. The budget will be handled for each club by the sports club director. A receipt must be provided for each expenditure of funds. Club members are not to disburse funds. Equipment and supplies will be purchased under the regulations of the state bid system. All supplies and equipment purchases become the property of the university. All such property will be stored in the checkout room for each club.

Section VII. Annual Reports

Annual reports on the standard sports club form number 2 are to be prepared and turned in to the sports club director two weeks prior to the end of school. Form 2 is as follows (Annual Report Form):

Club _____   Year _____

President _____   Faculty Advisor _____

Year Organized _____

Budget   Expenses   Balance

    a. Supplies _____   1 _____   _____

    b. Equipment _____   2 _____   _____

    c. Travel _____   3 _____   _____

    d. Lodging _____   4 _____   _____

    e. Officials _____   _____   _____

    Etc.

Number of Games Played _____

Score of Opponent _____   Your Score _____

_____   _____

----------------   ----------------

----------------   ----------------

----------------   ----------------

Injuries
Significant Events
Club Plans For Next Year
Future Needs

Section VIII.

This association charter can be ratified by a two-thirds vote of the majority of association members and the approval of the campus recreation director and dean of student affairs.

Another tool that can be a valuable aid in the administration of sports clubs is an operating code for *each* sports club. Such guidelines should be specific to the activity or sport. Here is an example of an operating code and guidelines for sports clubs.

Sports Club Operating Code and Guidelines

Purpose: The purpose of this sports club operating code is to provide sports clubs with an administrative guide. It is to be read and signed by all club members and then submitted to the coordinator or director of sports clubs. A duplicate is to be kept by the club.

Section I
Bylaws

Membership:

1. All sports club members must be students, faculty, or administration of their institution.
2. All sports clubs and their members must provide the information called for and meet the requirements for becoming a sports club (as provided for in Section V of the Charter).
3. All facilities, supplies, and equipment will be made available to club members insofar as this is economically feasible. Availability will be on a fair and impartial basis. It must be remembered, however, that other students' recreation needs must also be considered.
4. Scholarship varsity athletes may compete in all sports and activities except those closely related to the sport in which they have a scholarship.

5. No scholarships can be awarded by a sports club, nor can other enticements or rewards be given for participating in sports clubs.

Section II
Health and Safety Policies

Medical Exams:

1. All club members must have a valid medical exam prior to participation. The medical exam provided by the student health service will suffice, as will a personal exam by a general physician.

2. The standard medical exam form will be used, and a certified copy for each player will be on file in the office of the director of sports clubs.

3. The school does not provide medical or hospitalization insurance coverage; this is the responsibility of each player. Each participant engages in the sports club program voluntarily and at his or her own risk.

4. The sports medicine center can be used by all sports club members for treatment of injuries and accidents.

5. A physician from sports medicine will be present at all club competitive sports events, and the sports medicine center will be staffed by a trainer during this time.

6. Transportation for sports clubs will be provided by the school insofar as this is possible.

7. Any vehicle transporting club members must have adequate liability insurance.

8. All clubs and club members who participate in off-campus games or events must have their names and other information on the standard travel form (see the example below).

Example of Standard Travel Form

Name of team _____   President _____

                                 Advisor _____

Destination _____   Travel time _____

Lodging Agreement

Location of Lodging _____   Phone Number _____

_____   _____

Type of transportation used: School Bus _____

                              School Car _____

Private   ————

Cost of transportation
Cost of lodging
Cost of food

————————

Total

Section III
Funds

The proposed budget shall be submitted in accordance with the club association charter (Section VI). The budget is due January 15 of the following year.

Section IV
Facilities

1. All recreation facilities will be coordinated and scheduled through the director of club sports and the intramural department.
2. Neither the school nor the sports club association assumes liability or responsibility for practices or games held on non-campus-affiliated fields or space.
3. The facilities are scheduled on a priority basis, with sports clubs being provided their proportional share of time and space.
4. Court and field reservation cards for practice and play must be obtained from the director of sports clubs.

Section V
Equipment

1. The sports club director will purchase all equipment. Mutual use of equipment already on hand will be made to avoid excess duplication of equipment. Purchasing of equipment is based on the needs forecast in or by each club budget.
2. Purchased equipment is stored in the equipment checkout room for use by clubs. If special equipment for clubs is too large, such as equipment for crew, then safe storage will be provided by the school. The checkout system and the responsibility for club sports equipment is the same as for other physical education and recreation equipment. The individual is responsible for loss or neglect and damage.
3. The club equipment will become the property of the school.
4. The state bid system will be used to purchase equipment. (Private schools will use standard purchasing procedure.)

Section VI
Supplies

1. Office supplies that exceed normal usage will be provided to the clubs or requested in their budget.

2. Dressing facilities, use of towels, and other routine supplies will be provided to sports clubs and their legitimate opponents.

Section VII
Services

Administrative services in regard to correspondence, mimeographing of schedules, limited phone calls, and a common work space in which to produce these materials will be provided in the sports club director's office. Letterhead stationery may be used if purchased privately by the club.

Section VIII
Scheduling

1. Sports clubs can participate in a maximum of five away games or activities.
2. Contracts for these contests must be signed by both clubs and by the sports club director of each school. The contract will be filed in the sports club director's office. All contracts for the next year must be on file by January 15th of the preceding year. The contract, in the form provided by the sports club office, will be submitted with the proposed budget. The following contract may be used.

Sports Club Contract

The _____ Sports Clubs of _____
                                                        Institution

and _____ agree to meet in a _____
            Institution

contest on _____ at _____. The contest or
                Day, Month, Year   Time

event will be played or staged at _____. Officials will be provided by the home school.

Signed

_____ President of Sports Council

_____ Sports Club Director (home school)

_____ Sports Club Director (away school)

Place contest last played

Home-and-Home Basis _____   Single Visit _____

Housing Provided _____

Meals Provided _____

Section IX
Officials

Officials for home games or events will be provided by the director of sports clubs. Officials will be qualified and competent, and will be reimbursed by the school for their services.

Additional committees—for example, publicity and protest committees—may be established by the charter and the operating code as needed. The sports club charter and operating code are two excellent administrative vehicles with which to insure coordination and control of sports clubs and to see that sports club members receive their opportunity to participate in a safe, wholesome manner without impinging upon the rights of other students to play.

EVALUATING SPORTS CLUBS

Evaluating the effectiveness of and the need for sports club programs should be a continuous process. The traditional measurement and evaluation techniques of questionnaires, surveys, record analyses, interviews, and personal rapport, along with the "trained eyeball" or subjective evaluation of the club sports director, should all be used. In-depth study of participation patterns, cost statistics, recurring problem areas, and annual reports, budgets, and schedules is usually necessary. Likewise, the study of the effectiveness of the sports club association and the advisory council should be reviewed with the objective of continuing, constructive improvement. Sports clubs may or may not be temporal in nature, but they should be allowed to become inactive or die if they outlive their function. The club members, the sports club association, and the sports club director will know—through the ongoing process of evaluation, critical self-analysis, and subjective data—when the needs of the students are being well served and when and how services can be improved. Just as for every other phase of the total intramural program, constant evaluation is a necessary part of sports clubs.

FUTURE DIRECTIONS

What future directions will the sports club movement take? Will it remain static? Will it gradually die out as it did in the late 1800s? Will a national sports club federation be formed? Will either the National Collegiate Athletic Association or the American Alliance of Health, Physical Education and Recreation provide leadership in this area? Only time will tell. However, the professional campus recreation director, the concerned administrator, and all dedicated students must now begin to formalize play opportunities for sports clubs if the recreational needs of these special-interest groups are to be met. Sports clubs are an integral part of the present-day campus recreation scene. They too deserve to belong and to have safe, wholesome play opportunities provided for them by an effective, responsible organizational setup.

SUMMARY

Sports clubs are valid organizations on college campuses. Although their presence presents some administrative challenges and opportunities, the recreational needs of these special-interest groups can and should be served. Sports clubs present no threats, only opportunities for leadership. Leaders in campus recreation and intramural programs must provide the necessary organization and leadership to save sports clubs. "Where there is no vision, the people perish."

GENERAL BIBLIOGRAPHY

DENTON, HAROLD, "Promoting a Sports Club Program at the University of Tennessee, Knoxville," *National Intramural Association Proceedings,* XXIV (1973), 94–97.

FEHRING, W. P., "The Stanford Club Team Program," *National Intramural Association Proceedings,* XXIII (1972), 68–78.

GRAMBEAU, RODNEY J., "Encouraging the Development of Intramural Sports Clubs," *National Intramural Association Proceedings,* XVII (1966), 115–17.

HANIFORD, GEORGE, "Are Sports Clubs An Intramural Administrative Responsibility?" *College Physical Education Association Proceedings,* LXII, (1958), 105–8.

———, "Intramural Sports Clubs at Purdue University," *National Intramural Association Proceedings,* XXIII (1972), 64–67.

KLEINDIENST, VIOLA, and ARTHUR WESTON, *Intramural and Recreation Programs for Schools and Colleges,* Chap. 14. New York: Appleton-Century-Crofts, 1964.

LEAVITT, NORMA H., and HARTLEY D. PRICE, *Intramural and Recreational Sports for High School and College,* 2nd ed. Chap. 5. New York: Ronald Press, 1958.

MATTHEWS, DAVID O., "Sports Club Organization," *Scholastic Coach*, XXIV (January, 1965), 50–53.

MEANS, LOUIS E., *Intramurals: Their Organization and Administration*, Chaps. 15–17. Englewood Cliffs, N.J.: Prentice-Hall, 1963.

MUELLER, PAT, *Intramurals: Programming and Administration*, 4th ed. Chap. 13. New York: Ronald Press, 1971.

PARBERRY, CLEM, "Sports Clubs at the University of Idaho," *National Intramural Association Proceedings*, XXIII (1972), 67–68.

PHELPS, DALE E., "Current Practices and Recommended Guidelines for the Administration of Sports Clubs in Selected Four-Year Midwest Colleges and Universities," *National Intramural Association Proceedings*, XXI (1970), 32–36.

SLIGER, IRA T., "An Extensive Sports Club Program," *Journal of Health, Physical Education and Recreation*, XLI, No. 2 (February, 1970), 42–43.

STEVENSON, MICHAEL J., "The Impact of Sports Club Growth on Intramural Programs," *National Intramural Association Proceedings*, XXII (1971), 35–39.

ZYGADLO, RICH, "Students: The Best Solicitors of Public Support for Sport Clubs," *National Intramural Association Proceedings*, XXV (1974), 44–45.

17

Researching the
Intramural Experience

JOHN P. SMYTH
The Citadel
Charleston, South Carolina

At a research symposium not long ago, an exercise physiologist, a sports psychologist, and an intramural director were discussing the greatest contributions to mankind. The exercise physiologist acclaimed the magnificent scientific benefits of the treadmill. Both the intramural director and the sports psychologist agreed that much cardio-respiratory knowledge had accompanied and followed the use of the treadmill. The sports psychologist then suggested that the Skinner box was fundamental in the operant conditioning theory that is centermost in our behavior modification programs. The exercise physiologist and the intramural director agreed that behavior modification was a much discussed trend that is sweeping education today and that the Skinner box was obviously of fundamental importance. The intramural director was then asked for his contribution. He immediately nominated the thermos bottle, to the surprise and amazement of his associates. When asked why the thermos bottle, the intramural director responded by asking if the thermos bottle were able to keep a liquid hot if indeed a hot liquid were poured into its confines. The other two affirmed—indeed it would. Then the intramural director asked if the bottle would keep a cold liquid cold for a period of time should it be placed inside. Of course, the two scholars affirmed the simple query. Then, replied the intramural director, that was indeed amazing to him and justified the reverence of all posterity for the thermos bottle. But, the scientific scholars were quick to point out, the thermos bottle was designed to keep cold liquids cold and hot liquids hot. The intramural director, smiling, affirmed that this was what sealed its greatness. You put a cold liquid in and the bottle keeps it cold, and yet you put a hot liquid in and it keeps it hot; then he scratched his head and asked, "How do it know?"

"HOW DO IT KNOW?"

Philosophers have long pondered the source of ideas, prognosticators have long predicted the ingredients of success in the future, and the practitioner still must think and act out each day as a new one. Where does the evolution of ideas take place in education? What will it take to meet the needs of students in the future? How can the intramural director be most effective in his chosen profession? The enterprise of research and the intramural director have not realized their potential mutual benefits.

As the scientist researches in his laboratory, so should the physical educator research in his laboratory. The intramural director should take great pride in the realization that students are meeting many of their needs through the intramural experience, and are therein satisfying the goals of the profession. However, the intramural director has a professional responsibility to stay apprised of the true nature of student needs and of how the intramural experience relates to their fulfillment. The intramural experience is seldom studied by the sociologist for group interaction, nor by the psychologist for contributions to the self-concept, nor by the physiologist seeking to uncover biological data relative to individual or group cardio-respiratory fitness levels. Who then, can determine what outcomes are realized as a result of intramural participation? A review of the professional literature reveals a limited amount of research relating to program concepts in intramurals. Therefore, in addition to the intramural literature the program director must examine sociology, psychology, social psychology, physiology, anthropology, and the remainder of physical education and recreation research findings if he desires to gain new knowledge for program improvement. How else will the program director find new truths? Questions must be asked, answers must be sought, and curiosity, that love of understanding, must prevail.

Theory development is too vital to the future development of intramurals to be relegated to those few theorists who have the time and the inclination to take part. Theorists and practitioners must collaborate in theory development if a functional theory is to be derived.

It must be remembered that effective intramural directors have always operated from some theoretical base, even if their theory was not directly stated. Thus, the intramural director has a unique contribution to make to the process of theory development when he shares his thinking. This theory is more likely to be stated in language the layman and neophyte professional can understand and apply.

Most important, the intramural director can and should provide constant feedback to the theorist to insure that the theory, when developed, can be put into practice and modified. This chapter is an exploratory excursion. It is not a long and careful study and review of research methodology or intramural research. Rather, it is a series of reflections on parts of our heritage in intramural research. The intent of the chapter is to ask questions that must be asked and to suggest bases upon which some meaningful answers may be initiated.

RESEARCH AND INTRAMURAL RESEARCH

In research, as in other facets of life, the fact that no one method can work in every situation supports the need for a multiplicity of methods. With a broad scope, it is more likely that each person can find a technique that will work for his program. Also, each program and each program worker is at a different point of professional development. The technique must be appropriate for the person, time, and place. The proper selection and application of techniques can lead to future personal and program development.

The intellectual and creative activity of research is an attempt to reason systematically. The processes of inductive and deductive reasoning must contribute to their respective conclusions, and—perhaps like the hourglass, which must be inverted regularly in order to function— the two methods must periodically be combined (Metheny, 1967, p. 77).

Truth can be pursued by many methods. One can base truth on the observation of his personal experience, which is obviously shallow and inconclusive. Nonetheless, this method is used quite commonly. Authority is another source of investigation: truth is then what is read or heard from a referent of greater resources. The traditions and customs of generations gone by have become truth and law in many aspects of life. We follow a procedure simply because "that's the way we've always done it." A more comprehensive study of history brings references from past experiences, from other people and environments, to add testimony to what truth is. The study of philosophy devotes a field of inquiry to the evaluation of man, with a major emphasis on the epistemological search for truth. More recently, the scientific method has been conceived as the most valid and reliable mode of inquiry.

The search for truth in educational institutions appears to have followed an unwritten pecking order of scholarly prestige. Physical sciences, biological sciences, social sciences, humanities, and professional schools are paid tribute in decreasing proportions. Academia is replete with those who begrudgingly tolerate professional training, and training is sharply contrasted with educational contributions (Vanderzwagg, 1973, p. 73).

The contrasts and conflicts between science and philosophy are well documented but largely unresolved. It has been recommended that the sciences and the humanities coexist peacefully in the quest for truth (Thomas, 1973, p. 99). It has also been suggested that irrational man cannot be studied rationally by either method, as his significant acts are never relived or repeated in original form. Research remains charged with a quest for significance through accurate predictions and tested hypotheses for intelligent decision making. Research answers, with historical research reporting what was, descriptive research reporting what is, and experimental research predicting what will be (Best, 1970, pp. 14–15). Some proponents of research suggest that the major focus should be to determine what ought to be.

Research is basic and applied. Basic research seeks new knowledge and understanding through detailed fundamental processes; it is generally conducted in a laboratory setting with the goal of contributing to theory development. Applied research seeks control or prediction based on gross, higher-ordered macroprocesses that are situationalized around theoretical extrapolations (Carroll, 1968, pp. 271–72). The concepts of reliability, validity, objectivity, and appropriateness are essential throughout the many methods and types of research.

With this cursory glance at the research endeavor, the emphasis will be narrowed to physical education—more specifically, to the intramural experience. The research movement in physical education is gaining more scholarly plaudits, yet it remains essentially in the pecking order. The researcher in physical education, be he a sports psychologist or an exercise physiologist, takes an academic stance providing a view of all the practitioners in the field. The researcher, then, is often judged to be lacking in professional skill; conversely, the practitioner is seen as the intellectual inferior of his counterpart (Rothstein, 1973, p. 58). The absence of mutual respect is a serious deterrent to the emergence of a body of knowledge that can be applied at all levels. Within the ranks of the researchers there is much ado about superfluous jargon, superficial designs, monetary motivations, and a lack of relevant studies conducted and published (Massey, 1966, pp. 46–47).

The practitioner does no research because no time is scheduled or available, there is a lack of preparation in either research systems or processes, the relevance of research is not demonstrated, and/or the problems faced daily seldom show up in the acclaimed professional references (Rothstein, 1973, p. 56).

The confrontation between applied and basic research is continued by the practice of researchers jargonizing with one another to the exclusion of the practitioners, who are too incompetent or disinterested to read and interpret the professional literature (Locke, 1969, p. 163). What can be done to reconcile these basic differences? In-service clinics, faculty apprenticeships, interdisciplinary training, research seminars, and course work in higher-level systems have been suggested as mean of improving research and consumer competencies (Gutin, 1972, p. 66). Within intramural programs recommendations embrace a greater exchange of administrative and organizational materials, expanded reading habits, more collateral areas of academic pursuit, interdisciplinary research, and greater student involvement in research.

The interdisciplinary approach has permeated physical education and intramurals in the form of psychobiological, psychophysiological, and sociophysiological studies. The current labels for the interdisciplinary groups who have studied intramural activities have been limited generally to "sports sociologists," "sports psychologists," and "play theorists." The interdisciplinary approaches have struggled to apply the scientific method to human subjects with acceptable levels of experimentation error (Martens, 1973, p. 18). It can be hypothesized that human error has created research artifacts that have surely cast serious doubt upon the validity of human research; this problem is especially frequent with the commonly used volunteer subject (Williams, 1973, p. 26). Singer has grouped such errors of experimental contamination into the categories of prior manipulation, experimenter influence, and demand characteristics (1973, p. 34). With the recorded sources of errors achieving the status of catalog classification, the future use of human subjects will assuredly require stringent methodological testing.

What now is expected of the practitioner if the researcher is also being challenged? Can the practitioner be expected to do research? Many teachers and coaches would contend that none of this research is very new; consequently they have placed their reference base in experience and common sense. This pervasive negative attitude toward research among many professionals obviates a united front embodying research and practice (Stadulis, 1973, p. 52). The voices of the past still echo past philosophies for future application. The present alignment with the physiological emphasis has been challenged once again by the humanistic movement, which calls for better preparation in the humanities to deal with the art of physical education (Ogilvie, 1969, p. 186). The present preparation in methods is being challenged by the humanists and the exercise physiologists; yet the public is calling for accountability from the practitioner, who evidently is lacking in effective methods. In any event, research must be viewed as a viable part of the change process, for its quantity, quality, and nature are under constant challenge. Given a revisionary cycle of five years for a science and an everchanging humanity of unpredictable and irrational beings, it would appear that change is the only constant. Can we program for change? Programming for change requires that research be more than a charity that receives its last contribution on departing from graduate school.

Constructive criticism, the building variety, carries with it the obligation to provide positive approaches to a functional solution. A recommendation is made for the school system and specifically the practitioner to involve the student in clincial training situations that include, rather than replace, renewed concern for relevant theory and knowledge (Stiles, 1972, p. 12). Increased professional preparation is recommended in conjunction with improved, specialized curricula. Corresponding to the specialized curriculum is a request for professional licensing for each area within the profession (Ibid.).

The utilization of action research, the on-the-job approach of testing a hypothesis in a specific setting for a solution applicable to that setting, can promote a level of research that the practitioner can accomplish and appreciate (Brown and Cassidy, 1963, p. 114). Additionally, historical and descriptive research can be completed by the earnest practitioner. Historical research can lend a new perspective that relates current trends to past events and subsequently lays the groundwork for future planning (Lindsay, 1970, p. 139). An accurate account of everyday events, and the subsequent meaningful analysis of them, brings the practitioner actively into viable research utilizing the descriptive method. A chief difficulty of the descriptive method lies in the semantic, as opposed to the somatic, realm (Fishman and Anderson, 1971, p. 9). This descriptive-analytic method should not be confused with mere tabulation, as it requires recording significant behavior and demonstrating a relevant application of the analyzed data.

The case method has long existed in verbal form through the professional interchange at local, regional, and national conferences. For a more inclusive discussion of the case study method, see Chapter 4, pp. 30–44. This case method can be expanded and refined to transmit wisdom, that capacity beyond knowledge that provides for application in addition to comprehension (Gallup, 1964, p. 86). Zeigler has long been a proponent of the case method of study, and he advocates the appropriateness of the method in preparing athletic administrators and coaches (1968, p. 143). Intramural directors could well use the case study method to propagate the administrative and humanistic wisdom that contribute so heavily to a successful program.

The improvement and modification of research processes to fit intramural and physical education needs still does not answer the challenge made concerning the level of professional competency in research systems. How does the practitioner select designs and analyze data in attacking administrative problems? Complex problems are rarely solved through the application of a simple research design. Most problems are multifaceted and subsequently involve several dependent variables, yet the basic research designs cannot interrelate all of them. Multivariate analysis can provide a more theoretically based design, which reduces contamination of the study from uncharted data and their hidden relationships. These hidden relationships can be instrumental in determining the nature and extent of the explanation and prediction value of the independent variables relative to each of the dependent variables (Olafson, 1972, p. 195).

The publication and subsequent dissemination of research information can be greatly assisted by the specialist in and around the profession. Relative to research design and statistical procedures, the professional or educational units can provide resource centers that conduct high-level research and provide consultant services for professionals with complex problems about dynamic functions. The practitioner can then allay any anxieties concerning statistical or mathematical competencies and devote his energies to critical issues in the investigation. The practitioner can gain insight into the application of appropriate designs while he and the profession gain concurrently from practical and scholarly investigation.

The dissemination of results has and probably will continue to change through scientific achievement in the area of reproduction and storage forms. The six microcards at the 1969 AAHPER Research Council have volumed to 2,400 in 1973 and have just as quickly given rise to a more efficient microform for the future (Geser, 1973, p. 39). Research materials from the *Research Quarterly,* books out of print, professional periodicals, and some master's and doctoral theses from *Completed Research in Health, Physical Education and Recreation* are now to be reproduced in the negative form of microfiche at nearly a fifty percent increase in efficiency by Microform Publications of the HPER School at the University of Oregon (*Ibid.*). This availability of research materials should increase the ability of the practitioner to relate to professional problems and solutions. The master's thesis, currently not revered for its scholarly design, is, however, much more practical and meaningful to the practitioner; yet the master's thesis is relatively unavailable to the professional in the field. There remains a personal and professional responsibility to stay abreast of the supported methods of program improvement.

What is the status of research in intramurals? It has been suggested that the intramural profession is lacking in intellectual substance and is therefore transparent to all who observe its functioning (McGuire, 1969, p. 205). Yet a contention can be made that the true service motive and the resultant individualized values may serve to render the field opaque to those searching so diligently for academia that basic fulfillments become clouded. It may well be that the uniqueness of intramurals as a body of knowledge lies in its particular combination of other bodies of knowledge and its capacity to blend. Intramurals may not fly its own color, but it seeks to share in the hue of one more brilliant, or to refract and reflect yet the brightest light in a rainbow, more beautiful in its radiant arc. Can the profession follow that rainbow, or must we be more practical and less poetically naïve?

What then, have intramural personnel to research? What has been researched by intramural personnel in the young life of the profession? First evidence of intramural programs is traced to mid-nineteenth-century boating, baseball, and track interests in the barely tolerant Ivy League (Kleindienst and Weston, 1964, p. 31). Intramural research has been annotated and indexed from 1900 to 1957 by Leftwich (1958), and, more recently, from 1930 to 1965 by McGuire (1966, pp. 2–3). Articles on intramurals have been found in a wide variety of professional journals; some are quite repetitive of previous discussions but remain somewhat pertinent because the problems were and still are unresolved (Leftwich, 1958). Leftwich detected the expansion of the intramural program in direct relation to the fitness movement of the war years. McGuire noted the lack of philosophical, sociological, and historical research in an abundance of surveys conducted on high school and college programs (1966, p. 239). He found another serious limitation to be the restricted dispersion of the published research: most of the postwar publications were in the proceedings of the National Intramural Association and the National College Physical Education Association for Men (*Ibid.*). In McGuire's recommendations for future study, the fact that women intramural personnel and public school directors have not been frequent contributors to these publication efforts, and the void of studies related to junior high school and junior college intramurals were noted as areas of weakness (*Ibid.*, p. 240).

METHODOLOGICAL CONSIDERATIONS
IN INTRAMURAL RESEARCH

Intramural researchers must seek expertise in philosophical and sociological research methods. The theory and design of future research in intramurals should be generated from a sound knowledge of the focus of inquiry, the expected products, means of verification, and an understanding of prestudy assumptions (Fraleigh, 1970, p. 29). A taxonomy for research utilizing the philosophic method has been constructed to assist in the organization of future efforts and the classification of past research (Osterhoudt, 1973, p. 87). The criteria were distinguished as mutually exclusive classifications for future inquiry and were labeled construct, system, and concept analyses (*Ibid.,* p. 90). Methods, concepts, empirical generalizations, and typological models are not to be confused with an empirically testable series of statements capable of providing solid generalizations that contribute to theory (Loy, 1970, pp. 96–98). Loy further discusses the obligation of sociological theory to describe, discover, and explain (*Ibid.,* p. 95). Butler has proposed a model for future intramural research that is based upon the premise that the participant is centered among the use, meaning, modification, and opportunities of the program (1971, p. 112). It has been suggested that the traditional philosophical model for intramurals is presently inappropriate for the profession (Jones, 1971, p. 34). The traditional pyramid is obviously not the basis for program development in the present society. Although the intramural director cannot operate his program by relying on idealistic thinking, he must not compromise what "should be" for what "is" the working philosophy. Is there a valid rationale for bridging physical education and athletics with an intramural program? Are there priorities of participation privileges? The intramural director has a philosophy, and he must verbalize that philosophy to permit a valid investigation of the profession while it changes under his influence. Some intramural administrative personnel have been guilty of operating from personal and professional philosophies that are substantially inconsistent (Rohrer, 1973, p. 1). If the operational value system of the program director is schizoid, then obvious problems of consistency will plague the administration of the program. With an increase in the number of intramural directors holding the doctoral degree and with the majority completing the master's degree, sufficient graduate education is presently available to provide the profession with quality leadership. Graduate school emphasis in intramurals is becoming more pervasive. What is needed now is the application of that education to the problems of the profession.

THE PROBLEM WITH PROBLEMS

What is old and what is new? New problems look very much like old ones. The new leisure ethic is stated positively. Sports activities that contribute to the betterment of the individual are provided. Intramural activities are less frequently promoted as prevention and treatment services providing therapy, preventing juvenile delinquency, and generally keeping the youth off the street (Wilson, 1973, p. 64).

Are games of sufficient status for scholarly research? Such works as Huizinga's *Homo Ludens* ("Man the Player") paved the way for a multi-faceted source of investigation into such surface-level aspects as rules and boundaries, interaction-level characteristics such as cooperation and competition, and theoretical components such as strategy analysis (Ohm, 1966, p. 122). The movement movement has contributed its support to the medium of play by promoting the development of laterality, body image, spatial perception, motor patterns, classification and seriations, and cognitive development (Moffit, 1972, p. 47). The proof is yet to come. The increase in leisure time is likely to draw the researcher closer to the programmer in studying the quality and quantity of the play of young and old (Ellis, 1972, p. 29). Do participants seek catharsis in competition? Spectators of varsity and professional contests are thought to seek vicarious or secondary involvement. Does the participant seek primary-drive reduction (Butler, 1970, p. 97)?

What are the effects of games on children of varying intellectual levels and differing social environments? Are games always for fun? When is a game more than just a game? Does man seek stress? The stress herein is not the stress of Selye, which has negative connotations, but the pleasant stress of adventure, thrill, and excitement—the phenomenon of eustress (Harris, 1970, p. 34).

The enterprise of intramural research needs to focus upon the capacity of play to meet the psychological and social needs of the individual. Theory development becomes applied when it precedes practice and guides the experiences in positive programs.

"NEW" PROBLEMS IN INTRAMURAL RESEARCH?

Intramurals live in the philosophic ground between expressive legitimation, which is found in the fun and sociability values of intrinsic origin, and instrumental legitimation, which extracts functional importance from character development, delinquency reduction, and fitness and skill development (Ingham and Loy, 1973, pp. 7–9). An intramural experience is examined personally, for its contribution to meaning and dignity, and socially, for its acceptable and creative achievement. The humanistic approach focuses on people rather than program. Is play a basic human need? How does the student react to the subordination-superordination hierarchy? How do athletic success and failure affect the peer status? Does the intramural experience provide an emotional outlet with positive affiliation roles in human relationships? Caskey relates the attempts to re-habilitate inmates in penal institutions utilizing recreational therapy (1966, p. 109). The practice of withholding recreational privileges has come under study, with particular attention paid to the balance of syn-tonic and dystonic percepts. Normal functioning requires a delicate bal-ance of syntonic (pleasant, ego-rewarding) and dystonic (unpleasant, un-rewarding) experiences. Caskey suggests that provision for positive ego experiences is a responsibility of the institution in rehabilitating the personality (*Ibid.*, p. 111). The same assumption can be extended to society as an institution. Have you ever witnessed a student being pun-ished by withholding him from play? Has society done this in the inner city by its failure to provide the play experience?

The increasingly frequent incidence of disciplinary problems in in-tramural participation poses new challenges for intramural administrators. The behavioral antecedents and consequences of such participation should be identified and studied. Academic success and the patterns of intra-mural participation may correlate much more than intellectual and rec-reational patterns, if the designs are sophisticated enough for the experienced program director to apply comparisons to multiple be-havioral variables. Group cohesiveness has been isolated as a behavioral variable in the intramural experience, and conclusions have been drawn with respect to the motivational base, aspiration levels, and subsequent effects of winning and losing (Peterson, 1970, p. 78). How many times does a team that loses its first game or two drop from the league? What kind of leadership facilitates group participation?

"NEW" QUESTIONS FOR INTRAMURAL RESEARCH?

The growing independence of the student has modified the in-tramural program in several ways. The traditional program concept of competitive individual and team sports has been expanded to include many recreational and club sports. Many intramural and recreational facilities have been constructed. How does the program handle faculty participation? Are point systems still used, and if so, why? And are the traditional awards used as motivation for participation? If the stu-dent chooses not to conform to the traditional institutional units of dormitories and fraternities or sororities, how will team sport participa-tion be affected? Does the academic program require time formerly spent in recreational pursuits? Does intramural participation contribute to a balanced education?

Does the evolution of the new morality or the resurrection of the old one affect the demand for co-recreational activities at the junior high, senior high, or college level? What sports, if any, should remain segregated?

What is the moral and legal responsibility of the intramural director to provide a safe environment and adequate supervision for play? Is the adequate treatment of an injury a satisfactory substitute for the provision of planned preventive measures?

Does the intramural programmer have the privilege or the obligation to set up operant models to shape or modify behavior in the intramural-recreation situation? Is it a goal of the intramural program to seek behavior modification?

Has competition gone too far? Are institutional racism and ethnic hostility promoted when an all-black team plays an all-white team? What is the nature of play between segregated teams?

Questions beget more questions in unsatiable proportions, but answers lead to more answers if the curiosity to seek is nurtured. Who wins if we play this research game? Who loses if we do not?

THE WINNER IS . . . ?

The intramural program can relate to current issues and trends. Self-actualization through leisure activities can be accomplished through programmed intramurals. Intramural programs can relate to nongraded schools on modular schedules. Programs can be developed in inner-city schools with busing problems. Paraprofessionals and ability grouping have long been a part of the intramural program. Model school programs and facilities can have a positive effect on the junior and senior high school levels, where intramural programs are often nonexistent. The principle objective of the program should be to help the individual gain an awareness of his potential and to provide a practical means for achieving a fuller development of that potential. This discussion is not designed to promote progress by nomenclature or the invention of semantic solutions, but a positive position toward the relevance of intramurals to education today is reaffirmed.

RESEARCH AND THE TEN–HOUR WORK DAY

No attempt has been made to editorialize the concepts presented in this chapter. The reader has been given the opportunity to draw individual conclusions and hopefully to select aspects of the content for questioning or study. The material is offered for the consideration and stimulation of intramural program workers at all levels of education.

What are the opportunities for a high school or college teacher and a program director to do research? What are the practical problems and their possible solutions? Experienced program workers are painfully aware of the shortages of time and money. Time can be compromised through action research and/or team projects. Funding for research can be procured from local, state, and national educational sources. Specifically, the intramural director can apply to the National Intramural Association for a maximum grant of $300 for studies of regional and national scope. The National Intramural Sports Council and the Research Council present professional advisory services to the membership of the American Association of Health, Physical Education and Recreation. The National College Physical Education Association for Men and the National Association for Physical Education of College Women provide publication opportunities and reference sources for substantial scholarly enterprise.

Additional newsletters, proceedings, and state, district, and national journals for physical education, recreation, athletics, and intramurals should be considered for publication opportunities and resource documents.

The researcher should seek to avoid the "in-house" criteria of producing quantities of publications at the expense of quality and seeking federal or private funds merely because they are available. The profession has enough meeting men.

Beginning researchers can find help from experienced professionals, standard library sources, professional organizations, and related curricular discplines. Intramural programmers need to look back to history for perspective, to the present for relevance, and to the future to accommodate change. Well-conducted research efforts can provide reliability, validity, and objectivity in the quest for knowledge. Art or science; discipline or profession; academia or service—the intramural experience awaits the quest of the curious.

GENERAL BIBLIOGRAPHY

BROWN, CAMILLE, and ROSALIND CASSIDY, *Theory in Physical Education: A Guide to Program Change.* Philadelphia: Lea and Febiger, 1963.

BUTLER, K. NELSON, "Catharsis and Intramurals," *National Intramural Association Proceedings,* XXI (1970), 97–101.

————, "A Model for Intramural Research," *National Intramural Association Proceedings,* XXII (1971), 111–13.

CARROLL, JOHN B., "Basic and Applied Research in Education: Definitions, Distinctions, and Implications," *Harvard Educational Review,* XXXVIII (1968), 263–76.

CASKEY, ALAN R., "The Role of Intramural Activities in a Penal Institution," *National Intramural Association Proceedings,* XVII (1966), 109–14.

ELLIS, M. J., "Play: Practice and Research in the 1970's," *Journal of Health, Physical Education and Recreation,* (June, 1972), 29–31.

FISHMAN, SYLVIA E. and WILLIAM G. ANDERSON, "Developing a System for Describing Teaching," *Quest,* XV (January, 1971), 9–16.

FRALEIGH, WARREN P., "Theory and Design of Philosophic Research in Physical Education," *Proceedings of the National College Physical Education Association for Men,* LXXIII (1970), 28–51.

GALLUP, GEORGE. *The Miracle Ahead.* New York: Harper & Row, 1964.

GESER, L. RICHARD, "HPER Microcards, 1948–1972; Microfiche, 1973–," *Journal of Health, Physical Education and Recreation,* XLIII (April, 1973), 38–39.

GUTIN, BERNARD, "A Graduate School Seminar to Train Quality Researchers," *Journal of Health, Physical Education and Recreation,* XLII (May, 1972), 66–67.

HARRIS, DOROTHY V., "On the Brink of Catastrophe," *Quest,* XIII (January, 1970), 33–40.

INGHAM, ALLAN G., and JOHN W. LOY, JR., "The Social System of Sport: A Humanistic Perspective," *Quest,* XIX (January, 1973), 3–23.

JONES, TOM R., "Needed: A New Philosophical Model for Intramurals," *Journal of Health, Physical Education and Recreation,* XLI (November-December, 1971), 34–35.

KLEINDIENST, VIOLA R., and ARTHUR WESTON, *Intramural and Recreation Programs for Schools and Colleges.* New York: Appleton-Century-Crofts, 1964.

LEFTWICH, HORATIO F., "An Annotated and Indexed Bibliography of Intramural Literature from 1900–1957." Master's thesis, Springfield College, 1958.

LINDSAY, PETER L., "What Are We Trying to Do? (Theory, Design and Methodology of Historical Research),"*Proceedings of the National College Physical Education Association for Men,* LXXIII (1970), 132–39.

LOCKE, LAWRENCE F., "Researchers and Teachers at the OK Corral," *Proceedings of the National College Physical Education Association for Men,* LXXII (1969), 160–69.

LOY, JOHN W., "The Nature of Sociological Theory and Its Import for the Explanation of Agonetic Behavior," *Proceedings of National College Physical Education Association for Men,* LXXIII (1970), 94–105.

MARTENS, RAINER, "People Errors in People Experiments," *Quest,* XX (June, 1973), 16–20.

Massey, Benjamin H., "The Physical Educator as Researcher," *Quest,* VII (December, 1966), 46–52.

McGuire, Raymond J., "The Achievement of True Professional Status for Intramurals," *National Intramural Association Proceedings,* XX (1969) 199–206.

————, "A Retrieval of Selected Intramural Research and Literature." Master's thesis, University of Illinois (Urbana), 1966.

Metheny, Eleanor, et al., "Physical Education as an Area of Study and Research," *Quest,* IX (December, 1967), 73–78.

Moffitt, Mary W., "Play as a Medium for Learning," *Journal of Health, Physical Education and Recreation,* XLII (June, 1972), 45–47.

Ogilvie, Bruce, "The Mental Ramblings of a Psychologist Researching in the Area of Sports Motivation," *National Intramural Association Proceedings,* XX (1969), 173–93.

Ohm, Robert E., "Are Games Trivial?" *National Intramural Association Proceedings,* XVII (March, 1966), 120–23.

Olafson, Gordon, "Multivariate Applications to Research in Administrative Theory," *Proceedings of the National College Physical Education Association for Men,* LXXV (1972), 194–98.

Osterhoudt, Robert G., "A Taxonomy for Research Concerning the Philosophy of Physical Education and Sport," *Quest,* XX (June, 1973), 87–91.

Peterson, James, "Investigating the Behavioral Consequences of Participation in Intramural Activities: A Changing Emphasis for Intramural Research," *National Intramural Association Proceedings,* XXI (April, 1970), 75–80.

Rohrer, Susan J., "An Identification of Basic Administrative Philosophies Held by a Selected Sampling of College and University Intramural Administrators," *National Intramural Association Intramural Newsletter,* (March-April, 1973), 1–2.

Rothstein, Anne L., "Practitioners and the Scholarly Enterprise," *Quest,* XX (June, 1973), 56–60.

Singer, Robert N., "Methodological Controls for Social Psychological Problems in Experimentation," *Quest,* XX (June, 1973), 32–38.

Stadulis, Robert E., "Bridging the Gap: A Lifetime of Waiting and Doing," *Quest,* XX (June, 1973), 47–53.

Stiles, Lindley J., "State of the Art of Teacher Education," *Quest,* XVIII (June, 1972), 3–13.

Thomas, Carolyn E., "Science and Philosophy: Peaceful Coexistence," *Quest,* XX (June, 1973), 99–104.

Vanderzwagg, Harold J., "Sport Studies and Exercise Science: Philosophical Accommodations," *Quest,* XX (June, 1973), 73–78.

Williams, Harriet G., "Volunteerism, the Beneficent Subject and Ecological Validity," *Quest* XX (June, 1973), 26–31.

Wilson, George T., "The New Leisure Ethic and What It Means to the

Community School," *Journal of Health, Physical Education and Recreation* XLIII (January, 1973), 64.

ZEIGLER, EARLE F., "The Case Method of Instruction as Applied to the Preparation of Athletic Administrators and Coaches," *Proceedings of the National College Physical Education Association for Men,* LXXI (1968), 143–49.

SELECTED REFERENCES

Research Texts

AMERICAN ASSOCIATION FOR HEALTH, PHYSICAL EDUCATION AND RECREATION, *Research Methods in Health, Physical Education and Recreation,* ed. M. Gladys Scott, 1967, 536 pp.

BEST, JOHN W., *Research in Education.* Englewood Cliffs, N.J.: Prentice-Hall, 1970, 320 pp.

BORG, WALTER R., and MEREDITH D. GALL, *Education Research: An Introduction.* New York: McKay, 1971, 533 pp.

FOX, DAVID J., *The Research Process in Education.* New York: Holt, Rinehart & Winston, 1969, 758 pp.

GOOD, CARTER V., and DOUGLAS E. SCATES, *Methods of Research.* New York: Appleton-Century-Crofts, 1954, 920 pp.

VAN DALEN, DEOBOLD B., *Understanding Educational Research.* New York: McGraw-Hill, 1962, 432 pp.

Intramural Publications and Sources of Research

AMERICAN ASSOCIATION FOR HEALTH, PHYSICAL EDUCATION AND RECREATION, *Abstracts of Research Papers Presented at Annual Convention.* Washington, D.C., 1960–1975.

——, *Completed Research in Health, Physical Education and Recreation,* Vol. 1–15, 1959–1974, ed. Research Council. Washington, D.C.

——, *Intramural Messenger.* A Joint Project of the Division of Men's Athletics and Division for Girls' and Women's Sports. Washington, D.C., 1972–1974.

NATIONAL ASSOCIATION FOR PHYSICAL EDUCATION OF COLLEGE WOMEN, and THE NATIONAL COLLEGE PHYSICAL EDUCATION ASSOCIATION FOR MEN, *Quest* Editorial Board Monograph Series, 1963–1975.

18

Financing Intramural Programs

HARRY R. OSTRANDER
University of Iowa
Iowa City, Iowa

In reviewing the history of intramurals, one finds that serious problems in financing have existed throughout. The purpose of this chapter is to point out problem areas and to suggest some innovative methods of financing that have proved successful. There are two dimensions of intramural programs that in many instances have greatly influenced the mode and the degree of financial support: (1) the type of organizational structure and (2) the establishment of a student, faculty, and staff advisory committee.

ORGANIZATIONAL STRUCTURE

At many institutions, success in financing the intramural program depends to a large degree upon the type of organizational structure under which intramurals is governed. Intramurals started as a program under the wings of either physical education or intercollegiate athletics. In recent years, however, there appears to be a trend for the intramural director to report to some other authority within the university's central administration. Today, it is not uncommon to find intramural directors reporting to high-level university staff officers, such as the vice-presidents for student services and administration and the dean of students. There are several advantages to this type of administrative organization. It elevates the intramural director to department-head status, a status that he never enjoyed when he reported to either the chairman of the physical education department or the director of intercollegiate athletics. Under this type of organization, the intramural director is usually completely free of administrative accountability to the physical education and intercollegiate athletics departments. As such, he can attempt to fulfill his responsibilities as an advocate for quality intramural and campus recreation programs despite possible conflict with the existing physical education and varsity athletic program.

This type of organization also provides the intramural director with a direct line of communication to central administration, which can result (hopefully) in a greater understanding and consideration of intramural budgetary problems. If the organization and authority for intramurals lies within the physical education department, the intramural budget request must first be submitted to, and subsequently justified before, the chairman of that department. The physical education chairman must then evaluate the intramural request along with other requests he receives from his physical education staff. The next step in the budgetary process is for the physical education chairman to submit his department's request (including the intramural funding appeal) to the dean of the college to which his department is organizationally assigned. The dean then evaluates the physical education budget along with all the other departmental budgets within his range of control. The dean subsequently submits his college's budget to the vice- president of academic affairs, or to some other designated budgeting officer, for final consideration.

By the time the intramural budget request reaches the university budget officer, most intramural funding problems are usually either forgotten or deleted in favor of some other department's needs. However, in an administrative organization where the intramural director reports to the vice-president for student services, he is only one step away from the budgeting officer. The intramural director submits his budget to the vice-president, who in turn submits it to the budget officer. The vice-president should be well aware of the intramural budget needs, as he has worked frequently with the intramural director all year long. The chances of receiving favorable consideration should be improved in those situations where the vice-president is aware of the many dimensions of the intramural situation.

This type of organization also gives intramurals a stronger mandate to serve the largest number of students possible. Student intramural interests and needs should not be subordinate to the interests of either intercollegiate teams or physical education programs. In an administrative organization where intramurals is part of the department of physical education or varsity athletics, one could not reasonably expect the physical education or athletic director to give intramurals the same consideration that he would give to his own program.

ADVISORY COMMITTEE

The establishment of a student, faculty, and staff advisory committee can be extremely helpful in securing adequate funding for the intramural program. The advisory role of the committee should be twofold: first, to advise the university president on proposed recreation and intramural policies submitted by the intramural director; second, to advise the intramural director on the development of short- and long-range plans for campus recreation programs and facilities. Whenever possible, the members of the committee, particularly the faculty and staff members, should be highly respected and influential members of the university community. The advisory committee becomes extremely valuable as an advocate of the interests of the intramural department when negotiations are under way either with central administration over funding requests or with physical education and varsity athletics personnel concerning the use of athletic facilities. Because of the work of the committee in this respect, the intramural director is generally able to maintain a low profile throughout such controversial negotiations. As a result, he is often able to maintain good working relationships with both the central administration and the directors of physical education and athletics, even though heated exchanges may have occurred between these groups and the advisory committee. Another important advantage of such advisory committees are the benefits provided by the various members of the committees. For example, a university law professor could provide legal advice, a business administration professor could be very helpful in budget preparation, and so forth. In many cases, it is both easier and more effective to have the intramural advisory committee, rather than the intramural director, apply pressure for equitable financial support.

METHODS OF FINANCING INTRAMURALS

A number of current practices have contributed to the achievement of successful financial funding for intramural programs. The exact methods employed with each practice vary somewhat from school to school.

Equipment Rental

Items such as canoes, bicycles, toboggans, and camping equipment have proved very popular on many campuses. Usually, the income from rentals is enough to repair and replace the equipment as well as provide a margin of profit.

Annual Projects

Carnivals are popular at many schools. The Gymkana at Florida State University is one of the best organized programs of this kind. This type of activity usually takes a great deal of organization and volunteer help, but the financial benefits are usually well worth the effort.

Organized Trips

Some of the most common types of trips are skiing, canoeing, camping, and scuba diving trips. The type of trip depends on the location of the school and the popularity of the activity. These trips are usually scheduled during nonclassroom times—for instance, Christmas, spring vacation, or during the summer session.

Special Events

The promotion of special events that have wide public appeal has helped solve funding problems at a few schools. Promotion of such events as the Harlem Globetrotters, Roller Derby, and concerts have frequently been very successful. Some events of this type can be brought to the campus without any appreciable financial risk to the intramural department. Some promoters of this type of show are looking for places to hold these events and are willing to schedule the event with little or no guarantee from the local sponsor. The intramural department receives a percentage of the gate receipts for securing the facility, providing ushers and ticket takers, handling local publicity, and so forth. Intramural departments should be careful not to promote too many events of this type, as they may begin to infringe upon the informal use of the available recreation facilities by the students.

Intramurals Without Officials

In some situations, a program of intramurals without officials could result in the saving of several thousand dollars (Hopkins, 1972,

p. 51). Peter D..Hopkins of the University of Waterloo has started an intramural league without officials and has found the practice to work quite well. Hopkins believes that there is an "officials syndrome" in our society—a hate syndrome. According to Hopkins, the benefits of an intramural program without officials are as follows:

1. It is economical.
2. It teaches self-discipline.
3. It is an area of program for the radical element on campus.
4. It reduces the win-at-all-cost attitude that typically predominates in officiated programs.
5. It reduces injuries and fights in the activity. (questionable)
6. It creates a proper atmosphere for coed activities, which are more social in nature.
7. It increases playing time: there are no delays for officials' decisions, such as foul shots and penalties.
8. It simply puts fun into the activity. (questionable)

Entry and Forfeit Fees

Entry fees are usually just enough to cover the cost of providing trophies and awards. The purpose of the forfeit fee (it should be collected in advance and returned only if the team has no forfeits) is to discourage last-minute forfeits. Too many forfeits can be detrimental to the intramural program. Teams look forward to the competition. There is nothing more disappointing than the opposing team not showing up. Forfeits can also be expensive, as the intramural department has already hired officials for that game and in most cases must pay them whether the game is played or not.

Private Enterprise

The University of Minnesota is one school that has made extensive use of this method. During the 1972–73 school year, the Theodore Hamm's Company donated $25,000 for use by the University of Minnesota Intramural Department. The majority of these funds were used for publicizing intramural activities. The Hamm's Company paid for a weekly full-page ad in the University of Minnesota student newspaper. They also made posters containing intramural information and distributed them at various taverns that students frequented. The Hamm's Company also sponsored awards banquets for intramural managers and teams. They also sponsored the first Big Ten Intramural Basketball Tournament, which was held on the University of Minnesota campus. They paid all tournament expenses, including travel money for the teams, room and board, officials, individual jackets for team members, and other incidental expenses connected with the tournament. Obviously, the Theodore Hamm's Company felt that this was a worthwhile indirect means of advertising their product. The use of private enterprise to help finance the intramural department has tremendous potential, as demonstrated by the experience of the University of Minnesota. However, intramural directors must be careful that the terms of the arrangements are determined in concert by the university and the intramural department and not by the private enterprise.

Concessions

Concessions are a means of income that should be considered as a legitimate source of funding for the intramural program. Many intramural programs have several thousand students participating on a regular basis who would welcome a concession stand (or machine) nearby. The profit margin for concession items ranges from 10 to 50 percent, depending upon the product. The University of Illinois has a vending machine that dispenses handballs, squash balls, sweatbands, and other items. To date, the revenue generated from this machine, plus a score of typical food and snack machines, has been considerable. For many years, the Associated Student's Organization at the University of California (Berkeley) has operated a successful supply stand for quick snacks and (minor) athletic equipment in the basement of the university's gymnasium.

THE RECREATIONAL LESSON PROGRAM: A CASE STUDY

One of the less widely publicized methods of generating "intramural income," but still highly successful, is the recreational lesson program. Perhaps the biggest advantage of this program is that it enables you to expand your program offerings to all members of the university community and at the same time produce substantial income for the development of the total intramural program. This method has been used extensively at the University of Iowa. A review of the procedures, advantages, disadvantages, and problems of this program at the University of Iowa is presented below.

The initial step that is necessary to implement this program is for the intramural director to commit himself to the philosophy that intramural and campus recreation programs should meet the needs of the *entire* university community (students, faculty, staff, and the *families* of students, faculty, and staff). Student programs should retain priority, but programs that meet the needs of other members of the university community should also be initiated.

One of the first steps in developing a recreational lesson program is to establish a policy (many universities already have such a policy) that prohibits anyone from using university recreational-athletic facilities for his own private gain. Next, a policy should be established that enables only the intramural department to utilize recreational-athletic facilities for instructional programs for which a fee is charged. This is not to be confused with the instructional programs offered to registered students for academic credit by the physical education department.

Once these policies are established, you are ready to develop a recreational lesson program geared to the needs of your particular campus community. The type of program that proves successful will vary from campus to campus. Any such program must be structured and organized around the existing physical education, athletic, and intramural schedules. Some programs may be impossible to implement on your particular campus because of either lack of the proper facilities or a lack of program time on the available facilities.

The University of Iowa has based its recreational lesson programs on the following criteria:

1. Programs should not be scheduled on facilities during periods of peak student use.
2. Programs must be professionally administered and supervised.
3. Highly qualified instructors (students, whenever possible) should be employed.
4. All registration fees should be reasonable but must cover the cost of the program plus provide a margin of profit.

There are many ways to organize and structure recreational lesson programs. The following examples illustrate the methods used at the University of Iowa.

1. *Gymnastics*

Method: Seven-week session. Participants may register for one or two classes a week.

Available to: Preschool through adult (release form required).

Registration Fee: $13 for those attending once a week and $20 for those coming twice a week.

Instructors: There is one instructor for every eight participants. Wages vary between $3.50 and $5.00 per hour, depending upon experience. The director of the program is paid $10 per hour.

Number of Participants: Approximately 400 per session. There are four sessions per year. Each class has approximately 48 participants.

2. *Yoga*

Method: Conducted on a semester basis. Classes meet twice a week.

Available to: Family-oriented activity. Youth must be at least 10 years of age.

Registration Fee: $10 for individual registration, $15 for two from the same family, or $20 for all members of a family.

Instructor: One instructor, who receives two-thirds of the registration fees; the intramural office receives the other third.

3. *Women's Self-Defense*

Method: Eight-week session, meetings twice a week.

Available to: Women, tenth grade and above (release form required).

Registration fee: $10 per person.

Instructor: Instructors (2) receive two thirds of the registration fees and the intramural office receives one third.

Number of Participants: Approximately 15 to 20 per session.

4. *Karate*

Method: Conducted on a semester basis with participants meeting twice a week.

Available to: 16 years old and above (release form required).

Registration Fee: $25 for all new participants and $15 for anyone enrolled in any previous session.

Instructors: Instructors (5) receive two-thirds of the registration fees and the intramural office one-third.

Number of Participants: Approximately 50 per session.

5. *Aikido*

Method: Conducted on a semester basis with participants meeting three times per week.

Available to: 16 years old and above (release form required).

Registration fee: $25 for new participants and $20 for anyone enrolled in any previous session.

Instructors: One instructor, who receives two-thirds of the registration fees; the intramural office receives the other third.

Number of Participants: 10 to 15 per session.

6. *Scuba Diving*

Method: Classes meet once a week for ten weeks. Classes include one hour of lecture and two hours of pool time.

Available to: 16 years old and above.

Registration Fee: $50 per person, which includes tank, regulator, and air.

Instructor: Instructor receives two-thirds and the intramural office one-third.

Participants: Approximately 50 to 75 per session.

7. *Tennis*

Method: Offered on three levels: (a) group lessons meeting twice a week for four weeks; (b) individual instruction—participant may register for any number of lessons; and (c) on a clinic basis.

Available to: Third grade and above.

Registration fee: $5 per person for group lessons. $3 to $4 per half-hour individual lesson, and $10 per person for clinic instruction. Three group sessions are conducted—in May, June, and July. Individual instruction is offered during June, July, and August.

Instructors: Instructors receive $5 per hour for group lessons; $2.50 to $3.50 per half hour (intramural office receives $.50 of each individual lesson fee) for individual instruction; and two-thirds of clinic registrations—intramural office receives one-third.

Number of Participants: There are approximately 100 participants per group session (each class is limited to 10), over 700 enrolled in individual lessons, and approximately 60 in clinic instruction. Clinic instruction is for the more advanced player who wants special coaching in tournament strategy and other advanced areas. Clinics are usually limited to 20 participants.

8. *Golf*

Method: Golf is offered on both a group and individual basis. Group lessons meet twice a week for four weeks. Participants may register for any number of lessons for individual instruction.

Available to: Third grade and above.

Registration Fee: $5 per session for group lessons, $3 to $4 per half-hour individual lesson. Three group sessions are conducted—in May, June, and July. Individual instruction is offered during June, July, and August.

Instructors: Instructors receive $5 per hour for group lessons and $2.50 to $3.50 per half-hour (intramural office receives $.50 of each individual lesson fee) for individual instruction.

Number of Participants: There are approximately 100 participants per group session (each class is limited to 10) and about 50 enrolled for individual lessons.

9. *Adult Beginning Swimming*

Method: Classes meet three times a week for ten weeks. Classes consist of one hour of pool and lecture time.

Available to: 18 years old and above.

Registration Fee: $10.

Instructor: Instructors (one for every ten participants) receive two-thirds and the intramural office one-third.

Participants: Approximately ten per class.

Of all the factors that must be considered when developing a program of pay-as-you-go instruction (such as recreational lessons), perhaps none is more important than the legal and liability parameters of the program. It is an absolute necessity that this consideration be *thoroughly* investigated. Table 1 is an example of a release form used by the University of Iowa in its gymnastics program.

Table 1. Gymnastics Instructional Program Release Form

Division of Recreational Services
University of Iowa

Room 111   Field House

Iowa City, Iowa

I, _____ (name) _____, in consideration of the Division of Recreational Services of the University of Iowa granting me permission to participate in its Gymnastic Instructional Program, hereby assume all risk of personal injury (including death) that may result from participation in said Program; and acting for myself, my heirs, personal representatives, and assigns, do hereby release the University of Iowa, its Board of Regents, individually and collectively, the Division of Recreational Services, members of the University faculty, administrative officers, all other agents, representatives, and employees of the said University, gymnastic instructors and all other participants in the said Program from all liability, including claims and suits at law or in equity, for an injury, fatal, or otherwise, that may result from my taking part in said Program.

Signature _____

University Address _____

Home Address _____

IF PARTICIPANT IS A MINOR (IN IOWA, AGE 18 OR LESS), THIS RELEASE MUST BE SIGNED BY THE PARTICIPANT'S PARENT OR LEGAL GUARDIAN.

I, _____, as parent (or legal guardian) of

_____, the person executing the foregoing release, do hereby give my permission for said person to participate in the said Program, and consent to all terms and conditions of said release.

Signature _____

Address _____

PROBLEMS AND ISSUES

There are a number of fundamental problems and issues that must be considered when planning a funding program for the intramural department. Since the situation varies somewhat from campus to campus, however, each problem must be viewed within a conceptual framework if an appropriate solution is to be reached.

Relationship with Physical Education and Intercollegiate Athletics

Since campus recreation programs must usually share recreational facilities with both the physical education and the varsity athletics departments, it is desirable (whenever possible) for the intramural director to establish and maintain a cordial working relationship with the high-level staff of each department. Very few universities can afford separate facilities for intramurals, physical education, and varsity athletics. In addition, on many campuses equipment is utilized mutually by the three departments. In an arrangement of mutual use of equipment, intramurals typically benefits the most since physical education and athletics frequently have greater resources to purchase and maintain athletic equipment. Such arrangements can also have beneficial consequences for the "sharing" department. For example, if budget requests are granted priority on the basis of total usage data, the "occasional" sharing of equipment with the intramural department can increase the justification and legitimacy of requests for such equipment. Assisting such a visible program as intramural activities can also benefit a department's public relations—an area in which many varsity athletic directors can use help. Unfortunately, on many campuses the intramural director has failed to establish good interdepartmental working relationships, particularly with athletics. Frankly, such individuals have spent too much time blaming varsity athletics and physical education programs for their funding problems rather than addressing themselves to solutions to the problems. In universities where there are poor interdepartmental relationships, it is not uncommon to find considerable unnecessary duplication of facilities and equipment.

The Role of the Advisory Committee

The advantages of having a committee of independent university community members to advise the intramural department on funding matters have previously been discussed in detail. However, the establishment of such a committee may also lead to some problems. The role and the responsibilities of the committee must be clearly defined. Committee members should be encouraged to provide recommendations relating to intramural policy, but they should not become actively involved in *administering* the intramural program.

Unfortunately, on almost every committee, whether advisory or policy-making, there are one or two members who insist upon involving themselves in the active administration of the department. When this happens, the intramural director should remind these committee members in a diplomatic manner that their role is limited to advisory and support responsibilities. The function of the intramural staff is to carry out that policy and to administer the intramural program.

Since many matters that are occasionally discussed by the advisory committee also involve, to some degree, both the physical education and the athletic departments, it is recommended that the directors of each department (or their designated representatives) be appointed ex-officio members of the intramural advisory committee. This should facilitate communication among the three departments, prevent unnecessary misunderstandings, and provide the framework to coordinate all capital expenditure programs and efforts.

Attitude of Faculty and Administrators

Many faculty members and university administrators hold the attitude that since intramural programs are primarily service-oriented (as opposed to academic-oriented), they should receive a lower priority than requests relating directly to the academic program. In situations where such misguided attitudes affect equitable funding for his department's efforts, the intramural director must develop a strategy to convince those administrators in a position of financial power that the university does, in fact, have an obligation to provide leisure experiences for its students.

Programming for the Nonstudent

It is a universal proposition on most campuses that students should have priority regarding intramural programming opportunities and the use of recreational facilities. This assumption, however, is no reason for the remaining members of the university community to be completely ignored. Unfortunately, this is the case on far too many campuses. Usually, the excuse offered by the administrator is that he does not have adequate facilities for his own students, let alone "outside" interests. What many administrators do not consider is that sometimes one needs to create a problem in order to solve a problem. When the intramural director is content with the existing amount of recreational space (even though the limited facilities restrict the leisure opportunities only to students), what catalyst can prompt the university administration into providing additional facilities? A strong case can be made that vocal controversy over limited facilities is the one best technique at the intramural director's disposal for justifying the need for more facilities. The university has an obligation to its entire community membership: students, faculty, staff, and families of students, faculty, and staff. The intramural director has the responsibility of seeing that this obligation is met in regard to intramurals and recreation.

SUMMARY

In conclusion, it can be argued that the time has arrived for intramural directors to become innovative and to develop new methods of financing their own programs. Effective organizational accountability and a viable financial advisory committee are two of the most important components of successful funding efforts. A wide variety of some of the most successful methods have been presented in this chapter. Failure to provide adequate funding can no longer be blamed totally on an administration that is insensitive to the needs of the intramural program; rather, the intramural director must pursue alternate sources. The financial support to provide "leisure for all" must be found!

GENERAL BIBLIOGRAPHY

BALRIDGE, J. VICTOR, ed., *Academic Governance.* Berkeley: McCutchan Publishing, 1971.

HANIFORD, GEORGE, "Future Trends in Intramurals: Organization and Finances," *National Intramural Association Proceedings,* XIX 1968), 16–18.

HOPKINS, PETER D., "Intramurals Without Officials," *National Intramural Association Proceedings,* XXIII (1972), 51–54.

MAAS, GERALD M.; C. E. MUELLER; and BRUCE D. ANDERSON, "Survey of Administrative Reporting Sequences and Funding Sources for Intramural-Extramural Programs in Two-Year and Four-Year Colleges in the United States and Canada," *National Intramural Association Proceedings,* XXV (1974), 122–26.

MILLER, VAN, *The Public Administration of American School Systems.* New York: Macmillan, 1965.

MINER, JERRY, *Social and Economic Factors in Spending for Public Education.* Syracuse: Syracuse University Press, 1963.

OSTRANDER, HARRY R., "Innovative Methods of Financing Your Programs," *National Intramural Association Proceedings,* XXIII (1972), 62–66.

19

Procuring, Training, and Evaluating Intramural Sports Officials

LOUIS MARCIANI
University of Southern Mississippi
Hattiesburg, Mississippi

INTRODUCTION

"Officials threatened and abused . . ."
"Worst year for IM sportsmanship . . ."
"Brawl erupts at IM BB game . . ."
"Allen charged criminally in intramural incident . . . faces battery count . . ."
"ATO receives suspension . . ."
"Kappa Alpha Psi suspended . . ."
"Intramural officiating . . . a thankless job . . ."
"IM protest board suspends team . . ."

Above are but a few of the headlines that appeared in college student newspapers during the early 1970s. In every instance, the headline referred to a serious incident that occurred either during or as the result of an intramural contest. Unfortunately, the frequency of such incidences has been increasing in recent years. In many respects, the treatment accorded student officials is a microcosm of the manner in which officials are sometimes dealt with in professional sports. Student officials have been physically abused, cursed at, threatened, and generally intimidated. An avocation that was once an easy way for the athletic-oriented student to earn some spending money has been transformed, for many individuals, into an emotional nightmare where all but the very brave or the very foolish fear to tread. Since the quality of student officiating frequently plays a major role in the quality of the intramural program, what can the intramural director do to improve this critical aspect of the intramural program? This chapter attempts to answer that question.

A CASE STUDY

The stage was set for a typical fall afternoon intramural football game pitting the Hustlers against the Raiders, two arch rivals on the gridiron. Because of the publicity concerning the game, a large crowd appeared on the sidelines to witness the contest. While the teams prepared for the game, the intramural student supervisor was searching frantically for his three prospective officials for the contest. Eventually reporting to the supervisor were the referee and linesman. The prospective umpire did not show up for the game, leaving the student supervisor to go through the crowd looking for a "body" to act in the capacity of an official. Suddenly, the student supervisor persuaded a former varsity football athlete to officiate. The student supervisor was elated to have a "body" officiate rather than have the game rescheduled.

The touch football game was under way. Both teams demonstrated an explosive offense as they each scored twice in the first half. The complexity of the game changed drastically during the second half when both defensive squads "tightened their belts." No scoring took place in the third quarter, but as the fourth quarter began, the feeling was that the tight defensive battle would burst sooner or later.

Time was running short: only 25 seconds remained in the tied game. The Hustlers had the ball on the Raiders' 18 with a third-down situation. The Hustlers' quarterback rolled out to his left and heaved the ball downfield into the end zone. Although both the receiver and the defender ran for the ball, the receiver made a diving catch in the end zone. Unfortunately, all three officials were so preoccupied looking at the pass play develop in the end zone that they failed to realize that the Hustlers' quarterback was beyond the line of scrimmage when he released the ball. A touchdown was signaled, giving the Hustlers the victory as time ran out. Pandemonium broke loose as the final horn sounded. The air became punctuated with cries of "Hey, ref! Did you get your license at Sears?" The Raiders ran furiously to the student supervisor, asking that the game be put under protest. They were in such an emotional state that they lost all control and proceeded to assault one of the officials. The fight was broken up and order finally restored. Immediately, the student supervisor phoned the intramural director to explain the situation.

The following day, the intramural advisory committee met to re-resolve the question of the Raiders' alleged misconduct. The Raiders' defense of their action was based on their opinion that the game had been poorly officiated. The officials, explained the Raiders, lacked an acceptable knowledge of the rules and failed to use proper officiating mechanics and procedures. Upon investigation, the committee found that the charge was partially substantiated. The referee was an experienced official who had three years of touch football officiating experience and had successfully completed the training program. The linesman was in his first year of officiating and had also gone through the training program. He had, however, recently failed the preseason practical evaluation. Because of the shortage of officials, however, the supervisor was forced to use him. The umpire had no officiating training but was a letterman on the varsity football team. As a result of this investigation, the committee recommended that the intramural department undertake a reevaluation of the entire officiating program. In addition, the advisory committee suspended the Raiders from all intramural competition until the following semester. In this situation nobody won. The program received adverse publicity. An individual was assaulted. Several students were prohibited from further competition for a period of time.

Although this is a hypothetical situation, many intramural directors are probably familiar with several aspects of these circumstances. How many times are violent comments concerning the capabilities of student officials heard each year? How many protests each year are based on incompetent officiating? What effect has the number of incidents had on the difficulties in recruiting competent officials? Is there any rational way to limit the number of fights or temper flare-ups that result from the decisions of student officials? It can hardly be questioned that a major determining factor in the success of a competitive intramural sports program is the degree of competence displayed by the officials in game situations.

This chapter undertakes an in-depth analysis of the problem of procuring, training, and evaluating sports officials. Because of the differences in programs, facilities, personnel, and institutional traditions from school to school, a single model or solution to the problems attendant to student officiating cannot be identified. Hopefully, an examination of several practices that have been developed through the years and some of the techniques that are being developd today will provide the reader with the information necessary to functionally approach his own officiating situation. The practices or methods described in this chapter are limited in scope to the procurement, training, and evaluation of officials for the team sports.

PROCURING OFFICIALS

As in the case of the Hustlers-Raiders game, many intramural departments frequently are confronted with a shortage of qualified student officials. In order to have an adequate number of competent officials, it is critically important to initially attract as large a group of prospective officials as possible prior to the training and evaluation phase.

Intramural directors throughout the country utilize various methods to procure prospective intramural officials. These methods range from catch-as-catch-can techniques of accepting anyone, regardless of ability or background, to more sophisticated methods, such as attracting and signing up officials who are enrolled in accredited sports officiating courses. (Rhoads, 1963, p. 81). Among other recruitment methods that have traditionally been utilized are the selection of officials from the varsity athletes in that sport (Means, 1973, p. 42), volunteer officials (Mueller, 1971, p. 202), officials provided by the competing teams (Voltmer and Lapp, 1949, p. 66), the use of physical education majors (Sezak, 1968, p. 31), the assignment of officials through an officials' club (Sawyer, 1973, p. 53), and paid student officials (Thompson, 1968, p. 35).

The specific methods of procuring officials vary from school to school and depend on many factors. These variables include the school's programs, size of student enrollment, location of institution, finances available for officiating, intramural staff, and the degree of administrative commitment by the intramural director to excellence and competence in his student officials. Keeping these variables in mind, the reader should examine several of the more common methods of securing officials and identify those methods applicable to his situation.

Volunteer Officials

The practice of using volunteer officials is most prevalent in intramural programs at the junior and senior high school level, at small colleges, and at colleges with programs that have limited funds for this type of expenditure. There is usually little difficulty at the public school level in obtaining boys and girls who wish to officiate. Since many students at this age feel a sense of pride and importance when asked to assume such a severe responsibility, they are frequently eager to volunteer. Many intramural directors at this level improve the probability of success in attracting volunteers by offering awards and participation points to their student officials as additional incentives. Faculty officials are also used at this level. Many faculty members involve themselves in this type of activity in order to satisfy their extracurricular duty requirement (*Physical Education Newsletter,* 1965, p. 4; and *Physical Education Newsletter,* 1968, p. 2).

At the college level, the term "volunteer" can only be applied loosely. Most college intramural directors utilize this system more in a mandatory capacity. Two approaches exist in "attracting" volunteers. Each organization is required to provide an official either for its own contest or for inclusion into a pool of officials who will be assigned games by the intramural director (Thompson, 1968, p. 35). This system adapts itself well to colleges with a low enrollment and to institutions lacking adequate officiating monies. The disadvantages to this system, however, quite outweigh its advantages. Since many of the "volunteers" have been appointed by their teammates to act in the capacity of the required official, the intramural administrator must literally take what he gets. The administrator has no idea of the volunteer official's competence (Thompson, 1968, p. 35). In this author's opinion, the existence of these unknown factors can only produce a game of Russian roulette. Chance becomes the governing factor of the program. Quality officiating becomes only a haphazard by-product rather than a prime tenet of the competitive sports progam.

Another mandatory approach that is occasionally used to "attract" volunteers at the college level is the use of varsity athletes as officials. Many coaches feel that this type of internship improves the player's understanding of the game, and they are therefore willing to lend "their" athletes to the intramural program. Although these individuals have more than a casual insight into the rules that govern their respective sport, the element of chance is still a prominent factor in this type of selection. The intramural director is once again faced with the problem of ascertaining whether or not he has a quality officiating program. Although a strong background in a particular sport is certainly a desirable qualification for an official, it does not necessarily constitute a quality official (Thompson, 1968, p. 35). Once again, the intramural director is playing Russian roulette—taking what he can get and hoping it all works out for the best.

Paid Officials

One of the most widely used means of attracting student officials at the college and university level is financial reimbursement (Means, 1973, p. 42). Without question, paying officials for services rendered usually results in a more selective process. The intramural administrator, as employer, is provided the opportunity to interview and screen candidates. Obviously, this method is suited only to college and university programs that have ample resources to fund such a program. Although financial reimbursement is perhaps one of the most successful methods of procuring officials, intramural administrators are also discovering that in order to achieve acceptable results, they must have the funds available to offer a higher-than-average student employment wage scale (Cook, 1969, p. 36). This is particularly valid in an urban campus setting, where job opportunities exist in the community. The lack of funds to raise the pay scale, however, presents less of a problem on a rural campus, where job opportunities are usually somewhat limited.

Sports Officiating Course

Several intramural departments have been able to use an existing sports officiating course as a valuable source of student officials. Since the prospective officials in these courses are receiving academic credit for their training, they usually obtain more adequate preparation. Also, assignment and control problems are usually less difficult with this source. Another positive aspect of this method is that it can frequently provide the student official with an opportunity to be associated with a local officials' association. Where this option exists, the student can take the state examination for certification through the state high school athletic association and become an official in public school competition (Kurth, 1966, p. 51).

Unfortunately, this system does not represent the ultimate cure-all to procurement problems. In many instances, the intramural director cannot rely on the course to meet all of the officiating needs of his program. In addition, officiating courses exist only at colleges and universities that offer a physical education, recreation, or professional coaching major.

New Outlooks in Procurement

In order to give impetus to and enhance the success of the methods that will be used to attract competent student officials in the years to come, several courses of action may be taken. As indicated above, there appears to be a trend at many colleges and universities to rely less on "volunteers" and more on the use of financial reimbursement as a means of procuring adequate officials. In most instances, the latter method has been the most successful. With a few modifications (for instance, salaries above the student minimum wage, and incentive pay scales), this method would appear to be the most popular system currently and the most promising one for the future.

Although the paying of officials is being adopted by more and more institutions, there are still schools where this is impractical. Certainly, if no funds are available, volunteer officials will have to suffice. In spite of this obstacle, alternate means of attracting and utilizing "volunteer" officials should be examined.

A greater emphasis might be placed upon a college-accredited course in sports officiating. This has already proved successful in many colleges and universities, such as Long Beach City College, the University of Nebraska, Omaha; Ohio University; and California State College at Long Beach. This course has alleviated many of the problems associated with the procurement and training of intramural officials in highly organized team sports. The advantage of the course is the constant source of available officials, who are under the constant direction and supervision of a qualified instructor. The same approach has proved successful at the junior and senior high school levels: in certain schools, a sports officiating course is offered during the last period of the school day. The secondary schools in the Abilene, Texas, area offer this option through their physical education department. If for one reason or another it is impossible to institute such a course, an alternative method might be to offer academic credit in a different fashion for intramural officiating. For example, variable credit could be offered for an independent study or contract course that involved a certain amount of officiating.

If academic credit cannot be offered for sports officiating, another option is to organize a sports officiating club. These clubs have proved successful at several institutions. The funding of these organizations should not present a major problem. If these clubs are members of the student activities association, student funds should be available—either directly, from the student activities budget, or indirectly, through a transfer of intramural funds to the club for services performed, such as officiating activities. Even if funds were unavailable, sports officiating clubs could still be utilized. Using the spirit-of-service approach, club meetings could be held for the purpose of learning rules, observing films, making assignments, and so forth.

One of the most effective procurement systems currently in operation is the credit-plus-pay plan at California State College at Long Beach. Not only does this combined approach give a student credit for a course in officiating and organizing intramural sports, but the student also qualifies to receive pay for all games officiated after a minimum number to meet the course requirement. Ideally, the most satisfactory system for attracting officials would incorporate some of the desirable qualities of all three of the methods we have discussed: financial reimbursement, academic credit, and a sports officiating club.

Publicity and Procurement

Regardless of what system is utilized in procuring officials, the student population should be aware of the opportunities to officiate. Too many times, the methods used to attract officials are basically sound but still result in a shortage of competent officials.

In order for the officiating program to have some "breathing room," a large number of prospective officials should be enrolled in the training program. Good publicity for the college program is a must in attracting qualified applicants. There are several means of publicizing officiating opportunities. Kent State University contacts all known former officials and solicits their cooperation and help. This institution also sends letters to all fraternities, dormitories, and independent athletic managers asking their aid in procuring officials (Rees, 1968, p. 40). Other media that have been utilized for the publicizing of officiating opportunities are posters, hotlines, bulletin boards, handbooks, campus radio, and television (Figure 1). Some of the more recent and successful media techniques being used to attract qualified applicants are multimedia slide productions on intramural officiating; video-tape commercials on closed-circuit televisions located in the college union, classrooms, and halls; and a transparency bulletin board advertising the officiating program.

Too many intramural directors publicize their program to increase intramural participation but fail to pour an equal amount of energy into attracting good individuals to officiate. These administrators should remember that the success of a competitive intramural program is in large measure related to the level of excellence in the officiating program.

TRAINING OFFICIALS

Ask any administrator of an intramural program to list several problem areas in his program and the probability is high that the training of officials will be the major problem. Unfortunately, if situations such as those in the Hustlers-Raiders game continue to occur, intramural programs will eventually deteriorate in quality. One of the most influential factors in a successful program is excellence in officiating. On the other hand, the development of adequate methods of training student officials is one on the most difficult problems confronting the intramural administrator. Many intramural protests and conflicts result from a lack of competent officiating. When student officials exhibit a poor working

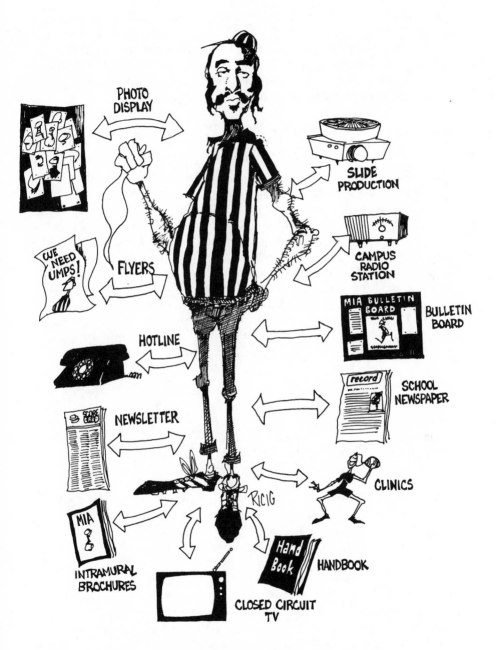

Figure 1. Promotional Media Used to Attract Officials

knowledge of the rules, poor positioning, and poor mechanics, the intramural director should examine the methods used to train them. When the officials are not properly trained, they cannot execute their responsibilities competently. In order for the intramural director to determine the best possible training method for his particular situation, he should review the various means of doing so.

Sports Officiating Association

An extremely popular method of training officials is through a sports officiating association. This volunteer organization can draw from a wide spectrum of the student population since it is not limited to certain academic areas, such as physical education. At the club meetings, which are arranged on a weekly basis, students discuss rules, observe films, make assignments, and learn the mechanics of officiating.

The key to a successful officiating club is a commitment by the director to make the organization as attractive as possible. The possibility of being paid for working intramural contests is one attractive characteristic. Another is the potential working relationship with local officiating chapters. Through these contacts an intramural official may become a certified member of the local officiating association, thereby making him eligible to referee nonuniversity athletic contests (Sawyer, 1973, p. 53).

Sports Officiating Course

Intramural directors who are fortunate enough to be at a school that offers a sports officiating course believe this to be a valuable tool in molding competent officials. This method provides the student with a full semester of instruction and training. Some of the techniques that are utilized in such a course are guest speakers—outstanding officials, coaches, and athletes—who provide their own insights, experiences, and philosophies of officiating; practice game situations on the field; and the media capability of reenacting plays and/or situations. Commercial officiating films can be shown along with the institution's varsity scouting films to provide students with a visual aid in learning the correct officiating positions and mechanics during game situations. Various rule books, casebooks, officiating guides, and textbooks can also be employed in this course. A few institutions video-tape several intramural contests and use the tapes as an instructional aid in the officiating class. Specially prepared transparencies and slides that illustrate proper officiating mechanics can be added to the instruction.

As with sports officiating clubs, this method provides the student with an opportunity to become associated with the local officials' association and to attend a local chapter's rule interpretation meetings. At some schools, the final exam for this course includes taking the state examination for certification, thus becoming eligible to officiate public school athletic contests. Another outstanding feature of the sports officiating course is that it generally provides the intramural program with an instant "crop" of student officials. One of the typical requirements of an officiating course is that each enrollee officiate a specific number of intramural contests.

One of the more innovative approaches to supplying officials is the aforementioned credit-plus-play plan being used at California State College at Long Beach. This program has proved successful not only in achieving high morale in the classroom but also in providing high-quality student officials. Unfortunately, adoption of this particular method is usually limited to those institutions offering a major in physical education.

Training Clinics

The most widely used method of instructing officials is by means of training clinics. As a new sport season approaches, the learning program for all prospective intramural officials, both volunteer and paid, starts with a clinic designed to prepare these student employees for the coming season. At the minimum, this intensive phase of preparation should accord attention to rule interpretations, officiating films, local rule modifications, mechanics of officiating, a practice game checkout, and a rules test. (Thompson, 1968, p. 36).

These clinics are usually conducted over a concentrated period of time. The length and duration of these sessions depend on situational factors (such as amount of experience of the applicants and level of competitiveness in the program). In most instances, it is desirable to require all prospective officials to attend these clinics.

These officials clinics are normally continued throughout the sport season. Either the intramural director or the supervisor of officials conducts the meetings. Many institutions hold these clinics either weekly or biweekly after the season is under way. A number of exams can be conducted at these meetings. Game assignments are made, rule interpretations and judgment calls are discussed in the context of experiences on the field, mechanics are reviewed, and video tapes are shown. A few intramural departments even pay their officials to attend these clinics (Wanamaker, 1969, p. 180). Additional assistance at many of these clinics can be obtained through the cooperative efforts of local officiating chapters. When this is the case, these organizations constitute an added attraction of the clinic. In these situations, members of the local association (prefer-

ably veteran officials) either are paid or volunteer to discuss and interpret the rules and to review proper officiating mechanics with the intramural officials (Sezak, 1968, p. 31).

The Use of Video Tape

As an aid to the aforementioned methods of training officials,
several colleges and universities are adopting video-tape procedures as
a means of preparing and evaluating their officials. Video-tape as an instructional tool has certain characteristics that can be beneficial in the
training of officials. Video taping permits the immediate playback (in
slow motion, if desired) of a recorded play. This playback capability
greatly facilitates the analysis of game situations and rule interpretations.
In addition video taping can provide a self-instructional means for the
training of officials (Hixson, 1971, p. 62).

The equipment needed to tape and view performance consists of
video tape, recording unit, camera, and monitor. In recent years, portable
equipment has been developed that allows video taping at nearly any
location.*

Several intramural administrators are also using video tape in providing instruction at their on-the-field clinics. Parts of practice games
are taped and viewed immediately. This "instant" review allows the official to watch the game in action as rules are presented. Many times, a
visual interpretation bridges the gap that exists in attempts to explain
and interpret rules (Cook, 1969, p. 34).

Video tapes are also being used as instructional aids in sports officiating courses. Several intramural contests are video-taped, reviewed
and edited, and shown, accompanied by appropriate instructor's comments on officials' mechanics. This project has proved successful in illus-
trating to prospective officials the proper field or floor positions and
mechanics (Tyler, 1971, p. 2).

Another innovative idea for utilizing video tape was conceived by
the intramural staff at Iowa State University. Getting all of the officials
together at one convenient time for the training clinics proved to be a
major problem at ISU. To solve this problem, the ISU staff video-taped
the training sessions and made video-tape cassettes of them available at
the convenience of each individual. These tapes are kept on file at the
ISU learning resources center.

The utilization of video tape in the training of officials is becoming
more refined and flexible; color has been added, for example. In addition, research is currently under way to explore the many potential uses

---

* The Sony Corporation has a portable video system on the market. This unit is
lightweight and features a zoom lens and freeze-frame capability.

of this valuable tool in all phases of education. The intramural director who wishes to improve this officials program should use this tool on the athletic fields and courts if he is to obtain a real conception of its potential value.

Individualized Learning Modules

Traditionally, intramural directors have been responsible for training a group of 20 to 150 student officials for each team sport, and they have attempted to provide instruction for this group at the same time, place, and rate of speed. Current instructional methods for training sports officials, such as an officiating course, an officiating club, clinics, or a combination of these methods, have been somewhat restrictive since they tend to place a major emphasis upon efficient group organization and in turn tend to neglect the importance of individual progress and achievement. A strong case can be made that drastic instructional and organizational change is needed to revise and improve the teaching-learning process so that it can adapt to individual differences.

Several "radical" changes were undertaken in the instruction of intramural sports officials at the State University College at Buffalo while this author was employed there. A sequence of competency-based learning modules was developed and implemented making a shift from traditional group learning to competency-based instruction.*

Two questions should be asked by the intramural director seeking assistance in this area: What is competency-based instruction? Does it have application to my program? Kliendienst and Weston have answered the first inquiry.

> It is based on the specification or definition of what constitutes competency in a given field. The way in which the agreed-upon level of competency is communicated is through the use of specific, behavioral objectives from which criterion levels of performance have been established. Once the required behaviors have been specified, an instructional sequence is planned that will help the learner achieve the desired behaviors. When the learner is ready, a test or self-analysis of some sort is administered to determine if the required level of competency has been achieved. (1972, p. 29)

In short, a learning module is a process by which specific competencies are transmitted to the student. The instruction is individualized and personalized.

The first step in the development of these learning modules is to

* This work was funded through the New York State University Faculty Grant for the Improvement of Undergraduate Instruction.

establish appropriate behavioral objectives for the program. These objectives should be specific and detailed so as to indicate precisely to the student what is expected, the conditions under which the expected performance is to occur, and the criteria by which the performance is judged to be acceptable. An example of this type of objective would be:

> Given a Pass Infraction Learning Module, the student will identify the basic rules associated with an illegal forward pass, an illegal backward pass, ineligible receivers, and pass interference. Evidence of identification will be obtained by completion of the ten-question video-tape self-analysis module on passing infractions. The lower limit of acceptable performance will be 80 percent accurancy.

The students' rate of progress through the program is determined by demonstrated competence rather than by time or course completion. These objectives should be understood clearly by the student before he enters the program.

The second step is the pre-assessment, which indicates the competence a student possesses upon entering the module. It is normally not necessary for students to repeat competencies already mastered. The instructor might suggest, however, that the student, although successfully demonstrating competency in that module, review the video-tape learning module to enrich and reinforce his knowledge. An example of pre-assignment for an intramural touch football module would be:

> The student will complete a self-analysis module on passing situation infractions. The lower limit of acceptable performance will be 80 percent accuracy.

Perhaps the essential part of the learning module sequence is that designated "instructional activities." Here the instructor and student agree jointly on how best to acquire the necessary skills—by studying the rule book, viewing the video-tape learning module, attending an officiating class, studying the officials' cartooned manual, and so forth. Although the student directs his own learning program, the instructor assumes the role of diagnostician, guide, and evaluator.

The student is held accountable for his performance, completing the prepared program when and only when he has demonstrated the competencies that have been identified. This is accomplished through the post-assessment, an example of which would be:

> The student will complete a self-analysis video-tape module on passing situation infractions. Satisfactory completion will be based on correct responses to 80 percent of the questions.

The learning experience of the individual depends on feedback for the correction of error and improvement of efficiency. Feedback in the competency-based learning module consists of having a student see and hear how others react to his performance, *and boy do they hear it!* In addition, feedback serves as a self-evaluative tool when the student checks his responses on the self-analysis video-tape modules or observes video-tape segments of his officiating experiences. On the basis of feedback, the instructor and student might plan remedial work that the student must complete satisfactorily in order to accomplish the objectives.

The emphasis in this program is on exit rather than entrance requirements. Performance is the criterion of evaluation. If the student is able to perform acceptably prior to, during, or at the conclusion, he is considered to have completed the competency area.

Figure 2 illustrates a competency-based learning module sequence. The candidates for officiating may come from various areas: training clinics, a sports officiating course, an officiating club, an independent study, or a contract course; or they may just be students who are interested in officiating. Each prospective student official is administered a diagnostic evaluation (step 2), which is designed to determine his degree of competency and the point at which he should begin the learning sequence. This diagnostic process consists of responding to a written test and responding to ten video-tape self-analysis modules. These self-analysis modules help identify specific competencies in certain sports. For example, in touch and flag football competencies would include kicking rules, penalty administration and enforcement, pass infractions, timing principles, and officials' positions and responsibilites.

These modules, together with the accompanying booklet, constitute the primary evaluating process. This process is then implemented in the following manner. The commentator asks a question while the student views the play on the screen. After viewing the play, the student completes the question by selecting one answer. He then checks his answer by referring to the accompanying booket. The correct answer is printed on the back of the question page. This assures the student immediate feedback. The lower limit of acceptable performance is 80 percent accuracy.

On the basis of the diagnostic evaluation results, the student either selects or is guided by the instructor to his appropriate starting point in the learning modules (step 3). At this point, the student is provided with an individualized prescribed method of study containing any or all of the following: participating in instructional classes or clinics; viewing a competency-based learning module; studying the rule book, casebook, and officials' manual. At this time, he is directed to the facility housing the competency-based learning modules.

STEPS

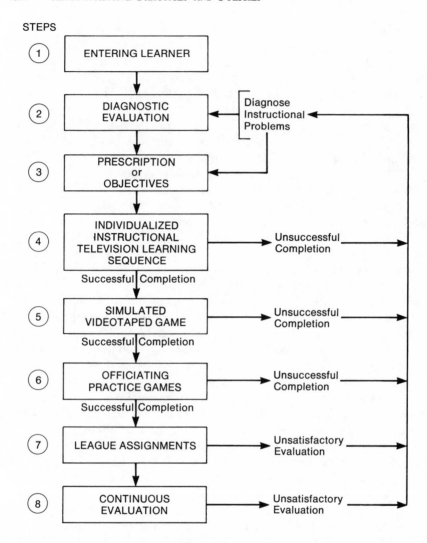

Figure 2. Outline of Sports Officiating Training Program

The student is now ready to begin viewing one of the prescribed learning modules (step 4). After viewing one of these modules, the student determines if he has successfully achieved the lower limit of acceptable performance. He does this by viewing the self-analysis module associated with the above learning module. If he answers eight of the ten questions successfully, he then advances to the next learning module. If he fails to answer eight questions correctly, he is directed to replay that learning module and/or study the various other learning alternatives.

When the student completes the ten competency-based learning modules satisfactorily, he must then officiate a simulated video-tape game (step 5). This experience measures the degree to which he has accomplished the terminal objectives. This concept places the learner in a contrived situation that is real or as nearly "lifelike" as possible and requires him to perform (a process) or produce (a product). In many instances, much can be inferred about a process from observing its product; the two are interrelated. Since competency is extremely important by this stage of learning, the lower limit of acceptable performance will be 98 percent accuracy. The procedure during the simulated game experience begins with the commentator verbally cueing the viewer as to his responsibility during the upcoming play. The commentator then asks the question while it appears on the screen. The play is shown, and the viewer proceeds to answer the question. The viewer's responses are recorded immediately on an electronic board. The responses are automatically recorded and a print-out of the individual and/or group achievement is given to both the student(s) and the instructor. If certain weaknesses are found in the officials' experience, the instructor will suggest that they replay certain individual learning modules and study other sources in order to obtain a better understanding of the specific content.

Step 6 is geared to actual officiating on the field. Several teams play preseason exhibition games, which the students officiate. Each student's performance is evaluated on the spot by the use of a standard rating form and by the review of video-taped game segments. From this feedback, the student and instructor should be able to formulate a remedial program to meet the needs of the individual.

Step 7 places the student in regularly scheduled games. This competency-based learning module sequence would be meaningless if student officials were not assessed continually throughout the season (step 8). This continual assessment is made by the intramural supervisor or class instructor and the game officials with the use of an evaluation check list and video taping. An analysis of these results often reveals areas where further review of material is necessary. The instructor and student agree jointly on a remedial program. Since officiating depends heavily upon accurate performance during the game, much of the assessment is conducted on the field.

The fact that the learning and self-analysis modules are available at all times during library hours enables the students to accomplish the prescribed objectives as well as review all aspects of officiating at times convenient to them. They can sharpen themselves prior to each assignment. This can reinforce their confidence and instill a higher degree of calmness in their officiating roles. Although competency-based learning modules may not be the complete answer, they have demonstrated in many instances that they are more successful with some individuals than the sole use of the old "spray and pray" lecture technique of the past.

EVALUATING OFFICIALS

Over the years, intramural directors have used many techniques and procedures to evaluate intramural officials. Possibly the most popular means of doing this has been direct observation. To lend a degree of objectivity to these efforts, various rating scales have been developed (Thompson, 1968, p. 36). In addition to direct observation, several more complex steps have been employed, such as filming and video taping, in an attempt to upgrade the quality of officials by identifying both the better officials and areas in which specific individuals should improve (Cook, 1969, p. 34). Written and practical tests have also been used in this task. Many intramural programs use both direct observation and the written rule test as the basis of their evaluation efforts (Rees, 1968, p. 41). Although many methods have been developed and tried, it appears that the majority of intramural directors have relied on their own intuitive feelings as their basis for evaluating their officials. Without question, there is a definite lack of systemized evaluation procedures in the field today.

The Intramural Director's Perspective of Evaluation

The intramural director should base his observation on specific criteria if his measurement program is to be both valid and reliable. In short, if his evaluation is to be effective, it must be related to the specific parameters of the task (Barrow and McGee, 1964, p. 24).

What are the basic criteria or qualities of officiating that can serve as guidelines for the intramural director? A list of the more commonly identified aspects of good officiating would include reaction time, confidence, calmness, consistency, judgment, cooperation, integrity and knowledge of the rules, duties, and mechanics of officiating. Although a cursory knowledge of the rules, duties, and mechanics of officiating can be measured most accurately through objective means such as written tests and practice situations, an examination of the remaining criteria suggests that many are intangible and do not lend themselves to the objective techniques of measurement. As a result, in order to obtain the best evaluation input, the intramural director has to consider both objective and subjective ratings.

Subjective Measurement

The rating scale is one of the best means of measuring subjective qualities and factors (Barrow and McGee, 1964, p. 526). Although the use of rating scales helps lend a degree of objectivity to observation results, this device is neither as accurate nor as reliable as most objective tests. It is, however, more reliable than a guess or random judgment made by the instructor without the help of a scale or check list.

Various rating scales are being used by intramural directors across the country. The type of rating scale to be employed should be dictated by the nature of the information desired and the characteristics of the individuals being rated. Figure 3 illustrates a sample of an evaluation rating form that could be used in most traditional team sports. It is based on the assumption that certain qualifications are conducive to effective officiating in almost any sport (Cable and Grzenda, 1972, p. 119).

The intramural director should approach ratings with a knowledge of their potential limitations as an evaluative tool. Rating scales can demonstrate limited reliability when the rater has limited experience and knowledge of the particular instrument to be employed or when the rater has only a peripheral understanding of the factor or item to be rated. The latter is the more important consideration. The rater cannot judge reliably what he himself does not know or understand (Scott and French, 1959, p. 402).

In the intramural programs utilizing paid or volunteer officials, the team managers or captains often assume the evaluative capacity (Thompson, 1968, p. 36). At other schools, someone from the intramural staff rates the officials. Some schools use a combination of both staff and student input. Regardless of the method used, the individuals involved as raters should be briefed thoroughly as to the principles involved in achieving objective, reliable results (Mueller, 1971, p. 202).

Since many individuals are often involved in the evaluation, it is advisable that a simplified rating form be used. Another approach to increasing the reliability of ratings is to have the same official evaluated by different raters. The results are then combined into a composite index. Kent State University incorporates such a rating system. If there is a discrepancy between the team captain's rating and the supervisor's rating, the two attempt to account for the disparity (Rees, 1968, p. 41).

In a sports officiating course, independent study, or contract course, the instructor should complete the rating (Clegg, 1967, p. 67). Long Beach City College is using yet another method for evaluating student

Name of Official _____   Date _____

Name of Rater _____

Team _____   vs. _____

Rating Scale:

5   *Superior*   (little or no constructive criticism needed)

4   *Good*   (slight weakness that should be corrected)

3   *Average*   (seems to know most of his responsibilities, is weak in some areas, but for the most part is fairly acceptable)

2   *Fair*   (seems unsure of himself and causes a great deal of confusion during the course of the game)

1   *Poor*   (totally unacceptable performance)

Directions:

Circle the number that most accurately reflects the official's performance on each of the criteria that appear below.

1. *Reaction Time*   (quick whistle or slow whistle?) 5   4   3   2   1

2. *Confidence*   (assured, meek, or withdrawn?) 5   4   3   2   1

3. *Calmness*   (chokes under pressure? not rattled?) 5   4   3   2   1

4. *Judgment*   (calls game too tight or too loose? game savvy?) 5   4   3   2   1

5. *Consistency*   (easily influenced? calls fouls evenly?) .. 5   4   3   2   1

6. *Cooperation*   (relies on other official? supports other official?) 5   4   3   2   1

7. *Knowledge of Rules*   (game sense or lack of it?) 5   4   3   2   1

8. *Mechanics of Officiating* (field position?) 5   4   3   2   1

9. *Appearance, Attitude, Condition*   (interest in game?) 5   4   3   2   1

10. *General Control of Game*   (game out of hand? assumes control and exercises full authority?) ... 5   4   3   2   1

Total Number of Points _____

Additional Comments:

Figure 3.   Official's Rating Form

officials. A "peer rating" approach has been adopted in the sports officiating course. Each student in the class rates each other member of the class in prescribed areas. The results of the ratings are confidential and are returned to the individual for his consideration (Thompson, 1968, p. 36).

Regardless of the specific evaluating approach the intramural director employs, it is desirable to transmit the information to the official as soon as possible. Since discussing the rating with each official offers another opportunity for individual instruction, it should not be neglected.

Hopefully, this procedure may also serve to stimulate the official to greater heights and to help him plan any necessary remedial procedures. The intramural director should, however, inform each student that the ratings are subjective in nature and, as such, have certain shortcomings.

Rating List

Since most intramural directors are concerned with providing the best possible officials, a rating list can be used. This list provides competition within the group of officials and encourages each official to do his best. This author agrees with Rees in that the rating of officials should occur throughout the season and that future assignments should be based on their performance. This can be achieved by determining the weekly average ratings for each official and by then averaging this index with the previous week's rating to obtain a new measure. This new rating should help determine assignments for the upcoming week. Each official is forced to do a good job in order to continue receiving desirable assignments. In addition, improvement, as well as a lack of it, should be considered as a factor by the director when he makes new assignments.

SUMMARY

The need for competent officiating will exist as long as organized intramural activity programs are offered as a leisure-time pursuit for students. The intramural director must make every effort to ensure that his officiating program reflects the most effective methods of securing and training student officials. Individual differences must be accounted for. Evaluation procedures should be made as reliable and as objective as possible. Efforts should be undertaken to ensure that program and individual evaluation is an ongoing process throughout the year. The success of the intramural program might well depend on who is blowing the official's whistle.

GENERAL BIBLIOGRAPHY

Barrow, Harold, and Rosemary McGee, *Measurement in Physical Education.* Philadelphia: Lea and Febiger, 1964.

Bunn, John, *The Art of Officiating Sports.* Englewood Cliffs, N.J.: Prentice-Hall, 1968.

Cable, Donald, and George Grzenda, "Simplified Scoresheets, Officials Evaluation Form, and Program Evaluation Form," *National Intramural Association Proceedings,* XXIII (1972), 110–19.

CLEGG, RICHARD, "Training Intramural Directors and Game Officials Through Physical Education Class," *National Intramural Association Proceedings,* XVIII (1967), 65–68.

COOK, ROBERT, "Intramural Officials and Intramural Rules," *National Intramural Association Proceedings,* XX (1969), 32–37.

Croft Educational Services, "Student Officials Play a Vital Role in Intramurals," *Physical Education Newsletter,* X, No. 16 (April 15, 1968), 2.

HIXSON, CHALMER G., "Television in Physical Education," *Quest,* XV (January, 1971), 58–65.

KLIENDIENST, VIOLA K. and ARTHUR WESTON, *Intramural and Recreation Programs for Schools and Colleges,* 2nd ed. New York: Appleton-Century-Crofts, 1972.

KURTH, BERT, "Ideas on Officiating Problems," *National Intramural Association Proceedings,* XVII (1966), 51–53.

MEANS, LOUIS, *Intramurals: Their Organization and Administration.* Englewood Cliffs, N.J.: Prentice-Hall, 1973.

MUELLER, PAT, *Intramurals: Programming and Administration.* New York: Ronald Press, 1971.

REES, TREVOR, "Procurement, Rating, and Payment of Intramural Officials," *National Intramural Association Proceedings,* XIX (1968), 40–44.

RHOADS, A. H., "A Method for the Improvement of Officiating in Intramural Team Sports," *National Intramural Association Proceedings,* XIV (1963), 81–82.

ROUSCH, ROBERT, "Research Using the Videotape Recorder in Teacher Education," *Educational Leadership,* XXVIII, No. 8 (May, 1971), 849–53.

SAWYER, THOMAS H., "Intramural Officials Association," *Journal of Health, Physical Education and Recreation,* XLIV, No. 6 (June, 1973), 53–54.

SCOTT, M. GLADYS, and ESTER FRENCH, *Measurement and Evaluation in Physical Education.* Dubuque, Iowa: William C. Brown, 1959.

SEZAK, SAM, "Training Intramural Officials at the University of Maine," *National Intramural Association Proceedings,* XIX (1968), 31.

THOMPSON, BILL, "Procurement, Training, Paying, and Rating Officials," *National Intramural Association Proceedings,* XIX (1968), 35–39.

TYLER, COULBORN, "Video Tapes," *Intramural Newsletter, National Intramural Association* (January 2, 1971), p. 2.

VOLTMER, CARL, and VERNON LAPP, *The Intramural Handbook.* St. Louis: C. V. Mosby, 1949.

WANAMAKER, GEORGE, "Toward Better Intramural Officiating," *The Physical Educator,* XXVI, No. 4 (December, 1969), 180–81.

20

Planning Intramural-Physical Recreation Facilities

JAMES A. PETERSON
United States Military Academy
West Point, New York

INTRODUCTION

Planning educational facilities involves more than designing and constructing a facility with X number of square feet to accommodate Y number of students. Rather, the process of creating educational facilities can be viewed as a continuous series of closely related but separate events or actions, some of which are prerequisite to others. Unfortunately, there is a wide variety of interpretations regarding either the identification of these events or the conceptualization of a coherent theory of facility development.

A perusal of the literature suggests that the numerous efforts to define the parameters of the process of planning facilities can be categorized into two divergent approaches. On one hand, a number of educators advocate that the proper administrative approach to facility planning is adherence to a semisequential order of steps. The primary tenet of this approach is that the planning process can be viewed as a specific number of administrative activities that must be undertaken

From *Administrative Theory and Practice in Physical Education and Athletics,* Earle F. Zeigler and Marcia J. Spaeth, eds. © 1975. Reprinted by permission of Prentice-Hall, Inc., Englewood Cliffs, N.J. The original article has been slightly revised.

before an optimal level of planning is achieved. In contrast with this approach, other educators postulate that the process for planning facilities should be conceptualized in terms of broad planning considerations. This viewpoint suggests that, depending on the level of competent leadership and effective communication among the individuals involved in the development of the facility, the essence of the task of the facility planner is the selection, coordination, scheduling, and timing of the diverse planning activities (Council of Educational Facility Planners, 1969, pp. 17–18).

Despite the relative disparity between the two interpretations of the basic elements of the process of planning facilities, one prominent commonality between the two exists: both emphasize that the cornerstone of a well-planned facility is an administrative commitment to careful planning. The need for careful planning in the search for and the subsequent expenditure of capital construction monies has never been more acute. With the cost of constructing educational facilities increasing to almost crisis proportions, there appears to be an immutable realization on the part of most administrators that the extant funds for capital construction must be employed efficiently. Accordingly, building programs must be geared towards the development of functional facilities.

Unfortunately, when the available funds are insufficient to meet all of the building needs of higher education, higher priorities are frequently placed on the construction of "academic" buildings. This pre-emptive judgment subsequently results in a lower priority for the development of student-service facilities, such as physical recreation buildings. As a consequence, if intramural administrators hope to be reasonably competitive in the quest for a share of the available capital construction monies, it is essential that they commit themselves to an administrative approach that insures that their facility planning efforts are thoroughgoing, efficient, and appropriate. This commitment should begin with efforts to justify the need for a particular facility and should be sustained throughout the life of the facility.

The usefulness of the instructional material that has been published to aid the physical educator in his attempts to achieve a maximum degree of efficient planning is unfortunately subject to question. In many cases, the material on facility planning can best be described as quite superficial. As a result, despite the voluminous amount of literature on the subject of planning facilities, the intramural director has very little information at his disposal regarding the inner workings of the process of planning and constructing a physical recreation facility. For the intramural director the question remains this: What is the proper administrative approach for developing a well-planned physical recreation building?

In order to gain a clearer insight into the dynamics of the process for planning a physical recreation facility, this chapter presents a study undertaken by the author that examined the facility planning efforts at several universities, each selected for having a substantially large intramural-physical recreation building (Peterson, 1971). Using the case study approach, the individuals who were involved in the planning of each facility were identified, and the extent of their participation in the planing process was determined. Insight into this latter aspect was gained by presenting an overview of the interrelationship between the facility planning efforts and the existing administrative structure of each school.

A CASE STUDY

Historical Background and Related Literature

The efficient planning of physical recreation facilities has long been an administrative concern for physical educators in general and intramural personnel in particular. One of the first references to the fact that the development of facilities was of interest to physical educators appeared as early as the late nineteenth century (*American Physical Education Review,* 1896–99). The literature suggests that since those initial efforts, there has been a substantial increase in the demand and need for information regarding the planning of physical recreation facilities. In response to this demand, many of the aspects attendant to planning educational facilities have been accorded extensive treatment in the literature.

The intramural administrator seeking assistance in the task of facility planning is confronted, however, with a contradictory dilemma. On one hand, as Boles suggests, "there is hardly a topic in education which has been written about so energetically and voluminously as school buildings" (1965, p. v.). On the other hand, despite the proliferation of information on facility planning, little agreement exists among educators regarding the proper approach to planning them. One plausible avenue of assistance for the intramural director who is seeking guidance in his facility planning efforts is to survey the literature on selected aspects of the process of planning educational facilities. The remainder of this section is devoted to a review of the literature concerning the specific aspects of the planning process that were investigated in the present study.

Administrative Approval for the Facility

A primary element of the process of planning facilities is the action that must be undertaken to achieve administrative approval for a proposed building project. On some campuses, this task involves nothing more than submitting a simplified request to an individual or agency with the authority to make the decision to proceed with plans to build the facility. This approach requires minimal preplanning or other action on the part of the applicant. At other schools, the process is more complex. These schools require that a more sophisticated, quantitative approach to the evaluation of the relative merits of their proposed projects be adopted. In varying combinations, this approach consists of surveys to assess needs, normative indexes to provide a comparison between the existing facilities and reasonable standards, and projections based on existing requirements, activity trends, and so forth, of how much activity space will be needed when the facility is completed. Although these various quantitative tools do not represent the complete answer, they do contribute substantially to efforts to make the approach to planning both comprehensive and objective.

A number of inclusive guides have been compiled that offer detailed instruction in how to conduct a space survey and inventory (Bareither and Schillinger, 1968; Dahnke et al., 1970). Within certain situational limitations, a utilization-of-space survey is developed to accomplish the following objectives (Schwehr, 1962, p. 140):

1. To determine the present utilization of existing facilities.
2. To determine how utilization might be improved.
3. To pinpoint institutional strengths and weaknesses in building utilization.
4. To provide information relative to space allocation standards.
5. To provide background data for future plant expansion based on need.
6. To use the findings as a guide in the development of an integrated building priority list.
7. To keep abreast of the rapidly changing educational scene.

Sumption and Landes suggest that an appraisal of existing plant facilities should include an evaluation of qualitative aspects, as well as a compilation of quantitative data (1957, p. 81). The literature reveals that the usual approach to evaluating the qualitative aspects of a facility has been to develop a check list of specific items and to assign an arbitrary value (score) to each item. A facility is appraised by being evaluated on those items. The total score thus obtained is, for assessment purposes, then compared with normative standards.

The use of "evaluation" forms, however, introduces a measure of subjectivity into the process of planning facilities, because the use of any qualitative appraisal is closely related to the selection of the standards that provide the comparative basis. For physical recreation facilities, the most well-known and widely acclaimed source of normative standards has been the guide prepared by Sapora and Kenney (1960).[1] From an extensive inventory of the existing facilities at all of the campuses of the Western Athletic Conference (more commonly referred to as the Big 10 Athletic Conference), they developed a list of standards based on what they considered to be the minimum desirable number of square feet per student required to conduct an adequate program in various physical activities. Relative to situational factors, the indexes developed by Sapora and Kenney serve not only as an aid in evaluating existing facility needs but also as a normative tool in the projection of future space requirements. For planning purposes, their standards are employed after an assessment of enrollment and activity trends has been undertaken.

The Design of the Facility

In this crucial phase of the planning process, the collective efforts of the planning participants are channeled into transforming the ideas for a facility into a tangible form that can guide the construction contractor. Among the more important matters that the facility planner must consider during this phase are the development of a program statement (educational specifications); the selection of the architect; the use of design consultants; the selection of the site; the establishment of aesthetic parameters for the design; and the formulation of landscaping guidelines for the project.

The literature suggests that there is widespread agreement that the planning efforts for a facility should utilize all persons who can contribute to the planning process. Students, as well as faculty and staff, should be involved. The most viable means of channeling such involvement is to encourage maximum input into the development of the program statement. Simply stated, educational specifications (collectively referred to as the program statement) are the guide the architect follows to design a new facility. They are the means by which an educator describes to the architect the activities to be housed, persons to be accommodated, space requirements, spatial relationships, equipment to be housed, and the special environmental treatment that should be accorded each space in the facility (Council of Educational Facility Planners, 1969, p. 49). In considering the wide variety of educational specifications that are developed, one basic guideline is appropriate: the greater the detail of such specifications, the greater the likelihood that the architect will be able to design a facility to meet specific needs (Leu, 1965, p. 34).

---

[1] The development of standards for physical recreation facilities by Sapora and Kenney was only part of a larger concurrent study that investigated the current and desired status of the intramural program at the University of Illinois.

Another of the critical aspects in the design phase of the planning process is the selection of an architect. This task confronts the facility planner with four basic problems: when to retain the architect for a project; what criteria to base the selection on; what selection method to use; and what services to require from the architect. Although in many cases specific legal regulations and guidelines govern the approach to these problems, in other situations such decisions are left to the discretion of the appropriate administrator.

The literature suggests that a prudent approach to the question of when to select the architect is to do so as soon as it can be determined that his services will be required. One of the primary advantages of selecting the architect very early in the planning process is securing his immediate assistance in the overall coordination of the planning efforts (Priest and Oglesby, 1967, p. 26).

Three general methods of selecting an architect are commonly employed: direct appointment, competitive selection, and design competition (American Institute of Architects, 1963, Chap. 5, p. 4). The particular method used is usually determined by the type of client and the type of project. The first two methods listed above are the procedures most commonly followed in selecting an architect for an educational facility. The direct appointment method bases the selection of the architect on the client's knowledge of the architect's reputation, ability, and experience. In the comparative selection method, the architect is selected from a list of architects who have been asked to submit to the client information and materials concerning their qualifications.[2]

The question of what services to require from the architect is based to a great extent on the type of project involved and when, during the planning process, he is hired. In most cases, the services of the architect usually begin before the actual design is started and normally continue until the facility has been completed and accepted by the client. In these cases, the architect has extensive involvement in several areas of service: predesign planning, schematic design, design development, construction documents, bidding, and construction.

Consultants and specialists sometimes join the architect on the "design team." Some facilities—physical recreation facilities, for example —necessitate that the architect possess expertise in the design of a number of different types of activity areas. When a client feels that its architectural firm does not have the expertise or breadth of knowledge to design a particular type of activity space, arrangements are made to employ con-

---

2 The subject of what constitutes a competent architect is accorded extensive treatment in the American Institute of Architects' *Handbook of Architectural Practice* (1953). This text examines in detail the appropriate areas of exploration concerning the proper qualifications of an architect.

sulting services to assist the architect. For example, the use of pool consultants in the design of physical recreation facilities appears to be a frequented practice.

Another integral element of the design phase of the planning process is the selection of the site. Although the literature suggests that a wide variety of factors should be considered, several criteria are particularly appropriate: accessibility to those who will use the facility (for instance proximity to the greatest density of residence halls), availability of utility services, proximity to related outdoor recreational areas (such as tennis courts and play fields), proximity to traffic hazards, proximity to safety and health facilities, cost, aesthetic appeal, environment, and suitability of soil for a building foundation. Responsibility for site selection varies from campus to campus. In varying degrees of collaboration with others, the design architect or someone from the school's planning department or physical plant may undertake this task. In some instances, a landscape architect or an outside consultant may be used to select the site.

Unfortunately, facility planners traditionally follow the approach that anything not essential to the immediate curriculum or not necessary to the efficient operation of the facility should be labeled as a frill or extravagance and omitted (American Association of School Administrators, 1960, p. 76). The literature implores facility planners to place a greater emphasis on aesthetic parameters in the design of their facilities. Accordingly, administrators should insist that architects not forget one of the most important elements in the design of new buildings—beauty.

The Method of Financing the Facility

Faced with limited monies for capital construction, most administrative officials view financial planning as the most critical step in the process of planning facilities. Quite obviously, if the necessary financing is not secured, the project cannot be consummated. Because the capital needs and resources of universities vary from campus to campus, the approach to financial planning also varies from school to school. Despite these differences, the literature indicates that there are several fundamental aspects that the facility planner must usually consider: estimating preliminary costs (translating planning proposals into dollar requirements), determining the sources of funding for a project (including an evaluation of the legal and program stipulations that apply to each source), and developing a feasible and effective financial plan that will sustain the building project.

In most cases, the initial step in the financial planning for a project is to calculate preliminary cost estimates. Following the development of preliminary plans and design specifications, these projections of costs are normally made by either the project architect or a financial officer of the university. Preliminary or rough estimates of costs are based on unit costs obtained from past experience. Although this approach does not yield a precise projection of the costs, it does enable the facility planner to proceed with the development of a feasible financial plan for the project.

Later, as more detailed plans are developed, the preliminary cost estimates are reworked in order to obtain a more realistic projection of the building's cost (Foreman, 1958, p. 41). The closer the specifications are to the final plans, the more precise the estimate of the project costs will be. A detailed cost projection usually involves (1) a determination of the time required for each item of work; (2) a calculation of the labor requirements; (3) a computation of equipment requirements; and (4) a determination of the materials required (De LaTorre, 1958, p. 1).

Once the cost estimates for a project have been determined, the facility planner must then formulate a plan to finance the project.[3] In general, the financial plan outlines what the sources of funding will be, how these sources are to be tapped, when they are to be utilized, to what part of the facility each is to be applied, and how the indebtedness is to be liquidated.

Though the procedures for determining the financial plan for a building project are strictly regulated on many campuses by state statutes and university policies, more often than not this process is simply one of procuring the funds from whatever source(s) is available. The literature suggests that the traditional sources of funding for university facilities are state appropriations, federal grants and loan assistance, debt services (bonds), private grants and gifts, and use-generated revenues.

The applicability of the various revenue sources for financing physical recreation facilities varies from state to state and from project to project. Most states appear to be reluctant to provide state funding assistance for any but "academic" buildings. These states usually stipulate that the financing of student-service facilities (such as a student union building) must come from the students themselves. Physical recreation facilities are normally considered to be "service" facilities. However, because most physical recreation facilities accommodate some part of the physical education instructional program, several states participate in the financing of these facilities to the percentage extent that they might be construed as serving the "academic" program.

Resulting from both pragmatic and philosophic factors, one of the most prevalent methods of financing physical recreation facilities is the

---

[3] On some campuses these steps are reversed. The financial plan is developed first; then the project (by necessity) is designed to accommodate the financial plan.

use of student-fee revenues. In a sense, many educators consider the student-fee assessment to be the charge for services rendered over and above the pursuit of "academic enlightenment." The essence of this position is that students should bear the financial burden for student-service facilities. Among the critical questions that the use of student-fee revenues raises for the facility planner are (1) when to initiate the student-fee assessment for a project, (2) when to sell the revenue bonds (before the project begins or when the best interest rates are available?), and (3) when to schedule the maturation of the bond issue(s). In addition, the literature suggests that facility planners should develop a "strategy" to minimize any student displeasure over the use of student-fee funding for a particular project.

In some instances, a major source of the funding of collegiate physical recreation facilities has been the federal government. Federal assistance in this area is administered under Public Law 88-204, also known as the Higher Education Facilities Act of 1963.[4] This law contains two provisions for providing assistance for recreational facilties, both of which are contingent on the percentage of time that a physical recreation facility is projected for use for instructional purposes. The Title I program provides for the appropriation of grants (up to one third of a project's cost) for the construction of undergraduate academic facilities. The Title III program provides for loans for the construction of academic facilities. These loans produce long-term (up to fifty years) low-interest assistance for up to 75 percent of the development costs for a project.

Two additional sources of funds for the construction of facilities for higher education are gifts from private sources and use-generated revenues. The literature emphasizes that although monies from these two sources are certainly welcome, they are normally not available in sufficient amounts to be considered a significant source of revenue for the development of physical recreation facilities.

Planning Input During the Construction Phase

In the construction phase of the planning process, the preceding planning efforts are expressed in terms of concrete, brick, and steel. The literature suggests that during this stage, facility planning includes a number of integral considerations: the awarding of the construction contract, the bidding process, the final contract, supervisory procedures during construction, arbitration of disputes concerning the construction documents, change-order procedures, and the final inspection and acceptance of the facility.

---

[4] Public Law 88-204, 88th Cong., H.R. 6143, December 16, 1963.

Two basic methods of awarding construction contracts are used: competitive bidding and direct appointment. Regarding the direct selection method, the American Institute of Architects (AIA) suggests that the contract be awarded on the basis "of the abilities of the contractor in those areas which are particularly important to the project at hand" (1953, p. 2). Under the competitive bidding system, each bidder submits a sealed proposal to execute the work for a specific sum. By law, all public works must be contracted for by competitive bidding.

For public works, the law prescribes awarding the construction contract to the lowest responsible bidder. The task of determining this is by no means a simple step, however. The exact parameters of this stipulation are somewhat ambiguous. The Supreme Court of Pennsylvania, for example, defines the "lowest responsible bidder" principle as requiring facility planners to exercise sound discretion. Furthermore, planners "should call to their assistance the means of information at hand to form an intelligent judgment" (Foreman, 1958, p. 26). The bidding documents usually provide, however, that the client has the right to reject any or all bids, or to accept the bid that in his judgment will be to his own best interests. If the client rejects all bids, he normally has three alternatives: resubmit the project as is for new bids, ask the architect to make changes in the specifications that (hopefully) will induce more bid proposals when the project is rebid, or drop the project altogether.[5] If he accepts a bid, the bid deposits of the unsuccessful bidders are returned and the contract is awarded.

For the great bulk of construction, bid proposals generally lead to one of four types of agreements: lump sum, guaranteed upset price, cost plus fixed fee, or management contract (McLean, 1958, Chap. 27, p. 1).[6] For the great majority of schools, the choice of a contractual agreement is regulated closely by both state statutes and university policies.

The agreement between a client and a contractor is usually stipulated, along with modifications to fit the particular project, on the standard contract form provided by the AIA. The construction contract normally includes the contract documents; a description of the scope of the contractor's work; the name of the contract architect; a commencement date and a tentative completion date for the work; stipulations (if any) regarding liquidated damages, penalty, and bonus clauses; the total contract procedures for progress payments; references to the final inspection, certification of completion, and acceptance of work; and references

---

[5] The choices of resubmitting a project as is for bid or of dropping the project altogether are normally rejected as being either unrealistic or undesirable. The process of changing the specifications is referred to as "developing a list of deductive alternates." Either less expensive materials are substituted in the specifications for a facility or items are dropped altogether in order to bring the project within feasible (money-wise) boundaries.

[6] An inclusive examination of the relative merits of each type of construction agreement is also offered by McLean (1958, pp. 1–8).

to the issuance of a final certificate for payment (AIA, 1963, Chap. 17, pp. 2–4). In addition, the contract includes provisions regarding the responsibility for cleanup after construction, the procedures for handling disputes over interpretation of the contract documents, the procedures for change orders, the client's ideas on the specific working relationship between the architect, the contractor, and himself, and the guarantees provided by the contractor.

Once construction actually begins, the responsibilities of the various major participants (architect, contractor, and client) vary somewhat from project to project, depending upon the contractual arrangements. An understanding of the scope and intent of all the contract documents is the primary cornerstone of all activity in the construction phase.

When a project nears completion, several procedures are followed. The contractor sends the architect and/or the client a statement claiming substantial completion of the project.[7] Subsequently, the architect and/or a representative of the client conducts a semifinal inspection to determine the status of completion. If the project is found to be substantially complete, a certificate of substantial completion is prepared. Attached to this certificate is a list (referred to as a "punch list") of the items to be completed or corrected by the contractor. This certificate also provides for agreement as to the time allowed for completion or correction of the items, the date upon which the owner will occupy the project or specified areas of the project, and a description of the responsibilities for heat, utilities, and insurance (AIA, 1963, Chap. 18, p. 10).

If for some reason the inspecting team does not concur with the contractor's claim of substantial completion, another semifinal inspection is scheduled after the contractor submits a new statement. On the average, the typical project does not require more than two such semifinal inspections. Once substantial completion is achieved, a final inspection is then conducted by the representatives of the owner and the architect. If everything is acceptable, a written certificate of completion is prepared. The contractor then submits an affidavit stating that all of his bills have been paid. He then prepares his final application for payment.

RESEARCH METHODOLOGY AND TECHNIQUES

The major purpose of the study was to examine, through case analyses, the process involved in the planning and construction of intramural-physical recreation buildings that were financed primarily by student-fee revenues. A second objective of the study was to determine which

---

[7] The date of substantial completion is defined by the AIA as the date when the construction is sufficiently completed in accordance with the construction documents— as modified by any change orders agreed to by the contractual parties—so that the owner can occupy the project or specified area of the project for the use for which it was intended.

individuals were involved in the planning of these facilities and to investigate the extent of their participation in the planning process. The following subproblems, stated in question form, were posed to direct the investigation:

1. How did each school gain administrative approval for its building?
2. How did each school arrive at the design of its facility?
3. How was the method of financing determined for each facility?
4. Who had planning input into the construction phase of the facility?

Preliminary Procedures

The initial step was to identify those universities that had a large physical recreation facility that had been financed primarily by student-fee revenues. Based in part upon geographical, time, and cost considerations, five schools were selected: University of Illinois (Urbana), Michigan State University, Oklahoma State University, Purdue University, and the University of Washington. The next step was to contact an individual at each school who had been an active participant in the planning of his institution's physical recreation facility and to request his assistance in the compilation of data pertinent to the planning of his school's facility. At four of the universities, the director of intramurals was the individual contacted; at Oklahoma State University, initial assistance was provided by the chairman of the department of physical education.

The means used to gather information on the dynamics of the planning process was the descriptive survey method. The specific descriptive survey techniques employed were the structured interview and content analysis and appraisal. A questionnaire was developed in order to standardize the data solicited from the interview survey and to achieve a sense of continuity in reporting the data collected at each university.

Survey Procedures

Each of the five individuals who had agreed to serve as an intermediary contact for the study was sent a copy of both the questionnaire and the horizontal analysis for the study. Requested to conceptualize the parameters of the information sought for this study, these individuals were asked to schedule appointments at which this investigator could meet with persons who could supply the desired information.[8] Based upon

---

[8] During the interviews, a number of individuals were identified who had provided input into the planning process for their school's facility and who had not previously been scheduled for an interview. Appointments were subsequently made to see these individuals.

prior arrangements, the author then visited each school for approximately one week.

In cooperation with the intermediary contacts, interviews were held with those individuals who were involved in the planning of their school's physical recreation facility. The approach to the interviews was based, in part, on the check list of recommendations for conducting an effective interview proposed by Good (1966, pp. 235–36). In order to achieve an accurate chronicle of each question-and-answer session, all interviews were tape-recorded. The tapes were subsequently transcribed. Among the numerous individuals who were interviewed at each university were the dean or director of the school or department of physical education, the dean or manager of facilities for the physical education administrative unit (or any other individual who had been assigned this responsibility), the director of intramurals and members of his staff, the director of the campus planning committee, the design architect and members of the university architect's staff, the design consultants who were used, the university comptroller or the chief financial officer involved in developing the financial plan for the facility, and the construction contractor. In short, an attempt was made to interview anyone who provided input into the planning of the five facilities.

The minutes of meetings of the various planning committees and agencies furnished a second primary source of information for the study. In addition, at a few of the schools several individuals made their personal archives and other pertinent planning correspondence available to the author.

Reporting of the Data

The information concerning each school's planning efforts was synopsized into a descriptive narration. Each narration was organized by topical headings corresponding to the study's main subproblems. Subsequent to the five synopses, a content and comparative analysis was completed that pointed out the similarities and differences among the approaches of the five universities to the main aspects of planning.

FINDINGS AND CONCLUSIONS

The approach of each university to planning its physical recreation facility depended on a number of factors: the administrative structure of the school, the extant university policies and procedures for planning facilities, federal, state, and local statutes and regulations, the existing state of technology, the personalities of the individuals involved in the planning efforts for each facility, the influence of cultural and political constraints, and various chronological considerations. Because situational factors at each university varied considerably, each school's approach to planning its physical recreation facility also varied. The remainder of this section is devoted to a succinct (and thus somewhat limited) presentation of the findings and conclusions concerning the approach of each school to the major elements of the process of planning facilities.

Administrative Approval for the Facility

The approaches that the five universities followed to gain administrative approval for their physical recreation facilities can be categorized into two distinguishable groupings. At Purdue, Michigan State, and the University of Washington, the decision to proceed with plans for a new recreational facility was reached by an administrative decree. A strong-willed administrator who possessed the necessary authority simply decided arbitrarily that his university would construct such a facility.

In contrast, officials at the University of Illinois and Oklahoma State were directed by the extant regulations to pursue approval for their physical recreation facility through the proper administrative channels. At Oklahoma State, these channels consisted primarily of directing all capital construction requests to the university's executive committee—an administrative body that included in its many functions the assignment of priorities to building projects. Subsequent to an evaluation by the university's board of regents, the state legislature appropriated a lump sum (as opposed to specific allocations) of state funds to Oklahoma State University for whatever capital projects the school officials deemed worthy.

In the procedure that was followed to gain administrative approval for the University of Illinois's physical recreation facility, the project had to be reviewed by both a campus and a university system–wide screening committee for capital development. After it had been analyzed and approved by both advisory groups and had received an appropriately favorable priority, the project was included in the university's biennial capital budget request. Unlike the other schools, both the Universities of Oklahoma State and Illinois compiled a detailed listing and assessment of their space needs.

The activity programs that generated space needs for each university also varied. Although all of the schools faced a critical lack of adequate indoor physical activity space, none of these universities, at the time of their efforts to obtain a new building, had constructed an indoor recreational facility in over twenty-five years. Designed solely to meet the recreational needs of the student body, Purdue's "co-rec" gym houses the free-time and competitive programs of the intramural department. It does not service either the intercollegiate athletics program or the instructional program offering of its department of physical education. In contrast, Michigan State's men's intramural building accommodates an extensive program of varsity sports. In addition, this facility provides space for the instructional program of its department of physical education and both the leisure-time and the organized activity offerings of the intramural department.

Though the University of Washington's intramural activities building was designed primarily to meet the needs of the intramural activities program, it does house some basic instruction classes. A policy was instituted, however, to limit the amount of instructional space allocated for classes. At all times, part of every type of activity space included in the building (for example, the swimming pool or handball courts) is available for free-time recreational use by members of the university community. Varsity athletics are totally excluded from the facility. Oklahoma State's Colvin Physical Education Center, designed to meet space needs similar to those of the University of Illinois's IM–PE Building, was developed to accommodate the professional preparation and instructional programs in physical education, the free-time and competitive activities of the intramural program, and the varsity swim team (the only intercollegiate users). The Colvin Center was designed to service (by such means as laboratories) the academic-related and instructional users of the facility, whereas the Illinois IM–PE Building stresses recreational aspects.

The Design of the Facility

Each school employed a somewhat different arrangement for the design of its facility. Purdue had members of its physical plant department develop the schematics and the preliminary plans for the co-rec gym. After these basic specifications of the building had been established, the university employed an outside architectural firm to produce the working drawings for the project. The selection of the design architect was made arbitrarily by a university vice-president. The architect chosen was an individual who had done practically all of the architecture on the Purdue campus since the early 1920s.[9] After the working drawings were finished, the bids taken, and the construction contract awarded, Purdue bought the drawings from the outside architect and turned the project over to its construction department, which supervised the facility to completion.

---

[9] Similar to architects used by the Universities of Washington and Illinois, Purdue's design architect had extensive experience with athletic facilities. Michigan State University and Oklahoma State University used design architects whose experience with athletic facilities encompassed only secondary school gymnasiums.

At the time of the men's intramural building project, Michigan State did not have its own staff of architects. A design architect was selected arbitrarily by the president of the university. This individual was expected to follow the project all the way through—from the development of the schematics for the project to the completion of the construction.

The University of Washington used its own university architect's office to direct and coordinate the development of the plans for the intramural activities building. An outside architect was hired to do the design work on the project. The selection of the design architect was made by the university's architectural commission, a group of independent architects who serve as an advisory committee to the university's board of regents. Their decision was based on a recommendation of three possible architects for the project submitted (in order of priority) by the university architect's office. The University of Illinois employed similar procedures to develop the architectural plans for the IM–PE Building. Illinois's university architect's office monitored the plans for the project, and an outside architect, appointed by the university's board of trustees, did the design work.

Oklahoma State University employs a unique arrangement for architectural services. Its university architect's office is independent, to the extent that it is not salaried. Receiving no budget, it is allotted a percentage of the costs for each project. For the Colvin Physical Education Center, it developed the schematics, did the preliminary plans, wrote the contract, and supervised the construction. The university hired an outside architect to develop the working drawings and detailed specifications for the facility.[10] Together, the outside architect and the university architect's office shared 6 percent of the construction costs for the project. The contract architect for the facility was appointed by the board of regents from a list submitted (in order of priority) by the university architect's office.

Two basic approaches to developing the specifications for their facilities were employed by the universities whose planning efforts were investigated in the study. At both Purdue and MSU, the director of intramurals was assigned (by the chairman of the department of physical education) the responsibility for developing a list of the activity areas that should be included in his school's proposed multipurpose physical recreation facility. Neither university devised a program statement per se. In both instances, these individuals were not given detailed instructions or guidelines on how to proceed with the task of determining the specifications for their project. In both cases, their primary source of in-

---

[10] The outside architect employed an aquatics consultant to assist in the design of the pools. Of the other schools, only Illinois employed a design consultant (also an aquatics specialist).

formation was input provided by the faculty of each school's department of physical education.

In contrast, the Universities of Washington, Oklahoma State, and Illinois appointed a committee to develop the specifications for their projects. The approach of each committee to its task was characterized by a strong commitment to maximize input at the various stages of the project. Information was solicited from several sources: the physical education faculty, pertinent university personnel, equipment and material representatives of independent companies, and several trips to survey and evaluate the facilities at other schools. All committee decisions were made by consensus.

At four of the universities, the design architect worked closely with representatives of the various campus agencies and departments that had input into the project. Oklahoma State was the only school whose outside architect did not meet regularly with someone from either the physical education or intramural department (its contract architect worked directly with the university architect's office). Regarding the specific arrangement for architectural services, the scope and type of input provided by the design architect into the project was generally the same for each of the five universities.[11]

The procedures for selecting the site of the project were somewhat similar for each of the schools. Either a high-echelon administrator, a university department, or a university governing body (such as the board of regents), acting upon the recommendations of the appropriate university personnel, made the decision as to where the facility was to be built. The criteria for site selection varied considerably, however. Among the site criteria employed, in varying combinations, at these schools were proximity to student residence halls, adherence to the university's master plan, accessibility to the various segments of the university community, proximity to outdoor play fields, availability of bus service, proximity to other physical recreation facilities, and accessibility to parking facilities.

The Method of Financing the Facility

Each university used a somewhat different approach for developing the preliminary budget for its facility. Based on a "ball-park" projection of a reasonable scope for the co-rec gym project, the Purdue University treasurer calculated that $2,500,000 of student fees could be allotted to the building. At Michigan State, the design architect developed the initial estimate of the cost of the men's intramural building project.

---

11 The work of each of the design architects was influenced to a certain extent by either formal policies or implicit understandings regarding "aesthetic considerations" in the design of the facility.

He devised his cost projection by multiplying the cubic footage area of the facility by a per-cubic-foot cost, which he had calculated by averaging the cubic footage costs of five large physical activity facilities. Unfortunately, the assumptions on which he based his cost projects were invalid. As a result, he grossly underestimated the cost of the project. In consultation with the comptroller, the business manager of the University of Washington developed a "ball-park" projection of the amount of funds needed to build the intramural activities building. Based upon cost estimates furnished by the university architect's office, Oklahoma State's vice-president of development prepared a preliminary budget for the Colvin Physical Education Center, which included a five-year escalation factor. The University of Illinois's university architect's office developed the preliminary projection of the cost of the IM–PE Building. This estimate was based on the space requirements that were generated by the program statement for that project.

The approach to developing the financial plan and the rationale behind that plan were very similar for both Purdue's co-rec gym and the University of Washington's intramural activities building.[12] In each instance, the school had a substantial student-fee revenue bond issue that was being retired within a few months of the time the university decided to proceed with the planning and constructing of a new multipurpose recreational facility. As a result, both schools had the bonding capability that would generate the necessary funds for such a facility. It was a relatively simple administrative procedure to arbitrarily reallocate the existing student-fee revenues to a new project once the old bond issue had been retired. Officials at both universities did not attempt to look for alternate sources of funding for two reasons: (1) they felt that this was a legitimate student expense because the building would be used primarily by students; and (2) they did not want to secure money that would have "strings" attached, which might lessen the recreational emphasis of the facility.

With the concurrence of Michigan State University's executive committee, Michigan State's vice-president for business and finance developed the financial plan for the men's intramural building. With the exception of $345,000 of private monies, the entire project was funded by student-fee revenues.[13] At that time, Michigan State had no other source of funding for the project. Neither the state of Michigan nor the federal government provided assistance for this type of capital development.

---

[12] The total project costs for the co-rec gym (148,700 sq. ft. gross area) and the intramural activities building (153,165 sq. ft. gross area) were $2,739,723 and $4,681,096, respectively.

[13] Total project costs for the men's intramural building (198,600 sq. ft. gross area) were $3,957,133.

Oklahoma State's business manager devised the financial plan for the Colvin Physical Education Center. His primary approach to this task was to "look under every rock." With assistance from the university's office of development and research, funds from four sources were obtained: a state appropriation, a Title I grant, a Title III loan, and the sale of private bonds.[14] Both the Title III loan and the private bond issue are being retired entirely by student-fee revenues. In the largest student referendum in the school's history, the Oklahoma State student body voted to assess themselves a fee for the Colvin Physical Education Center.

Subject to the agreement of the president, the university's comptroller developed the financial plan for the University of Illinois IM–PE building.[15] Initially, some administrative support existed for funding the project entirely through student fees. Because of a dramatic rise in costs, which resulted from a lengthy delay in awarding the construction contract, the university was forced to look elsewhere for funds. Based upon the proposed recreational-instruction usage mix of the facility (75 percent and 25 percent, respectively), the university subsequently asked the state for an appropriation for the "academic" portion of the building. In addition, because the state-appropriation for the project was less than that included in the university biennial capital budget request, the university also applied for federal assistance in financing the building. As a result, the IM–PE Building was financed from three sources: a general revenue appropriation from the state, a Title I grant, and a private bond issue. Debt service for the bond issue is being provided entirely through student-fee revenues.

Planning Input During the Construction Phase

As public institutions, each of the schools included in the present study had to award the construction contract for its facility on the basis of open competitive bidding. The bidding system of each university was governed by the public works statutes of its state. These statutes stipulate that if a construction contract is awarded, it must be granted to the lowest responsible bidder.

The type of bids that were taken on these projects differed among the schools. Purdue University, the University of Washington, and the

---

14 The total project costs for the Colvin Physical Education Center (153,000 sq. ft. gross area) were $3,272,481: state appropriation, $683,394; Title I grant, $873,087; Title III loan, $1,155,000; and student-free revenue bonds, $500,000.

15 The total project costs for the IM–PE Building (262,484 sq. ft. gross area) were $11,100,000: state appropriation, $909,200; Title I grant, $1,082,615; and student-fee revenue bonds $9,100,000.

University of Illinois requested a single bid on the entire project. Michigan State University, however, took separate bids on each of the five major components of the men's intramural building project. Michigan State used this component-bidding procedure for two reasons: to develop strong competition in the various trades and (hopefully) to have the bid shopping result in a cost savings to the university. After the bids were taken, a single contract was written with subcontractors being assigned to the general contractor. Oklahoma State took both types of bids—components and a lump sum for the Colvin Physical Education Center.

None of the universities included penalty, liquidated damages, and/or bonus clauses in their contractual agreements with the construction contractors. Each of the five contracts included a provision that suggested a tentative completion date. None of the contractors met this deadline.

The schools varied somewhat in the procedures they followed to handle problems and/or disputes during the construction phase. The three universities (Michigan State University, the University of Washington, and the University of Illinois) that hired outside architects to do all of the design work on the project gave final-decision authority to that architect and/or his appointed representative. These design architects were required to interpret the contract specifications and to arbitrate any disagreements over the contract documents. On the other hand, the two schools (Purdue and Oklahoma State) that employed an outside architect only to do the working drawings had a different arrangement for resolving problems and/or disagreements. During the construction phase, the only responsibility of these outside architects was to answer all questions regarding an interpretation of their drawings. At Purdue, all other matters were handled by the superintendent for construction. The university architect's office managed all other questions concerning the Colvin Physical Education Center.

Except for the University of Illinois, all of the schools employed a similar arrangement for monitoring the construction of their facilities. Each university appointed an individual as the overall "director" (also referred to as a manager, supervisor, and/or superintendent) of the project during the construction phase. In addition, a full-time on-the-site supervisor was hired to represent the university's interests. Together with inspectors from the physical plant department and/or the university's architect's office, these supervisors had the responsibility for quality control on materials and work.

In contrast with this arrangement, the University of Illinois required that the design architect maintain a full-time field representative at the site of the project. This representative was responsible for monitoring the progress of the contractor and maintaining quality control on all materials and work. In addition, the university employed field inspectors to provide cursory supervision of the progress of the contractor.

On all of the construction projects, someone from either the physical education or intramural department provided almost daily on-the-site inspection of the progress of the work. At every school but OSU, the director of intramurals assumed the task of vigilant watchguard over the project.[16] The extensive efforts of these individuals served as a valuable source of input and quality control over the project.

The procedures for change-order requests were fairly standardized among the schools. All of the schools required that any change in the contract specifications be written up and submitted to the appropriate representative of the university. And finally, although the individuals involved in processing the change-order requests varied from school to school, the approach to conducting the semifinal and final inspections was basically similar among the schools.

Conclusions

Within the limitations of the study, the following conclusions may be drawn:

1. There appeared to be an increasing sophistication of the techniques and tools used for planning physical recreation facilities.
2. There seemed to be a growing tendency toward the decentralization of the administrative approach to planning multipurpose recreational facilities.
3. Each of the facilities investigated in the present study appeared to be a product of more than the "formal" parameters of planning, such as statutes, regulations, policies, and guidelines. The design of each facility was also affected, to a large extent, by the personalities of the people involved in the planning efforts.
4. Although limited somewhat by the policies of each university, the practice of having the intramural director or chairman of the department of physical education involved in the daily inspection during the construction phase served as a valuable source of quality control over work and materials.
5. In the 1960s, the use of student-fee funding for multipurpose recreational facilities necessitated an increasing administrative commitment to involve students in the decision-making processes of the planning aspects.
6. With the exception of Michigan State, which has a separate intramural building for its women students, the planning efforts at each school emphasized the development of a totally co-recreational facility.

---

[16] At OSU, the chairman of the physical education department provided the daily on-the-site inspection.

IMPLICATIONS FOR THE
INTRAMURAL ADMINISTRATOR

The findings of this study suggest that although a number of factors influence the approach that a college employs in developing its facilities, effective facility planning results from the cooperative efforts of many individuals and groups. Stated another way, effective facility planning is the product of many individuals working together to devise an "inclusive plan" for guiding the development of a well-planned building. Accordingly, one of the primary tasks of the administrator is to identify and enlist the cooperation of *anyone* who can contribute to the planning of a proposed facility.

The administrative commitment to achieve a well-planned facility, however, requires more than just securing the services of interested and qualified persons. It is essential that competent leadership be appointed to coordinate the efforts of the individuals who participate in the planning process. The most critical quality required in such leadership is a thorough understanding of the dynamics of the process of planning facilities. This understanding provides the foundation for organizing the collective planning efforts into a unified, objective-oriented approach. The facility planner faces two tasks in this regard. The working relationships between the planning participants must be determined. In addition, guidelines for facilitating communication and coordination among all participants should be formulated.

The actions of the facility planners who were investigated in this study suggest that there are several steps that an administrator should pursue in order to enhance his planning efforts. He should keep abreast of the extant techniques and tools for planning and developing facilities. Manufacturers' representatives for materials and equipment that are appropriate to the facility should be encouraged to present a documented case for the use of their products to the committee (or a designated committee member) developing the program statement. The design architect should be hired early in the process of developing the project so that he can lend his expertise and experience to the collective planning efforts. In addition, it is desirable to employ a design architect with extensive experience in the design of athletic facilities.

Equally important, the administrator must involve the students in the process of planning facilities. If for no other reason than feasibility, university officials cannot continue to plan buildings, create schools, and attend to all the other "traditional" college matters without consulting with and involving those young men and women who are affected the most by what is done and how it is done. The relatively demure acceptance of the dramatic (more than 100 percent) increase in the amount of student-fee revenues required to fund the IM–PE Building by the University of Illinois's student body stands in sharp contrast with situations where little or no effort was made to induce student input into the planning process. The violent confrontations at Columbia University over the location and construction of a gymnasium and the tumultuous conflicts concerning the People's Park athletic field controversy at the University of California (Berkeley) offer two dramatic illustrations of the negative potential of the latter approach. Illinois's planners, on the other hand, made numerous attempts to involve students in their planning efforts and to inform the student body (as a whole) of the progress of the IM–PE Building project at every stage.

The study's findings also raise several significant considerations regarding the financing of college intramural-physical recreation facilities. Opinion is divided over the usefulness of student-fee monies as a source of funding for higher education facilities. Several high-level administrators forecast a diminishing reliance on student-fee revenues as a funding source for university facilities. These officials submit that the administrative headaches that accrue when students are involved extensively in decision-making processes for the buildings they finance are simply not worth the trouble. (Unfortunately, these officials do not speculate on tenable alternative funding sources.) In contrast, other administrators see an expanded role for student-fee revenue in the financing of facilities. They surmise that in light of the financial difficulties facing higher education, state officials (for instance, those from the state of Indiana) will become increasingly willing to finance "academic," as well as student-service facilities, with student-fee revenues. If this procedure is actually adopted, administrators will face even more difficulties in their attempts to obtain adequate financing for physical recreation facilities, because there will be more applicants for the student-fee dollar.

Another aspect of the financial phase of planning is a growing realization on the part of administrators that students are becoming increasingly reluctant to provide funding assistance for space that services intercollegiate programs. Perhaps this is because of a lessening of interest in traditional college activities of all forms. On the other hand, organized and free-time physical recreation programs appear to be growing at an unprecedented pace. Accordingly, the need for indoor physical recreation space has never been more critical. Administrators who wish to fulfill that need, however, must commit themselves to developing a facility that will provide opportunities for all rather than competitive arenas for the "gifted few."

GENERAL BIBLIOGRAPHY

ALEXANDER, CHRISTOPHER, *Notes on the Synthesis of Form*. Cambridge, Mass.: Harvard University Press, 1964.

AMERICAN ASSOCIATION FOR HEALTH, PHYSICAL EDUCATION AND RECREATION, *College and University Facilities Guide*. Washington, D.C., 1968.

———, *Planning Areas and Facilities for Health, Physical Education and Recreation*. Washington, D.C., 1965.

AMERICAN ASSOCIATION OF SCHOOL ADMINISTRATORS SCHOOL BUILDING COMMISSION, *American School Buildings*. Twenty-Seventh Yearbook, National Education Association. Washington, D.C., 1949.

———, *Planning America's School Buildings*. Washington, D.C., 1960.

AMERICAN INSTITUTE OF ARCHITECTS, *AIA School Plant Studies: A Selection 1952–1962*. Washington, D.C., 1962.

———, *Architect's Handbook of Professional Practice*. Washington, D.C., 1963.

———, *Handbook of Architectural Practice*. Washington, D.C., 1953.

American Physical Education Review, Vols. 1–4, 1896–99.

ASSOCIATION OF AMERICAN UNIVERSITIES, *The Federal Financing of Higher Education*. Washington, D.C., 1968.

THE ATHLETIC INSTITUTE, *Planning Areas and Facilities for Health, Physical Education, and Recreation*. Chicago: The Athletic Institute, and Washington: American Association of Health, Physical Education and Recreation, 1965.

BAREITHER, HARLAND D., and JERRY L. SCHILLINGER, *University Space Planning*. Urbana, Ill.: University of Illinois Press, 1968.

BEACH, W. W., *The Supervision of Construction*. New York: Scribner's, 1937.

BEYNON, JOHN, "Campus Planning: Review and Preview," in *Report from the School Laboratory*. Palo Alto, Calif.: Educational Facilities Lab. Inc., School of Education, Stanford University, 1967.

BOLES, HAROLD W., *Step by Step to Better School Facilities*. New York: Holt, Rinehart & Winston, 1965.

BROWN, J. DOUGLAS, *The Liberal University: An Institutional Analysis*. New York: McGraw-Hill, 1969.

BRUMBAUGH, A. J., "Estimating Capital Construction Costs," in *Establishing New Senior Colleges*. Atlanta: Southern Regional Education Board, 1966.

BULAT, DONALD C., *Architecture and the College*. Urbana, Ill.: Department of Architecture, University of Illinois, 1966.

CASTALDI, BASIL, *Creative Planning of Educational Facilities.* Chicago: Rand McNally, 1969.

————, *The Road to Better Schools.* Cambridge, Mass.: New England School Development Council, 1955.

CASTETTER, WILLIAM B., *Public School Debt Administration.* Philadelphia: University of Pennsylvania Press, 1958.

Council of Educational Facility Planners, *Guide for Planning Educational Facilities.* Columbus, Ohio, 1969.

CRAWFORD, WAYNE H., *A Guide for Planning Indoor Facilities for College Physical Education.* New York: Bureau of Publications, Teachers College, Columbia University, 1963:

DAHNKE, HAROLD, et al., *Higher Education Facilities Planning and Management Manuals, Preliminary Field Review.* Boulder, Colo.: Planning and Management Systems Division, Western Interstate Commission for Higher Education, November, 1970.

DE LA TORRE, M., "Estimating Building Construction Costs," in *Building Construction Handbook,* ed. Frederick S. Merritt. New York: McGraw-Hill, 1958, Chapter 26.

DOI, JAMES I., and JOHN DALE RUSSELL, *Manual for Studies of Space Utilization in Colleges and Universities.* Athens, Ohio: Ohio University, 1957.

EDUCATIONAL FACILITIES LABORATORIES, *Bricks and Mortar Boards.* New York, 1964.

ENGELHARDT, N.C., et al., *School Planning and Building Handbook.* New York: F. W. Dodge, 1956.

FOREMAN, CHARLES M., *A Procedure Guide for School Plant Construction for the State of Wyoming.* Laramie, Wyo.: The Curriculum and Research Center, College of Education, University of Wyoming, 1958.

GOOD, CARTER V., *Essentials of Educational Research.* New York: Appleton-Century-Crofts, 1966.

HANDLER, BENJAMIN, *Economic Planning for Better Schools.* Ann Arbor, Mich.: University of Michigan, 1960.

HARRIS, SEYMOUR E., *Higher Education: Resources and Finance.* New York: McGraw-Hill, 1962.

HERRICK, JOHN H., et al., *From School Program to School Plant.* New York: Henry Holt and Company, 1956.

HOLY, T. C., and W. E. ARNOLD, *Standards for the Evaluation of School Buildings.* Columbus, Ohio: Ohio State University, 1936.

Industrial Recreation Association, *Standard Sports Areas.* Chicago, 1944.

KEEZER, DEXTER M., ed., *Financing Higher Education: 1960–70.* New York: McGraw-Hill, 1959.

LEU, DONALD J., *Planning Educational Facilities.* New York: Center for Applied Research in Education, 1965.

MacConnell, James P., *Planning for School Buildings*. Englewood Cliffs, N.J.: Prentice-Hall, 1957.

McClurkin, W. D., *School Building Planner*. New York: Macmillan, 1964.

McGuffey, C. W., *A Review of Selected References Relating to the Planning of Higher Education Facilities*. Tallahassee, Fla.: Florida State University, 1968.

McLean, Robert, "Construction Management," in *Building Construction Handbook,* ed. Frederick S. Merritt. N. Y.: McGraw-Hill, 1958, Chapter 27.

McLeary, Ralph D., *Guide for Evaluating School Buildings*. Cambridge, Mass.: New England School Development Council, 1952.

Merritt, Frederick S., ed., *Building Construction Handbook*. New York: McGraw-Hill, 1958.

Mushkin, Selma J., *Economics of Higher Education*. Washington, D.C.: U.S. Department of Health, Education and Welfare, 1962.

National Citizens Commission for the Public Schools, *What Are Our School Building Needs?* New York, 1955, 74 pages.

National Council on Schoolhouse Construction, *Guide for Planning School Plants*. East Lansing, Mich.: Michigan State University, 1964.

———, *National Inventory of School Facilities and Personnel*. Washington, D.C.: U.S. Department of Health, Education and Welfare, Office of Education, Spring, 1962.

New Hampshire Department of Education, *Guide for Planning the Construction of School Buildings*. Concord, N.H., 1956.

New York State Education Department, *School Building Projects: A Guide to Administrative Procedures*. Albany: The University of the State of New York Press, 1955.

Peterson, James A., "A Case Analysis of the Process Involved in the Planning and Construction of Intramural-Physical Education Buildings Which Were Financed Primarily Through Student-Fee Revenues." Doctoral dissertation, University of Illinois (Urbana), 1971.

Phelon, Philip S., *Campus and Facilities Planning in Higher Education. The Process and Personnel. An Annotated Bibliography*. Albany: New York State Department of Education, 1968.

Pierce, David A., *Saving Dollars in Building Schools*. New York: Reinhold, 1954.

Priest, William J., and Edward O. Oglesby, "Selecting the Design Team," *Junior College Journal*, XXXVIII (September, 1967), pp. 26–30.

Romieniec, Edward J., and James Patterson, *Higher Education Facilities: Library of Source Documents. Summary Report*. College Station, Tex.: School of Architecture, Texas A & M University, 1968.

RUSSELL, JOHN DALE, *The Finance of Higher Education.* Chicago: University of Chicago Press, 1954.

SADLER, WALTER C., *Legal Aspects of Construction.* New York: McGraw-Hill, 1959.

SAPORA, ALLEN Y., and H. E. KENNEY, *A Study of the Present Status, Future Needs and Recommended Standards Regarding Space Used for Health, Physical Education, Physical Recreation and Athletics at the University of Illinois.* Champaign, Ill.: Stipes Publishing, 1960.

SCHNEIDER, RAYMOND C., "Factors Affecting School Site." Doctoral dissertation, Stanford University, 1955.

SCHWEHR, FREDERICK E., "Planning Educational Facilities," *Journal of Experimental Education,* XXXI (December, 1962), 140–44.

SCOTT, HARRY A., and R. B. WESTKAEMPER, *From Program to Facilities in Physical Education.* New York: Harper & Brothers, 1958.

SIMONDS, JOHN ORNSBEE, *Landscape Architecture.* New York: McGraw-Hill, 1961.

STOLLER, DEWEY H., *Managing School Indebtedness.* Danville. Ill.: Inter-State Printers and Publishers, 1967.

STONEMAN, MERLE A., *Planning and Modernizing the School Plant.* Lincoln, Neb.: University of Nebraska Press, 1949.

STREVELL, WALLACE H., and ARVID J. BURKE, *Administration of the School Building Program.* New York: McGraw-Hill, 1959.

SUMPTION, MERLE R., and JACK L. LANDES, *Planning Functional School Buildings.* New York: Harper & Brothers, 1957.

WIDDALL, KENNETH R., *Selected References for Planning Higher Education Facilities.* Columbus, Ohio: Council of Educational Facility Planners, 1968.

YOUNG, GORDON, *Planning School Plant Construction.* Frankfort, Ky.: State Department of Education, 1955.

21

Intramural Athletic Injuries: Prevention and Control

JOHN W. POWELL
United States Military Academy
West Point, New York

INTRODUCTION

A person tracing the development of sports participation in the United States over the past seventy-five years would easily see the integral role of intramural play. As athletics have become more sophisticated and complex over the years, several supporting disciplines have developed. One of these is that phase of the medical profession that has come to be called "sports medicine."

In the early 1900s, the proper treatment of athletic injuries was an area of sports about which little was known. Very seldom were doctors associated with sports teams. The injuries that occurred were generally handled by a "trainer." Being little more than a masseur, this individual usually had no specific training regarding injury care. Athletes who were injured were probably told to "shake it off" and return to the game, unless the injury was dramatic.

As athletic programs at colleges and universities began to prosper and as the money realized from ticket sales became essential to the "growth" of the school, the athlete's health and safety became a major concern of college administrators. Since good athletes make good teams and good teams typically produce large gate receipts, having the "star" players ready for competition became extremely important. Thus, money became available to develop medical coverage for those athletes who were participating in the intercollegiate athletic programs.

The popularity of competitive sports has received two significant boosts in the past fifty years, one after each world war. During these two armed conflicts, high levels of physical fitness and a strong sense of competitive spirit were considered the cornerstones in the armed services' effort to develop leadership, courage, and endurance in the fighting units. At the conclusion of each of the two "wars to end all wars," thousands of service veterans flocked to the colleges. Their enthusiasm for sports programs provided a solid basis for developing an extensive number of competitive teams. Accompanying this enthusiastic growth was a concommitant emphasis on physical fitness, conditioning, injury control, and safety. The "trainer" of early times developed into a highly educated and specialized sports therapist. As the medical profession followed sports more actively, the athletic trainer became even more skilled and eventually became the mainstay for injury control programs.

SPORTS MEDICINE TODAY

Today, the field of sports medicine is an integral aspect of athletic programs. The sports medicine team consists of surgeon, physical therapists, nurses, and athletic trainers. In most programs, the athletic trainer provides for the centralization of records and follow-up care of the injured athletes. In other institutions, this injury control responsibility may be handled by any of several persons, from a team physician to a campus administrator.

At the present time, almost every university, college, and junior college, and in some areas even high schools, have some type of specific injury prevention program for their competitive teams. Most of these programs include full-time team physicians hired by the institution and a fully staffed athletic training department. These programs often include individuals who have complete responsibility for the safety and maintenance of equipment. The sad part of these extensive programs is that in most areas, intramural participants are not allowed full access to the professional prevention teams.

SPORTS MEDICINE AND INTRAMURAL ATHLETICS

What is the relative status of intramural programs in the field of sports medicine? How many institutions have actively functioning injury prevention programs for intramurals? What kind of on-the-field emergency medical facilities are provided for the intramural athlete? What about medical coverage, facility and equipment safety, and rehabilitation for intramural athletes? All of these questions must be answered if we are to establish the status of intramural injury control. If an assumption is made that intramurals are an integral part of the university community and that all students should have an equitable opportunity to participate, then it is also the responsibility of the administration to provide those who participate in intramural programs with reasonable assurance that maximum safety standards and good medical care are present. In the remainder of this chapter, the basic concepts of injury prevention programs will be discussed as well as essential aspects of administration of such a program.

INTRAMURAL INJURY CONTROL

The topic of injury prevention and control in intramural activities is an area that includes many different concepts. Embodied in it are the basic philosophies of any good intramural experience. One of the more common philosophies of an intramural program is that each institution sponsoring a program should provide for the health and welfare of all of the participants. Scott (1951 p. 423) lists several features of an intramural program that, if adopted, will lead to a *quality* experience for each participant. His list includes the following items regarding medical care:

1. Periodic and thorough medical examination and supervision of all participants.
2. Classification of participants with reference to physical characteristics, degree of motor ability, and athletic experience in order to assure equality of competing units.
3. Provision of practice periods of considerable length at which expert instruction is available upon request.
4. Improved equipment for participants, including proper protective equipment where indicated.
5. Improved maintenance of fields, courts, and other facilities in order to make possible participation in properly prepared and marked surfaces under official game rules.
6. Improved officiating of games and contests by competent officials.
7. Improved guidance of students in and supervision of all phases of the program by professionally competent members of the faculty.

If Scott's ideas are indeed sound premises for intramural programs, then to fully realize them a specific program designed for injury prevention and control must be implemented by each institution.

INJURY PREVENTION TEAM

The effectiveness of any injury prevention program depends greatly on the coordination and communication among the medical, paramedical, intramural, and (where applicable) physical education staffs. This kind of communication can best be developed through the efforts of an injury prevention team. A team of this nature would be charged with the responsibility for the health and welfare of intramural athletes. The doctor, the athletic trainer or paramedic, coaches, officials, and administrators all work together for the benefit of the athlete and the program.

The real key to the success of the injury prevention team is the division of responsibility among the individual members and the close communication between each member and the remainder of the team. The ultimate responsibility for the injured athlete lies with the physician. The other members of the team provide the physician with a means for daily supervision of the patient.

The athletic trainer or injury coordinator's job includes maintenance of records, use of follow-up procedures for those who are injured, and provision for immediate emergency field coverage for the intramural games. Behind this phase of the program lies the intramural staff and the support its members provide for the whole "team." They must be able to enforce the limitations that are placed on participants by the medical department. Collectively, the injury prevention team has complete responsibility for the health and welfare of the intramural athlete.

The key person in the whole operation is the athletic trainer or the individual charged with similar responsibilities who is directly accountable to the intramural department. In addition to providing for emergency medical care, his job is to inform the respective teams of any limitations that have been placed on their players. He must also see that the individuals are fully aware of the scope of their limitations, and in larger programs he may even provide space, time, and supervision for the rehabilitative programs for injured athletes. A secondary but critical task to be assumed by this individual would be to evaluate all aspects of the intramural program for safety "consciousness" and to institute remedial programs wherever necessary.

THE ADMINISTRATION OF AN INJURY PREVENTION PROGRAM

The details involved in the administration of an injury prevention program depend on the size and philosophy of each sponsoring institution. Schools with large budgets can afford to develop an extensive, in-depth program. Institutions with smaller budgets can also develop programs that will be meaningful for them. The significance of any injury prevention program in intramurals lies not in the mere existence of the program, but in how much detail can be developed in it. Every organized athletic program should have some type of established policies to prevent or lessen the chances of injury to the participants. To assist in sorting out the needs of an injury prevention program, the following pages will be devoted to a more detailed explanation of each of Scott's criteria for a quality intramural experience.

Medical Examination and Supervision

Medical examination and supervision in a healthful intramural environment encompasses three basic areas:

1. Preparticipation screening and evaluation of the individual's history of injury and illness.
2. Safety policies and practices, along with medical supervision regarding all playing equipment and facilities.
3. Accurate records of injuries, and follow-up procedures for returning the injured athlete to competition.

The preparticipation evaluation is probably the most difficult of these to achieve, especially with large numbers of participants. However, it can be the most beneficial technique in minimizing the risk of injury. There are several different approaches to this type of screening. One might be a review of health and medical records that were submitted for college or high school entrance. Special note should be taken of any condition that would be aggravated by sports participation. Another means of obtaining this injury history might be to require a written survey of those individuals who will participate. This can easily be accomplished through a simple questionnaire that includes categories regarding injury history. Another method might be to require a written survey of those individuals who will participate in high-risk sports such as football, wrestling, lacrosse, soccer, rugby, or hockey. Each of these three techniques will provide adequate screening information; unfortunately, all have as a limiting factor the number of individuals participating. Obviously, the screening of all individuals is far more difficult than to screen only those who will compete in high-risk sports. The intramural director should adopt the screening method which is most appropriate to the particular situation. A careful review of the injury survey will help eliminate serious injury to those individuals who have had recent surgery, concussions, dislocations, fractures, or serious illness. The requiring of a current medical examination by the health center or team physician if the screening exam shows the need will also aid in preventing serious injury to the athlete.

In developing these injury survey forms, special consideration should be given to the areas of the knee, shoulder, back, and neck. Specific attention should be given to current limitations, recency of injury, and frequency of occurrence in each category. In addition to joint injuries, consideration should be given to head injuries of all types, mononucleosis, hepatitis, allergies, asthma, diabetes, epilepsy, and loss of one of a pair of organs. Decisions regarding the types of sports in which individuals may compete must be made by the individual, the intramural office, and the physician. This interdisciplinary team insures that the doctor, who has the final say, is completely aware of the physical capabilities required by the sports in which his patient wishes to compete. By means of such intelligent medical management, the individual who participates can do so with a reasonable assurance of the minimized risk of serious injury.

Safety: Equipment and Environment

With the rapid expansion of intramural sports programming comes a growing need for the adequate supervision and regard for the health and safety of each participant. The responsibility for this supervision lies with the sponsoring institution. Safety in athletics or in any other field does not occur automatically through some process in nature; rather, it must be planned and developed with specific goals in mind. In order to practice safety effectively, someone must be assigned the task of maintaining safety practices. This duty becomes important in overall injury control.

In athletics, two areas exist in which safety must be practiced routinely: the type of equipment used for participation, and the general conditions under which the games are to be played. The amount and type of equipment required to play the particular game will dictate the emphasis placed on the equipment aspect of safety. A large number of injuries can be prevented if the equipment that is used by the intramural participant is in good repair and properly fitted. For example, a thigh guard in football, if not properly placed, can lead to a long-range disability. That is, if the thigh were unprotected, bruised, and not cared for or protected, the result could be permanent disability. This kind of injury is also a good example of the need for immediate care of what appears at the time to be a relatively minor injury. A more detailed discussion of injury care will be presented later in this chapter.

The biggest problem with equipment safety is that proper repair and fitting must be done while the equipment is in use. It is very difficult to check all equipment every day. Therefore, it is the responsibility of the safety supervisor to provide some form of education regarding safety of equipment for each of the participants. Once the player knows what his equipment is for and how it is to be maintained, he can then take care of it himself. However, to insure the safest standards, the supervisor should perform periodic spot checks of all equipment.

Developing a safe environment in which to participate is probably the easiest aspect of safety in sports. The routine cleaning of gymnasiums and court floors, the mowing and seeding of playing fields, and the cleaning and sanitizing of locker and shower rooms should receive priority attention in any intramural as well as intercollegiate program. Just assuming that these tasks will automatically be completed can lead to a breakdown in high safety standards. Therefore, it is the job of the safety coordinator to see that these programs are undertaken and completed on a regular basis.

Other considerations in the development of a safe playing environment should be the frequent marking of playing fields, maintenance of good light for evening competition, and good outdoor field preparation. Each of these categories is important to the overall safety program in intramurals.

The most important point to remember is that safety in sports does not happen by accident, nor is it maintained automatically. Safety must be thoughtfully planned and painstakingly executed by individuals who have the health and welfare of each participant as their main objective.

Injury Reporting and Follow-Up Procedures

Regardless of the prevention techniques used at any level of competitive sports, there will always be some injuries. One of the most important roles of an injury prevention program is to see that the injured athlete has adequate emergency first aid, proper supervision during his recovery, and detailed rehabilitation (as well as extra protection), whenever indicated, before he returns to competition.

In order to maintain this kind of supervision, each member of the injury prevention team must be informed when an injury occurs. The circumstances surrounding the injury, the extent of the injury, the limits that are placed on further participation, and the period of time the player should be exempt from playing must all be known if the management of the injured athlete is to be effective. To implement such a management program, there must first be a centralized and coordinated system for reporting and filing injuries. The athletic trainer or injury supervisor must develop some kind of injury report form that can be used by each coach. On this form, information must be filled out at the time of injury regarding the circumstances surrounding the injury. The form must be written in terms everyone can understand. Therein lies the importance of good communication.

The development of such a communication system is imperative and must have as its central force the intramural office representative. The rapport that he establishes throughout the team is the key to success. It is also his job to coordinate a system governing the graded return to competition of the injured athlete. A serious injury that occurs because the injured athlete returned to play before he was completely rehabilitated is totally unnecessary. For example, being able to accelerate and decelerate while sprinting and being able to run a variable-speed diminishing figure eight without favoring a recently sprained ankle, would indicate that recovery was adequate and the athlete could return to activity. However, as an added precaution the athletic trainer should probably offer some type of tape support, at least for the remainder of the season.

Only through an organized program for the prevention of reinjury can a complete program to minimize injury be fully effective. If centralization of information, communication among injury prevention team members, and the cooperation of the intramural office cannot be established, an injury prevention program is doomed.

Emergency Field Care

Emphasis must be placed on minimizing injury on the field by seeing that it is not complicated by a person poorly trained in emergency first aid. Expert care administered to an injured athlete on the field can be a very critical factor in the total treatment of the injury. Knowing how to recognize what is serious and what is relatively minor and being able to administer to fractures, dislocations, concussions, and the like is essential to good injury prevention programs. Having a knowledgeable person on hand when a neck or back injury occurs may prevent permanent disability or even death. Granted, these types of injuries are not frequent in intramurals, but is having a tragedy occur because of a lack of trained personnel worth the risk? It becomes imperative, then, that the sponsoring organization provide adequate medical or paramedical support for their intramural games, especially for the contact or semi-contact games.

Some larger institutions may have the capability of placing a doctor on the field of competition. Others may be able to use some upperclass medical student to meet the medical needs on the field. With the academic demands such individuals face, their extensive use is probably somewhat limited. However, in many situations their coordinated use would provide at least a partial means of providing support for intramural participants.

A more feasible intramural program might gain its medical support through the physical education department's student trainer or through apprentice physical therapist programs. The young men and women who are in these programs possess the skills necessary to provide emergency first aid. A more detailed discussion of the implementation of the student trainer program will be presented later in this chapter. In any case, those individuals charged with the responsibility for field care of the injured should have, as a minimum, background training in American Red Cross first aid. To insure the best coverage, these individuals should also be equipped with some means of communicating with the nearest emergency vehicle or medical facility. Remember, communication is the key to the success of injury prevention.

NONMEDICAL ASPECTS OF INJURY PREVENTION

So far, our discussion of injury prevention has centered in the injury prevention team and its responsibility for minimizing the risk involved in competitive athletics. At this point, consideration will be given to responsibilities that should be assumed in the general administration of intramural competition. The specific areas to be considered are (1) the classification of participants, and (2) physical conditioning for competition, and (3) officiating. All of these areas are important in the overall concept of injury prevention.

Classification of Participants

The early identfication of the skill levels of participants in sports is essential in order that each individual obtain maximum benefit for his efforts. This classification becomes extremely important in sports that call for individual competition, such as wrestling, tennis, golf, and handball. There is nothing more frustrating than for a beginner to have to compete with a highly skilled performer. For a novice wrestler to compete against a champion is not only frustrating but dangerous. Also, a skilled squash player sometimes suffers from the wild swinging of the beginner's racquet. Grouping by weight for such sports as wrestling and boxing is essential for the protection of the participants.

In team sports, the lack of experience of an individual may be masked by the efforts of the team, especially in the won-loss column. However, there is a certain degree of extra risk for the novice due to his inexperience. In a game such as flag football, the individual who is not fully skilled in the techniques of blocking becomes a risk not only to himself but to his opponent as well. In any case, it is important that some equitable system be devised to protect the novice from the expert, as well as vice versa. This system will naturally vary with each sport, and therefore the exact techniques for grouping should be left to the administrators of each program.

PHYSICAL CONDITIONING FOR COMPETITION

In any competitive game, whether it be football, track, swimming, or bowling, good physical condition is the mark of a winner. Physical fitness and readiness for competition are important for all ages and at all levels of competition. Although it is not the function of the intramural office to operate year-round physical fitness programs, a program of guidance should be available upon request. Some of the popular ways of maintaining relative fitness are jogging, running, swimming, cycling, or just plain walking. Whatever method is used, the goal of each is to improve the general physical fitness of the individual. However, certain sports require some special physical conditioning. Specifically, these would be sports requiring hand-held implements (golf, tennis, squash) body contact sports (football, soccer), or a combination of both (lacrosse, hockey). A person who enjoys a good level of physical fitness will not necessarily be fit for contact without first engaging in a period of specific conditioning.

This specific conditioning for competition should be considered when intramural competitive schedules are drawn up. Within each schedule should be "strongly recommended" days of practice prior to game competition. During these practice sessions, players would have the opportunity to condition themselves for contact. In addition, it would be wise for the intramural staff to provide some guidance to the team as to types of practice programs to use in order to obtain the best results.

Specifically, the routines for practice should include warm-up drills, events to teach the skills of each sport, and one or two practice game situations. Through this kind of scheduling, teams have the opportunity to truly practice. In addition, the practice game can provide an opportunity for the officials who will be working that sport to become proficient.

Obviously, this kind of regimen is more important for the more physically oriented sports. However, procedures for warm-up prior to competition can be important to the health and welfare of any individual participating in any type of sport.

Officiating

The officials given the responsibility of supervising the play are a very important aspect of injury prevention. No matter what level of competition, it is the officials' job to control the game. To call infractions of the rules when they occur, to regulate substitution, to be observant to dangerous players or unsafe playing areas, to act positively to prevent injury—to do all this and still regulate the general tenor of the game is a very complex task. It is the job of the intramural administrator to screen and train officials for the intramural program. These officials must have knowledge of the sport they are working, as well as the skill to regulate the game in the safest possible manner.

It is especially important in intramural competition to insure that the highest standards of officiating skill be maintained. Since most intramural officials are paid only a nominal fee (and as such, are not professionals), some form of supervisory board should be established in an attempt to standardize the officiating.

AN APPROACH TO AN INJURY PREVENTION
PROGRAM FOR INTRAMURAL ATHLETICS

The whole concept of injury prevention at any level of competition is only as good as the design of the program and the support given it by the sponsoring organization. It is the responsiblity of this sponsor to provide policies and practices for its program that will take into consideration the health and welfare of each individual. The sponsor must select the types of sports to be played, assign coaches, officials, and assistant or student administrators, and develop schedules of competition that will benefit the largest number of participants.

Any successful intramural injury prevention program will have as its focal point the development of a first-class team of professionals who are dedicated to the task of injury prevention and control. As mentioned earlier, the "main man" in this team must be able to communicate with medical personnel as well as professional intramural staff. Most logically, this individual will be the product of an athletic training background. More and more young men and women are being educated as professional athletic trainers. These individuals possess the skills necessary to develop and manage injury prevention programs. It is time that intramural directors began to avail themselves of the skill of these young professionals. It is too late to wait until after a series of serious accidents, or possibly a death, occurs.

The major problem with the development of any new program is, of course, money. The question of where the money will come from is one that must be answered in order to begin to develop a quality program. Some of the possible answers might be to charge entrance fees for teams who wish to participate, to make an appropriation from the existing intramural budget, or to develop programs with other departments for time sharing. Perhaps a senior student athletic trainer could be given the responsibility for intramurals, or possibly a special graduate assistantship could be established in the area of intramurals. Regardless of how the program is to be financed, the *first* capital outlay should be to hire an athletic trainer or injury supervisor for intramurals.

To elaborate all of the possible ways of starting the injury prevention program would be an endless task, especially since each institution is governed by its own set of conditions. However, one aspect of the program should be detailed in order to provide a common starting point for many different situations. That is the selection of the "key man."

Most varsity athletic programs, no matter how large or small the institution, have some form of athletic training facility for their participants. These staffs (regardless of size) typically support some kind of student trainer program, which, when properly developed, can provide injury control for intramurals. This kind of program provides two valuable ends: intramural injury control and experience for students of athletic training.

As an example, assume a relatively large institution where several student trainers are hired by the varsity staff. Most of these individuals will stay with the varsity program through graduation. Therefore, not many slots open each year. If more students apply than there are openings available, why not offer the students similar experience at the intramural level? Obviously, these students would need expert supervision, which could easily come from one of the varsity trainers or graduate student trainers. Many times, these young students jump at the chance just to gain some experience under the supervision of a professional. As these students become more proficient, more responsibility can be allocated to them. These freshman or beginning trainers could come from physical education classes, athletic training curricula, or first aid classes. Wherever these students are found, the important point is that the program will work for the *benefit of the student* and the intramural program if properly organized. Smaller institutions could probably set up a similar program on a lesser scale.

Intramural programs operated outside the realm of a university or college might draw on the experience of existing staff or establish a work-study program with a nearby institution's physical education department. Here again, intramural programs and students benefit from a combined, even if nominal effort.

To fully implement the programs discussed thus far requires the allocation of space from which to operate. Some room within the intramural area must be set aside as a training room or injury control center. This room could result from the conversion of a small locker room, old office, or small storage area. The basic requirements are adequate light, heat, ventilation, drainage, water supply, and electrical outlets. The extent of each depends on whether the room will be used strictly as an office or whether it will also double as a training room. Whatever the use of the room, it must be operated on a full scale. Injury prevention is not a part-time problem; it requires constant supervision by qualified personnel and the complete support of the intramural administration.

SUMMARY

Throughout this chapter, a wide variety of topics concerning injury prevention in intramural athletics have been discussed. The essence of each is that injury prevention entails complete communication and cooperation among those individuals charged with responsibility for administrating the intramural program. Each member of the injury prevention team must be willing to listen and take counsel from the other members. It is through this communication that the participants will benefit most.

Based on the discussion in this chapter, several ideas should have uppermost priority when an institution develops an injury prevention program.

1. The institution should be willing to give its full support to the operation of the program.
2. The program should be developed and operated by a team of professionals from the areas of medicine, intramurals, and (wherever applicable) physical education.
3. Health exams should be given to all participants. These exams should include preparticipation screening of those individuals who will be playing high-risk games.
4. Levels of competition should be defined in terms of age, experience, and skills of the individual participants.
5. Special care should be taken to see that the highest safety standards are maintained for all playing areas and equipment.
6. A program must be set up to provide for emergency field care, provisions for follow-up and rehabilitation, and graded return to competition of those who are injured.

One of the first textbooks on athletic training contains a passage that, though written and intended for athletic trainers, embodies the spirit that intramural programs and their sponsors should feel toward the individuals who participate.

> Conscientious, intelligent care of the athlete is, admittedly, a vital responsibility of those connected in an official capacity with the conduct of competitive sports. The youngsters (individuals) are entrusted to our care by parents who have faith in our ethics, our sincerity, our fitness. Life, limb and happiness depends on our appreciation of this responsibility and its conscientious fulfillment. (Bilik, 1948)

It is critical that injury prevention programs should exist at some form at all levels of competitive sports. Every participant has the right to expect that his health and welfare will be protected in every way possible. Remember, the best possible insurance plan that the intramural program can have is to operate with a blanket of protection provided by an actively functioning injury prevention program.

GENERAL BIBLIOGRAPHY

ANDERSON, BRUCE D., "Touch Football Injury Survey: A Product of NIA Research," *National Intramural Association Proceedings,* XIX (1968), 94–96.

BILIK, S. E., *The Trainer's Bible,* 8th ed. New York: T. J. Reed, 1948.

BUCHNER, CHARLES A., *Administration of School Health and Physical Education Programs,* 5th ed. St. Louis: C.V. Mosby, 1971.

COLBERG, GARY, and JESS KRANS, "The Incidence of Injury in a Rural College Intramural Football Program," *National Intramural Association Proceedings,* XXII (1971), 117–27.

DAYTON, WILLIAM O., *Athletic Training and Conditioning.* New York: Ronald Press, 1965.

HIRATA, ISAO, JR., *The Doctor and the Athlete.* Philadelphia: Lippincott, 1968.

KLAFS, CARL E., and DANIEL D. ARNHEIM, *Modern Principles of Athletic Training: The Science of Injury Prevention and Care.* St. Louis: C.V. Mosby, 1973.

POWELL, JOHN W., "Injury Prevention: The West Point Program," *National Intramural Association Proceedings,* XXV (1974), 106–13.

ROOKER, A. A., and M. WAYNE JENNINGS, "Fact Finding Study on Intramural Football (Touch and Flag) Injuries," *National Intramural Association Proceedings*, XX (1969), 134–37.

SCOTT, HARRY, *Competitive Sports in Schools and Colleges*. New York: Harper & Brothers, 1951.

SHEPARD, GEORGE, and RICHARD E. JAMERSON, *Interscholastic Athletics*. New York: McGraw-Hill, 1953.

STEVENSON, MICHAEL J., "The Effects of Artificial and Natural Turf on Injuries, Player Opinion, and Selected Game and Team Variables in College Intramural Touch Football," *National Intramural Association Proceedings*, XXIV (1973), 178–87.

VOLTMER, EDWARD F., and ARTHUR A. ESSLINGER, *Organization and Administration of Physical Education*, 4th ed. New York: Appleton-Century-Crofts, 1967.

YOST, CHARLES P. ed., *Sports Safety*. Washington, D.C.: American Association for Health, Physical Education and Recreation, Division of Safety Education, 1972.

22

Awards and Participation Incentives

NORMAN C. PARSONS, JR.
University of Miami
Coral Gables, Florida

INTRODUCTION

Today's student, at all educational levels, has a multitude of activities and endeavors in which he can spend his leisure time. In view of this, the intramural director is challenged to attract his student body to the participation opportunities available in their school's campus recreation program. Because of the variety of demands on the leisure time of the students, all intramural personnel must be attuned to the factors that, either directly or indirectly, affect the student's decision to participate in an activity. Many of these factors have been examined in prior chapters of this text. This chapter examines the usefulness of awards and tangible participation incentives as motivators for student involvement in the intramural program.

Traditionally, intramural directors have directed their "incentive efforts" to promote their programs to the use of point systems and trophies. It can be argued, on one hand, that many "mediocre" intramural programs have been aided greatly by a well-planned program of point systems and awards. On the other hand, many individuals are quick to point out that award and point systems have many negative attributes. Point systems and awards, they claim, are worthwhile only when their use acts as a positive incentive for continued or increased involvement in the intramural program by the university community. Without question, there are other factors that influence the student's decision whether or not to participate in an intramural program. Many intramural programs, for example, have continued to prosper even though they have eliminated both point systems and the awarding of trophies. Such an occurrence provides support for those who argue strongly against the need for an "artificial" framework for participant incentives. These advocates claim that neither awards nor point systems are essential to the intramural program.

If one were to examine the total arena of participation incentives, every potential positive and negative influence on the attractiveness of the program should be investigated. It would be, however, a boundless and perhaps impossible task. This chapter will focus on the utility of using either point systems or awards as part of the administrative effort to involve people in intramurals. Some of the positive and the negative aspects of each endeavor will be presented. This chapter will also look at other techniques or tools used by intramural directors to increase participation. Finally, several administrative implications of the use of participation incentives will be suggested.

POINT SYSTEMS

Pont systems are an integral part of many intramural programs. Grambeau reports, for example, that over 80 percent of the schools included in a study purporting to investigate selected intramural programs reported that they used a point system of one kind or another. The literature appears to suggest, however, that the use of such systems has decreased in recent years. The purposes of this section are (1) to discuss several of the types of point systems currently in use, (2) to examine some of the pros and cons of point systems in general, and (3) to present suggestions for incorporating a point system into the intramural program.

In order to look at several types of point systems, it is first necessary to answer this question: What is an intramural point system? Traditionally, intramural point systems have consisted of efforts to quantify "rewards" both for participation in general and for successful participation in the competitive aspects of the program. Designed to serve primarily as an incentive factor, point systems typically give X number of points for entering a sport or an activity and award X number of points (on a graduated scale) for successful participation in that sport. The desired by-product of such a system is increased interest resulting from the incentive of a team striving to accumulate points. Tables 1–3 illustrate three examples of point systems.

Table 1 is an example of the point system used in the intramural

Table 1. The Point System Used in the United States Military Academy's Intramural Program

BANKERS TROPHY POINT DISTRIBUTION

Sport	1st	2nd	3rd	4th	5th	6th	7th	8th	9th
Fall									
Football	162	144	126	108	90	72	54	36	18
Orienteering	72	64	56	48	40	32	24	16	8
Soccer	144	128	112	96	80	64	48	32	16
Tennis	72	64	56	48	40	32	24	16	8
Track	126	112	98	84	70	56	42	28	14
Triathlon	72	64	56	48	40	32	24	16	8
Winter									
Basketball	108	96	84	72	60	48	36	24	12
Boxing	108	96	84	72	60	48	36	24	12
Handball	54	48	42	36	30	24	18	12	6
Squash	56	48	42	36	30	24	18	12	6
Swimming	90	80	70	60	50	40	30	20	10
Volleyball	90	80	70	60	50	40	30	20	10
Wrestling	108	96	84	72	60	48	36	24	12
Spring									
Boat Racing	54	48	42	36	30	24	18	12	6
Cross Country	72	64	56	48	40	32	24	16	8
Lacrosse	144	128	112	96	80	64	48	32	16
Touch Football	144	128	112	96	80	64	48	32	16
Water Polo	108	96	84	72	60	48	36	24	12

program at the United States Military Academy. Each team in each of the company units within a regiment receives a proportional number of points for its relative degree of success in each activity. Typical of most point systems, this system awards a greater number of points to those activities involving more individuals. Table 2 offers an example of another point system (Van Nostrand, 1970, p. 46). The number of points awarded for each sport in this system depends on the total number of teams and (where applicable) individuals who enter the activity. A moderate level of success in a highly popular activity can be worth more point-wise) than a high level of success in a less popular activity. This concept is based on the premise that there is a sliding scale of difficulty which is directly proportional to the number of entrants competing in an activity. The point system in Table 3 places a greater emphasis on achieving "victories" than on finishing in a certain place (Endres, 1971, pp. 104–5). Only the first three places in the "championship round" receive additional points.*

If as Endres surmises there are indeed "as many point scoring plans in existence as there are schools using them" (Ibid., p. 103), what system should be adopted for the reader's institution? Before answering that question, however, we must raise a more fundamental inquiry. Should any point system be used? Unfortunately, no crystal ball exists that would enable an individual to organize the "best" intramural program. What may be proper and effective for one institution may be totally inappropriate for another. In his quest for an answer as to whether or not to use a point system for his school, the reader should examine the arguments pro and con concerning the utility of intramural point systems. Curry has compiled a list of several of the most widely expressed views in the literature (1972, pp. 59–63).

In Favor of Point Systems

1. Interest is *created* and *maintained* through point systems (Leavitt and Price, 1958, p. 245).
2. Giving participation points attracts individuals who might not otherwise become involved in the intramural program (Mueller, 1971, pp. 182–83).
3. Points offer a system of giving (deserved) awards (Endres, 1971, p. 103).
4. Offering points draws participants into the less popular sports.
5. A motivating device in intramurals is not only helpful but necessary.

---

*In order for this system to be completely equitable, it would be necessary for all organizations to play the same number of games in an activity. Readers who wish to examine additional examples of point systems are referred to Louis Means's *Intramurals: Their Organization and Administration* (Englewood Cliffs, N.J.: Prentice-Hall, 1973), pp. 134–60.

Table 2. The Point System Used at
the University of Missouri (Rolla) Prior to 1970

INTRAMURAL POINT AWARDS

Each organization is given a number of points for entering a sport. The number of points that they may receive depends upon the final standing in the competition of that sport.

	1	2	3	4	5	6	7	8	9	10	11	12	13	14	15	16	17	18	19	20	21	22
Horseshoes	300	275	250	225	200	175	160	140	100	90	80	70	60	50	40	30	20	10	5	0	0	0
Table Tennis	300	275	250	225	200	175	160	140	100	90	80	70	60	50	40	30	20	10	5	0	0	0
Basketball	850	750	700	675	650	625	500	475	450	425	400	375	350	325	300	275	250	225	200	150	100	50
Football	850	750	700	675	650	625	500	475	450	425	400	375	350	325	300	275	250	225	200	150	100	50
Softball	850	750	700	675	650	625	500	475	450	425	400	375	350	325	300	275	250	225	200	150	100	50
Volleyball	850	750	700	675	650	625	500	475	450	425	400	375	350	325	300	275	250	225	200	150	100	50
Track	450	400	350	325	300	275	250	225	200	175	150	125	100	90	80	70	60	50	40	20	10	5
Swimming	400	350	325	300	275	250	225	150	125	100	90	80	70	60	50	40	30	20	10	5	0	0
Boxing	400	350	325	300	275	250	225	150	125	100	90	80	70	60	50	40	30	20	10	5	0	0
Wrestling	400	350	325	300	275	250	225	150	125	100	90	80	70	60	50	40	30	20	10	5	0	0
Cross Country	300	275	250	225	200	175	160	140	100	90	80	70	60	50	40	30	20	10	5	0	0	0
Tennis	300	275	250	225	200	175	160	140	100	90	80	70	60	50	40	30	20	10	5	0	0	0
Handball	300	275	250	225	200	175	160	140	100	90	80	70	60	50	40	30	20	10	5	0	0	0
Golf	300	275	250	225	200	175	160	140	100	90	80	70	60	50	40	30	20	10	5	0	0	0
Rifle	300	275	250	225	200	175	160	140	100	90	80	70	60	50	40	30	20	10	5	0	0	0

Table 3.   The Catholic University of America's
Intramural Point System

ORGANIZATIONAL SPORTS

Sports	Entrance Points	Victory Points	Championship Points
Touch Football	20	10 per game	100–60–40
Basketball	20	10 per game	100–60–40
Softball	20	10 per game	100–60–40
Swimming	20	6 for first *	100–60–40
Track	20	6 for first *	100–60–40
Volleyball	20	10 per game	75–45–30

INDIVIDUAL SPORTS

Sports	Entrance Points	Victory Points	Championship Points
Badminton	20	10 per match	50–30–20
Foul Shooting	20	10 per match	50–30–20
Handball	20	10 per match	50–30–20
Horseshoes	20	10 per match	50–30–20
Table Tennis	20	10 per match	50–30–20
Tennis	20	10 per match	75–45–30
Wrestling	20	10 per bout	75–45

* Note: Second, third, fourth, and fifth place victory points of 4, 3, 2, and 1 will be awarded in track and swimming. The relays in both sports will be scored 12, 8, 6, 4, and 2.

6. Since point systems are so widely used, they must be necessary.

7. Point systems are merely another extension of the American ethic of "competition brings out the best in us."

8. The end-of-the-year point championship is the high-water mark of student enthusiasm.

9. Point systems add "zest and spice" to the intramural programs (Means, 1973, p. 134).

In Opposition to Point Systems

1. It is possible to develop a good intramural program without the use of point systems (Hall, 1966, p. 102).

2. Since several intramural programs do not use a point system, such incentives are unnecessary.

3. When point systems are a part of the intramural program, quite often

the participants cease to enter for the fun of participation (Curry, 1972, p. 61).

4. The use of point systems leads to an increase in the number of forfeits since many individuals enter only to obtain the points and not for the competitive aspects of the activity. Once the participant concludes that the points "just aren't worth the trouble," he or she is more apt to drop out than the individual who is competing for other reasons.

5. Maintaining reliable, up-to-date records of the point system is frequently a time-consuming task—time that could be better spent by the director.

6. The battle for points increases the competitive nature of the program and frequently leads to an increase in the number of disruptive incidents on the playing field.

7. Students may tend to enter an activity in which they can get the most points rather than an activity that would provide them with immediate enjoyment and would be of value later (Leavitt and Price, 1958, p. 246).

8. Point systems discriminate against residential units that have fewer potential participants.

9. The spirit of play is often lost in the mad rush to accumulate points.

10. "Forced" competition is contrary to the traditional intramural philosophy of "fun for all."

11. Point systems are "artificial devices" to attract participants (Stumpner, 1960, p. 6).

In conclusion, it is apparent that many arguments can be advanced to either support or reject the use of a point system in the intramural program. Unfortunately, there is no way to objectively weigh the relative merits of point systems in a manner that would be valid from school to school. No matter what criteria are used, the intramural director must ultimately make what is essentially a subjective decision as to whether or not to use a point system at his school.

Administrative Suggestions

If the decision is made to incorporate a point system into the intramural program, the following suggestions are recommended for the intramural administrator:

1. Make a careful study of existing point systems and apply the best procedures to your situation.

2. Select the point system that will best complement the other facets of the intramural program.

3. Develop a point system that is both basic and practical. Do not devise a system that no one can understand or that is too time consuming to administer.

4. Insure that the system is equitable for all groups and individuals within the intramural "community."

5. Remember that in some instances it is both possible and desirable to administer point and nonpoint leagues in the same sport. At the University of Illinois, for example, a residence can enter only one team in the point league but is encouraged to enter as many teams as possible in nonpoint leagues of the same sport. Since in most institutions individuals are not allowed to compete on two teams, a medium for the less competitive or less skilled player is provided.

6. Structure and administer a total program whose primary emphasis is on meeting student needs, not on the accumulation of points by students.

AWARDS

In many respects the problem of whether to use awards in the intramural program is similar to the question regarding the merits of point systems. For the most part, the intramural director need only substitute "award" for "point system" in the previous section's discussion in order to view the traditional arguments. One additional argument is traditionally attributed to awards. On the plus side is the contention that awards are highly conducive to motivation because of their tangible quality. An award is an object that you can see and touch, an item that can be exhibited, viewed, shared with others, and kept as a tangible remembrance of achievement. On the other hand, the actual and potential cost of some of the more common types of awards can harm some intramural programs.

The argument against the use of awards (e.g. cost, misplaced program emphasis) does not, however, appear to be as strong or as debatable as that against the use of a point system. Louis Means provided a succinct and yet inclusive case for awards when he wrote:

> Some argue that awards in sports are objectionable, but it cannot be denied that awards are a great motivating force in intramural sports. Achievement is recognized in almost every other walk of life. Academically, we still recognize merit with grades, certificates, diplomas, and scholarships. We still select valedictorians and members of local and national honor societies. Retail business often uses similar devices to increase sales. The human desire for recognition is most natural. (1973, p. 161)

It is important to note that nowhere in Means's statement is there a suggestion that awards should become an end in themselves. Rather, they should be considered a measure of achievement. To the extent that intramural directors focus on the giving of *awards,* as opposed to *rewards,* the use of such awards can contribute significantly to the intramural program.

Types of Awards

As many types of awards and recognition exist as there are imaginations to consider these at each institution. Many of the "best" awards are the product of nothing more than a clever mind and a resourceful intramural director. They need not be expensive. The specific type of award that should be used varies from situation to situation. Possibly the two most important factors in the ultimate determination of which award(s) to use are cost and the degree of esteem in which the award is held by the school's intramural participants.

Many types of awards have traditionally been employed as a means of recognizing achievement in the intramural program. Trophies and plaques are perhaps the most popular type. They are given for many areas of achievement, ranging from relative team success to individual proficiency (in terms of sportsmanship, service, or athletic skill, for example). Medals are another type of award. They are most frequently used to award achievement in individual activities, such as track and swimming. A third method of making awards is to give the designated recipient a school emblem or insignia. Styled with an intramural accent, these awards are typically worn on jackets or sweaters (similar to varsity athletic monograms). The primary advantages of emblems are their high degree of visibility and their strong emphasis on individual recognition. Photographs are another type of award.* Their great popularity with students, coupled with their relatively low per-unit cost, has resulted in their more frequent use by intramural directors across the country. A novice photographer with access to basic darkroom equipment can turn out an 8-by-10 black-and-white photograph for less than a quarter. Mounted on heavyweight paperboard or placed in an inexpensive picture frame, photographs offer a flexible, nonextravagant means of recognizing achievement. Other objects that have traditionally been used as awards are pins, ribbons, banners, certificates, mugs, and various items of athletic equipment.

Administrative Suggestions

1. Awards should be selected that are held in esteem by the students.
2. Proper planning dictates that the awards be on hand before the activity begins.
3. The specific number of awards to be given out for each activity should be stipulated *before* the activity begins.

---

* Kooman Boycheff of the University of California (Berkeley) has used photographs as intramural awards for almost two decades.

4. Wherever this is possible, it is desirable to display the awards in a designated showcase or intramural area.
5. Specific policies on the administration of awards should be established.
6. Whenever possible, the intramural department should provide teams with the option of *purchasing* additional awards for any extra team members.
7. In order to maintain the status of emblems and insignia, intramural directors should provide specific regulations on how they should be worn.
8. The entire system of awards should complement, rather than inhibit, the goals of the program.

OTHER INCENTIVE FACTORS

It is not the intention in this section to attempt to identify all of the reasons why an individual decides to participate in the intramural program. Such an endeavor would be an endless if not impossible task. However, four factors with the demonstrated potential to influence student participation should be examined further: personal contacts, the quality of the program, publicity, and opportunity for student input.

Personal Contacts

Individuals tend to reflect on past negative experiences and to relate these to similar situations in the present. How many people refuse to shop in a particular store or buy a certain product because of the way they were once treated while dealing with a person associated with that store or product? This simple concept has tremendous potential impact for intramural programs.

Students are frequent visitors to the intramural office. If the student becomes dissatisfied with the treatment he receives while visiting the office and having contact with intramural personnel, he may decide to spend his time pursuing nonintramural activities. The office should have a warm, friendly atmosphere that encourages student visits and thus, hopefully, student participation. An individual's impression of the intramural office should fortify his impression of the intramural program. Such an atmosphere is achieved through a combination of factors: a friendly, attractive receptionist; a colorful, orderly office; easy listening music played throughout the offices; an efficient, attractive system of posting notices and other pertinent information; and the assurance that every student has access to vent his or her criticisms and thoughts regarding the program to an appropriate staff member—not just to the secretary! In short, an administrative commitment to serve the student must be made and sustained. Since a majority of students who participate in intramural activities may never visit the intramural office, this ethic of "service to the intramural community" must also be understood clearly and followed by *all* individuals who represent the intramural program—officials, gym supervisors, field personnel, student managers and others.

An evaluation of all departmental policies and actions that relate to the image of the intramural department should frequently be made. The total intramural approach toward the student consumer should be discussed. Ineffective handling of personal contacts can be a serious stumbling block to a successful program.

Quality of the Program

The readers are undoubtedly familiar with the old saying, "It only costs a nickel more to go first class." Although, due to inflation, the price today may be a dollar, the philosophy is relevant to intramural programs. Students are likely to continue participating in quality programs and are just as likely to discontinue their involvement with what they perceive to be inferior programs.

The intramural staff should strive to ensure the best possible programs for the students. The facilities should be maintained as efficiently as possible, and the best equipment should be provided whenever possible. The advantage of having participants play softball on a well-kept field with good equipment, as opposed to playing with poor equipment on a field resembling a test-bombing range, is immeasurable.

Care must be exercised when scheduling teams or individuals. If at all possible, schedule contests at times when participants indicated they are available. For example, avoid placing the participant in the predicament of choosing between an intramural game and other, equally pressing demands on his time. This can be accomplished by providing on the entry sheet an area in which the participant can circle convenient times to play and cross out conflicting times. The administrative time required to coordinate playing times will be rewarded by a lower forfeit rate and, thus, greater satisfaction with the program.

The following should also receive administrative attention:

1. Insure that all officials used in the program are properly trained.
2. Strive to make all employees aware of basic human relations principles.
3. Try to keep participants (student leaders in particular) aware of the basis for certain departmental policies.
4. Solicit student input whenever possible and desirable.
5. Continue to search for means to improve the program.

In short, a positive experience can reinforce the desire to participate again. The best salesman for the intramural program is the satisfied participant.

Publicity

Publicity plays an important role as a participation motivator in three major areas: preactivity publicity, para-activity publicity, and postactivity publicity. Adequate preactivity publicity is necessary in order to afford the student the most informed (from an intramural director's standpoint) choice of whether or not to participate. Obviously, before such an inquiry can ever be raised, every student on a campus must be aware of the various opportunities available in the intramural programs. Publicity is the means by which the existence of these opportunities is made known to the potential participant.

Publicity during the season is also extremely important. Campus newspapers, departmental newsletters, bulletin boards, and direct interpersonal contacts are some of the more traditional forms publicity assumes during the season.

Postactivity publicity serves to recognize accomplishments and achievements by both teams and individuals. Care should be exercised to recognize as many participants as the situation warrants. If, for example, the playoffs were divided into six classes, each class should be represented in the publicity. All-star teams can be selected from the various divisions that have competition between teams. The designation of a most valuable player is another method of stimulating interest.

Perhaps the most important means of publicity and the most important participation incentive for any program is the voice of approval from students to students. If a program is providing quality experiences for the participants, the word soon spreads. Intramural departments should strive to create satisfied customers, who will subsequently broadcast the virtues of participating in the intramural program.

Student Input

The enthusiasm and ideals of students can serve as a catalyst for participation in intramural programs. A student actively involved in the program beyond the participation level can serve as an invaluable resource. Student involvement through officiating and supervising is extremely common throughout the country. However, we need to allow the student to demonstrate further leadership in the program.*

---

* *Editor's Note:* The reader is referred to Chapter 9 of this text for a more detailed examination of student input.

Students should be involved in the establishment of the rules and regulations of the intramural program. If it is their program, why not let them play the way they want? Existing rules and regulations should be discussed, modified, or eliminated at periodic meetings held throughout the academic year.

Students should also have the opportunity to provide input into the conduct and administration of the program. The student disciplinary-protest board has become increasingly popular and in most instances is proving to be quite successful. A representative group of students serve on a board that is chaired by a student. The intramural director serves on the board as an ex-officio member. Parenthetically, the students tend to be more strict with their peers than would an administrator.

Participation incentives can also be obtained from student-run tournaments. Many students have special interests that may not lie within the current framework of the competitive program. Whenever possible, encourage and help these students to set up and run a special-interest tournament. Their enthusiasm will be a tremendous asset to the program.

Increased student participation can occur as a direct result of student involvement. Individuals tend to identify with and place more importance on activities that they have an opportunity to influence. Another potential benefit of student input is the decrease in the number of conflicts and complaints, which frequently occurs as a result of student feeling that the program is a reflection of student input and not just the opinions and desires of the intramural director.

SUMMARY

In essence, the intramural administrator should not look only at point systems and awards as participation incentives, but should closely examine all phases of the intramural program. Everything that the intramural director does influences in some way the student's decision to participate or not participate. If the director takes time to talk with his students, to involve them personally in his program, and to provide a truly quality program, he will reap the benefit of increased participation.

GENERAL BIBLIOGRAPHY

Boycheff, Kooman, "Aspects of Photography with Application to the Program of Intramural Sports," *National Intramural Association Proceedings,* XXV (1974), 9–11.

CURRY, NANCY L., "What's the Point of Points?", *National Intramural Association Proceedings*, XXIII (1972), 59–63.

DALRYMPLE, ROBERT, "Points for Participation," *National Intramural Association Proceedings*, XXV (1974), 73–77.

ENDRES, ART, "Intramural Point Scoring System," *National Intramural Association Proceedings*, XXII (1971), 103–5.

GUNSTEN, PAUL, "Credit for Intramurals," *National Intramural Association Proceedings*, XXV (1974), 61–62.

HALL, J. TILLMAN, *School Recreation: Its Organization, Supervision and Administration*. Dubuque, Iowa: Wm C. Brown, 1966.

KAMISH, LOREN F., "An Intramural Scoring System That Creates Student Interest," *National Intramural Association Proceedings*, XIX (1968), 91–94.

KLEINDIENST, VIOLA K., and ARTHUR WESTON, *Intramural and Recreation Programs for Schools and Colleges*. New York: Appleton-Century-Crofts, 1964.

KURTH, BERT, "Motivation for Participation in Intramurals at a Commuter University," *National Intramural Association Proceedings*, XX (1969), 16–18.

LEAVITT, NORMA M., and HARTLEY D. PRICE, *Intramural and Recreational Sports for High School and College*, 2nd ed. N.Y.: Ronald Press, 1971.

MEANS, LOUIS, E., *Intramurals: Their Organization and Administration*. Englewood Cliffs, N.J.: Prentice-Hall, 1973.

MUELLER, PAT, *Intramurals: Programming and Administration*. New York: Ronald Press, 1971.

STUMPNER, ROBERT, "Philosophy of Intramurals at Indiana University," *National Intramural Association Proceedings*, XI (1960), 6.

TILLMAN, ALBERT, *The Program Book for Recreation Professionals*. Palo Alto, Calif.: National Press Books, 1973.

VAN NOSTRAND, BURR R., "Developing a Flexible Point System," *National Intramural Association Proceedings*, XXI (1970), 44–51.

III

A Look to the Future

23

The Road Ahead:
Administrative Implications

JAMES A. PETERSON
United States Military Academy
West Point, New York

In the previous chapters, the contributors have reviewed the present status of intramural administration, the achievements to date, and the opportunities for greater effectiveness. An attempt has been made to emphasize the nature of the challenges that intramural directors are currently facing and will be encountering in the years ahead. The need for the development and use of conceptual skill, for more inclusive knowledge, understanding, and insight, and for more effective ways of thinking and acting—all of these keys to effective intramural administration—has been stressed.

This final chapter consists of two sections. In the first, the basic requirements for a new framework as suggested by the literature on administration and management) for improving the capability of intramural directors to fulfill their professional responsibilities are identified and briefly discussed. In the second section, five challenges confronting the administrator are presented for the reader's consideration.

A NEW APPROACH

If intramural directors are to execute their professional responsibilities in the most effective manner possible, an orderly approach to the training and continued development of administrators should be adopted. Such an approach must be designed to prepare intramural directors to meet the fundamental challenges of today and tomorrow through the use of conceptual skill. In this context, conceptual skill involves three essential attributes: (1) an inclusive, working familiarity of the subject, (2) a thorough knowledge of the subject, and (3) an organized way of thinking about the subject.

The framework for this new approach must provide a learning experience that includes five basic requirements. *Initially*, the intramural director must reexamine and reevaluate his knowledge, values, experience, attitudes, and thinking concerning the scope and the nature of intramural administration. Learning begins with questioning what we know or think we know. The *second* requirement is that intramural directors develop a systematic way of acquiring new knowledge, understanding, and insight essential to effect intramural administration. Currently, it appears that the most popular way of approaching this task is by means of professional interactions. Although attendance and involvement at the annual meetings of the National Intramural Association and at gatherings of other professional groups are certainly worthwhile and viable endeavors, the intramural director must not overlook other resources of potential equal importance. Personal contacts with colleagues in other disciplines (for instance, business, law, ethnic studies, and humanities) can provide the administrator with a valuable means of new input. Interdisciplinary readings are yet another. *Third,* the intramural director must be accorded the opportunity to grasp the new input within the framework of conceptual understanding. This goes beyond mere learning of more information about more things. To be able to use new information requires that the administrator learn to organize and interpret information and experience within a conceptual framework. *Fourth,* intramural directors must develop an organized approach through which they can apply and master this new knowledge, understanding, and insight in their daily work in order to develop conceptual skill and form new habits and patterns of thought and action. This is no easy task. Forming new habits and developing new attitudes requires courage, patience, a degree of humility, and an open mind. *Last,* attention should be focused on processes, relationships, and change in order to facilitate the intramural director's ability to form the habit of thinking in terms of essential concepts. The administrative efforts of intramural directors are limited by established ideas, customs, habits, prejudices, and assumptions. Removing these barriers is the way to understanding and dealing with change and is the key to effective leadership.

ADMINISTRATIVE CHALLENGES

In this section, I will examine five challenges facing every intramural administrator and discuss the potential implications of each for the intramural director.

The Need to Construct a Consistent, Persistent Philosophy

The basic premise of this challenge holds that before the intramural administrator can make sound and *consistent* value judgments concerning the execution of his professional responsibilities, he should have a basic understanding of the philosophical foundations of life, education, and sport. The interrelationship among these elements should be understood clearly if the intramural director is to determine where he stands on the important issues facing intramurals. This determination enables the administrator to act in a manner compatible with his personal and professional goals. In this way, intramural directors will be better prepared to direct their energies in the most effective channels possible. Unfortunately, many administrators think of philosophy as something that is beyond them—too difficult an intellectual activity. As a result, they fail to fully achieve a logical, consistent, well-ordered approach to their responsibilities.

Many intramural directors have taken a basic course in the philosophy of education or the philosophy of physical education. Unfortunately, the ivory tower approach (and its attentiveness to "isms") that is frequently the *modus operandi* for such courses fails to examine the empirical problems facing the practicing intramural administrator. As a result, the intramural director tends more often than not to discount the utility of philosophy as a professional tool or aid. On the contrary, intramural directors should view "philosophy" as an essential tool in their handbag of managerial skills rather than as an unattractive alternative to common sense.*

If the intramural director hopes to avoid the pitfalls attendant to making decisions on the basis of convenience and immediacy, he must decide where he stands in relation to the various problems and positions that confront the field of intramural administration and allied interests. Then, and only then, will the intramural administrator be able to direct

---

* Earle Zeigler's *Philosophical Foundations for Physical Health, and Recreation Education* (Englewood Cliffs, N.J.: Prentice-Hall, 1964) offers the intramural director one of the most inclusive examinations of the entire issue of the role of philosophy in society, education, and sport.

his energies within a framework of professional consistency that does not compromise individual beliefs and values.

The Need to Identify Organizational Objectives

If a profession is to know where it is going, what it is striving for, what it hopes to accomplish, and how it might proceed in its tasks, it should have goals that have been clearly defined. The field of intramural administration is no exception. Unfortunately, the objectives that might normally be considered as attendant to leisure-sports participation —fun, enjoyment, fitness, self-esteem, excitement, diversion, exercise, and so on—are, at best, difficult to quantify. As a result, intramural directors have focused primarily on the number of participants as a basis for self-evaluation and goal setting. It is not atypical for the intramural director to concentrate his managerial efforts at achieving *more* individual participation, *more* teams, and *more* activities. Such unwavering obeisance to a single criterion can be attributed to several factors: lack of concern in the determination of organizational objectives; inability to quantify apparent by-products of intramural participation; and a less-than-adequate capability for articulating organizational objectives. Gross collectively refers to this latter factor as the "lack of a well-developed language of organizational purposefulness" (1965), p. 195).

Gross suggests that one of the best responses to such a deficiency is to adopt a systematic approach to organizational purposes.* The basis for this approach is the development of a general systems model—that is, a model that brings together in ordered fashion information on all dimensions of an organization. It provides the basis for managerial action by organizing and furnishing the data needed to appraise the state of a system and guide it towards the attainment of desirable future system states. Inherent in such a model are two general categories of objectives: performance and structural. In a particular situation, each of the goals or objectives in both categories may partially answer two basic questions: Where does the organization want to go? How well is it accomplishing its desired tasks? Performance objectives include satisfying interests, producing output, making efficient use of inputs, investing in the system, acquiring resources, observing codes, and behaving rationally. Concurrent with the attention given the aforementioned goals, the intramural director must also exhibit concern for "structure" objectives. These include people, nonhuman resources, attentiveness to subsystems, internal relations, external relations, values, and the quality of the guidance

---

* Since space does not permit an extensive examination of this question, the reader is referred to Bertram Gross, "What Are Your Organization's Objectives," *Human Relations*, XVIII, No. 3 (1965), 195–216.

subsystem (the means by which the management process is executed). Intramural administrators who guide their organizations on the basis of the inclusive dimensions of both performance and structure will be provided with the framework for efficient and effective decision making.

The Need for Leisure-Services
Programming for the Community

This challenge can be expressed by two fundamental questions: What are the responsibilities of the intramural director in regard to providing leisure-service opportunities to individuals who reside in the community adjacent to the university? Are programming efforts by the intramural administrator for the community a right that has accrued to the community because of the social responsibilities of our educational institutions, or a special privilege arising from the prerogative of each intramural administrator?

Without question, it may be concluded that there is an increasing tendency on many campuses towards university involvement in providing recreational services for the community. In a great majority of these campuses, the intramural administrator is expected to be an active participant in that involvement. This presumption—on the part of both the community and certain individuals within the university—places the intramural director in somewhat of a dilemma. On the one hand, the demands of his primary function—to provide organized and free-time leisure-service opportunities for the students and faculty—exhaust most of his time, most departmental funds, and most of the available facilities. Consequently, the intramural administrator is faced with the question of how to justify his providing services and activities for the community, since they usually result in a reduction of the resources available to his university "constituents."

Traditional reasoning has held that the commitment of the intramural department to the university community precludes a major share of its social responsibility to society. Within the last few years, however, the resonant demands of our changing society have necessitated that intramural administrators reexamine their position on this question. In order to accomplish this task, it is imperative that a delineation of the role of the university within society be made.

Basically, the university and its personnel are finding that there are two contrasting educational philosophies within the institutional walls. The first asserts that the unversity should concern itself essentially with research and with the training of individuals to facilitate their integration into society as professional persons of one sort or another. This view holds that "social purpose" will evolve indirectly from the attainment of these objectives. Subsequently, individuals subscribing to this position become involved in recreational programming for the community largely as the result of empirical rather than ethical or social considerations. On several campuses—the University of Chicago, for example—the vocal temperament of the adjacent community is such that a lack of attention by the intramural administrator to the leisure-time demands of the community would result in the serious impairment of his capacity to administer his program. Such impairment assumes many forms from mere threats to violent confrontations. Understandably, such coercion is not always conducive to meaningful, constructive cooperation.

A second, quite different assessment of the role of the university concludes that the university is an institution of society. Thus, society, as its creator, has the right to demand and expect certain responsibilities and duties from it. This author finds himself in essential agreement with this second position. The time has come for intramural administrators to reject the rhetoric of traditional thinking—a demeanor which is being challenged persistently as problems in our communities multiply. Rational inquiry indicates that there should no longer be artificial lines between the rights of mankind and the responsibilties of the university. What is needed is a careful balance to help us achieve an encompassing degree of social justice. Our actions and commitments must focus on more than shallow rationales of either convention or expediency.

If universities are to play a meaningful role in our changing society, they must concern themselves with the problems of the community. This commitment is imperative if both entities hope to survive. One manifestation of such involvement is to provide leisure opportunities, whenever possible, to residents of the community.*

The Need to Consider the Legal Ramifications of Departmental Actions †

The days when the intramural director could thoughtfully comply with his department's legal responsibilities merely by acquiring minimal

---

* Some of the methods by which such opportunities may be developed are described by this author in "Intramural Programming for the Community: A Right or a Privilege," *Proceedings of the National College Physical Education Association for Men,* LXXIV (1970), 261–63.

† Originally, it was considered that an entire chapter might be devoted to the legal aspects of intramural administration. In view of the multiplicity of laws, statutes, and regulations affecting such actions and the rapidly changing status of these factors, the idea was eventually abandoned as a limitless, hopeless task.

participant medical insurance and employee liability coverage are over. In these times of increased consciousness of human rights, it is imperative that the intramural administrator consider the legal aspects of the actions and decisions of the intramural department. Unfortunately, the difference in situational factors from campus to campus precludes a listing of specific legal guidelines. The intramural director, however, would be wise to reflect on the potential legal ramifications of *all* aspects of his program. Among the considerations that are likely to have a greater impact for the intramural department are adherence to fair employment practices; compliance with all sections of Title IX of the Educational Amendments Act of 1972; negligence and liability cases; medical and liability insurance; and the equity and legality of existing procedures for conducting intramural programs.

Before problems arise, the intramural director should adopt an administrative posture that is both legally sound and pragmatically appropriate. What, for example, are the rights of the intramural department in suspending a student's opportunity to participate in the intramural program? Several intramural directors have discovered in recent years that there are specific instances in which higher authorities either could not or would not support such student suspension, regardless of the reason. Another question that appears to be raised more frequently is this: What policies or procedures should govern instances of actual assault (for example, against a student official) or criminal damage (for instance, a broken window)? Is it appropriate to bring criminal charges against the offender? What role should the intramural director have in such procedures? Should intramural personnel be briefed on the proper procedures for collecting evidence in a potentially criminal situation? While the editor was employed at the University of Illinois, two specific cases (one concerned with the discovery of a large cache of drugs by a student intramural gymnasium attendant, the other involving the apprehension of a sex offender in the gymnasium) occurred where the proper handling of evidence by intramural personnel was important. Another important area of legal concern to the intramural director is how to respond to injuries. Intramural personnel have traditionally been attentive to preventing accidents, but once these injuries are a *fait accompli,* what steps should the intramural administrator take to minimize the danger to the injured participant? Is there any way to identify and ingrain in the minds of departmental personnel the legal differences between prudent and bad judgment? Since the list of legal considerations confronting the intramural director appears to be boundless, the administrative vigil in this area should remain constant and intense.

The Need to Maintain a Commitment
to "Sport for All"

Through the years, a number of slogans have been accredited to the intramural experience—"something for everybody," "down in the arena are the doers," "an activity for every person and every person in an activity," "every student an athlete," "sport for all," and so on. In these challenging and exciting times, it is imperative, however, that intramural directors examine their efforts to insure that such slogans are more than shallow babbling. "Sport for all" should be more than an idealistic goal; it should be both the cornerstone of the intramural department's administrative focus and the by-product of its efforts. The intramural director should evaluate his efforts to insure that every member of the university community has an equitable opportunity to participate in the intramural program. Quality programming that will attract members of minority sex, race, and religious groups must be an integral part of the total program. In addition, steps should be taken to plan both programs and facility modifications that will enable handicapped members of the university community to participate in campus recreation activities. In short, an administrative commitment must be undertaken and sustained to service the leisure needs of the entire university community. It's a matter of simple justice.

EPILOGUE

Since intramural administration is still a relatively young professional endeavor, there will always be something exciting to anticipate: the development of new programs or procedures; the construction of new facilities; the accomplishment of desired goals; the pride of viewing previous progress. As a field we still have our problems, and there will continue to be difficulties in the months and years ahead. But the field of intramural administration is progressing, and the substance of certain intramural hallmarks is unwavering. The quality of our offerings, the commitment to our task, our concern with channeling the best of the university's resources toward leisure services—these must never change. Hopefully, we will strive to achieve and maintain a level of excellence that will enable us to meet the opportunities and challenges of the 1970s.

Selected Bibliography

This bibliography is classified into three sections: (1) books, (2) unpublished theses and dissertations, and (3) articles included in the annual proceedings of the National Intramural Association. For a more complete bibliography of "intramural references" see McGuire and Mueller, *Reference Directory for Intramurals and Recreational Sports.*

BOOKS

AMERICAN ASSOCIATION FOR HEALTH, PHYSICAL EDUCATION AND RECREATION, *Intramural Sports for College Men and Women.* Washington, D.C.: National Education Association, 1964.

ANTON, THOMAS, and LOUIS TOSCHI, *A Practical Approach to Junior High School Intramurals.* Richmond, California: Anton and Toschi, 1959.

BEEMAN, HARRIS F., CAROL HARDING, and JAMES H. HUMPHREY, *Intramural Sports: A Text and Study Guide.* Dubuque, Iowa: William C. Brown, 1974.

BOYDEN, E. DOUGLAS, and ROGER C. BURTON, *Staging Successful Tournaments.* New York: Association Press, 1957.

HUNT, VALERIE V., *Recreation for the Handicapped.* Englewood Cliffs, N.J.: Prentice-Hall, 1955.

KLEINDIENST, VIOLAK, and ARTHUR WESTON, *Intramural and Recreation Program for School and Colleges.* New York: Meredith, 1964.

KRAUS, RICHARD, *Recreation and Leisure in Modern Society.* New York: Appleton-Century-Crofts, 1971.

LEAVITT, NORMA M., and HARTLEY D. PRICE, *Intramural and Recreational Sports for College.* New York: Ronald Press, 1958.

McGUIRE, RAYMOND J., and PAT MUELLER, *Reference Directory for Intramurals and Recreational Sports.* Cornwall, N.Y.: Leisure Press, 1975.

MEANS, LOUIS, E., *Intramurals: Their Organization and Administration.* Englewood Cliffs, N.J.: Prentice-Hall, 1973.

MUELLER, PAT, *Intramural Sports.* New York: Ronald Press, 1971.

POMEROY, JANET, *Recreation for the Physically Handicapped.* New York: Macmillan, 1964.

SCHEERER, WILLIAM W., *High School Intramural Program.* Minneapolis: Burgess, 1951.

THOMPSON, WILLIAM, and RICHARD CLEGG, *Modern Sports Officiating.* Dubuque, Iowa: William C. Brown, 1974.

YUKIC, THOMAS, *Fundamentals of Recreation* (2nd ed.). New York: Harper & Row, 1969.

UNPUBLISHED THESES AND DISSERTATIONS

AMATO, BENJAMIN P., "The Relationship Between Academic Grades and Intramural Participation of Fraternity Men at the Pennsylvania State University." Master's thesis, Penn State University, 1965.

ANDERSON, JOHN DICKASON, "An Evaluation of Participation in Extracurricular Activities by Secondary School Students." Doctoral dissertation, University of Pittsburgh, 1941.

BAILEY, GORDON ARTHUR, "Analysis of Data Basic to Organization of Intramural Athletics in a Senior High School." Master's thesis, University of Texas, 1946.

BAKER, JOHN ALOYSIOS, "Sociological Aspects of Intramural Sports." Master's thesis, University of Kentucky, 1940.

BEACH, LOWELL W., "The Nature and Status of Co-Recreation in the Michigan High School Physical Education Program." Master's thesis, University of Michigan, 1946.

BEEMAN, HARRISON F., "An Analysis of Human Relations in the Administration of Intramural Sports Programs of the Western Conference." Doctoral dissertation, University of Michigan, 1960.

BERG, JAMES O., "Differences Between Male Participants and Non-Participants in a College Intramural Sports Program in Regard to Academic Achievement and Academic Ability." Doctoral dissertation, University of Missouri, 1969.

CABLE, DONALD L., "Intramural Sport Courses in Selected Institutions of Higher Education." Master's thesis, University of Illinois, 1965.

DULLES, FOSTER R., "America Learns to Play: A History of Popular Recreation." Doctoral dissertation, Columbia University, 1940.

FIELDS, FOREST E., "The Cost of Intramural Sports Per Man Hour Participation." Master's thesis, Purdue University, 1946.

FRATZKE, MEL R., "Personality Traits of Intramural Basketball Officials." Doctoral dissertation, University of Indiana, 1973.

FRYE, MARY V., "A Proposed Plan to Coordinate Student Recreation on the Campus of the University of Illinois." M.S. thesis, University of Illinois, 1955.

GRAMBEAU, RODNEY J., "A Survey of the Administration of Intramural Sports Programs for Men in Selected Colleges and Universities in North and South America." Doctoral dissertation, University of Michigan, 1959.

HANHILA, MATT O., "A Study of the Intramural Sport Programs in the High Schools of Arizona." Master's thesis, University of Arizona, 1940.

HANIFORD, GEORGE W., "The Utilization of the Recreational Gymnasium by Purdue University Undergraduate Students." Doctoral dissertation, University of Indiana, 1962.

HASSING, JAMES, "A Determination of Attitudes of Intramural Administrators towards Education, Physical Education, Varsity Athletics, and Recreation." Master's thesis, University of Minnesota, 1972.

HAY, W. THOMAS, "Differences in Grade Point Averages of Participants and Non-participants in Intramural Activities." Master's thesis, Bowling Green University, 1966.

HEITHOLD, DOROTHY, "Factors Related to Intramural Participation for High School Girls." Master's thesis, Illinois State Normal University, 1960.

JARBOE, PRISCILLA S., "Student Involvement in Administration of Women's Intramural Programs." Master's thesis, University of Illinois, 1967.

KORSGAARD, ROBERT, "Tournament and Schedule Making." Master's thesis, Ball State Teachers College, 1955.

KRAUS, JESS F., "An Epidemiologic Investigation of Predictor Variables Associated with Intramural Touch Football Injuries." Doctoral dissertation, University of Minnesota, 1967.

KRAFT, HAROLD, "Administration of Intramurals in North Dakota and Minnesota." Master's thesis, University of North Dakota, 1953.

Lux, LLOYD H., "The Application of Guides for Development of Intramural Activities for College Men." Doctoral thesis, Teachers College, Columbia University, 1950.

McDONALD, CHARLES E., "A Study of Intramural Flag Football Injuries Which Occurred During the Fall of 1963 at Washington State University." Master's thesis, Washington State University, 1964.

McGUIRE, RAYMOND J., "A Retrieval of Selected Intramural Research and Literature." Master's thesis, University of Illinois, 1966.

MARTIN, LA VERLE, "An Evaluation and Comparison of Men's Intramural Programs in Four-Year State-Supported Institutions in the United States." Master's thesis, Texas Technological College, 1969.

MATHEWS, DAVID O., "Programs of Intramural Sports in Selected Ohio Public Schools." Doctoral thesis, Western Reserve University, 1958.

MAURER, BRUCE L., "A Multivariate Analysis of Student, Faculty and Administrators' Attitudes Toward the Division of University Recreation and Intramural Sports at the Ohio State University." Doctoral dissertation, Ohio State University, 1972.

MILLER, J. O., "Study of College Recreation Programs." Master's thesis, Indiana University, 1951.

NORDLY, CARL L., "The Administration of Intramural Athletics for Men in Colleges and Universities." Doctoral dissertation, Teachers College, Columbia University, 1937.

ORTMAYER, ROLAND L., "Intramural Sports Participation at the State College of Washington with Special Reference to Scholastic Attainment." Master's thesis, Washington State University, 1959.

PEACE, JAMES S., "A Manual of the Organization and Conduct of an Intramural Program for Colleges and Universities." Doctoral dissertation, New York University, 1943.

PETERSON, JAMES A., "The Process Involved in Planning and Constructing Intramural-Physical Education Buildings Which Were Financed Primarily Through Student-fee Revenues." Doctoral dissertation, University of Illinois, 1971.

PHELPS, DALE, "Current Practices and Recommended Guidelines for the Administration of Sports Clubs in Male and Co-educational Four-Year Colleges and Universities." Doctoral dissertation, Indiana University, 1969.

————, "An Investigation of the Intramural Program as Related to Married Male Students Living in University Housing." Master's thesis, Michigan State University, 1962.

PINK, RALPH J., "A Survey to Determine the Current Status of Intramural Recreational Programs in Selected United States Colleges and Universities." Doctoral dissertation, University of Utah, 1969.

POLLACK, BERNARD, "A Method for Obtaining and Utilizing Student Information in Intramural Program Development in an Urban

College Setting." Doctoral dissertation, Teachers College, Columbia University, 1968.

PREO, LAWRENCE S., "A Comparative Analysis of Current Status and Professional Preparation of Intramural Directors." Doctoral dissertation, University of Illinois, 1972.

REZNIK, JOHN W., "Junior College Intramural-Recreational Programs: A Survey and Analysis." Doctoral dissertation, University of Illinois, 1972.

RISKEY, EARL, "Participation in Intramural Sports at the University of Michigan, 1936-1941." Master's thesis, University of Michigan, 1942.

RYAN, ROBERT R., "The Effects of Participation in Selected Intramural Sports upon Physical Fitness, Social and Emotional Adjustment of College Fraternity Men." Doctoral dissertation, Colorado State College, 1963.

SEIDEL, BEVERLY L., "Development of Intramural Sports for Women, with Particular Emphasis on Participation." Master's thesis, University of Michigan, 1946.

SMITH, WARREN E., "A Survey of Post-War Trends and Changes in College and University Intramural Programs." Master's thesis, University of Michigan, 1947.

SPRANDEL, WALTER B., "Status of Intramural Sports in Ten Denominational Colleges in Michigan." Master's thesis, University of Michigan, 1941.

STEVENSON, MICHAEL J., "The Effects of Artificial and Natural Turf on Injuries, Player Opinion, and Selected Game and Team Variables in College Intramural Touch Football." Doctoral dissertation, University of Minnesota, 1973.

UHRLAUB, DAVID, "Recommended Criteria for Directors of College Intramural Activities for Men as Compared with Present Practices in Selected Colleges and Universities of the United States." Master's thesis, Kent State University, 1969.

WAGNER, FRED, "The Status of Intramural and Extramural Sports Programs at Washington State Community Colleges." Master's thesis, University of Washington, 1971.

WEATHERFORD, TERRY LYNN, "A History of the Intramural Sports Program at the University of Illinois, 1903-1965." Master's thesis, University of Illinois, 1966.

WELCH, MARYA, "Guides for the Organization of Campus Recreation." Doctoral dissertation, Teachers College, Columbia University, 1952.

WILKERSON, JAMES LEE, "Intramural Point Systems." Master's thesis, Texas Technological College, 1969.

WILLIAMS, JACK, "Evaluation of Intramural Sports of Colleges in the Lone Star Conference." Master's thesis, University of Texas, 1947.

ANNUAL PROCEEDINGS OF
NATIONAL INTRAMURAL ASSOCIATION (1950-1974)

ADAMS, GARY, "Eligibility Rules: Are They Enforceable?," XVII (1966), 100-2.

ALDRIN, LT. COL. EDWIN E. ("Buzz"), "The N.A.S.A. Mercury, Gemini, and Apollo Programs," XIX (1968), 112-18.

ANDERSON, BRUCE D., "Touch Football Injury Survey: A Product of NIA Research," XIX (1968), 94-95.

AQUILA, LAWRENCE DELL, "Sky Diving Intramurals at Nassau Community College," XXIV (1973), 146.

ARNOLD, CHARLES G.. and ROBERT E. WEAR, "Inner-Tube Water Polo," XX (1969), 218-25.

BALOGH, JOSEPH, "Prison Intramurals," XII (1961), 27-30.

BANKHEAD, WILLIAM H., "Club Sports Program at L.S.U.," XVIII (1967), 58-61.

BARNEY, FREDERICK A., "High School Intramurals: The Decade for Decision," XVII (1966), 103-6.

BECK, CECIL M., "Intramural Promotion Aids at Harding College," XIII (1962), 18-22.

BEEMAN, HARRISON F., "An Analysis of Human Relations in the Administration of Intramural Sports Programs of the Western Conference," XI (1960), 27-31.

————, "The Philosophy of Intramurals at Michigan State University," XI (1960), 9.

BERG, J. OTTO, "Differences Between Male Participants and Non-Participants in a College Intramural Sports Program in Regard to Academic Achievement and Academic Ability," XXI (1970), 80-87.

————, "Future Trends in the Administration of Intramural Sports at the College Level," XX (1969), 74-78.

BERRAFATO, PETER, "Community Recreation in the Commuter Institution," XXII (1971), 19-20.

————, "Problems of the Commuter Colleges and Junior Colleges—Introduction," XX (1969), 15-16.

————, "Problems Unique to the Commuter College," XVIII (1967), 52-54.

————, "Rating an Intramural Basketball Referee," XIX (1968), 32-34.

————, "Sixteen—inch Slow Pitch Softball," XVII (1966), 37-40.

BERRES, LARRY, "A Summary of the Ideas Expressed in the Four Discussion Groups of the Commuter Colleges," XXII (1971), 26-27.

————, "Five Considerations for Commuter College Programs," XXIV (1973), 52-55.

BERRES, LARRY, and THOMAS SATTLER, "Discussion of Five Topics Unique to Commuter College Program," XXIII (1972), 46-47.

BEUTTLER, FRED C., "Results of a Study of Boys' Intramural Programs in Iowa High Schools," XI (1960), 31-44.

BIRDY, EARL J., "Three-Man Volleyball," XXIII (1972), 136.

BLANKS, WILLIAM, "Bowling in the Intramural Program," IX (1958), 12-16.

BOWIE, EMBRA, "Scoring Systems," VIII (1957), 8.

BOYCHEFF, KOOMAN, "Aspects of Photography with Application to the Program of Intramural Sports," XXV (1974), 9-10.

———, "Program Administration Procedures," XIX (1968), 22-26.

———, "The University of California Intramural Sports Festival," XXI (1970), 143-46.

BOYER, EUGENE, "Scheduling—Time and Space," XIV (1963), 95-97.

BRONZAN, ROBERT, "Game Plans for Getting the Facilities You Need," XXIII (1972), 9-13.

BROWN, ROBERT, "Safety in Intramurals," VIII (1957), 5.

BRUHN, WILLIAM J., "The Learning of Other Nations' Cultures Through Intramural Activities," XIV (1963), 100-3.

BUCHANAN, EDSEL, "Co-recreation," XII (1961), 58.

———, "New Sports Activities for the Intramural Program," XVII (1966), 31-36.

———, "Point Systems, Awards, and Records," XIII (1963), 50-54.

———, "Psychological Implications of Participation to the Student Engaged at the Intramural Level," XV (1964), 45-47.

———, "The Relationship of Intramurals and Physical Fitness," XIII (1962), 61-67.

———, "Structure for Women's Intercollegiate Athletics," XXV (1974), 149-52.

BUCK, CHARLES R., "Coeducational Intramurals: Trend or Topic," XX (1969), 52-55.

BUFFA, HAL, "Awards Systems for the Commuter College," XX (1969), 22-23.

BUGGE, ELWYN, "The Administration of Intramurals at Stanford," XI (1960), 26.

———, "Intramural Disciplinary Provisions," XIV (1963), 35.

———, "Scheduling," XII (1961), 54.

BULGER, HOWARD J., "Athletic Clubs," XIX (1968), 100.

BUTLER, K. NELSON, "A Model for Intramural Research," XXII (1971), 111-12.

———, "Catharsis and Intramurals" (Doctoral dissertation), XXI (1970), 97-100.

CABLE, DONALD, "Field Work Form," XXII (1971), 92-100.

CABLE, DONALD, and GEORGE GRZENDA, "Simplified Scoresheets, Officials' Evaluation Form, and Program Evaluation Form," XXIII (1972), 110-19.

CALDWELL, SANDRA, "Co-Rec Intramurals—Emphasis Fun," XXV (1974), 43.

CAMPBELL, LOREN D., "Selling the Intramural Program to the Students," X (1959), 3.

CASKEY, LT. ALAN R., "The Role of Intramural Activities in a Penal Institution," XVII (1966), 109-14.

CLARK, DON, "The Present Years, 1962-1968," XIX (1968), 72-73.

CLARK, DONALD A., "Public Relations and Publicity in Intramural Sports," XIV (1963), 34-36.

CLARK, JAMES, "Records," XXI (1970), 73-74.

CLEGG, RICHARD, "Methods of Involving Students in College Intramural Programs," XVII (1966), 87-90.

———, "Training Intramural Directors and Game Officials Through a Physical Education Class," XVIII (1967), 65-68.

CLEMENT, TONY, "The Black Athlete in Intramurals," XXIV (1973), 71-72.

CLEMENT, WILLIAM K. "Unstructured Activities in the U.S. Navy," XXI (1970), 36-41.

COBB, JUSTIN L., "Publicity and Public Relations—Its Relation to the Intramural Program," XIV (1963).

COLBERG, GARY, "Co-Ed Flag Football," XXIII (1972), 129-30.

———, "Co-Ed Innertube Water Polo," XXIII (1972), 131-32.

———, "Powder-Puff Football," XIX (1968), 96-99.

———, "Rec-Reality 1975," XXIV (1973), 38-43.

COLBERG, GARY, and JESS KRAUS, "The Incidence of Injury in a Rural College Intramural Football Program," XXII (1971), 117-30.

COLGATE, JOHN, "160-LB Football and Basketball," XIX (1968), 81-82.

COLGATE, JOHN A., "Coordination of Programs With Union Activities," XVIII (1967), 55-57.

CONRAD, CARLSON, "A Message From the President's Council on Physical Fitness and Sports," XXIII (1972), 27-35.

COOK, ROBERT, "Karting Goes to College," XXI (1970), 20-22.

———, "Intramural Officials and Intramural Rules," XX (1969), 32-36.

COONEY, LARRY, "Kaleidoscope of Leisure," XXV (1974), 24.

CORLEY, VAUGHN, "Is the Intramural Program Keeping Pace with the Fast Growth of Universities and Colleges?" XVI (1965), 14-15.

———, "Motivating the Intramural Program," XV (1964), 32-33.

CORRINGTON, DENNIS, "Touch Football at Iowa State University," XX (1969), 124-25.

COTTRELL, EDWIN B., "Viewpoints on Intramurals," XIV (1963), 12-14.

COWARD, BILLY, "Knee Tackle Football," XVIII (1967), 12.

COWEL, B. C., "New Developments at Colorado State University," XII (1962), 24-26.

CUBBON, EDWARD, "Report on the National Intramural Sports Council," XX (1969), 239-42.

CURRY, NANCY L., "What's the Point of Points?," XXIII (1972), 59-63.

DALRYMPHE, BOB, "Points for Participation," XXV (1974), 73-76.

DANIEL, F. C., "Riflery in an Intramural Program," XII (1961), 16-27.

DAVIS, EDWARD L., "Separation But Cooperation," XX (1969), 36-30.

DENIKE, HOWARD R., "Values of Intramural Handbooks—Publication and Problems," XIV (1963), 110-15.

DENTON, HAROLD, "Promoting a Sports Club Program at the University of Tennessee, Knoxville," XXIV (1973), 94-97.

DEXTER, WILLIAM H., and STEVEN A. SHERMAN, "A Community Within a Community—The Urban University," XXIV (1973), 44-48.

DROSCHER, KEN, "Implementation and Utilization of Intramural Facilities," XXIII (1972), 17-19.

EICHMAN, EDWARD, "The Temple University Program," VIII (1957), 7.

ELLIS, FRED, "Scoring Systems," VIII (1957), 8.

ENDRES, ART, "Intramural Point Scoring System," XXII (1971), 103-4.

ENGLAND, ROBERT, "Eastern Michigan University Float-a-thon," XXIV (1973), 142.

ENGLAND, ROBERT W., "Intramural Newspaper and Hotline," XXIII (1972), 50.

FEHRING, W. P., "Club Sports," XX (1969), 49-51.

———, "The Stanford Club Team Program," XXIII (1972), 68-78.

FELSHIN, JANET, "Girls' Sports Organization Handbook," Division for Girls' and Women's Sports, American Association for Health, Physical Education and Recreation, 1961.

FIDLER, MERRIE A., "Selected Survey of the Organization and Administration of Women's Intramural Programs," XXIV (1973), 170-77.

FINDER, EARL F., "Student Unions and Their Impact on Intramurals," XIV (1963), 28-31.

FISHER, STAN, "Floor Hockey as an Intramural Sport," XIX (1968), 83-87.

———, "Promoting Intramurals," XXI (1970), 42-43.

FLORY, C. M., "The Social Aspect," XIX (1968), 49-50.

FOGARTY, DAN, "Intramural Sports—Fort Knox, Kentucky," IX (1958), 16-20.

FRATZKE, MEL R., "Personality Traits of Intramural Basketball Officials," XXV (1974), 114-15.

FRED, KEITH, "Winning Isn't Everything," XXIII (1972), 99-104.

FREDERICK, NORMAN, "How to Integrate the Intramural Program with Required Physical Education Courses. How?," XVIII (1967), 13-15.

———, "Motivating the Intramural Program," XV (1964), 35.

———, "Selection of Student Leaders," XIX (1968), 59.

FRI, ROSEMARY, "Co-educational Intramurals," XV (1964), 9.

FUDGE, LARRY, "The Positive Side," XX (1969), 13-14.

FULLER, WILLIAM F., "Intramurals and the Union, A Common Goal," XIV (1963), 25-28.

GAITHER, A. S. ("Jake"), "Sports Contribution to the American Way of Life," XVI (1965), 7-8.

GARRITY, JOSEPH, "The Norwich University Program," VIII (1957), 8.

GEUSS, SANFORD, "Awareness and the Intramural Director," XXII (1971), 55-56.

———, "Intramural Promotion and Publicity," XVIII (1967), 62-64.

GOEHRS, WARREN J., "Program Promotional Gimmicks," XIII (1962), 67.

———, "Recorder's Report," XIX (1968), 64-65.

———, "Recreational Aspects of the Intramural Program," XIX (1968), 51-52.

GRAHAM, PETER J., "The Old and the New—The Past, Present and Future of the NIA," XXV (1974), 93-94.

GRAMBEAU, RODNEY J., "Encouraging the Development of Intramural Sports Clubs," XVII (1966), 115-17.

———, "Faculty-Staff Intramural Programming," XXI (1970), 137-42.

———, "Panel on Student Unrest," XXII (1971), 78.

———, "The Relationship of Physical Education to Intramurals," XIV (1963), 103-7.

———, "A Survey of the Administration of Intramural Sports Programs for Men in Selected Colleges and Universities in North and South America," XI (1960), 44-46.

GRAY, RICHARD L., "An Architect Plans an Intramural Physical Education Building," XIX (1968), 101-7.

GREEN, RAY E., "Are Intramural Programs Keeping Pace With Fast Growing Universities?," XVI (1965), 18-20.

GROVES, BARNEY R., "An Investigation of Personality Changes Resulting from Participating in a College Intramural Program for Men," XVII (1966), 129-30.

GRUBER, ALAN J., "Proposals for Improving Fairness in Single and Double Elimination Tournaments," XX (1969), 98-109.

GUNKLER, OSCAR, "The Berea College Intramural Program," IX (1958), 23-28.

GUNSTEN, PAMELA C., "A Commuter School Program," XXII (1971), 28-29.

GUNSTEN, PAUL H., "Credit for Intramurals," XXV (1974), 61.

———, "Flying on Feathers," XXIV (1973), 56-57.

———, "The Impact of 'Title IX' on Intramural and Extramural Programs," XXV (1974), 142.

———, "Motivating the Intramural Program," XV (1964), 33-35.

———, "Participation Records," XVII (1966), 19-20.

———, "Public Relations with Faculty and Administration," XVIII (1967), 5-7.

———, "Scope of Intramural Programs and Budgets in Small Universities and Colleges," XVI (1965), 43-47.

———, "Values of Bowling in a Small College Program," XII (1961), 62.

HAIGH, BARTON, "Co-education Programs," XV (1964), 14.

HALL, LINDA, "Serving Student Wives," XXV (1974), 77-78.

HANIFORD, GEORGE W., "Co-Recreation and Intramural Sports," XIV (1963), 19-22.

———, "Intramural Sports Clubs at Purdue University," XXIII (1972), 64-66.

———, "Keynote Speech: The Changing Complexion of the School Intramural-Recreational Program," XVI (1965), 1-3.

———, "Letter to Past Presidents," XXV (1974), 139.

———, "One Man's Viewpoint of Women's Intramurals," XXIII (1972), 98.

———, "Organization and Finances," XIX (1968), 16-18.

———, "The Role of Sports Clubs," IX (1958), 8-10.

HARDING, CAROL, "A Woman's View of Men's Intramural Sports," XXII (1971), 39-40.

HARPER, DON, "Co-Recreation Activity Stagnation," XV (1964), 13.

HART, DONALD E., "How One School Went About Upgrading Its Facilities," XXII (1972), 14-16.

HASKINS, HAROLD, "Extramural Program in Florida and Unique Activities," XX (1969), 24-26.

HAUBENSTRICKER, JOHN L., "The Place of Intramural Handbooks in Small Denominational Colleges," XVII (1966), 78-81.

HEFFERNAN, JOHN M., "The Middle Years, 1956-1961," XIX (1968), 69-71.

———, "Officiating," XIV (1963), 80.

———, "Psychological Implications of Participation to Students Engaged at the Intramural Level," XV (1964), 47-49.

————, "Recreation, Intramurals, and Student Unions," XVI (1965), 9-11.

HEFFINGTON, MARVIN D., "Training and Responsibility: The Combination to a Successful Manager Program," XVII (1966), 24-26.

HEWATT, CAROLYN, "A Woman's View Point of Men's Intramurals," XXII (1971), 41-45.

HIGGENS, JOSEPH R., "Intramural Sports and New Dimensions in Residential Education," XVII (1966), 82-86.

HILL, EUGENE L., "Factors Involved in Selecting Units of Competition for Intramural Competition," XVII (1966), 21-23.

HISAKA, LLOYD I., "One-on-One Basketball Championship," XXIV (1973), 143-45.

HOLLINGER, J. CLINTON, "More Emphasis and Financial Aid for Intramurals," XXV (1974), 140.

HOLMES, ALLEN, "An Investigation of the Effect of Intramural Sports Participation on Selected Criteria," XXI (1970), 89-95.

————, "A Method of Evaluating the Intramural Program," XVIII (1967), 25-27.

HOLSBERRY, WILLARD M., "Remuneration of Student Leaders," XIX (1968), 60.

HOOVER, WILLIAM R., "A Positive Perceptive Experience in Intramural Bowling," XXIV (1973), 131-32.

HOPKINS, PETER D., "Intramurals Without Officials," XXIII (1972), 51-53.

HUDDER, GERALD D., "Activities, Programs, and Participating Units," XIX (1968), 27-30.

————, "The Meaning and Purpose of Intramurals as They Relate to the Recreational Program in Small Colleges," XVII (1966), 94-96.

————, "Special Events—The Spice in the Intramural Program," XVIII (1967), 8-11.

HUDSON, JACKI, "Computer Time and the Livin' Is Easy," XXIII (1972), 105-9.

HYATT, RONALD, "Special Events at University of North Carolina," XXIII (1972), 146.

JAMES, LARRY A., "Intramural Playgrounds at the University of Northern Colorado," XXV (1974), 62-64.

JAMISON, H. TOI, "The Organization of a Women's Intramural Policy Board and Manager Program," XXV (1974), 35-37.

JANETOS, DIMITRI A., and KEITH S. GLASS, "Campus Recreation and Outdoor Recreation: Concepts in Total Programming," XXV (1974), 57-60.

JEVERT, J. A., "Guideposts for Intramural Eligibility," XVII (1966), 97-99.

JOHNSON, JUDY (Ford), "Former Miss America Looks at Intramurals," XXIII (1972), 48-49.

KAMEN, RICHARD, "Production and Use of the Intramural Sports Film," XXV (1974), 21.

KAMISH, LOREN F., "An Intramural Scoring System that Creates Student Interest," XIX (1968), 91-93.

KAMRAD, DENNIS R., "Crew as an Intramural Activity and Extramural Sport," XXIV (1973), 138-41.

KARAS, FRANK, "Orientation of Intramural Officials at Ferris Institute," XIV (1963), 87-90.

———, "Problems of Small Universities and Colleges," XV (1964), 29-32.

KEEN, PAUL V., "Contributions of Intramurals to the Education Program," XIX (1968), 53-57.

———, "Intramurals and Its Relation to the Student Affairs Department," XIII (1962), 47-50.

KRAFT, HAROLD, "Handbooks, A Means of Information and Publicity," XVII (1966), 134-35.

———, "Proceedings From the North Central Conference Intramural Director's Workshop," XXI (1970), 54-58.

KRAUS, JESS F., BRUCE D. ANDERSON, and C. E. MUELLER, "An Investigation of the Effectiveness of a New Helmet to Control Touch Football Head Injuries," XX (1969), 83-97.

KRZOSKA, RAY, "Problems in Administering an Intramural Program in a Rapidly Growing Urban University," XIII (1962), 23.

———, "Scheduling, Eligibility and Facilities," XIV (1963), 97.

KURTH, BERT, "Ideas on Officiating Problems," XVII (1966), 51-53.

———, "Motivation for Participation in Intramurals at a Commuter University," XX (1969), 16-18.

LAFLEY, JOHN C., "Student Directors' Program—Buzz Session 1972," XXIII (1972), 56.

LAFLEY, JOHN C., and CAROL L. ANDREWS, "Integration—Catch 22," XXV (1974), 49-53.

LAMBERT, KEITH, "Care and Prevention of Intramural Participation Injuries in a University of 6,000 Students," XVII (1966), 133.

LEIBROCK, PHILIP, "Publicity and Public Relations," XIV (1963), 47-50.

LEIGHTON, CAP, "Intramural Tennis, A Joint Project," XII (1961), 7-16.

LEMBACH, MICHAEL, "Organization," XV (1964), 18-20.

LITTLE, GORDON SCOTT, "Planning the Natatorium," XX (1969), 162-67.

———, "Stretching the Physical Plant," XVIII (1967), 69-72.

LINTA, NED A., "Scheduling and Publicity," XX (1969), 43-48.

———, "A Small College Intramural Program," XIII (1962), 57-61.

LOFT, BERNARD, "Motivating Safety in Intramural Competition," IX (1958), 33.

Lo MAGLIO, A. PETER L., "Contrary Views to Compulsory Intramural Programs," X (1959), 16.

LUDWIG, DONALD FREDERICK, "Summary of Findings of Men's Intramural Recreation Program Study Among the California State Universities and Colleges," XXV (1975), 126-28.

LUMLEY, ALBERT, "Knotty Problems for Rural Colleges," IX (1958), 12.

———, "Intramurals' Place in Education," IX (1958), 28.

MAAS, GERRY, "Commercial Involvement in Intramurals: McDonald's Restaurant Involvement in Intramural Sports Publicity at Iowa State University," XXV (1974), 68-69.

MAAS, GERRY, C. E. MUELLER, and BRUCE D. ANDERSON, "Survey of Administrative Reporting Sequences and Funding Sources for Intramural-Extramural Programs in Two-Year and Four-Year Colleges in the United States and Canada," XXV (1974), 122-25.

McAVADDY, JIM, "An Adaptive Program for Intramurals," XXIII (1972), 36-41.

———, "Facility Consideration for Handicapped Intramural Participants," XXIV (1973), 5-9.

McCONNELL, WAYNE J., "How Do You Allow Varsity Lettermen to Participate Without Dominating Your Intramural Program?" XXV (1974), 81-85.

McCUBBIN, WILLIAM, "Intramural Program at the University of Kentucky," IX (1958), 20.

McCUTCHEON, TOM O., "Physical Fitness Pentathlon," XX (1969), 147-52.

MACDONALD, GEORGE M., "Intramural Injuries: Your Responsibility," XVII (1966), 131-32.

McGUIRE, RAYMOND J. ("Ben"), "The Achievement of True Professional Status for Intramurals," XX (1969), 199-206.

———, "Communiversity Programming," XXII (1971), 33-34.

———, "The Reestablishment of Intramural Ice Hockey at the University of Illinois," XIX (1968), 108-11.

———, "The University of California Strawberry Canyon Recreation Area," XVIII (1967), 46-51.

MACINTYRE, CHRISTINE M., "Co-Recreation—A Must for the Future," XVII (1966), 126-28.

MALLETT, D. R., "An Educator Views the Contributions of a Campus Intramural Sports Program," XI (1960) 46-48.

MANJONE, JOE, "Five Man Soccer," XXIII (1972), 137-40.

MANNING, WILLIAM, "The 70's—Changing Times," XXIII (1972), 57-58.

———, "Suggested Administrative Approach for Solving Racial Tension in College Intramural Programs," XXII (1971), 62-64.

MANNING, WILLIAM, and SANFORD GEUSS, "Workshop on Films," XXV (1974), 11-13.

MARCIANI, LOUIS, "Competency-Based Learning Module Sequence for the Training of Sports Officials," XXV (1974), 116-21.

——, "Independent/Mediated/Training of Intramural Officials," XXIV (1973), 58-61.

——, "Promoting Intramurals: A Publicity Slide Production," XXIV (1973), 109.

——, "A Study of the Men's Intramural Program at an Urban Commuter College," XXII (1971), 23-25.

MARCIANI, LOUIS, and BEN McGUIRE, "How to Develop and Implement a Multi-Media Presentation Workshop," XXV (1974), 14-17.

MARCIANI, LOUIS, TOM SATTLER, and BILL THOMPSON, "Impact of the Energy Crisis," XXV (1974), 46-48.

——, "Single Elimination Tournaments Organizational Scoring," XXI (1970), 52-53.

MARCINIAK, JAMES, "Questionnaire Results of the Small College Problems," XXI (1970), 103-8.

MARTIN, LA VERLE, "An Evaluation and Comparison of Men's Intramural Programs in Four-Year State Supported Colleges and Universities in the United States," XX (1969), 116-22.

MARTIN, STEVE, "Rugby—An Intramural Sport," XVII (1966), 27-30.

MATHUS, DON, "Promotion of Intramurals in the Community College," XXIV (1973), 110-13.

MATSUNOBU, YOICHI, "Intramural Sports in Japan," XXV (1974), 86-92.

MATTHEWS, DAVID O., "Campus Recreation Department or Division," XXV (1974), 143-48.

——, "The Impact of Applied Intramural Research at the University of Illinois," XVI (1965), 48-51.

——, "Status Report—Planning and Construction of a Corecreation Building and a Pool Addition to the Women's Gymnasium at the University of Illinois," XVI (1965), 52-59.

MAURER, BRUCE L., "A Multivariate Analysis of Student, Faculty and Administrator's Attitudes Toward the Division of University Recreation and Intramural Sports at the Ohio State University," XXIII (1972), 151-53.

MAXIMON, HILLEL, and BERNARD POLLACK, "The Assignment of Officials —A Computer Program," XXIII (1972), 121-28.

MECHEM, EDWIN, "The Value of Intercollegiate and Intramural Athletics to the State of New Mexico," XIII (1962), 3.

MENDELSOHN, E. J., "Softball: Slow Pitch vs. Fast Pitch," VIII (1957), 7.

MENDELSOHN, ELLIS, "Intramurals—A Metroversity Concept," XXV (1974), 79-80.

MERKI, DON, "Scheduling, Eligibility and Facilities," XIV (1963), 92-95.

MERRIMAN, JOHN S., JR., "Selling the Intramural Program to the Varsity Coaches," X (1959), 5.

METZ, ROBERT V., "Getting the Message," XVII (1966), 68.

———, "Intra and Intermurals Conducted at F. D. U., a Tri-Campus Institution, XIV (1963), 107-10.

MEYER, C. B., "The Product of Intramurals and Selling the Program to the Academic Faculty," X (1959), 6.

MEYER, JOHN T., "The Conception and Conducting of an Intramural Facilities Survey at Iowa State University," XXV (1974), 133-38.

MEYERS, TOM, "Relationship of Intramural and Student Union Programs," XII (1961), 41-54.

MILES, E. H., "University Housing and Intramurals," XVII (1966), 124-25.

MILLER, HARVEY, "Student-Administered Intramural Programs," XXIII (1972), 120.

MILLER, J. CLOYD, "Intercollegiate and Intramural Athletics in the Eyes of the College President," XIII (1962), pp. 41-43.

MILLER, NORMAN P., "Intramurals and Campus Recreation, XX (1969), 243-46.

MOFFITT, BARBARA BRIMI, "Communication in Intramurals Through Video Tapes," XXIV (1973), 99-100.

MOORE, KENNETH M., "Intramurals Ala South Pacific," XVIII (1967), 28-30.

———, "Motivating the Intramural Program," XV (1964), 38-40.

———, "The Organization of Intramural Sports at U.C.L.A.," XVI (1965), 39-42.

———, "Recorder's Report," XIX (1968), 45-46.

———, "USAREUR Intramural Sports Clinics," XVII (1966), 3-4.

MORTON, MAX, "The Relationship of the Athletic Trainer to the Intramural Program and Related Problems," XV (1964), 40-42.

MUELLER, C. E. ("Pat"), "Facilities and Equipment," XIX (1968), 13.

———, "Ideation In Intramurals," XX (1969), 193-98.

MULL, RICHARD, "Innovative Programming," XXII (1971), 30-32.

MURDOCH, ALAN, "Audio-Tutorial Systems Approach to Recreational Learning," XXIII (1972), 43-45.

———, "Iowa State 'Cyclone 500'," XXII (1971), 109-10.

NAYLOR, JAY H., "Co-education, Why No Co-Recreation," XIV (1963), 24.

———, "How We Improved Our Officiating and Scheduling Problems at Brigham Young University," XIII (1962), 22.

———, "Is the Intramural Program Keeping Pace With the Fast Growing Universities?" XVI (1965), 16-17.

NEWMAN, STEVE, "Communications Principles and Tools for Intramurals," XXIV (1973), 101-6.

NEWMAN, STEVE, and BOB WALLACE, "Radio, T.V. and Video-Tape," XXV (1974), 18-20.

NEWTON, DON, "Intramural Program Highlights at the University of Saskatchewan," XIII (1962), 33.

NEWTON, DONALD M., "Public Relations–Publicity–Promotion in Intramurals," XVII (1966), 69-72.

NITCHMAN, NELSON W., "How Intramurals Tie In With Physical Education at the United States Coast Guard Academy," XIII (1962), 37-41.

———, "Hybrid Lacrosse (Claw Ball)," XXI (1970), 11-12.

———, "Problems in the Small Colleges or Universities," XV (1964), 28-29.

———, "Problem Solutions in Intramurals," XXIII (1972), 54-55.

———, "Student Unions, Recreation, Intramurals," XVI (1965), 12-13.

NOWKA, JACK, "Programming for Student Unrest at Wisconsin," XXII (1971), 65-69.

O'DELL, MICHAEL W., "A Survey of the Physical Activities of University Personnel," XXIV (1973), 151-54.

ODENEAL, WILLIAM T., "A Challenge to Intramurals," XVII (1966), 54-58.

———, "The Intramural Handbook—Its Purpose, Function, and Assets," XVIII (1967), 16-19.

OGILVIE, BRUCE, "The Mental Ramblings of a Psychologist Researching in the Area of Sports Motivation," XX (1969), 173-92.

OGLESBY, R. R., "Speech to National Intramurals Luncheon," XVI (1965), 21-24.

OHM, DR. ROBERT E., "Are Games Trivial," XVII (1966), 120-23.

OSBORNE, MURPHY M., JR., "Faculty—Staff Programs," XVII (1966), 118-19.

———, "Intramurals and the Trimester System," XIV (1963), 65-67.

OSTRANDER, HARRY R., "Innovative Methods of Financing Your Programs," XXIV (1973), 62-65.

PALMER, GARY K., "Flag Football at Brigham Young University," XX (1969), 131-32.

PALONE, JOE, "Intramurals at West Point—Scheduling, Eligibility, Facilities," XIV (1963), 90-92.

PARBERRY, CLEM, "Sports Clubs at the University of Idaho," XXIII (1972), 67.

PARSONS, NORMAN C., JR., "Mini-Soccer—The In Game," XXIII (1972), 141.

———, "Tell It Like It Is—Why 'Intramurals'?" XXIV (1973), 116-17.

PEDERSON, ELDON E., "Equipment and Facilities," XX (1969), 37-43.

———, "The Intramural Point System," XIV (1963), 58-62.

PETERSON, JAMES, "Investigating the Behavioral Consequences of Participation in Intramural Activities: A Changing Emphasis for Intramural Research," XXI (1970), 75-80.

PETERSON, JAMES, and HARVEY ROGOFF, "Developing a Multi-Dimensional, Sound-Coordinated Publicity Technique," XXII (1971), 46-49.

PETERSON, JAMES A., and HERBERT J. KROETEN, "Every Man an Athlete: The United States Military Academy's Intramural Program," XXIV (1973), 49-51.

PHELPS, DALE E., "Current Practices and Recommended Guidelines for the Administration of Sports Clubs in Selected Four-Year Midwest Colleges and Universities," XXI (1970), 32-35.

PINK, RALPH J., "A Survey of Current Trends in Intramural-Recreational Programs for Men Among Large Colleges and Universities of the United States," XXI (1970), 108-20.

PITCHER, DICK, "All-Campus Frisbee," XXIV (1973), 128-30.

PITCHFORD, KEITH, "Intramurals with the Trimester Plan at Florida State University," XIV (1963), 62-64.

———, "Intramural Trends in the Colleges of Florida," XIII (1962), 15-18.

POLLACK, BERNARD, "How Not to Build a New Physical Education/Recreation Complex," XXIV (1973), 15-17.

———, "The Quality of the Intramural Experience," XXII (1971), 50-54.

———, "The Role of the Questionnaire in Improving Intramural Sports Programs at Commuter Colleges," XXII (1971), 21-22.

———, "The Student View of Intramural Sports at an Urban College," XX (1969), 110-15.

———, "The Use of the Q Sort in Assessing the Influence of Ressentiment on Student Experiences in Intramural Programs," XXIII (1972), 173-79.

POLING, DOW P., "The Extent and Effectiveness of Student Involvement in the Administration of the University Intramural Program," XXIII (1972), 165-71.

POST, ARCHIE, "The University of Vermont Program," VIII (1957), 5.

POTTER, JIM, "Try It, You'll Like It," XXV (1974), 25-26.

POWELL, JOHN W., "Injury Prevention: The West Point Program," XXV (1974), 106-13.

PREO, LAWRENCE STEVEN, "A Comparative Analysis of Current Status and Professional Preparation of Intramural Directors," XXIV (1973), 150.

———, "Gay Liberation in Intramurals," XXV (1974), 65-66.

READING, LYNN, "Fraternities and Intramural Probation," XVII (1966), 16-18.

————, "Tackle Football," XX (1969), 133.

REES, TREVOR J., "Procurement, Rating, and Payment of Intramural Officials," XIX (1968), pp. 40-44.

REESE, TREVOR, "Programming for Student Unrest at Kent State," XXII (1971), 75-77.

REGNA, JOE, "A Faculty-Staff Recreation Program," XXIV (1973), 98.

RENNER, KENNETH H., "Essential Prerequisites for a New Intramural Program," XXIII (1972), 80-81.

————, "The Past, Present and Future of NIA," XXIV (1973), 120.

REZNIK, JOHN W., "Junior College Intramural-Recreational Programs: A Survey and Analysis," XXIV (1973), 164-69.

RHOADES, A. H. ("Jack"), "The Safety Aspects of the Experimental Touch Football Helmet," XVIII (1967), 31-37.

RHOADS, ARTHUR H., "A Method for the Improvement of Officiating in Intramural Team Sports," XIV (1963), 81-83.

RIDGEWAY, ART, "The Development and Application of an Intramural Sports Score Card," XXII (1971), 101-2.

RIORDAN, WILLIAM G., "Extra-Mural Sports Festivals," XII (1961), 30-41.

————, "Program Aids in Intramural Sports," XIV (1963), 36-45.

RIVET, RUSSELL L., "New Direction in Faculty Participation," XX (1969), 56-74.

ROHRER, SUSAN J., "Re-creation in Intramurals," XXIV (1973), 114-15.

————, "What Is the Philosophy of the Intramural Director?" XXIV (1973), 124-27.

ROKOSZ, FRANCI M., "Tournament Calculations Single Elimination," XXV (1974), 95-99.

ROOKER, A. A., and M. WAYNE JENNINGS, "Current Trends in College Intramural Athletics," XVI (1965), 25-34.

————, "Fact Finding Study on Intramural Football (Touch & Flag) Injuries," XX (1969), 134-37.

————, "Historical Review of Women in the National Intramural Association," XXIII (1972), 82.

————, "Safety in Touch Football," XIII (1962), 4.

————, "What Are the Areas of Responsibility of Intramural Departments in Large Universities?" XV (1964), 20-23.

RURAK, RICHARD, "100 % Participation," XXV (1974), 67.

SALEM, LEROY J., "Development and Use of Individual Sport Handbooks," XVII (1966), 73-77.

SALZLER, HENRY A., "A Survey of the Intramural and Interscholastic Programs for Boys in Selected High Schools in the State of Florida," XXIII (1972), 154.

SAMBORSKI, DOLPH, "The Harvard University Program," VIII (1957), 14.

SATTLER, TOM, and LARRY BERRES, "Important Issues for Commuter College Programs," XXV (1974), 129-32.

SATTLER, THOMAS P., "Basic Olympics," XX (1969) 143-46.

SCHAAKE, LARRY D., "Form Follows Function: An Overview of the Recreation Facilities Building at Southern Illinois University at Carbondale," XXIV (1973), 10-14.

SCHELSKY, CHARLES F., "The Philosophy of Intramurals at Purdue University," XI (1960), 4-10.

——, "Problems of Large Universities and Colleges," XV (1964), 26-28.

SCHMITT, TED A., "A General Appraisal," XX (1969), 9-10.

SCHUMACHER, DICK, "Student Involvement in Intramural Sports," XXII (1971), 60-61.

SEIDLER, JANET, "Viewpoints on Intramurals," XIV (1963), 6-9.

SERENA, J. ROBERT, "Lacrosse," XX (1969) 226-29.

SEZAK, SAM, "Training Intramural Officials at the University of Maine," XIX (1968), 31.

SHARPHORN, DAVID, "Communications," XX (1969), 19-21.

SHAW, JOHN H., "Rugby's Place in the Intramural Program," XX (1969), 208-14.

SHERIFF, AL, "Training of Student Leaders," XIX (1968), 61-62.

SHIRLEY, MAX, "Co-educational Programs," XV (1964), 9.

SHUCK, EMERSON, "Conveying the Values of Intramurals," XII (1961), 64-66.

SIENNA, PHILLIP, "Century Clubs for Promoting Physical Fitness," XXIV (1973), 83-93.

SIERRA, LAWRENCE, "Touch Football at Michigan State University," XX (1969), 126-30.

SIERRA, LAWRENCE, and THOMAS VANDER WEELE, "Visual Aids Used in Training Touch Football Officials," XXV (1974), 22-23.

SIMON, J. MALCOM, "Coaching of Intramural Activities," X (1959), 28.

SIMON, MALCOLM J., "Intramurals—Jamaica: A Peace Corps Experience," XXIV (1973), 66-70.

SLAUGHTER, EDWARD R., "Motivation of Intramurals at the University of Virginia," XV (1964), 36-38.

——, "The Relationship of Rapport Between the Intramural Department, the Administration, the Faculty, and the Students," XIII (1962), 18.

SLIGER, IRA, "A University Recreation Program," XXI (1970), 151-57.

SMITH, EMERSON P., "A New Look at Boxing," XXI (1970), 16-17.

——, "Officiating at the Naval Academy," XIV (1963), 83-87.

Smith, Harry E., "Physical Education, Intramurals, and Intercollegiate Athletics," XXIV (1973), 107-8.

Smyth, John P., "Team Handball: A Vigorous and Popular Team Sport," XXIV (1973), 146-49.

Sorensen, Jacki, "Aerobic Dancing and Aerobics in Intramurals," XXIII (1972), 20-26.

Starr, J. Howard, "Intramural Eligibility," X (1959), 28.

Steckbeck, John S., "Physical Fitness and Intramurals," XIV (1963), 73-76.

———, "What Happens to the Intramural Sports Program When the Physical Education Requirement Is Dropped," XXIV (1973), 121-23.

Steilberg, Peter, Jr., "A Comparison of the Intramural Sports Program at the University of Washington Prior to 1967," XXI (1970), 146-50.

———, "Some Negative Arguments," XX (1969), 11-12.

Stevens, Leonard W., "An Analysis of Eligibility Rules Used and Penalties Invoked in Twenty Representative Colleges," XIII (1962), 27-33.

———, "An Analysis of Safety Practices in Intramural Flag and Touch Football Programs in Eighteen Western Colleges," XIII (1962), 10-15.

———, "The New Look in Intramural Sports Programming at the University of Washington," XVI (1965), 35-38.

———, "Survey of Intramural Officiating Practices in Selected Colleges," XVII (1966), 41-47.

Stevenson, Michael, "The Effects of Artificial and Natural Turf on Injuries, Player Opinion, and Selected Game and Team Variables in College Intramural Touch Football," XXIV (1973), 178-90.

———, "The Impact of Sports Club Growth on Intramural Programs," XXII (1971), 35-38.

———, "Outrigger Canoeing," XXI (1970), 23-27.

Stewart, Ralph E., "Applications of Rules Modifications in Intramural Sports," XIX (1968), pp. 88-89.

———, "An Investigation of Student Discipline and Intramural Sports Participation," XXII (1971), 79-91.

———, "Some Officials Are Not as Bad as Others," XVII (1966), 48-50.

———, "Some Practical Applications of Rules Modifications," XIX (1968), 89-90.

Stewart, Sherri, "Women in Sports," XXV (1974), 30-34.

Stumpner, Robert, "The Philosophy of Intramurals at Indiana University," XI (1960), 5.

———, "Point Systems," XII (1961), 55.

Sullivan, Joseph M., "Awards, Their Value and Meaning," XX (1969), 231-33.

TAKOVICK, JOHN, "A Dynamic Intramural Program for Junior College Men and Women," XVII (1966), 107-8.

TAYLOR, DAVID H., "Special Events—A New Dimension in Intramural Programming," XXV (1974), 70-72.

TEMPLETON, JOE G., "Handball," IX (1958), 10.

THEIBERT, DICK, "New Concepts," XXII (1971), 10-17.

THOMPSON, BILL, "Communication Gimmicks," XX (1969), 234-38.

———, "Procurement, Training, Paying and Rating Officials," XIX (1968), 35-39.

———, "Unique Events that Succeed," XXIII (1972), 147-50.

THOMPSON, BOB, KENT BUNKER and DAVID C. PESHKE, "Mass-Media in Intramural and Recreation Programs," XXV (1974), 27-28.

TOWNES, ROSS E., "Advantages and Disadvantages of Point Systems," XXV (1974) 141.

———, "An Appraisal of Intramural Activities," XIII (1962), 52-57.

———, "Competition," XXIII (1972), 79.

———, "Fitness Programs—Way of Life," XX (1969), 138-42.

———, "Publicity, Public Relations, and Records," XIV (1963), 31-34.

———, "Student Interest and Student Involvement," XVII (1966), 91-93.

———, "Student Leadership," XIX (1968), 58.

TREVOR, DEAN S., "Increasing the Prestige of the Intramural Manager," XIII (1962), 50-52.

TRUMP, CLIFFORD, "Procedures to Strengthen High School Intramurals," XX (1969), 153-55.

———, "In Search of Leadership," XXI (1970), 61-64.

TUNE, ROBERT C., JR., "Lincoln Job Corps Intramural Program," XVIII (1967), 38-45.

TUOMI, WILL, "Units of Competition," XII (1961), 61.

TURNER, EALA D., "Co-educational Programs," XV (1964), 16.

TUTT, ROY, "Modified International Basketball Rules and Other Rules Changes," XXII (1971), 105-8.

TYLER, COULBOURN, "An Asset to Any Program," XIX (1968), 79-80.

———, "A Look to the Future," XIX (1968), 74-78.

———, "For the Winners," XXI (1970), 59-60.

———, "The Maintenance and Structure of a Successful Intramural Softball Program," XVIII (1967), 20-24.

———, "Problems of Large Universities and Colleges," XV (1964), 23-26.

TYRANCE, HERMAN, "Standards," XII (1961), 59.

UHRLAUB, DAVID, "Qualifications and Status of College Men's Intramural Directors," XX (1969), 79-82.

———, "Wheelchair Intramurals," XXI (1970), 13-15.

Unruh, Dan, "Programming for Student Unrest," XXII (1971), 70-74.

———, "Research and Development," XIX (1968), 19-21.

———, "A Survey of Techniques and Problems Involved in Promoting Intramural Programs in NIA Member Institutions Having 1000 Men," XVII (1966), 59-67.

Van Bibber, George, "Fitness and Intramurals," X (1959), 24.

Van Nostrand, Burr R., "Developing a Flexible Point System," XXI (1970), 44-51.

———, "Intramural Budgets," XXIII (1972), 91-97.

Van Whitley, Ada, "Our Goal: Women in Sports," XXV (1974), 29.

Varnes, Paul R., "Unstructured Activities," XXI (1970), 28-31.

Varnes, Paul R., and Seigfred Fagerberg, "Drug Abuse: Intramurals as an Alternative," XXV (1974), 100-5.

Varnes, Paul R., Linda Hall, John D. Hester, and Gene Newman, "Innovative and Exemplary Practices for Intramurals," XXIII (1972), 83-90.

Vattano, Frank J., "Psychological Implications of Participation to the Student Engaged at the Intramural Level," XV (1964), 42-45.

Vendl, Bill C., "A Systems Approach to Intramurals," XXIV (1973), 155-63.

Volo, Steven A., "The New Breed," XXV (1974), 38-40.

Wakefield, Markham C., "Sigma Delta Psi—An Intramural Activity," IX (1958), 6-8.

Walbaum, Richard S., "Intramural Participation at Purdue," XVII (1966), 5-15.

Wallace, Bob, "Co-Rec Basketball at Illinois State University," XXIII (1972), 133-35.

Wasson, William N., "The Formative Years, 1950-1955," XIX (1968), 67-68.

———, "A New Recreation Building," XX (1969), 160-61.

———, "A Survey to Determine the Trends Which Have Been Incorporated in Intramural Programs During the Past Ten Years,"

———, "The Use of Television in Promoting Intramurals," XX (1969), 207-8.

Weber, Edward, "Intramurals at Bellarmine College," IX (1958), 21-23.

Wedemeyer, Ross, "Budget," XII (1961), 57.

———, "Contribution of the Intramural Program to Education," XIX (1968), 47-48.

———, "The Philosophy of Intramurals at the University of Denver," XI (1960), 10.

———, "Play With a Purpose," XIV (1963), 99.

Wells, Harold, "Modified Water Polo," XXIII (1972), 142-45.

386   SELECTED BIBLIOGRAPHY

WHITE, JANICE L., "Women's Intramurals—Past, Present and Future," XXIV (1973), 73-82.

WIEMER, M. WAYNE, "High School Intramurals: The Need, and Meeting It," XX (1969), 156-59.

WILKERSON, JAMES L., "Assistant Director's Buzz Session: Contemporary Intramural Problems," XXIII (1972), 42.

———, "Duties of Student Leaders," XIX (1968), 63.

———, "The Future of the National Intramural Association," XXIV (1973), 118-19.

———, "Intramural Participation and Physical Fitness," XXII (1971), 113-16.

———, "Intramural Recreation Non-Participation: A Quality Factor," XXII (1971), 57-59.

———, "Student Director's Buzz Session: Major Items of Emphasis in the 70's," XXII (1971), 18.

WILKIE, DAVID R., "Broomball—The Great Equalizer," XX (1969), 215-17.

WILKIE, DAVID R., JAMES P. HASSING, BRUCE D. ANDERSON, and C. E. MUELLER, "Attitudes of Intramural Programmers Toward Recreation, Intramurals, Physical Education, Varsity Athletics," XXIII (1972), 155-62.

WILLIAMS, HENRY G., "Innovations in Outdoor Field Lighting," XXIV (1973), 18-29.

WILSON, FLOYD, "The Harvard Way," XXI (1970), 69-72.

WITTENAUER, JIM, "Point Systems, Awards, and Records," XIV (1963), 54-58.

———, "Professional Preparation," XXI (1970), 65-68.

WOOLISON, RICHARD L., and WILLIAM T. SELLS, "Broomball," XXIV (1973), 133-37.

———, "Innovations in Outdoor Lighting," XXIV (1973), 30-37.

ZIMMER, BARBARA J., "Recreate in the Craft Shop," XXV (1974), 54-56.

ZIMMER, WILLIAM R., "Beating the System—They Can't Fire Students," XXV (1974), 41.

———, "Student Input—It Makes the Program," XXV (1974), 41-42.

ZUARO, A. C., "Knotty Problems of Urban Institutions," X (1959), 10.

———, "The National Intramural Association Story," XIX (1968), 66.

ZYGADLO, RICH, "Students: The Best Solicitors of Public Support for Sports Clubs, XXV (1974), 44-45.

Index

Date Due